UNFINISHED BUSINESS

State Killings
and the
Quest for Truth

Bill Rolston
with Mairead Gilmartin

First published in 2000
by
Beyond the Pale
BTP Publications Ltd
Unit 2.1.2 Conway Mill
5-7 Conway Street
Belfast BT13 2DE

Tel: +44 (0)28 90 438630
Fax: +44 (0)28 90 439707
E-mail: office@btpale.ie
Website: http://www.btpale.ie

British Library Cataloguing-in-Publication Data.
A catalogue record for this book is available from the British Library.

ISBN 1-900960-09-5

Front cover photograph by: Kit De Fever
The photograph was taken on the 25th anniversary of Bloody Sunday (1997). Relatives
of the deceased burst through a banner showing the front cover of the Widgery Report.

Printed by
Colour Books Ltd, Dublin

CONTENTS

Acknowledgements   iv

Introduction   v

  1.   Bloody Sunday, 30 January 1972   1

  2.   Louis Leonard, 15 December 1972   23

  3.   The Dublin/Monaghan Bombings, 17 May 1974   31

  4.   Seamus Ludlow, 1 May 1976   45

  5.   Gary English, 19 April 1981   55

  6.   Carol Ann Kelly, 22 May 1981   65

  7.   Nora McCabe, 9 July 1981   75

  8.   Shoot to Kill: Gervaise McKerr, Sean Burns and
        Eugene Toman, 11 November 1982;
        Michael Tighe, 24 November 1982;
        Seamus Grew and Roddy Carroll, 12 December 1982   87

  9.   John Downes, 12 August 1984   106

10.   Charles Breslin, Michael Devine and David Devine,
        23 February 1985   115

11.   Patrick Kelly, 8 May, 1987   129

12.   Aidan McAnespie, 21 February 1988   143

13.   Mairéad Farrell, Daniel McCann and Seán Savage, 6 March 1988   155

14.   Pat Finucane, 12 February 1989   175

15.   Seamus Duffy, 9 August 1989   189

16.   Brian Robinson, 2 September 1989   199

17.   Peter Thompson, John McNeill and Edward Hale, 13 January 1990   207

18.   Fergal Caraher, 30 December 1990   225

19.   Kevin McGovern, 29 September 1991   233

20.   Peter McBride, 4 September 1992   241

21.   Pearse Jordan, 25 November 1992   251

22.   Diarmuid O'Neill, 23 September 1996   261

23.   Robert Hamill, 8 May 1997   275

24.   Raymond Murray   285

25.   Clara Reilly   293

26.   Denis Faul   303

Conclusion   309

Bibliography   326

Index   330

ACKNOWLEDGEMENTS

T his research emerged originally from conversations I had with Paddy Kelly, now a committee member of the Human Rights Commission. Without her encouragement and enthusiasm, I might not have persisted.

At a more material level I am indebted to the Joseph Rowntree Charitable Trust, which provided the finances for employing a research assistant. As often before in relation to the conflict in the North of Ireland, the Trust's involvement has made a difference.

The research assistant was Mairead Gilmartin. Every researcher should have the experience, at least once in their career, of working with someone of her calibre. She conducted all the interviews and most of the transcriptions. Her commitment, reliability and empathy meant that my task was made so much easier than it might have been.

My thanks to Don Mullan and Philomena Gallagher for permission to reproduce some material in chapters three and eight respectively. And I am grateful to Mike Tomlinson and Anna Eggert for reading drafts of what follows and for urging me to keep going with the project.

There are many contentious issues raised in the book and every effort has been made to verify the details of incidents and any names mentioned.

Finally, some of what follows makes for emotional reading. But if they are difficult stories to read, they were also difficult stories to tell. At least three seasoned campaigners who would have no difficulty arguing their case in front of the most antagonistic audience broke down and cried on tape. This project gave them the chance to reflect, a luxury they rarely had in the midst of the war when they were engaged in what was often tantamount to full-time campaigning. Telling their story now that the war is over brought emotions to the surface which had lain apparently dormant, often for decades. I am immensely grateful to all those who agreed to be interviewed.

INTRODUCTION:

VICTIMS, TRUTH AND PREJUDICE

It was business as usual in police room 619. (Peter Gabriel, 'Biko').

During the West Belfast Festival in August 1998, a campaign group called Relatives for Justice organised an event—'Forgotten Victims'—for people who had lost friends and relatives at the hands of British state forces during the previous three decades of conflict over the North of Ireland. Over two hundred people attended the meeting and many spoke of their experiences—not only of the killing itself, but of what happened to them subsequently. They spoke of being ignored, marginalised, vilified and harassed by the same state forces which had killed their loved ones. For some, it was a difficult task to speak in public, even though the audience was sympathetic. One speaker, Cornelius Rooney, had lost his nine year old son Patrick on 15 August 1969. The RUC had driven up the Falls Road firing into Divis Flats. Patrick was hit in his own home by a heavy Browning machine-gun round fired indiscriminately from a Shoreland armoured car. Cornelius Rooney had never before spoken publicly of the events of that night 29 years before.

Like the rest of the audience I listened, close to tears, as he spoke. I recalled the words of Antje Krog, a South African poet and broadcaster, as she listened to the testimony of victims and survivors at the Truth and Reconciliation Commission (TRC) hearings in her country. 'Over months we've realized what an immense price of pain each person must pay just to stammer out their own story at the Truth Commission. Each word is exhaled from the heart, each syllable vibrates with a lifetime of sorrow.' And I remembered too one criticism that had been made of the TRC. The majority of those who spoke about state killings were women; the stories they told were of their husbands, fathers and sons. But their own stories went untold. Nowhere was it recorded adequately or acknowledged fully that they had survived, doubly victimised by the killing and by a regime intent on silencing them when they demanded justice. The most telling proof of their marginalisation was that sometimes their accounts to the TRC were carried in newspapers only as those of 'the widow' or 'the mother'; not only were their own stories unimportant; they did not even have names.

Unlike the South African case, the venue at which Cornelius Rooney spoke was not a Truth Commission. It had not been set up formally as a result of the ongoing peace process. It was not chaired by a person of international standing, the winner of the Nobel Peace Prize. There were no state functionaries present to listen or to tell their own stories in the hope of amnesty. Above all, apart from a small amount of media coverage, there was no public acknowledgement that the meeting had even taken place. All of which could lead to dismissing the political importance of the meeting. Surely this was simply a case of relatives talking among themselves. It was a collective catharsis, an exercise in group therapy. It was indeed that, but it was also more. If ever there is a TRC for Ireland it will only be because these people told their stories when no one else wanted to listen. From that, they gained the political strength to insist that others listen, to demand a place in the debate about the future.

Throughout the conflict there have been groups such as Relatives for Justice which struggled to disclose the truth about state injustice and repression. The end of the conflict provided space for such campaigns to move up a gear, as it were. If the demands for truth and justice are to be met, then the message has to be carried beyond the audiences which are sympathetic, to the same state functionaries and institutions which have marginalised these people in the past. There are undoubtedly many in those institutions who are fearful of change, or more, who have something to hide and who would prefer if the relatives continued talking merely among themselves. From events like the 'Forgotten Victims' meeting, people can, by talking to each other, gain the strength and courage to take the message to others much less open or less sympathetic. As the example of South Africa's TRC revealed, the *sine qua non* of truth and justice, is that the story of the most marginalised victims has to be officially acknowledged by society as legitimate.

Who killed whom?

Those killed by the state during thirty years of conflict over the North of Ireland are a relatively small proportion of all those who have died. Perhaps surprisingly, there is some disagreement concerning the exact number of people who were killed. This arises from the fact that there are different definitions used by various authors regarding what constitutes a conflict-related death as well as difficult decisions about inclusion and exclusion once the definitions have been set; for example, should a person who dies from a heart attack during an explosion be included? That said, the number of people who died as a result of the conflict is approximately three and a half thousand.

State forces accounted for just over 10 percent of all the deaths in the conflict—357 people in all, according to Sutton. (McKitttrick et al give a slightly higher number, but given that their total for all deaths in the conflict is also higher, the percentage is identical.) The major perpetrator in relation to state killings was the British army, responsible for over 82 per cent of all such deaths (294 people in all). This compares to approximately 15 percent of state killings carried out by the next most active perpetrator, the Royal Ulster Constabulary (54 deaths). The UDR was responsible for eight deaths, the B-Specials one, and the RAF one.

The worst year for state killings was 1972, when 83 people died—23 percent of all state killings. This was also the worst year for overall deaths; 472 people died, 14 percent of the total for the entire conflict. In the three years 1971-1973, there were 160 state killings, 45 percent of the total for such deaths. In the same period there were 894 deaths overall, 27 percent of all the deaths in the conflict. Thus it is clear that state killings figured largely in the early days of the conflict. Ten of the 16 deaths (62.5 percent) which occurred in 1969 were carried out by state forces: seven by the RUC, one by the B-Specials, and two by the British army (compared to two killings by republicans and four by loyalists). In fact, there were 62 deaths attributable to state forces before the most-publicised instance of state killing, Bloody Sunday, occurred in January 1972.

There were no state killings in the following years: 1993, 1995, 1997, 1998 and 1999. At the same time, it is clear that state killings did not end with the declaration of ceasefires in late 1994. Dermot McShane was crushed by a British army vehicle during disturbances in Derry on 13 July 1996 and Diarmuid O'Neill was shot dead by Metropolitan Police in London on 23 September 1996.

Civilian deaths constitute the largest category of victims of state killings, over 50 percent of all such deaths. One such civilian was a robber armed with a sawn-off shotgun. Four other robbers carried imitation firearms. The remaining civilian victims, 189 in total, were unarmed. The vast majority—86 percent—of civilian victims of state killings were Catholic. The next largest category of victims is that of republican military activists, approximately 37 percent of all state killings. Remarkably few loyalist military activists became the victims of state killings, only 4 percent in all. All but two of the state killings of loyalists occurred before 1975.

If it is presumed as a shorthand calculation that republican activists were likely to have been Catholic while loyalist activists were likely to have been Protestant, it follows that the Catholic or nationalist community experienced the overwhelming bulk of killing by state forces; 88 percent of victims of state killings were from the nationalist community.

Deaths resulting from collusion between state forces and loyalist paramilitary groups are not included in the above figures. To do so would be to add at least the same number of deaths again. Collusion has been a factor in loyalist killings since early in the conflict, but reached a peak in the early 1990s. As Arthur Fegan and Raymond Murray documented, between March 1990 and September 1994, loyalists killed 185 people. Of these deaths, 168 (91 percent) were sectarian or political in nature, and in 103 cases (56 percent of all the loyalist killings in the period) there is evidence of some form of collusion.

Categorising State Killings

It is possible to categorise deaths from state killings in a number of different ways. In addition to the state agency involved in the killing and the method of killing used—plastic bullet, gun shot, etc.—the deaths could be categorised in relation to the geographical area in which they occurred. The Cost of the Troubles Study (Fay et al.) opts for a geographical break-down. Although it does not consider state killings *per se*, it provides some interesting information. The patterns of death are markedly different in the five areas selected: West Belfast, North Belfast, Derry, Newry/South Armagh and 'Mid-Ulster'. In all but one of the areas, the majority of killings resulted from republican action; only North Belfast was different, where loyalists were the main perpetrators. In Newry/South Armagh loyalists and the British army accounted for almost the same proportion of deaths (6 per cent and 5 per cent respectively), while in Derry loyalists were responsible for 8 per cent of the deaths and the British army for 21 per cent.

Ní Aoláin does focus on state killings and uses a chronological approach to categorise these killings. She groups them into three broad chronological periods based on the different strategies used by the state and the consequences in terms of the number and form of state killings.

Phase 1, 'militarisation', is from 1969 to 1974. During this period of street confrontations and escalating conflict, the British army was responsible for 90 percent of the 188 state killings. Phase 2, 1975 to 1980, is the period of 'normalisation', when the number of state killings dropped dramatically to 54. The range of state agents responsible for the deaths widened, with the uniformed British army responsible for 65 percent of the deaths, the SAS and 14th Intelligence Company 29 per cent, and the RUC 9 per cent.

In phase 3, 'counter-insurgency', from 1981 to 1994, tactics and results changed again. At the beginning of the period the RUC was convinced that it could take on a more robust counter-insurgency role. But after their brief spate of killing in North Armagh in 1982, regarded by British Intelligence as amateur and counter-productive, the British army was given primacy in counter-insurgency operations. The emphasis was on specialist units killing (rather than arresting) paramilitary members (in particular republicans). Although 51 percent of those killed were civilians, there were also 150 paramilitary deaths, 80 percent of whom were republican. What Ní Aoláin terms 'set piece' operations—stake-outs and ambushes by undercover British soldiers—came to account for 40 percent of all the state killings in this period. Throughout all three periods, she concludes, the average victim of state killing was male, Catholic and aged 18 to 25.

One further method of categorisation can be considered—organising the deaths by the nature of the incident. On this basis, six categories of state involvement in killing can be identified. An example drawn from the stories in this book is provided for each category, as follows:

- Planned shoot-to-kill operation; for example, the killing of Mairead Farrell and her companions in Gibraltar.

- Excessive use of force in a public order situation; for example, the killing of John Downes.

- Individual action by an armed member of the state forces, whether out of revenge, loss of temper, bravado, the result of an altercation, or a 'mistake'; for example, the killing of Peter McBride.

- Collusion with loyalists in advance of the death; for example, the killing of Pat Finucane.

- Actions by loyalists acting alone, but with security force cover-up after the event; for example, the killing of Seamus Ludlow.

- Other reasons, including dereliction of duty; for example, the killing of Robert Hamill.

It is sometimes difficult to allocate specific instances of state killing to each of these categories; there is frequently a question over, for example, the intention of the state forces involved. Did they go out to kill, or was it an arrest operation which 'went wrong'?

None of the above methods of categorisation is used in the presentation of the stories in this book. The incidents of state killing examined are simply presented in chronological order. Despite the simplicity of that organising device, the significance of different strategies employed by the state in various periods is often revealed; for example, the three accounts of deaths from plastic bullets occur in three out of four consecutive chapters on the early 1980s. Arranging the accounts chronologically also underlines two important points. First, state killings went on throughout the whole of the conflict, and were not confined to the high-profile incidents such as Bloody Sunday, or shoot-to-kill in North Armagh, and Gibraltar. Secondly, in one important sense, any form of categorisation can help to conceal an important fact: as the stories which follow show, no matter the period, the perpetrator, the method of killing, the status of the victim, etc., the post-killing experience of relatives of those killed by state forces is practically identical.

The relatives' stories

Those who have *campaigned* over state killings are the focus of this book. For the most part they are not professionals, involved because of their jobs in legal or human rights organisations, but ordinary people, recruited by circumstances into campaigns for which they would never have willingly volunteered. They have been dragged into human rights activism by what was done to their relatives and in the process have displayed tenacity, skill and determination in pursuit of truth and justice.

The book looks at examples of the full range of victims of state killing—from student Kevin McGovern on his way to a disco with a can of beer in his hand and schoolgirl Carol Ann Kelly returning from a shop with a pint of milk, to Mairead Farrell preparing for a bombing mission in Gibraltar, and Patrick Kelly attacking what he believed to be an empty RUC barracks. It would be easy to focus on the former—the 'innocent'—victims and leave out the latter as somehow fouling the humanitarian pitch. I have not done so. All were subjected to excessive or unnecessary force by a state which has signed up to international protocols relating to the use of appropriate levels of force. Moreover, in media representations, official accounts and unfortunately also in popular memory there is often little distinction made between the various victims of state killing. After all, Peter McBride 'had a coffee jar bomb', and Kevin McGovern 'took up the standard aiming stance for a pistol/revolver'. Such justifications are not totally removed from those articulated in relation to the 'less innocent' victims: Gervaise McKerr 'crashed through a police roadblock'; Pearse Jordan 'was transporting guns and ammunition in a car'. Not one of these widely disseminated 'facts' stood up under the weight of careful scrutiny.

Forgotten victims

In retrospect, it is amazing how little attention was paid to the concerns of victims for much of the duration of the conflict. But as the conflict came to an end, there was a flurry of recognition. The Good Friday Agreement asserted that 'it is essential to acknowledge and address the suffering of the victims of violence as a necessary element of reconciliation'. Prior to the Agreement, Sir Kenneth Bloomfield, former head of the Northern Ireland civil service, had already been given the task 'to look at possible ways to recognise the pain and suffering felt by victims of violence'. His Report in October 1997 made 20 recommendations, and led to the security Minister, Adam Ingram, being given the added responsibility of looking to the needs of victims. His Victims' Liaison Unit launched a number of schemes—many of them financial—to enable victims and dependants to access education, business start-up, etc..

The apparent centrality of the issue of victims was soon a very public symbol of the change of political atmosphere. Yet there were problems. The debate on victims has been very much state-led. And although there was an attempt to engage the views of victims themselves, the suspicion soon emerged that that engagement was on the state's own terms. For example, Bloomfield met with a wide range of victims' groups, including those representing people injured or killed by state forces. Part of his brief was to represent the concerns of members of the security forces who had been killed and injured and he does so frequently and sensitively in his Report. He also summarises considerately the views of other categories of victims, for example, unionist families living near the border who regard themselves as victims of a republican campaign of ethnic cleansing. He specifically refers to them: 'Those affected have made representations to Government for some form of special help. I would hope that those representations are given sympathetic consideration'. But compare this to the case of victims of state killings; he notes the scepticism of such groups regarding his ability to represent their concerns adequately to government. He insists he has not been given 'a steer' by the government and is capable of so doing. But he adds, coolly and almost dismissively, that their views about 'state terrorism' 'are no doubt already well known to Government, but I promised to convey in this report their firm view that revelation of the full truth of controversial events was more important for the victims they represented than any other consideration. This I now do.'

This differential treatment of victims has its roots in the three decades of the war itself. It was apparent in a number of ways, not least the way in which victims were described. Countless reports in the media stressed that the victim was 'innocent', that 'he only had time for his family', that 'she was never interested in politics', that 'they were just going about their daily work' when killed. There was in effect the social construction of the ideal victim. The two key elements in that construct were 'innocence' and 'passivity'.

Of course, the corollary of this is that there are in fact two classes of victims, deserving and undeserving. The latter are presumed to be less than innocent, or worse, downright culpable, implicated in their own suffering. Thus, at the top of the hierarchy of victims were those who were 'innocent'—usually women and children and usually killed as a result of paramilitary violence. At the bottom were members of those same paramilitary groups killed by state forces; they attracted little widespread sympathy outside the communities where those groups drew support.

Raising the issue of state killings while the war raged was thus a difficult task because of a number of factors. First was the unquestioned belief that the state does not act as a terrorist, does not kill without reason or justification. Second was the presumption that 'there is no smoke without fire', that for all the protestations of innocence these victims had been somehow less than angelic. Third was the dissemination of these deep prejudices and presumptions by powerful institutions, especially the media. Fourth and finally was the deliberate misinformation and manipulation of the media by state forces, ensuring that a partial or downright false story was the first in the public domain and therefore the most likely to be believed and remembered.

Such was the power of this ideology that it was possible in the cases of state violence to override even the most obvious criterion of 'innocence'. Thus, it was usually presumed and often stated in official accounts that children killed by plastic bullets were involved in, or at least caught up in riots—the implication being that there was an element of contributory negligence involved.

Victims of state killings were often forgotten and ignored while the war was raging. To draw attention to them was to risk being labelled as 'soft on terrorism'. Criticising the state's human rights record was usually condemned on the grounds that it 'played into the hands of the terrorists'. It was even worse for relatives who dared to demand disclosure or prosecutions. To agitate was to draw down the wrath of the state forces on themselves, to become as marginalised and victimised as those for whom they fought. The vilification of the dead was echoed in the treatment of those who sought truth and justice. The fact that there were risks involved was undoubtedly one reason that agitation was less than might have been expected. Shock, powerlessness, marginalisation, harassment and fear were powerful deterrents. That powerlessness registered in different ways with different categories of victims. But it had a specific resonance in the case of relatives of members of paramilitary groups killed by state forces. Even if they believed that their relatives could have been arrested rather than killed, it was often difficult to find a sympathetic hearing for that view outside their own community, and sometimes even within.

In short, within the general ignorance and lack of official acknowledgement of victims in the past, the case of victims of state violence was even worse. They were not merely ignored, but there was a determination to exclude them and those who raised their plight from the debate. Despite those odds, there were brave individuals who fought to force their way into the debate, who worked often for years to ensure that their items were included on the agenda. There were campaigns, and even some successes, in the midst of the war itself. More often there was failure, frustration, dashed hopes and a gnawing sense of unfinished business.

When wars end is the time to turn to that business. Old campaigns were given new momentum, and new groups emerged; sometimes they dealt with recent killings, but more often with killings which had occurred years, even decades before. Peace not only provides the space for such politics without fear of reprisal; it also enables a real shift in consciousness. This is because one other reason for inaction in the past, apart from fear, was that the war had become part of the normality of people's lives. It was not so much that death and suffering were accepted, but that there seemed no alternative. Because the war was ongoing, all too often yesterday's victim became yesterday's news as the news of today's victims emerged. With peace this inertia was questioned—and rejected.

Peace creates the political space to raise the case of 'forgotten victims' and thereby win a place in the public debate for the first time. This is no easy task; the articulation of the needs and demands of victims of state violence has been a source of unease in a situation where the issue of victims has become increasingly colonised by the language of social work, psychology and counselling. Despite that, there has been a determination to argue for inclusion at every turn. Campaigning groups have organised conferences and meetings on the issue of state killings. They have demanded to be heard in the new venues and institutions resulting from the Good Friday Agreement, such as the Touchstone Group, set up to advise the Minister for victims. If the victims of state killings are no longer as invisible as they once were, it is not because of the largesse of the state but because of the persistence of campaign groups.

Focusing on state killings

It might be argued that it is elitist, perhaps even sectarian to focus only on state killings. Henry McDonald, *Observer* correspondent, has been a vocal proponent of such a criticism. For example, referring to the loyalist bombing of Dublin and Monaghan in 1974, and the Irish government's decision to hold an inquiry, he asks: 'Why was this atrocity any different to Bloody Friday, Enniskillen and Claudy?', all examples of mass killing by IRA bombs. He concludes: 'Either we draw a line under the past or we open up everything for examination' (*Observer* 8 August 1999).

Arguably, the same criticism can be levelled directly at this book. There are after all other victims' groups, for example: Disabled Police Officers Association, Families Acting for Innocent Relatives (FAIR), Londonderry Victim Support, Northern Ireland Terrorist Victims Together, and Homes United by Ruthless Terror (HURT). In addition, there are many other groups working with victims, such as: An Crann/the Tree, Cost of the Troubles Study, Families Against Intimidation and Terror (FAIT), Kairos, Survivors of Trauma, WAVE, Victim Support Northern Ireland, and South Down Action for Healing Wounds. Why leave out their stories?

There is nothing to prevent any victims' group telling their stories. Moreover, there is every reason to expect that the telling of those stories is a necessary part of dealing with the past. My focus is not on all victims, but solely on those killed by the state. There are two main reasons for this: first, they are qualitatively different from other killings because they have been carried out by an institution which, uniquely, claims to protect all citizens; and second, these victims have often been forgotten in the past, while those who have sought to keep the memory alive have been marginalised by the state and its institutions. None of this is to insinuate that the suffering of other victims and their relatives is necessarily any less than that of those killed by the state, even if in recent years some groups have had a more sympathetic hearing.

At the core of this issue is the question of equivalence. What truth is there about IRA massacres like Enniskillen and La Mon which needs to be uncovered and revealed? As a result of police investigations, court cases, etc. everything that can be known is known, except in some cases the names of the actual perpetrators. But there is no question of excessive force by a democratic state, no insinuation of state support or cover-up, no police or army harassment of those who demand justice in these cases. Moreover, in cases of killings by republicans it has been the presumption of the state, the media and large sections of public opinion that the victim is innocent, even if a uniformed and armed member of the security forces. Conversely, the victims of state violence have usually been presumed to be less than innocent, even if they were civilians. The state had the power to carry out these killings with impunity, to block, legally and otherwise, any investigation, and to vilify and harass those who opposed its actions. To focus on these cases is to counterbalance the exclusion of such cases in the past.

It should not be surprising that most of those interviewed are nationalist or republican, given that the vast majority of victims of state killings have been from that community. Moreover, given their relationship to the state, nationalists and republicans have been the most likely to agitate over the issue of state killings, not least because their communities have suffered disproportionately. Few loyalists were killed by state forces, and very few campaigns emerged around those killings. One such campaign—over the death of Brian Robinson—is considered in this book.

There are more such stories which have not been told here—for example, that of joyriders Karen Reilly and Martin Peake, shot dead by British paratroopers on 30 September 1990, and the saga of the imprisonment, release and legal vindication of Paratrooper Lee Clegg. Some long-running campaigns have not been considered, for example, that of Kathleen Stewart over the death of her son Brian by plastic bullet on 10 October 1976; Kathleen Stewart died in 1999 after a long illness and an even longer campaign for the truth. And new campaigns gather momentum each day, such as that over the murder of republican Sam Marshall in Portadown on 7 March 1990; although carried out by loyalists, there is powerful evidence of the involvement of state forces in his death. But time, space and on occasions emotional exhaustion have conspired to ensure that some stories have been left out.

The structure of this book

This book is built around the stories of 23 instances of state involvement in killings associated with the conflict over the North of Ireland. The stories are told by people—in most cases relatives—who have campaigned over these killings. Interviews were recorded and transcribed, after which they were carefully edited. The final version of each story was returned to the person interviewed for approval; not a word of their story is reproduced here without their agreement.

In addition, each story has an introduction. As much information about the case as currently exists in the public domain is summarised in order to put each instance of state killing in context.

Three accounts stand out from the others in that they are not based on individual incidents of state killing. Raymond Murray, Denis Faul and Clara Reilly are seasoned campaigners who have devoted years of effort to documenting and highlighting cases of state abuse and killing.

Finally, there is one solicitor whose name looms large in a number of the stories in this book—Pat Finucane. Had he lived, he would have been approached for an interview.

The basis of this book is that these stories are important, not just at the level of pain and suffering—a fact that is equally true of many other stories which could be told—but because they starkly exemplify a number of factors about the past. They reveal how far the state degraded the ideal of human rights over three decades and how some people struggled to uphold that ideal in the most hostile of environments. The lesson is a timely and essential one: that part of the unfinished business we as a society face is the task of finding ways to ensure that this past culture of the abuse of human rights will never again be repeated.

1

BLOODY SUNDAY
30 January 1972

Fourteen shot dead by British soldiers

On Sunday 30 January 1972, a major civil rights march took place in Derry, organised by NICRA, the Northern Ireland Civil Rights Association. It brought an estimated 15,000-20,000 people onto the streets to protest at internment without trial which had been introduced the previous August. The march left the Creggan area in carnival mood and the men, women and children wound their way down towards the centre of the town. The original intention was to converge on Guildhall Square for speeches from leading civil rights activists and MPs, but the centre of the town was blocked off by the British army. There were 1,800 British soldiers, including 320 members of the 1st Battalion of the Parachute Regiment, in town. Consequently the march swung into the Bogside and the rally began at Free Derry Corner.

The march was thus confined entirely to the no-go area of nationalist Derry on the west bank of the River Foyle. For almost two years, since the Battle of the Bogside in August 1969, barricades had kept out British troops and RUC and the area was effectively policed by the Official and Provisional IRA. Free Derry Corner was a potent symbol of resistance before Bloody Sunday, and even more so afterwards.

The march organisers had appealed for a peaceful demonstration, and the evidence is that there were no Provisional IRA weapons in the immediate vicinity. But as the march swung into the Bogside, approximately 200 marchers, mostly

1

young men, stayed behind at the William Street barricade to stone the British troops. This, however, was neither a major incident nor a particularly unusual one; rioting occurred at that corner regularly. The British army responded to the rioters with CS gas, rubber bullets and water cannon.

At 3.45 p.m., as the rally got under way, British soldiers fired two shots at civilians near William Street. Two civilians were injured, one of whom, John Johnston, died almost six months later, on 16 June 1972. Shortly after 4 p.m., British paratroopers swarmed into the Bogside. As the marchers scattered, the soldiers opened fire. In the next 27 minutes 13 people were killed and 14 seriously wounded. The dead were:

Gerard Donaghey, aged 17, killed as he ran towards a house in Abbey Park;

Jack Duddy, aged 17, shot as he ran for safety across the courtyard of the Rossville Street flats;

Hugh Gilmore, aged 17, killed as he ran up Rossville Street;

Michael Kelly, aged 17, killed near a pile of rubble near Glenfada Park;

Kevin McElhinney, aged 17, killed as he crawled towards a doorway in Rossville Street;

John Young, aged 17, **William Nash**, aged 19, and **Michael McDaid**, aged, 20, shot as they stood beside a rubble barricade at Rossville Street;

James Wray, aged 22, shot and wounded as he ran from Glenfada Park and shot again and fatally wounded as he lay on the ground;

Patrick Doherty, aged 31, killed while crawling towards Rossville Flats;

Gerald McKinney, aged 35, shot as he ran with hands raised towards Glenfada Park;

William McKinney, aged 26, shot dead as he bent over the body of Gerald McKinney;

Bernard McGuigan, aged 41, shot in the back of the head when he went to the assistance of Patrick Doherty;

and **John Johnston**, aged 59.

The following day, British Home Secretary Reginald Maudling spoke of the event in the House of Commons. He stated that the British army opened fire only after having been fired on themselves, and only at identified targets who were attacking them with firearms and bombs. Bernadette Devlin, MP, who had been preparing to address the rally at Free Derry Corner as the shooting began, attempted on numerous occasions to respond to Maudling's allegations. Denied the opportunity to speak, she eventually crossed the floor to the government front benches, struck Maudling, and left the House.

British Information Services immediately elaborated on Maudling's initial statement. 'Of the 13 men killed in the shooting that began after the bulk of the 3,000 [sic] marchers had been peacefully dispersed, four were on the security force's wanted list. One man had four nail bombs in his pocket.' The statement went on to itemise individual instances of 'gunmen' being 'hit' and 'nailbombers' being 'shot'.

As far as the British establishment was concerned, this incident was represented as an open-and-shut case. British troops followed their operational instructions to the letter, firing only to defend themselves and others from attack by 'terrorists'. At the same time, such was the international outcry about the massacre that the British government had to be seen to do something. Consequently, an Act of Parliament was passed hurriedly on 1 February 1972, setting up a tribunal of inquiry. The Lord Chief Justice, Lord Widgery, was appointed to head the tribunal. Widgery immediately moved to restrict the operations of the tribunal. Although he could have invited two or more other judges to sit with him, and was urged to do so by the leaders of the Labour Party, Harold Wilson, and Liberal Party, Jeremy Thorpe, he elected to sit alone. In addition, he decided to restrict his investigation solely to 'the period beginning with the moment when the march first became involved in violence and ending with the deaths of the deceased and the conclusion of the affair'. All questions about the planning of the military operation against the marchers were thus ruled out.

Widgery also seemed to be in an intense hurry to produce a report. In itself this may have appeared reasonable, but it had one further major negative consequence. Within weeks, Widgery's tribunal was taking evidence in Coleraine—Derry was felt to be an unsafe venue given local people's shock and anger over the killings. Part of that evidence was a submission of approximately 700 eyewitness statements painstakingly collected by NCCL and delivered to the tribunal at the start of March. But Widgery concluded that they had arrived too late and added little that he did not know already, and therefore ignored them.

The Widgery Report was published in April 1972. At first sight it would seem to confirm the evidence of civilian eyewitnesses on the march rather than the British Information Services statement.

> Although a number of soldiers spoke of actually seeing firearms or bombs in the hands of civilians none was recovered by the Army. None of the many photographs shows a civilian holding an object that can with certainty be identified as a firearm or a bomb. No casualties were suffered by the soldiers from firearms or gelignite bombs. In relation to every one of the deceased there were eye witnesses who said that they saw no bomb or firearm in his hands. The clothing of 11 of the deceased when examined for explosives showed no trace of gelignite.

The Widgery Report stated that 'None of the deceased or wounded is proved to have been shot whilst handling a firearm or bomb'. The careful wording gave the clue to Widgery's logic: that the British soldiers fired only at identified targets who were in the process of or preparing to attack them. The fact that the weapons they supposedly carried were never recovered was of itself no proof of innocence. Widgery thus verified the initial British Information Services statement about 'gunmen' and 'nailbombers'. He was at pains to exonerate the British soldiers from any blame. His Report stated that it was likely that 'as many rounds were fired at the troops as were fired by them', and that it was only their professionalism which saved them from injury.

The Coroner, Major Hubert O'Neill, came to a very different conclusion during the inquest into the deaths in August 1973.

> This Sunday became known as Bloody Sunday and bloody it was. It was quite unnecessary. It strikes me that the Army ran amok that day and shot without thinking what they were doing. They were shooting innocent people. These people may have been taking part in a march that was banned but that does not justify the troops coming in and firing live rounds indiscriminately. I would say without hesitation that it was sheer, unadulterated murder. It was murder.

Despite this unambiguous conclusion, there are questions over some of O'Neill's characterisation of the British army actions, in particular:

– why were all the deceased men?

– why were most of them young men?

– why did the majority of them die as the result of single, aimed shots to the head or upper part of the body?

In short, this did not look like a situation which got out of hand but rather like a premeditated and ruthless military operation.

For most nationalists in Ireland, north and south, the Widgery Report added insult to injury; in the words of Father (later Bishop) Edward Daly, Widgery 'found the innocent guilty and the guilty innocent'. They had seen, in person or in the media, Paddy Doherty shot dead as he tried to crawl to safety, a handkerchief around his nose and mouth to protect himself from the effects of CS gas. They had seen Barney McGuigan lying by Rossville Flats, his head demolished by a dum-dum bullet and his life blood flowing on the pavement; he had been shot while trying to go to Paddy Doherty's assistance. They had seen Father Edward Daly, clearly shell-shocked, waving a bloody handkerchief as he led a group of men carrying the body of Jackie Duddy. The denial of all this suffering and trauma had profound repercussions. The day after Bloody Sunday a crowd estimated at 35,000 surrounded the British Embassy in Dublin and burnt it to the ground. The IRA was swamped with recruits in the aftermath of Bloody Sunday. And 1972 turned out to be the worst year of 30 years of conflict as regards the number of deaths.

Don Mullan, who as a 15 year old had witnessed the deaths of some of the Bloody Sunday victims, summed up the political effect of the incident.

Bloody Sunday was the beginning of the end of British colonialism in my heart and soul. Henceforth, whenever I looked at the Union Jack flying in Ireland, it became symbolic of one abiding memory of that day: our blue-and-white civil rights banner stained by the blood of Barney McGuigan. Any faint hope of purchasing my loyalty to the British Crown through superficial reforms died on that day.

For the families of the dead the trauma was even more pronounced. Not only had their relatives been murdered, but official lies and innuendo had besmirched their good names. Widgery's Report became for them little more than a propaganda document on behalf of the British government to cover up what was a premeditated military operation, the planning of which went to very high levels.

Bloody Sunday marked the end of mass rallies and marches for many years and indeed the beginning of the end of NICRA itself. Each January there was a commemorative march to remember Bloody Sunday. It kept the spark alive until the time came for mass action again. Often the relatives of the dead could not bring themselves to go on the annual march nor even to observe it. As one told Joelle Gartner: 'I used to stand on the Creggan and watch them go down. I stopped doing that because what I was doing was, I was scanning the crowd looking for my dead brother.'

Twenty years after Bloody Sunday, in spring 1992, the campaign for truth and justice finally took off with the formation of the Bloody Sunday Justice Campaign. This had three aims:

- that the British government should publicly and unambiguously exonerate those killed and injured,

- that the British government publicly repudiate the Widgery Report in its entirety,

- and that those responsible for the murders and attempted murders on the streets of Derry on 30th January 1972 be brought to justice.

A book by Derry journalist Eamonn McCann—*Bloody Sunday in Derry: What Really Happened*—was published in 1992 and helped to revive interest. Don Mullan's *Eyewitness Bloody Sunday* was another book which boosted the campaign. Using the 700 eyewitness accounts which had been gathered in 1972 by NCCL and later ignored by Widgery, Mullan pieced together an account which helped to answer a number of crucial questions. In particular, he concluded that:

- there was overwhelming evidence that three of the victims—Michael McDaid, William Nash and John Young—were shot not by paratroopers in the Bogside, but by other British soldiers on the walls overlooking the area;

- there was strong suspicion that seven of the dead—Gerard Donaghey, James Wray, Kevin McElhinney, William McKinney, Jack Duddy, Patrick Doherty and Bernard McGuigan—were in fact murdered rather than merely shot by soldiers involved in an indiscriminate operation.

Mullan followed up his suspicions regarding the shooting from the walls by consulting with Dr. Raymond McClean, a Derry general practitioner who had ministered to four of the dead on Bloody Sunday and who was present at the post mortem examinations of all the dead. At the same time, Mullan sought the advice of Robert Breglio, a ballistics expert from New York. Both men agreed with the conclusion that three of the dead were shot from the walls. Further confirmation came from a member of the Royal Anglian regiment who had been stationed on the walls and approached the media to report that he had witnessed an army sniper at work on Bloody Sunday.

In August 1995 Jane Winter, Director of British Irish Rights Watch, went through 65 files on Bloody Sunday in the Public Record Office in London. Among them were statements by British soldiers which had not been made available to the lawyers for the families during the Widgery tribunal. Some of these statements had been rewritten four times. The statements and other evidence were then examined meticulously by law professor Dermot Walsh in 1996. He concluded that during the Widgery inquiry vital information had been withheld which could have led to charges of murder or attempted murder being brought against some soldiers.

The Irish government eventually decided to re-examine the Widgery Report in the light of Don Mullan's book, Dermot Walsh's report, the files located by Jane Winter, the reports from British army eyewitnesses and a further 101 eyewitness accounts which had been in the possession of the Irish government. On the basis of this new information it produced a report demolishing Widgery's conclusions and handed this to the British government in June 1997. Subsequently, on 29 January 1999, 27 years after the event, Prime Minister Tony Blair announced that there would be a new inquiry into Bloody Sunday. It was to be chaired by Lord Saville of Newdigate, assisted by Sir Edward Somers from New Zealand and Mr Justice William Hoyt from Canada.

Since its inception the Saville inquiry has come up against opposition from the British soldiers involved in Bloody Sunday and from the Ministry of Defence. In May 1999, Saville ruled that soldiers would not be granted anonymity when they appeared before his tribunal. The following month, a judicial review brought by 17 soldiers who had fired live rounds on Bloody Sunday was heard at the High Court in London. The High Court overturned Saville's ruling, ensuring anonymity for the British soldiers on the grounds that their lives would be in danger if their names were known. Ironically, shortly beforehand it was revealed that the names of at least 15 of these soldiers had been known in Derry for some years and were currently being distributed on the internet by Sinn Féin's RM Distribution e-mail service.

The British soldiers' campaign was backed by Defence Secretary George Robertson and by a number of British newspapers, in particular the *Daily Mail*.

Lt Col Derek Wilford, who had been in charge of the paratroopers in Derry on Bloody Sunday, stated in the *Daily Mail* on 31 May 1999:

> I have no regrets about what we did. If that situation existed again, I would do the same. Indeed, I would do more and go into the flats after the gunmen.

He said that he would gladly go to jail for contempt of court rather than reveal the names of his soldiers on duty that day.

Two months later Wilford was in the news again. On 10 July 1999, Michael McKinney, brother of Bloody Sunday victim William, was interviewed on Radio 4's 'Today'. He said his brother was not involved in any republican group. Derek Wilford responded:

> He may represent his dead brother, and a very, very tragic situation it is. But I do not accept that he merely represents him. He represents the republican organisation. They will all say that, won't they? I mean, every republican, every—I regret to say—almost every Ulster Catholic will say that.

Preliminary hearings of the Saville inquiry were held in the Guildhall in Derry for one week in September 1999. At this point, there was already a great deal of information in the public arena which vindicated the campaigners' case that Bloody Sunday involved both planning and cover-up. The evidence of cover-up begins with the Widgery tribunal and report. From time to time other evidence was unearthed. For example, Jane Winter's research in the Public Record Office in London in August 1995, already referred to above, also uncovered the minute of a meeting held on 1 February 1972 when Lord Widgery agreed to head the tribunal. He met with the British Prime Minister Edward Heath and the Lord Chancellor, Lord Hailsham. The minute was taken by the Prime Minister's private secretary, Robert Armstrong. It notes that Heath told Widgery that:

> It had to be remembered that we were in Northern Ireland fighting not only a military war but a propaganda war.

Similarly, in September 1999, Eamonn McCann revealed that in 1973, Attorney General Sir Peter Rawlinson had given his opinion on the issue of possible actions by relatives over the Bloody Sunday deaths. He concluded:

> – that the Crown had no prospect of a successful defence in the case of the deaths of James Wray, Gerald McKinney, Gerard Donaghey and William McKinney;
>
> – that a successful defence was highly unlikely in the case of Jackie Duddy, Patrick Doherty and Bernard McGuigan;
>
> – and that the Crown's position was not strong in relation to the cases of Kevin McElhinney and Hugh Gilmore.

This opinion was not made public at the time. Instead the British government continued to insist that the dead, as originally stated, were not innocent.

Information about planning trickled through from other sources. An anonymous paratrooper contacted the *Sunday Business Post*, which carried his statement on 16 March 1999. He stated that:

- the paratroopers had been briefed by a senior officer the day before they went to Derry to get some kills;
- that the three men shot at the barricade at Glenfada Park had their hands in the air when they were killed;
- that one victim had died as a result of a non-issue dum dum bullet;
- that the paratroopers had successfully concealed from Widgery that they had fired many more than the 108 bullets he had acknowledged.

The Saville inquiry began in earnest in March 2000. For three weeks, the inquiry's counsel, Christopher Clarke QC, made a lengthy opening submission. During this, he produced more evidence of the high level of planning which had led up to Bloody Sunday. In October 1971 General Michael Carver produced a memo for Prime Minister Ted Heath prior to a meeting between Heath and Northern Ireland Prime Minister Brian Faulkner. Carver concluded that,

> It may become imperative to go into the Bogside and root out the terrorists and the hooligans.

Clarke also produced a memo written by General Robert Ford after a visit to Derry on 7 January 1972 to assess the security situation. Ford wrote:

> I am coming to the conclusion that the minimum force necessary to achieve a restoration of law and order is to shoot selected ring leaders amongst the DYH [Derry young hooligans] after clear warnings have been issued.

Ford went on to add that that the use of high-velocity bullets would be justified, but that, given their devastating effect, it would be better to use bullets of a lower velocity. In fact it is now known that 30 guns, modified to take a .22 bullet, were delivered to Derry for potential use on Bloody Sunday.

In another submission, the former commander of the Royal Anglians in Derry in 1972—referred to only as Colonel 1347—made a statement to the inquiry that he was both surprised and upset that the Paratroop Regiment had been assigned to duty on the day of the march. Despite being the longest serving officer in Derry at the time, he had not been consulted. Nor was he happy with the Paratroopers' tactics, as revealed the week before Bloody Sunday when they had aggressively halted an anti-internment march at Magilligan Strand. The colonel stated that he had been assured at the time that the decision to use the regiment had been taken 'at the highest level', namely government.

That the Paras meant business—and were sent to Derry precisely for that reason—was made clear from a recording of British army radio messages made by a local Derry man, James Porter. He had made these tapes available to the Widgery tribunal but had been told not to continue publicising them as he was open to prosecution for taping the radio messages. One tape was of a radio conversation between a soldier and his officer. The soldier states that he is under attack from nailbombers in an alleyway. He reports seeing a youth emerge from the alleyway unarmed, but is positive that this is one of the nailbombers. 'Shoot him dead', commands the officer. The soldier fires and misses by 'about two inches'. 'Bad shooting, over', is the officer's comment.

Despite the boost that such revelations give to the campaigners' case, it is unlikely that the inquiry will proved to be plain sailing, not least because of the continued ability of the MOD to block disclosure. Shortly before the inquiry began, on 18 February 2000, it was revealed that the guns used in the Bloody Sunday killings had been deemed obselete and that most of them were no longer in existence. Of the 29 rifles fired by paratroopers that day, 10 had been sold to private firms and 14 had been destroyed a matter of days before Tony Blair's announcement of the Saville inquiry. When the Saville inquiry discovered this, they demanded the retention of the remaining five rifles for forensic testing. Despite MOD assurances that they would be kept under lock and key, a further two were destroyed. In addition, Christopher Clarke revealed on 31 March 2000, that although there were 10 military photographers on duty on Bloody Sunday, the MOD had destroyed all photographs of the march.

In the face of such obstacles, the crucial question is: will Saville manage to get at the truth of what happened on Bloody Sunday? He has clearly shown himself to be more independent than Widgery. For example, he reprimanded the MOD for not identifying and locating most of the soldiers present on Bloody Sunday, leaving it to his inquiry to find them. On the other hand, his inquiry was originally less than generous with relatives as regards the extent of legal representation they could have and only conceded more after being challenged by the relatives. Despite that, the very existence of the Saville inquiry is a realisation of the first demand of the Bloody Sunday Justice Campaign—a repudiation of Widgery.

Speaking of the original whitewash, Derry woman Maureen Shiels stated:

> People in our area did not wait for the Widgery Report to find out the truth.
> They waited to find out if he would tell the truth.

Widgery failed this test miserably. It remains to be seen if Saville can do better.

The story of Bloody Sunday and the campaign is told by Kay Duddy, sister of murdered teenager Jackie Duddy, and by Tony Doherty, whose father Patrick was shot dead by paratroopers.

Kay Duddy

Jackie has been called a bomber and a gunman. To me it is so important that his innocence is declared. We were naive enough to believe that the Widgery Tribunal would establish their innocence and then we would get justice and they would get their just desserts. We know the truth; we know what happened that day. I want the world and its mother to know what happened that day.

That Sunday, I don't know whether my daddy had a premonition or not. Daddy was a man who always said he fought his own civil rights and there was no call to go out on the streets. He'd been on night shift—he worked in one of the local hospitals—came home from work, had a bite to eat and went to bed for the afternoon, but with a warning that nobody was to go on the march. So of course, a few of the brothers decided that they were going to go anyway. Jackie was carrying on and he said, 'Do you think that me girlfriend will like the gear I've on me the day?' So away they went. We watched the march leaving. We had a vantage point; we were two storeys up. It was like a carnival. There were women and children and prams.

After we rid up the dishes, we sat down and played a hand of cards, generally passing the afternoon. At some stage, one of the younger brothers came in—he was ten, I think, at the time—and he said, 'Our Jackie was shot down the town'. We all swiped at him, and went, 'God forgive you; don't be saying things like that'. He said, 'I'm only joking'. It wouldn't have been maybe an hour after, an aunt and uncle came to the door and I said, 'Come on in. What's the crack with youse?' And she said, 'Kay, I don't want to alarm you or anything, but we've reason to believe that Jackie was hurt down the town'. My first instinct was, 'Ah Jesus! Me daddy will go off his head!' We didn't have a phone in the house and we went down, and the shop that was underneath the maisonette where we were living was packed to the door. I said, 'We'll not get into the phone there'. So we went to the community centre and I phoned Altnagelvin and said, 'Could you put me through to Casualty?' Whenever they answered the phone, I could hear the bedlam. I says, 'I'm enquiring was there a Jackie Duddy admitted today'. And she said, 'Who is asking, please?' I said, 'It's his sister, Kay'. She seemed to be a couple of minutes; she went away and when she came back she said, 'Jackie Duddy was dead on admission'. I remember throwing the phone and screaming. I said to me Aunt Dolly, 'You may tell me daddy'. She had to go and waken him out of his sleep. Ah God, he went crazy!

The ironic thing was that Jackie had an appointment to go and see the careers officer with the intention of joining the Merchant Navy, because he was getting that much hassle going to his work and the boxing club. He was a great wee amateur boxer. The appointment was for the second of February, the day he was buried.

It must have been my coping mechanism, but basically, I feel I've lost three days out of my life, because I can't remember going to the hospital, his remains coming home or his remains being at home. It's terrible. I picked myself out, as I thought, in a photograph of the funerals and the same aunt that had given us the word said, 'No, you collapsed in the chapel and had to be taken home'. My daddy's way of trying to help us was, you don't talk about it, because he knew that they would have gone out looking for vengeance.

The Widgery Tribunal came and went. To be honest, I'm not sure that my daddy went to it; everything's sort of hazy with me. As everyone knows now, it was one of the biggest whitewashes that ever was. It left us that my brother was murdered and as well as murdering him, they then besmudged his name. He was classed as a bomber or a gunman. The rest of them were the same, the wounded were the same. So, everybody's sort of waiting and saying, 'Someone's going to do something about this'. Time went on and nothing was happening. At the twentieth anniversary, a few of the family members got together and decided, 'Let's see if we can do something about this'.

We got together and arranged a meeting in the Pat Finucane Centre. And one meeting led to another. We put a wee itinerary together: anybody that had any ideas as regards fund raising, who we should talk to, who we should meet. It didn't matter how silly your idea was, put it on the table and discuss it and if a result came out of it, so be it. It was trial and error. We were stumbling along and as time went on, we seemed to come up against hurdles. The first hurdle that we reached was finance. So we started fund raising—a sponsored quiz, an auction, concerts, begging round the doors. When we got a wee bit more established, we tried to get permission from the police for a flag day. We were very surprised they did grant us a permit. For the twenty-fifth anniversary, we thought we had to do something special. We went to a woman in Scotland to get the wee logo, the dove, and we designed the badge. Another thing that we did over the Bloody Sunday weekend, the Bloody Sunday lecture and that, we didn't actually put a charge on that, but people gave us a donation. The people of Derry have been absolutely excellent, I have to say. They give their time, money, stuff for raffles.

The next thing that happened was that Don Mullan came along. One day he was in Derry and he met someone he hadn't seen in a long time and he says to him, 'I was just reading your statement there the other day'. He said, 'I must get a look at that', and he came up to the Pat Finucane Centre and there were all the original statements [to the Widgery Tribunal]. Don started going through them. Now Don, in his own line of work was always meeting various people and he was saying, 'Right, I'll see if I can get you a meeting with so and so'. We met Teddy Kennedy, who came to Derry, and Kerry Kennedy Cuomo. We went to Dublin and met Jean Kennedy Smith, Mary Robinson; we met all the TDs, Bertie Ahern, Mary Harney.

Don then got us invites to America. He even got us sponsored over; great fund-raiser he is! Some of our group were in the White House and some in Capitol Hill. If someone had said to me seven years ago, 'Some day you'll be standing talking on Capitol Hill', I'd have said, 'You're out of your mind, mucker'. They asked me if I would tell the story of what happened to Congressmen. So I stood up at the podium and I looked round and I went, 'Oh my God!' Of course, I went to pieces, to be perfectly honest. I basically cried my way through it. I was apologising at the end of it and every one of them said the same thing, 'Don't apologise; it was a very sad story; it never should have happened'.

We were in New York to participate in the St Patrick's Day parade. We also took part in Boston's St Patrick's Day parade, and through that, Mickey McKinney, who is the present chairman of the campaign, got connections with the A.O.H. in America. It was amazing how things seemed to roller-coaster all of a sudden.

We went to Downing Street and handed in a petition. Don Mullan got Cherokee Indians and everything to sign it. We got these postcards printed up demanding a new inquiry. We addressed them to John Major. We gave them to people and said, 'All you've to do is write your name'. I could have just pictured them in Downing Street going, 'Ah dear Jesus! Not more of them!' Then we had the meeting with Mo Mowlam and I took a photograph in my bag. After the meeting, I walked up and said, 'Excuse me, Doctor Mowlam'. She looked at me and I set Jackie's photo down and I said, 'That's what we're talking about. We're talking about human beings here. I'm sick listening to people talking in numbers'. You just have to grit your teeth and get on with it and develop a brass neck and go in and say to people, 'This is my story and this is what I want you to do for me', and just hope that they don't say, 'Bugger off'.

When eventually the actual date of the Saville Inquiry was announced, it was the strangest sensation, because there was really no joy or elation. We just sat in stone silence and looked at one another. I think what was going through everybody's mind was, 'What do we do now?' We just hadn't a clue, not a clue. Then the solicitors came on board; Madden and Finucane know what they are at and what we need from them. They are not going to let them away with anything this time. The first hurdle was legal representation; we had to go in and argue our case for legal representation. At the beginning the Saville Inquiry team only offered us three senior and three junior counsel. So we had to say, 'No, that's not sufficient; we can't accept that under any circumstances'. That was another battle that we had with Saville. They promised us that everything they got, we would get, but they were very reluctant to hand it over; they kept us waiting on it.

I wish there had been a way of not having to go through an inquiry again. I am dreading it. We got a wee insight of the distress that people were still going through when Eversheds—a private firm of solicitors employed by the Saville team to take statements—came to Derry. We put out appeals on the radio for anybody that had anything to say please come forward. There were people who had made previous statements and they were the first to come forward. There were a lot of people out there, because they hadn't actually seen anyone being shot, felt what they had experienced on the day didn't count. For instance, I was talking to a girl who was fourteen; her and her sister had gone to the march that day. They were standing at the platform at Free Derry Corner when Bernadette Devlin said, 'Jesus, everybody get down on the ground; they are shooting from the walls'. They thought this wasn't particularly important, but we have been saying to people 'It is. It's like a big jigsaw and we have to put all the pieces into the jigsaw. No matter how trivial you feel the thing is, come and tell it. This is what is going to put the picture together.'

As I said, the dread about the inquiry was the weeks Eversheds were in the Guildhall. We worked out a wee rota so that a couple of members of the families would be there during the day. When people came in and recognised us, it helped them to relax a wee bit and they felt the necessity to tell us the same story that they had told the Eversheds team. They were so upset by it all, I thought, 'Oh God! This is only the statement thing! What is the actual inquiry going to be like?' At this moment in time I'm not one hundred percent sure what the actual format of an inquiry is, but I'd say its going to be very traumatic. Needless to say, I'm not looking forward to it.

They so limited the witnesses at the Widgery Tribunal they never got a chance, never got their day in court to say what they'd seen. He selected something like seventeen statements out of a batch of between five or six hundred. That's what his findings were based on and of course, on lies that the soldiers told. Apparently some of the soldiers changed their statements up to two or three times. Some of them told exactly what had happened but were told, 'No, you can't say that. This is what you are going to say'. The paratrooper that got in touch with the *Newsletter*, and then came on the David Dunseith programme, 'Talkback', said that nothing that happened that day justified what took place after. He said, 'Even if', and he emphasised, 'Even if', there were one or two gunmen there after the shootings, 'it wasn't enough to justify fourteen lives'.

I find the saddest part of it all was that they were prepared to sacrifice all those lives over the years for this cover-up. I'm not just talking about Bloody Sunday, also about the subsequent deaths since. I'm not saying that there might not have been any other deaths, but I just think so many deaths could have been prevented, because there were people went out and did things in the name of Bloody Sunday. That's not what we wanted. I felt so responsible for so many deaths. Then I thought, 'How dare they do that to me? That's their burden, not my burden'. It took me a long time to convince myself of that.

The sad thing about it is that all that knowledge is there; they know it's there. I really do feel if there had been a Conservative government still in power there is no way we would have been granted the inquiry. The change of government was what helped and I think that Tony Blair realises it's time to lay this to rest. There were times we despaired, times we felt that we were up against a brick wall, that we weren't going to get any further. Then you would get a wee glimmer of light and you carry on. But it was something that had to be done.

My mother died in 1968; she was just forty four years old. She died from leukaemia. It was only when Jackie's death occurred my daddy was able to come to terms with my mummy's death. He said, 'Now I know why the Sacred Heart took your mother. He did not want her to go through what we were going through'. When you think of things like that, you've got to push on.

We lost my mummy in 1968, we lost Jackie in 1972 and we lost my daddy in 1985. When my mummy's anniversary comes round, we do what we have to do. We go and give the priest the money and we go to a wee mass; we take the flowers to the cemetery and get an acknowledgement in the paper. We do the same with my daddy's, all done in our own private way. With Jackie's, you can't; unfortunately, it's different. You see, Jackie has been called a bomber and a gunman. To me it is so important that his innocence is declared. We were naive enough to believe that the Widgery Tribunal would establish their innocence and then we would get justice and they would get their just desserts. I would love to be able to go and see the priest, get his mass said, go up the cemetery, say a wee private prayer—to have peace to grieve, deal with it, the same as we did with our parents and then hopefully, get on with the rest of my life. We know the truth; we know what happened that day. I want the world and its mother to know what happened that day.

I want truth and justice, plain and simple. I feel that we blew Widgery out of the water; Widgery's dead twice over. Our three demands were always repudiation of the Widgery Tribunal, the truth and justice. We want prosecutions; we deserve prosecutions. Being realistic, there are none of them that are ever going to serve a day in jail. My opinion is, if we get the truth, and get rid of Widgery and people realise it was the farce that it was, as long as I know that they were proved guilty in my heart, I would nearly settle for that. As I said, 'They can put all those soldiers into jail, but they have to put Ted Heath etc., etc. along with them'.

After the talks started up in Stormont, we met with Rita Restorick—her son was one of the last soldiers to be shot—to let her know that we knew what she is going through and also to let her know what we had gone through. I think it's so very sad that because people are shot by somebody in a uniform, that makes it okay. They have literally got away with murder for far too long. It's time to put a stop to it.

Tony Doherty

For most of the years it hasn't really been dealt with by the city. For most of its history there was almost a shame about the thing. You can't expect people to just support you; you have to reinvent your campaign in terms of PR and profile. You have to find different ways of reproducing the same story. As it turned out for us, sooner or later the issues will click and all the different elements will just come into place.

I suppose we need to look at where the issue was at in the years preceding the start of the campaign. For most of the years it hasn't really been dealt with by the city. For most of its history there was almost a shame about the thing. Bloody Sunday was very much a non-issue in real political terms. There was the annual commemoration in the city which was organised since 1973 by Sinn Féin, and at that stage you had two Sinn Féin's, Provisional and Official. The Northern Ireland Civil Rights Movement, which had run into the sand by 1974, would have been the most appropriate body for continuing on, but history didn't allow for that.

What you had then, from around the mid-1970s to the late 1980s, was a single commemoration. That was fine. We should be thankful that somebody was doing something on some level. But people started to focus on the possibility of doing something on a more serious level about Bloody Sunday around 1988-89 and '90, with a particular concentration on the twentieth anniversary in 1992. A possibility existed at that stage of comparing the issue of the Birmingham Six and the Guildford Four with Bloody Sunday. That era posed questions as to what possibilities existed here in terms of directly addressing Bloody Sunday as a real issue and not just as a historical issue. That's what the commemoration I think up until then was becoming; it was historical, in the past and while it was still a live political issue for many people, it really wasn't a campaigning or live human rights issue.

We started off with fairly limited objectives, that was just to create the broader platform coming up to the anniversary. There was no overall game-plan. There was no grand conspiracy to set about uncovering the truth about Bloody Sunday. Fairly simple tools were to be used to promote the issue. I think people involved in campaigning have to be clever as well; you can't expect people to just support you; you have to reinvent your campaign in terms of PR and profile and have short-term goals as well. You have to find different ways of reproducing the same story. As it turned out for us, sooner or later the issues will click and all the different elements will just come into place.

Since 1989, we built upon the Bloody Sunday march and weekend itself, broadened out the events, looked at the issue in a broad and international context and organised events accordingly. From that period until 1992, this worked very successfully. The attendance at the march alone, for instance, was clearly increasing; from a few thousand people it was becoming an event people wanted to identify with. When we came up to 1990 and 1991, we had sometimes fifteen thousand people on the streets, which was great for that time.

The twentieth anniversary was a very good local, national and international event. At that stage Eamonn McCann's book, *Bloody Sunday: What Really Happened*, was published. I had been involved in organising the research for the book. What we discovered was that most of the people who had been directly affected by it—the families—hadn't really been brought into the equation. That is nobody's fault, and in some sense it's everybody's fault. The families hadn't spoken collectively about this for years and years and you could see there was evidently quite a lot of raw emotion there, when people were speaking about their loss. It still was very deep; it hadn't healed. One could also detect a sense of resignation at that stage—that it had gone on unchanged for years that they were always going to carry the burden. There was no clear critical path there for people to identify with and so they felt very much on their own. Eamonn's book was the first time that the full spectrum of opinion had been taken into consideration and I suppose that started sparking off ideas in my mind, and I'm sure in other people's as well, about the potential that issue had.

It angers me when I look back. I was only nine when the Widgery Report was published. The families were really shafted. The sad thing was that, first of all, Bloody Sunday happened, and in the aftermath of Bloody Sunday, you had an explosion of conflict. 1972 was the worst year of the war. In that sense its importance as a justice issue was overshadowed by hundreds of other events that year and in subsequent years.

Everybody in Derry was shell-shocked and there was no clear attempt to advise the families at that time beyond the very limited confines of the Widgery Inquiry. Clearly the families weren't in any position to govern their own circumstances. People were badly traumatised by Bloody Sunday and they were very badly treated by the Widgery Tribunal. The overall outcome of Bloody Sunday left a lot of people damaged. There was no impetus for people to come together over that period between 1974 and 1992. When the book was eventually launched in 1992, it became the occasion in the city when the families actually met again. A lot of them actually would have passed one another and would have said, 'There's such-and-such; it's ten years since I saw her'. The book was a timely intervention. At its launch we rediscovered one another and found out that practically everyone felt that this issue needed to be taken up. The families decided they would begin the process of reconvening themselves, trying to set out some strategic objective for the emergence of a new campaigning group. People like Johnny Walker of the Birmingham Six, who had been released the previous year, and Robin Percival were involved in advising the families on what was the best type of structure, format, objectives and so on.

There was an energy around that suggested it was definitely going to go somewhere. However, people were realistic: this is going to take a terrible long time. There was a whole perception to be turned around. The popular perception was that Bloody Sunday was a republican issue. It didn't need to be a republican issue but had become so because republicans historically were the only group who were consistent for almost twenty years. In my view republicans had a right to campaign, but others should be encouraged to support the issue also. We went out of our way; even the republicans within the families, of which there are quite a lot, said this is about justice and the city of Derry, not about promoting one brand of politics over the other. But that was easier said than done. It was a slow process of reconstituting the issue, allowing support to come from the SDLP tradition as well as the Sinn Féin tradition, as well as others who might not identify with any particular category. As an example of that, we approached the council, which was majority SDLP, in May 1992. Certain members of the SDLP were very hostile towards the council funding the campaign and it became something of an argument—very undignified for everybody and certainly for us in approaching what is our council, looking for funding. It was also short-sighted for those who took a contrary and niggardly view of the matter to the extent of displaying open hostility towards the families. They just refused to understand how this issue was important twenty years later and allowed their petty politics to dictate how the council would or would not interact with the campaign. It was nothing short of a disgrace.

Suffice to say, we didn't receive funding from the council and I think the individuals involved may regret what they did. Even in terms of the Republic, we have created a platform there in accepting support from everybody, no matter what their politics were. That's where we wanted to go; some people couldn't see that at the time and they may regret their actions now.

From 1992 onwards, we established the objectives of the campaign: bringing about a declaration of innocence from the British government for those who were killed and wounded on the day; to have the government repudiate the Widgery Report; and for the government to bring about prosecutions of those who were involved in the events of that day. In terms of campaigning, it became quite highly profiled between 1992 and 1994-5. We petitioned the British government, travelled to other parts of the country, gathering signatures, etc. We had straightforward projects, like a postcard campaign to Downing Street with the aims of the campaign emblazoned on the cover and addressed to John Major.

From about 1993 onwards as well there was an exchange of correspondence between John Hume and John Major. I suppose the first chink in the armour came about just after that, where for the first time the government attempted to change the terminology that had been used previously. In terms of our correspondence with the British, they would have just used the same phraseology, you know, 'The government has found in terms of the Widgery Report this or the other', you know, 'piss off' type of thing. Around 1993, when Major replied to Hume he said something like, 'The government views the deceased as having been found innocent of the accusation of possession of weapons, etc'. It was a clever move on behalf of the government which didn't work however, because they applied that particular term which was used in the Widgery Report about the point where people were actually shot. What Widgery was saying was that the deceased should be considered found not guilty at the point of being killed; but went on to say there was sufficient evidence to suggest that several of the deceased were involved at some stage during that day. Major's reply didn't deal with that; he just repeated that the deceased should be considered innocent of the charges of possession of weapons at the point of being killed. Nothing had changed; it was a clever play with words. Members of the families were saying, 'This doesn't come anywhere near achieving our aims'. What it did suggest was that the government was becoming edgy.

We got the Derry City Council to support us in principle, which is very different to supporting us in practice. They supported our aims and we put pressure on the council to circulate the aims of the campaign amongst the other councils in the North; it then became a debating point in a wider arena. It was also circulated in the South where it became a debating point. In reality the only people who would propose the motions were Sinn Féin councillors, which was good, but it also demonstrated how hostile people had become towards dealing with issues from the North within the South.

During the first year of the campaign, December 1992, the RUC special unit raided our premises. There was a lot of loyalist killings at the time and they kicked their way in armed with sub-machine guns and without standard RUC uniforms. We thought they were loyalists and we were all going to be shot. I was standing at the window and saw all these people running up the steps. I thought, 'This is the end'. As it happens, they didn't shoot us, but they arrested everybody. When we were brought out, we were in those forensic white suits. The RUC were clearly trying to put across to people that they had captured an IRA unit. We were held in Gough Barracks for five or six days. While we were in Gough, the Special Branch concocted a cock and bull story of phones being tapped from the Campaign's office; whatever it was, they made a terrible hash of it, as they quickly dropped it and it was never heard of again.

The Campaign had over these years attracted the support of other individuals and organisations such as the CAJ, and I would like to mention Mike Ritchie in particular. Another is Jane Winter, who works with the British Irish Rights Watch in London and who has acted in a supportive way towards the campaign over the years. She happened to visit the Public Records Office in 1994. A document she discovered provided a real impetus for the families and for everybody involved, where Lord Hailsham was basically setting out the parameters for the Widgery whitewash. He had Heath, Widgery and a few others discussing the Tribunal and the immediate aftermath of Bloody Sunday. This was a confidential document obviously, but you had Heath advising Widgery that he needed to be careful because Britain was fighting not just a military but a propaganda war. He was clearly being told that, 'Your report better vindicate what we are doing there'. This was a real breakthrough.

In 1995 I was working at the Pat Finucane Centre and came across National Council for Civil Liberties' statements which were taken in the immediate aftermath of Bloody Sunday in Derry. I had met Don Mullan one day at a bus stop and told him I happened to be reading his personal statement of what he witnessed on Bloody Sunday. He was intrigued, for he had forgotten he had made a statement at all. His was actually quite a clear and detailed statement. I arranged with him to come up to the Pat Finucane Centre to look at it. When he came up, he was doubly intrigued by the mass of material that had been gathered over the years. He looked at the other statements, photocopied his own and left. We met one another a month afterwards, again casually and he said he had been thinking very seriously about the statements for they were 'a very important part of the hidden history of a very important event that happened in this town'. By sheer coincidence, we were actually talking in Rossville Street where Bloody Sunday occurred. He said he would like to talk to one or two people about the potential of reproducing the statements in book form as a contribution to the twenty fifth anniversary in 1997.

Don eventually received all the eye witness testimonies and set to work on the book, trying to compare the statements with what was carried in the Widgery Report. These statements were actually presented to Widgery and he didn't take any of them into consideration. Upon reading some of the statements, he realised that a major element of the eye witness accounts had been completely ignored by the Widgery Tribunal—that was the shooting from the walls. Don said he remembered the shooting from the walls and I think about 50 or 60 of the four hundred or so statements said there was shooting from the walls. Don takes a very technical approach to his work and he wasn't satisfied with his own sort of lay person's interpretation of the evidence, so he engaged other people with a greater knowledge of ballistics. It turned out that in the case of some of the people who were shot at the front of Rossville Flats the trajectory of the bullet strongly suggests that it did indeed come from a height. When the book was about to be published, Channel Four started to take a very active interest in the issue. Channel Four, a British company, deserve great credit for the work they did, independently investigating some of the anomalies within the Widgery Report and looking at Don's book and other publications with a view to exploding the whole state version of Bloody Sunday.

All of the material that was coming forward through Don, through Channel Four, through our own legal advisers, people working on our behalf in London, it wasn't being challenged any more by the British government. The game was practically up at that stage; it was just a matter of them trying to limit the damage and steer a diplomatic course around the whole thing. I think none of this would have happened if the campaign had not been there, because one good idea will attract another. It's what Mike Ritchie once described as a 'confluence'. People working on ideas will ultimately start collaborating with others. The campaign, in my estimation was the clear impetus for all of this to happen; if the campaign hadn't have been there, arguably Don wouldn't have worked on his book, and Channel Four wouldn't have picked up on it at all. That is why grass roots activity is vitally important.

1996 and 1997 were key years. As a result of the ceasefires and steady strides towards lasting peace, a new politics was emerging, the politics of peace and possibility. In the Republic as a result of Don's work, the issue of Bloody Sunday was being looked at differently; now there was space there for people to look at it differently. But it wouldn't necessarily have happened if our people hadn't been active on it. We then sat down and plotted a course of lobbying the Irish government. This was the Fine Gael government under John Bruton, who was supportive. Dick Spring was the Tanaiste; he was very supportive. Of all those at government level, he struck me as the most proactive and energetic.

All the families came down to Dublin for one of the key meetings we had with him. I think that was very important for people to see that there was a groundswell of opinion in Derry. We put forward what we felt needed to be brought about by the British government in order to resolve this. We put across the notion that a resolution of Bloody Sunday would be beneficial for everyone concerned, not just in Ireland, but in Britain. I think people recognised that this was an issue that was clearly not going to go away: we were living in a relatively more peaceful era, but what we were saying was that, even if we go back to the worst of what had happened in the previous twenty five years, this was still going to be an issue that needed to be resolved and which would always be a major injustice and therefore a barrier to lasting peace. Those sentiments were taken on board. The Irish government, under the directive of Dick Spring, drew up its own report. It concluded by calling on the British government to establish a new inquiry—which was completely unprecedented in British judicial history—and that the inquiry should also have an international dimension.

In late 1996 and 1997 Bloody Sunday became a recurring item on the agenda for the British-Irish inter-parliamentary council and the Anglo-Irish secretariat in Maryfield. We also understand that it was raised by Martin McGuinness with the British on several occasions. All of this, combined with lobbying at Westminister facilitated by John Hume and supported by Derry City Council, was clearly having an effect. But Britain was still not keen to move.

Circumstances changed when the Labour government came in 1997; we were dealing with a government which was concerned with image—new Labour with a sort of niceish, Mo Mowlamish feel to it. But the Labour government genuinely didn't appreciate the immensity of the issue of Bloody Sunday in Irish national terms. They were soon toying about with various ideas such a review of evidence, which was a meaningless, non-judicial mechanism; it wouldn't have any status whatsoever. We knocked it down right away. There were suggestions that the British government would apologise for what had happened and for the way people were treated subsequently. Some people within the Labour government genuinely believed that this was a radical way out of the issue. On the face of it, it looked like a positive thing, someone apologising for something they had done, seeking forgiveness, etc. But we were saying this is not the way things should be; we aren't involved just to make people feel better about it. This is about the truth. The British government was very close to issuing an apology, even up to a few days before the decision was made on the inquiry. So, between December 1997 and January 1998, we were involved in quite intense discussions with the Irish government and remained adamant if an apology was offered, it would actually exacerbate the situation, not make it better, because we, as the offended, are actually saying to the offender, 'We don't want an apology; this is what we want: tell us the truth'. The idea of an apology had a certain amount of currency; it was quite an effort for us to keep the emphasis on the truth. Some within the British Labour Party thought an apology would be appropriate. It took some intense education of those particular individuals about what was actually going to resolve it.

When he came into lead the country, An Taoiseach, Bertie Ahern, to his credit, took up this issue with gusto. According to reports in December 1997, he personally passed his government's file on Bloody Sunday to Tony Blair. The story goes that Blair took the file home with him over the weekend, went through the whole business and after a couple of telephone conversations with Bertie Ahern, the two of them agreed that the best course of action was a new independent inquiry.

I think it's going to be quite a long, difficult, gruelling process for everyone involved. It will go on for anything up to two years. It is a very personal issue for everyone concerned and different families will place different emphases on what they actually want. What we have all agreed on was that the inquiry won't immediately bring about the aims of the campaign. But it could be a significant stepping stone in that direction.

The British government introduced two international figures onto the panel. That was the key to get our support for it; if it had been a single British judge, the families could have adopted a very hostile attitude to it. It could be, though, that they will get us in the long grass. The emphasis has to be how we conduct ourselves during the inquiry and how our case is to be presented; that's no easy task. For the inquiry is bigger than us; it is unprecedented in British legal history. It's a major event for the city of Derry as well as for the whole country and it is going to attract major international attention. Obviously we don't want to make any mistakes; what we are trying to do is look at what support we need, counselling and legal support. We have been through an educational process in terms of the campaign; people have picked up skills from the experiences along the way and I think these have been invested in a positive way in terms of this tribunal. The British aren't going to simply lie down and wave the white flag and the temptation is that the British government will try at times to influence the outcome of the inquiry unduly. We have to guard against that. It would spell disaster again if there is a negative outcome. If it is another whitewash, it could probably set back relations between Britain and Ireland for a long time to come.

What I want may be somewhat different from what someone else wants. I suppose for me it's about closure. What I'd like is for the British government to be seen for what it is and that is not from a perspective of seeking revenge, but clearly there was a major crime committed within this city—two crimes committed, in terms of the massacre and of Widgery. What I would like to see is the full truth emerging about what happened on the day and in the immediate aftermath, including the Widgery Tribunal itself. There has to be accountability established around that. Personally, I don't want to see anybody suffer as a result of what has happened, either physically or psychologically. It could become a positive process for everyone concerned but I'm not sure that will happen. In saying that, we all have to live in the real world and the real world as we now see it was established last Easter, in terms of the Good Friday Agreement.

I wouldn't like to see the soldier who killed my father go to prison because, if that was the case, I would still have to deal with the consequences in a human and personal way. As well as that—he would get out some day. Would I then be back to square one? I'd rather say to myself, 'I have reached this point. I now know not just what happened but how and why it happened. Let's put it into the past and move on.' What I want to do is get away from that negative experience—not by burying it, but by realising that the event and the aftermath were major injustices. I think there is a danger as well of devolving or diminishing the responsibility of what happened on to people on the ground. It's like blaming the screws in H6 for batoning people during the blanket protest when in reality they were part of an uglier system which allowed this to happen. I would be more concerned that those who allowed the situation to develop would not be brought to account for what they had done; this to me would be more important. The individual who killed my father is not important to me. The British government must accept responsibility and be prepared to atone for its actions.

A favourite quote, penned originally by Bobby Sands, sums it up for me: 'Let our vengeance be the laughter of our children!'

2

LOUIS LEONARD
15 December 1972

Killed by loyalists with suspected British army involvement

Louis Leonard was a 26 year old butcher in Derrylin, County Fermanagh. He also captained the local GAA football team. And he was, unknown to his family until after his death, a member of the IRA.

In December 1972 he and his wife Betty were about to celebrate their first Christmas together in their new home along with their infant son Tony. In the weeks leading up to Christmas, both Louis and Betty worked overtime preparing and delivering meat to customers in the Derrylin area. On the evening of 14 December, Louis was working late at the butcher's shop. At 10.40 p.m. his brother Barry called in for a brief chat. But when Betty returned at 11 p.m. from making deliveries, there was no sign of her husband. Next morning, Betty's brother Tom and Louis' brothers Hugh and Ciaran broke into the shop and found Louis' body in the freezer among the Christmas turkeys. He had been shot eight to ten times at close range in the back and head. There was no sign of a struggle.

The RUC were called but showed little urgency then or in the days immediately following to investigate the murder enthusiastically. They did not seal off the murder scene nor interview key witnesses; crucial forensic evidence went unexamined.

Relatives of the dead man were able to piece together a partial sequence of events on the evening of the murder from witnesses. An expensive black car had been seen at the shop. It drove off, but returned shortly afterwards. Two men, one well-dressed, the other in overalls, entered the shop. A few minutes later they drove off. Later still, a van was seen parked beside the shop and three men, one wearing a white shop coat, stood nearby.

The RUC version was that Louis Leonard had been assassinated by loyalists, perhaps from as far away as Belfast. But from early in the story, Louis' wife and other relatives suspected a more sinister element. Louis' brother Desmond was in jail on bomb charges. As an IRA member, Louis himself had been harassed by state forces in the months before his death. In particular, a shadowy figure in the Welsh guards, Captain Reese—who seems to have played a role similar to that of undercover operative Captain Nairac in South Armagh in the mid-1970s— targeted Louis. Reese had warned Louis that he was going to 'sort him out'. Three weeks before the murder, Reese had entered Louis' shop with an army patrol and photographed Louis, refusing to tell him why he had done so. The RUC's lack of enthusiasm to investigate the murder seemed to complete the picture.

1972 was perhaps the bleakest year of the 'troubles'. 472 people died as a result of political violence, 180 more than in the next worst year, 1974. Less than two months before Louis' death, on 23 October, Fermanagh had witnessed the horrific murder of farmer Michael Naan (aged 31) and his farm labourer Andrew Murray (aged 23) on Naan's farm near Newtownbutler. Michael Naan had been a prominent member in the civil rights movement locally. The details of their deaths were particularly gruesome. Naan had died of 17 stab wounds, apparently from a pitchfork, to his heart and chest; his body was found in a byre. Murray's body was found in a slurry pit nearby with 13 similar stab wounds. It was presumed that the murder was the work of loyalists

Some years later the truth emerged in the most unlikely of circumstances. In 1978 police in England were investigating the murder of Huddersfield prostitute Helen Rytka, the latest victim of the Yorkshire Ripper. They received a phone call from a soldier in Scotland suggesting that there might be a link between the Yorkshire Ripper murders and those of Michael Naan and Andrew Murray in Fermanagh six years earlier. Although it emerged that there was no such connection, the investigation eventually led to the trial in 1981 of four Argyll and Sutherland Highlanders for the murders of Naan and Murray. The four were Staff Sergeant Stanley Hathaway, Sergeant John Byrne, Lieutenant Corporal Iain Chestnut and Captain Andrew Snowball. During the trial it emerged that the four had been on an undercover operation, camped on Naan's farm. When Naan confronted them at one point, they claimed, he threatened them with a pitchfork. So he was stabbed with a bayonet. Murray came on the scene at this point and both were stabbed repeatedly until they died.

Hathaway and Byrne were sentenced to life imprisonment, the first British soldiers to be convicted of murder in the 'troubles'. Chestnut was given four years for manslaughter and Snowball a one year suspended sentence for withholding information.

These revelations convinced the family and friends of Louis Leonard that there may indeed have been collusion involved in Louis' death. This conviction was eventually articulated by a campaigning group set up in the mid-1990s, VOICE (Victims of Injustice Campaigning for Equality). Their claim is that the deaths of Louis Leonard, Mickey Naan and Andy Murray are among 12 cases of murder in

Fermanagh in which there was direct state involvement. Another murder to which VOICE points is that of Jim Murphy, a 42 year old Sinn Féin member and friend of the late Louis Leonard, who was found dead at his garage near Kinawley on 21 April 1984. They contend that these murders were carried out by British army or police personnel in the guise of loyalist assassinations, and that the RUC played a major role in the cover-ups which followed.

An inquest in 1973 did little to solve the mystery of Louis Leonard's death. Every attempt was made by the RUC to curtail anything which called into question their contention that the murder was solely the work of loyalists. After almost 30 years the file on Louis Leonard remains open.

The story is now told by Ciaran Leonard, brother of the dead man, and chair of VOICE, and by another member of the same organisation, Loretta Lynch.

Ciaran Leonard and Loretta Lynch

It's not until you get a period without conflict and stress that you realise how abnormal the whole situation was. Nationalists have now got the strength to say: 'Just one minute. I suffered too'.

Ciaran: It was 1972, December the fifteenth, when Louis was murdered. It was just before Christmas. He wasn't long married. He and his wife Betty had a baby son, Tony, four months old. They had a butcher's shop and Louis was working hard trying to get the Christmas orders of turkeys and that ready. He had suffered a lot of harassment from the UDR, the RUC and the British army and from one particular British army officer, a Captain Reese, who seemed to be a type of Captain Nairac in the area at the time.

Betty had left that evening to do the country run, for they delivered meat. At nine o'clock she was stopped in Lisnaskea by an RUC patrol and she was let go. Then on her way back to Donagh, she was stopped again by a mobile patrol of the RUC; they were mad, she said. They jumped out in a very aggressive manner. They held her for ten minutes or so and then let her go. Some time after Louis' death we went to the sergeant of the Lisnaskea police and he said they had had no mobile patrols in the area at the time.

By the time Betty came back, there were no lights from the shop. It was very unusual for Louis to do this. Betty went to the local hotel to enquire about his whereabouts; there was no one about. So she went home to Derrylin to her mother's place and she and her brother Liam came back. They still couldn't find any trace of Louis. They knew something was wrong. Betty left the van she was driving at the side of the shop and came over towards Donagh where we live to find out if Louis was there.

This is what we have found out afterwards. Someone saw a big black car with two men in it and one of the men getting out, going to the window of the shop

and looking in, then getting into the car and driving off towards Kinawley. The car returned shortly afterwards and there were two men, one well dressed, fitting the description of a man from the Lisnaskea area, and the second a taller man with a boiler suit. Two girls walking down the street heard a sharp crack like a bulb being broken. A man came out of the shop and the car moved off towards Lisnaskea. The girls didn't see how many people were in the car.

At ten past one a local farmer came past the shop and noticed nothing only Betty's van parked at the side of the shop. At twenty past one he drove back in the other direction with his mother. He noticed three men standing outside the shop. The man in the middle was wearing a shop coat, like a butcher's coat. He also noticed that there was a blue Morris Minor van parked at the front of the shop, not Louis' van. At a quarter to two there was another neighbour driving by and there were lights on in the shop, but the outside lights weren't on and the blinds were pulled down. The van was still parked outside the shop. This van had been seen in the area three or four weeks before Louis' murder. In actual fact it had pulled in very irrationally one evening in front of Betty. The driver jumped out and said she had pulled out in front of him. She hadn't. He had a very aggressive manner. We believe that this person was connected to Louis' death. Later that evening this van was seen stopped outside the local Orange Hall.

The next morning Betty went and reported Louis missing at Kinawley RUC station. They didn't seem one bit annoyed. So Tom Rice, my brother-in-law, Hugh, my eldest brother, and myself went over to Derrylin. I was only fourteen but I had been working in the shop and I knew the ins and outs of the shop. Hugh and Tom Rice broke into the shop and found Louis' body lying in the chill area. The local doctor was called; he said Louis had been murdered. He had been shot something like eleven times in the head and body at point blank range. Then the RUC arrived. At no time did they attempt to seal off the scene of the crime. They didn't take any finger prints and the electricity had been turned off by the mains switch. They took the counter flap away a couple of days after the murder, after a couple of hundred people had passed through the shop. That was it.

Louis was waked at home in Donagh; it was a huge wake and funeral. The RUC basically harassed the funeral the whole way from Enniskillen. The morning after the funeral my father and I were going into town to get a few groceries. We met a British army Saracen in our lane coming in to raid our house. Here we had a person allegedly murdered by loyalists and the British army was coming to raid our house! My father got out of the car and stopped them. That night seven bullets were left on our clothes line with a note saying that each one of us was next. We sent them to our solicitor and all the evidence was passed on to the RUC; nothing was ever traced. We are definite that there was British army/RUC involvement in Louis' murder. We believe Captain Reese was the person who manipulated things and got this murder gang together in this area because loyalism wasn't really organised.

The Captain Reeses and the Nairacs weren't just doing these things because they were bad people. They were doing it as a directive of the government. So somebody was telling them what to do, either through the Secretary of State or through British Intelligence. There was a concerted effort to intimidate and terrorise us. We believe there was most definitely an inner circle working in the area in the early seventies.

Louis was an IRA man. The family didn't know that at the time. He was a leader in the GAA and in the community. He was a young nationalist who was making a name for himself and it seemed to us that it was a case of a leader of nationalism being taken out. All of his friends suffered huge harassment, even those who didn't hold the same views as him. I remember that period being a dark era; it was as though someone turned out the light. People were on the verge of crying. I mean, people did not go out at night; they were scared, intimidated. Louis lived six miles from where Naan and Murray were murdered by British soldiers, stabbed to death.

Loretta: That is probably why those murders took place; it was a warning to everyone else, to put the fear of God in people and say, 'This is what you will get as well'.

Ciaran: Inspector Curry, who was in charge of investigating Louis' murder, took our solicitor, Terry Gibson, who was in Enniskillen one evening seeing another client, and kept him in the RUC station for four hours. He told Terry Gibson to let Louis' case drop, that Louis Leonard deserved to be killed. Also, during the police investigation of Louis' case, a certain woman was approached three times to try to get her to change her description of the car. They tried to suppress evidence during the inquest, to suppress statements of those people who had passed by the shop.

Loretta: There was no investigation. Even in a domestic incident that doesn't happen. Not only was there no investigation, but there was a concerted effort not to investigate. Louis' case was a murder in a small village and it was never treated like you would imagine a murder to be treated. It was like they knew what had happened and there was nothing necessary.

Ciaran: The inquest came to nothing other than the factual evidence of how he was killed—that is, is gunshot wounds. There was no forensic evidence uncovered. There was no serious investigation. I found out that Inspector Curry was running his investigation on the lines that it was two butchers who had fallen out and that one had shot the other. It was the same as Naan and Murray, a family feud.

Our family has never been notified by the RUC as to the state of the investigation into Louis' murder which happened 27 years ago. We are as heart-broken today as we were on that terrible Christmas in 1972. On the 25th anniversary of his death we wrote to the RUC on the matter. We received this one line reply:

Dear Madam,
Letter Regarding Your Late Husband, Mr Louis Leonard

I acknowledge receipt of your letter dated 18 March 1999, the subject of which will receive attention.

Yours faithfully,

G G O'Callaghan. Chief Superintendent
(Dated 29th March 1999.)

We've never heard another word since!

Two years after Louis' death, Louis' friend Jim Murphy from Derrylin, was shot in similar circumstances. Jim was one of those behind *Concern*, which was a nationalist civil rights paper at the time. Jim was found lying alongside the petrol pumps outside the garage by someone who had stopped for petrol. Inside the garage there had been a struggle and shots had been fired. There was no sealing off of the scene of the crime. The neighbours landed there and one of them was done with no number plate light. There was never any investigation in Jim Murphy's case either. People went in and looked round and where the struggle had taken place in the wee office, they found bullets. The RUC couldn't do that. There was a cudgel left at the back door with blood on it. The RUC didn't find it. Again Inspector Curry was over the team and the same officers were involved.

The Murphys were totally shattered. Jim Murphy was a leading light in the community. He was the man who had dug deepest into Louis' death and maybe he was getting too close to the truth. Again a van was seen speeding away from the area and Jim's car was found about two miles away. People are adamant that the UDR/RUC were involved in Jim's death. The UDR were seen outside the shop before the murder that night.

Loretta: There are four very obvious murder cases in the area—Louis, Jim Murphy, Naan and Murray. But there are up to a dozen other cases. My own brother died in a car crash. He had been threatened several times and told he would be taken out. There were three actually killed in the car. After they took the car away, there was a note on RUC-headed note paper saying, 'We told you we would get you'. There was a young girl from Clones who actually stopped at the scene that night. There were two men standing in the road; they told her everyone was okay and to drive on. When my mother went to see her, she told her that same story. When they went back to her after the funeral, she denied all knowledge of having seen anything.

There have been other cases which looked like ordinary hit and run accidents. We know of a woman who had two family members killed in separate incidents. She believes there was RUC involvement and when she tried to raise the issue through her MP, Frank Maguire, and her solicitor, she herself was threatened. They actually tried to run her off the road when she wasn't going to change her story. The RUC insisted that she had made a mistake about the number plate but she had a very good head for remembering numbers. As it turned out, it was an authorised police car which had tried to run her down.

VOICE was formed nearly two years ago. It came about because there was so much talk about victims and the nationalist voice wasn't being heard. It was as if we didn't exist. So a lot of people here said, 'Hold on, there have been a lot of murders in this county'. A lot of them were made to look like accidents but as far as the families were concerned, there was enough evidence to point to the involvement of the RUC, UDR, British army—state involvement.

Ciaran: One of the problems is—and I found this among my own family—people say, 'Ah, you'll never find out'. My attitude is if we don't speak out for these people, then who is going to speak for them? We have short and long term objectives. One of our short term objectives was to attempt to put together some sort of interim report—listing incidents, naming names, the inconsistencies in the investigations and the complete unprofessionalism in the approach to the investigations. The whole thing actually got bigger than what we thought.

Loretta: We thought we should document not only the murders but also the displaced people, those people who had to leave because of intimidation. Around the Rosslea area, which is a small area, there are around fifty such people, a couple of members of my own family among them. We tried to document what each family went through, but it is a mammoth task.

Ciaran: There is a lot of drudgery work but it's amazing how much interest there is out there. People want to tell their story. Our next step is taking those four cases, putting together a case file on each of them as best we can, and taking them to the Helsinki Watch, the British Irish Rights Watch, Amnesty International.

We don't want revenge. There was a war going on. As an individual, I'm not asking who pulled the trigger. But I am asking for the state to acknowledge its part in this. We are not out for vengeance; we want accountability. To get that overall acknowledgement I think a number of things have to happen, especially an independent investigation into the RUC's handling of the cases, whether some disciplinary action would follow or not, although a number of those involved are still serving. Then the reopening of the cases and if that isn't possible, the state has to acknowledge its role. We would like to get in touch with some ex-British army or RUC personnel who served here at the time. We don't want to know their names for we are not out for any sort of revenge. We just want to know what happened. It's going to be a long haul.

There is a great thing in Fermanagh now, an umbrella group of victims run by the Fermanagh Partnership. We went to them as a group. They didn't want to acknowledge that we were there but we made them. We participated and made them acknowledge that they had not got the monopoly on suffering.

Loretta: VOICE is probably the only group in this area dealing with victims of state violence. I went to the last meeting and it was interesting. We were broken down into workshops and some of them said they had a real problem with what I represented. I said I understood this but that I was not taking away what their group represented and that I didn't think they should do that with me. They say people aren't victims who were stopped on the roads, whose houses were raided, IRA men who were murdered, nationalists, Sinn Féiners who were murdered—these are not victims. One of the more prominent unionists from this area said that the people who she represented wouldn't even sit down with me. We talked about where we could see this thing going and to my mind things are being led too much by support agencies and victims' groups than by victims themselves. I pointed out that they shouldn't assume that all victims wanted the same thing. Don't assume that all victims want counselling, that all victims want a building that they could walk into. The victim support agency was saying. 'Forget all the conflict', but we haven't got to that stage yet. We are a long way from being able to sit down with each other and say, 'This is what happened to me. What happened to you?' But they were jumping the gun and saying, 'Assume we are all at that stage, move on past. What building can we get?' It's a long way off. We have only got to the stage of standing up and saying, 'I am a victim'.

Ciaran: In some ways it's looked at as employment for counsellors, etc. They have wonderful buildings in Enniskillen with counsellors in them and I said there would have been no need for a group such as ours if they had worked.

Loretta: Walking into a building and saying, 'I'll go in here and tell my story to a stranger'—people are even finding it difficult telling their stories to friends.

Ciaran: My family is only starting to acknowledge. Members of my family would probably still react to it in hatred. I would say we never grieved. I remember we just stopped having Christmases. For about seven years we didn't have a Christmas tree up in our house. Our mother just wouldn't have Christmas. That was her second child named Louis that she had buried and a couple of years later her grandson named Louis was killed in a car accident.

Loretta: It's not until you get a period without conflict and stress that you realise how abnormal the whole situation was. Nationalists have now got the strength to say: 'Just one minute. I suffered too'. I think it would be a wonderful thing for my children and myself to have these things documented—that they can lift it and say, 'This is what happened'.

Ciaran: And we also want to ensure that it will never happen again to anybody. At times I really hate the British army, the RUC and the UDR for what they have done to our people and the years of suffering they have inflicted on us in the name of the law. But in human terms, I wouldn't want to see any of their relatives suffer what we've endured. One of the important things on reconciliation I feel is the need for people to tell their story. I mean, it's doing me good telling my story now.

Loretta: My mother said she thought she was mad until she could sit down and say, 'This is what happened' and someone else said, 'No, you are not mad'.

Ciaran: The important thing is that people are being listened to. Then others can say, 'Yes, I remember that and let's hope it doesn't happen again'. We as survivors of the conflict have a duty, I believe, to speak out on behalf of those who lost their lives at the hands of state forces, because they cannot speak for themselves. Furthermore, it is our responsibility to ensure that the British government is forced to acknowledge its role in the conflict, a role which in many instances has led to the authorised murder of our loved ones.

3

THE DUBLIN/MONAGHAN BOMBINGS
17 May 1974

Thirty-three people killed by four car bombs in Dublin and Monaghan

O n a Friday afternoon in May 1974, a series of connected bombings in Dublin and Monaghan led to the biggest single loss of life in thirty years of conflict. At 5.30 p.m. three car bombs exploded in Dublin in quick succession; the first was in Parnell Street, followed by those in Talbot Street and South Leinster Street, all in the heart of the city. It was rush hour and the start of the weekend, so the streets were packed. The congestion was even greater than usual because of a strike by Dublin bus drivers which was in its second week. Responding to the strike, the government had relaxed car parking restrictions in the city, thus making it even easier for the bombers to place their car bombs unnoticed where they could cause the maximum number of casualties. The Dublin bombs left 26 dead and 134 injured.

Almost ninety minutes later another car bomb exploded in the centre of Monaghan town, near the border. Seven people died as a result.

Those dead in Dublin included an entire family, the O'Briens: John (aged 23), Anna (22), Jacqueline (17 months) and Anne Marie (5 months). In fact, more than 24 hours after the bombs, there was concern and surprise that no one had come seeking to identify the bodies of the two children. Then the reason became clear; their parents lay dead in the same morgue. There were also two foreign nationals who died in Dublin: a French woman named Simone Chetrit (31) and an Italian, Antonio Magliocco (37). The others who died in Dublin were: Josephine Bradley (21), Marie Butler (21), Ann Byrne (35), John Dargle, Concepta Dempsey (65), Patrick Fay (47), Elizabeth Fitzgerald (59), Bernadette Grace (35), Ann Marren

31

(20), Anna Massey (21), Mary McKenna (55), Dorothy Morris, Colette O'Doherty (21), Christina O'Loughlin (51), Edward O'Neill (29), Marie Phelan (20), Siobhan Rice (19), Maureen Shields (44), Breda Turner (21) and John Walsh (27). Concepta Dempsey was nine months pregnant.

The Monaghan dead were: Patrick Askin (53), Thomas Campbell (52), Jack Travers (29), Margaret White (46), George Williamson (73). Archibald Harper (72) died two days later, and Thomas Croarkin (35) two months after the bomb.

The finger of suspicion seemed to point naturally at northern loyalists. The bombs occurred on the fourth day of the Ulster Workers' Council (UWC) strike, organised to topple the power-sharing executive led by unionist Prime Minister Brian Faulkner. The UWC leaders were particularly opposed to the creation of cross-border institutions which had resulted from the Sunningdale Agreement of the previous year and which were to be enacted under the new executive. On the day before the bombs, Ulster Vanguard leader and UWC member Bill Craig stated: 'The British government will have to recognise that it cannot ratify the Sunningdale Agreement or implement it in any way. If they do there will be further actions taken against the Irish Republic and those who attempt to implement it'.

Loyalists had been active in bombing Dublin before. On 1 December 1972 two bus conductors—George Bradshaw and Thomas Duffy—had been killed and 72 people injured by a bomb in Sackville Place. One hour later the Fine Gael opposition withdrew their objections to the Offences Against the State (Amendment) Act being discussed in the Dáil, thus ensuring its successful passage. As a result, a person could be jailed on the word of a senior policeman that it was believed that he or she was a member of an illegal organisation. On 21 January 1973, another bus conductor, Thomas Douglas, was killed by a further bomb in Sackville Place; 13 people were injured.

On hearing the news of the bombs in Dublin and Monaghan in 1974, UDA spokesperson Sammy Smyth said:

> I am very happy about the bombings in Dublin. There is a war with the Free State and now we are laughing at them.

He denied UDA involvement and advised the authorities in the Republic to look 'a bit closer to home' for the culprits. The UVF stated that they were 'appalled' by the news and denied responsibility. They had, they said, been 'engaged in the political field' and were therefore not involved in any military actions.

At the same time, it was known from the start that the cars used in the bombs had been hijacked in loyalist areas of Belfast and Portadown. Despite this, the government seemed wary about pointing the finger at loyalists. Defence Minister John Cooney said on the Monday following the bombing that, although it was possible that loyalists had been behind it, the government was keeping 'an open mind' on the matter. In a deft sleight of hand, he then went on to single out the IRA for condemnation:

I think that the IRA bear a very heavy burden of responsibility. I would regard it as hypocrisy to hear their condemnation of these acts when they are a mirror pattern of what they have been doing in Belfast and in other Northern Ireland streets and in London.

The Taoiseach, Liam Cosgrave, was less specific in his condemnation, but added his voice to the general condemnation of all paramilitary groups, even those clearly not involved in this atrocity.

The government are as yet unaware of the identity of those responsible for these crimes. But everyone who has practised violence or preached violence or condoned violence must bear a share of responsibility for today's outrages.

Opposition leader Jack Lynch of Fianna Fáil agreed that 'every organisation involved in the campaign of bombing in any part of our country over the past four years has the blood of these innocent victims on their hands.'

The collective trauma of the event was compounded by such official statements. It became almost impossible for anyone in subsequent years to ask questions for fear of being branded a fellow traveller of terrorists. This neatly fitted with the state's agenda at the time. The Cosgrave government had been wedded to a strong law-and-order approach. It suited the government that people would not distinguish between perpetrators of violence or acts of violence, but simply condemned all, leaving the state forces to pursue members of republican and other groups unhindered.

On the Tuesday after the bombs, the Gardai initiated a country-wide swoop on homes of known republicans and arrested 10 people for questioning. In the North, the RUC took statements from some people, including those whose cars had been hijacked, but there was little follow-through. No one, North or South, was charged in relation to the bombing. Three months later the Garda investigation was wound down and the detectives involved redeployed. There the matter rested for some years.

The shock of the events plus the atmosphere of indiscriminate condemnation of opposition to the state made it next to impossible for relatives and others to campaign for disclosure of information about the killings. Until the mid-1990s, some of these relatives continued to be convinced that the bombs must have been the work of the IRA. Others were clearer that loyalists had been the perpetrators, but even they had to worry that if they campaigned for the truth, they would be open to accusations of being IRA supporters. The Special Branch photographed relatives who attended the annual mass in Dublin in memory of the victims, thereby adding to the sense of fear and reticence.

Then in 1993, Yorkshire Television's 'First Tuesday' produced a documentary (*Hidden Hand: the Forgotten Massacre*) in which it was claimed that, although the UVF carried out the bombings, MI6 was also involved. According to the programme makers, the names of the bombers—including a number of members of the UDR who were involved—were known to the Gardai shortly after the events. The UVF unit included William Marchant, a UVF leader in Belfast, who was shot dead by the IRA on the Shankill Road, Belfast on 28 April 1987, and who was reputed to have been the leader of the unit; William Hanna, a UVF leader in Portadown, shot dead in an internal UVF dispute on 27 July 1975; Robin Jackson, the UVF commander in the Portadown area, nicknamed 'The Jackal'; and Wesley Somerville and Harris Boyle, blown up with their own bomb on 31 July 1975 in an attack on the Miami Showband. The programme makers concluded that the Gardai had been less than meticulous in following up these early leads. A later RTE 'Primetime' documentary (*Friendly Forces*) added to the allegations that the UVF was behind the bombings and that the Gardai had known for almost two decades. In response to the Yorkshire TV programme, the UVF acknowledged for the first time that they had carried out the bombings; however, they denied the assertions of British Intelligence involvement and stated that they acted alone.

The claims of both documentaries meshed well with the earlier revelations by Fred Holroyd and Colin Wallace, both of whom had worked for British army Intelligence in the north in the mid-1970s. Holroyd in particular provided details of dealings he had with the Commissioner of the Garda Siochána in 1974, Ned Garvey. He also revealed his contacts with gardai in border areas, in particular one nicknamed 'The Badger'; they had regularly exchanged information on republicans and loyalists. But British Intelligence in the North was involved in more than information gathering and dissemination. There were also clandestine operations against republicans which involved kidnappings and assassinations carried out by British undercover personnel. Holroyd claimed that another undercover operative, Captain Robert Nairac, had personally boasted of his role in the murder of IRA man John Green in County Monaghan on 10 January 1975. Nairac was also known to have close relations with loyalist paramilitaries in the Portadown area and was reputed to have been involved in the loyalist attack on the Miami Showband near the border in July 1975. Robert Nairac was himself killed by the IRA on 14 May 1977.

As a result of these revelations, a number of suspicions about the Dublin and Monaghan bombs came to the fore:

- that the bombings were not merely the work of loyalists, but also involved collusion with British Intelligence;

- that the government of the day did not to pursue the Dublin and Monaghan bombers for fear of compromising some of their clandestine relations with British Intelligence;

- and that, on account of the collusion which existed between loyalists and British forces, the RUC, which in 1974 enjoyed good relations with the Republic's government, did not vigorously investigate the bombings.

The Yorkshire Television documentary served to galvanise some of the relatives of the dead into initiating a campaign, Justice for the Forgotten. They met with Justice Minister Nora Owen, but on the 21st anniversary of bombings, May 1995, she issued a statement to the effect that departmental files showed no evidence of collusion. The relatives then initiated court proceedings to gain access to government documents on the bombings, but failed in both the High Court (1997) and the Supreme Court (1998).

Despite these set-backs, the campaigners had a number of legitimate questions which required answers:

- Did the gardai know the names of the UVF suspects involved in the bombs at an early stage in the investigation
- If so, did they pass those names on to the government?
- If not, why not?
- If the government was in receipt of those names, why did they not pursue the matter further?
- Was the government aware at an early stage of the possible hand of British Intelligence in the bombings?
- Why was the garda investigation wound down after three months?
- Why was forensic evidence from the four bombs sent to RUC laboratories when the Republic's own forensic service was perfectly capable of testing it?
- Why was that evidence not delivered to the RUC laboratories until 11 days after the bombing, when the best results for forensic tests are achieved within six hours of an explosion?

In 1999, some reassurance that their questions were not unrealistic emerged as a result of the report of the government-sponsored Victims Commission led by former Tanaiste John Wilson.

> My information on what happened comes, in the main, from reportage which suggests, among other things, that the Garda investigation had identified the probable culprits very quickly but that it then ran into difficulties. This reportage also suggests that the Garda did not receive all appropriate co-operation from the RUC, that the Irish Government did not press the British government on this point, and that agents of a friendly Government may have had a hand in planning and executing the crime.

The Report concluded that the Government should chose a former Supreme Court Judge to enquire privately into the Dublin and Monaghan bombing. The relatives immediately rejected this recommendation, stating that they wanted nothing less than a public inquiry.

The government subsequently agreed to a private inquiry and appointed former Supreme Court Justice Hamilton to chair it. The families refused to participate. Through their solicitor Greg O'Neill, they stated:

> The relatives and victims cannot and will not engage in a private inquiry into mass murder and compromised police inquiries into these murders.

There are clearly matters of public interest in the case of the Dublin and Monaghan bombings to warrant a public inquiry. The reluctance of the government is bizarre and in the view of many may be explicable only in terms of maintenance of secrecy over that which should be revealed. It adds insult to the injury suffered by the bereaved and wounded.

As stated earlier, one of those killed in the bomb at Parnell Street was an Italian citizen, Antonio Magliocco (38), a father of three children. Antonio owned a restaurant in Bray, but was visiting his brother Mario's fish and chip restaurant, The Venezian Café, in Parnell Street when the first of the three Dublin bombs exploded. He died instantly.

Antonio's body was taken to hospital. A few hours before, he had changed a cheque, so he had a considerable amount of money with him. The money was stolen. This happened not only to him, but to other victims as well.

A week later, his brother Mario, his sister Savina Borza and brother-in-law, Vittorio Borza, accompanied Antonio's remains back for burial in his native Casalattico.

On 13 February 1999, President Mary McAleese interrupted, at short notice, a very busy schedule, to meet with Anna, Antonio's widow, her son Tommassino and Savina Borza's son, Claudio. Later that day Irish writer, Don Mullan and Italian journalist, Silvia Calamati, visited Casalattico and interviewed Anna Magliocco and Savina Borza. These interviews are reproduced below. Following them, Don Mullan recounts the experiences of the campaign group, Justice for the Forgotten.

Anna Magliocco

I just would like to know the truth. I want to know who killed Antonio and why I have to live without him for the rest of my life.

When I first met Antonio in Casalattico he had come back to Italy on his summer holidays. He was working in Ireland with his brother and sister. They had a little fish-and-chip shop in Dublin.

After getting married I went with him to Dublin. It was hard for me to go to a foreign country and leave my little village, as I had never been anywhere else before. I remember the day I said goodbye to Casalvieri and to my family. It was a very sad day.

When I got to Dublin it took me some time to settle down. The first encounter with the new language and the people was not easy. I had no English at all, so I could not understand what people were saying. Even though I could not learn much, I remember I tried my best and forced myself to go to the shops to get food for my family and for the restaurant.

Little by little I got used to the new situation. Things changed and my children were born. I used to spend most of my time looking after my three little ones and helping Antonio in the restaurant. I liked and still like Ireland very much, though now I have so many bad memories that I cannot go back yet.

It was a Friday, a very busy day for us. I was working in the restaurant with another girl, while my mother-in-law was minding the children. At six o'clock we got a phone call from my brother-in-law Mario. My mother-in-law answered the phone and then she wanted me to talk to him. It was then I got to know that Antonio was dead.

At first I thought he had died in a car crash. I would have never imagined Antonio being killed by a bomb. After the phone call I had rushed to Parnell Street. It was in complete chaos. No one was allowed to stay. Everybody was pushed back by the police. I did not want to go away. I wanted to go forward to see if Antonio was still there. I was stopped by a policeman who slapped me on the face and sent me away. I didn't see Antonio until we went to the morgue. A few months later, however, while I was watching a television documentary on those explosions I could recognise him being lifted from the ground and put on a stretcher. That was a very distressing moment for me.

After he was taken back to Italy I found myself alone in a foreign country. Sorrow and grief never left me. I got great help from Antonio's family. From time to time I had some other Italian people coming to visit and comfort me. After some time I had to rent the restaurant. I could not keep it as I had to look after my children.

The Irish police never phoned or got in touch with me. At the same time I was very distressed and I had so many problems to solve that I did not get in contact with them myself. For one year I got free dental care for my children and free bus fares. That was all. Then I was granted some money for myself and for each of my children, but only when they would be eighteen years of age.

I was left alone, far away from home. I wanted to stay with my parents. I had so many bad memories there that I had to leave Ireland. I returned to Italy and went to Forosinone to talk to someone in the trade unions. I thought I might be entitled to some form of social security, being a widow with three children. He said he could not help me and suggested I should go to the Irish embassy in Rome. There, again, I was told that there was nothing they could do for me. The money granted to us was the only benefit we were entitled to. In Forosinone I was also told that I could not get help in Italy since my husband had died in Ireland and Ireland was not part of the European Economic Community.

I also applied for my second son Corrado to be exempted from military service, but with no success. I knew that in Italy orphans of war do not have to do their military service, but my application was turned down because they told me there was no war in Ireland.

I wish I could be entitled to a pension. I do not know how I will be able to manage when I get older. My husband was a worker. He had a regular permit to stay in Ireland and always paid his taxes to the Irish government. He was not there to do anything wrong. He was there to work for his family and his children.

I just would like to know the truth. I want to know who killed Antonio and why I have to live without him for the rest of my life.

Savina Borza

Twenty-five years have passed and we still do not know the reason why so many innocent people lost their lives and who planted the bombs.

That morning Antonio came to my shop to give me some help. At two o'clock he told me he had to go and buy some food for his own shop. He said he would be back at tea-time.

At six o'clock we got a phone call instead. I do not remember who phoned. I think it was either my mother-in-law or my sister-in-law Anna. I was told that an explosion had taken place in Parnell Street.

My husband set off for the centre of Dublin, but there was so much traffic that he could not get there. He had to leave the car far away from Parnell Street and walk. As he got to the scene of the massacre he saw the place totally devastated. The bodies had already been taken away.

When my husband came back he was as white as a sheet. He did not answer my questions. He just took the key of the shop and closed it down, without saying a word. It was then I understood that something serious had happened to Antonio. I hoped that he might be just injured, although no one was able to give us more information.

The following day my brother Mario and my husband tried to find out where Antonio had been taken. Someone said he was at the Mater Hospital, some others in Amiens Street. Finally we were told where he was. The place was off Wexford Street. We got into a room and saw a coffin, carrying a little label with an official Irish print and a foreign name. It was the name of the French woman who had been killed in the explosion. We moved to the next room and Antonio was there, lying in a coffin with a white robe on. So I could see him only the day after he had been killed.

A week later Antonio's coffin was taken to Italy. My husband made all the arrangements. After landing in Rome we drove to our native village, Casalattico, where Antonio was buried.

Problems started soon afterwards, as his wife Anna was left alone in Dublin with three little children. The oldest, Tommassino, was four years old, his sister, Marinella, was two and a half, and the youngest, Corrado, was just seventeen months. We tried to help her as much as we could. She had to rent the shop as it was impossible for her to keep it going without Antonio. Nine months later my mother died. Antonio's death killed her. She was well and got sick all of a sudden. She just could not cope with it.

At the beginning, after Antonio's death, I could not look Irish people in the face. I got angry with everybody. I was devastated and shocked. For me Antonio was a father, not only a brother. Our father died when I was thirteen. We were very close to each other. Antonio's murder left us stunned. Our minds were totally deranged by sorrow. We kept asking ourselves, 'Why did it happen to us?' We had nothing to do with what was happening in Ireland at the time.

We feel very abandoned. We hope that justice will be done. For us it was so terrible. Our family was totally, devastated. Antonio's young children were left without a father.

We decided to return to Italy in 1983, nine years after the bombs. My husband and I felt it was better to go back. All my family were just stunned. Nothing mattered for us anymore. We had lost all motivation and interest. Our little shop was not a good reason anymore for us to stay in Ireland. So we came back. Three years after my husband died of a heart attack. So I was left alone again. Life is really very hard sometimes. After my husband's death my sister died too.

I just hope that one day we will get to know something about my brother's death. Twenty-five years have passed and we still do not know the reason why so many innocent people lost their lives and who planted the bombs.

This is why I find it very encouraging that the President of Ireland agreed to meet my nephew Tommassino and his mother Anna during her visit to Italy.

Don Mullan

If the forces of a supposedly friendly state were involved in a covert operation to kill and maim innocent human beings, then it's not only in the interest of our state to know what was happening but also in the interest of the British state to know that there were people within their forces who actually did this and to weed them out.

It was suggested by a few people who had an interest in the Dublin/Monaghan bombs that maybe I would have a look at it because of my work on Bloody Sunday and the book that I had written. It's not that I was reluctant in the beginning but I wasn't sure if I wanted to do it. To be honest, I was as ignorant as most of the other people in the country in terms of the facts surrounding Dublin/Monaghan. Over the years the families had tried to make some kind of response, but they lacked a lot of direction and they weren't quite sure how to put a campaign together. Of course we were lucky in the North in that we had experience and had to learn a lot of skills very quickly. There was another problem the Dublin/Monaghan people had; the attack on the families on Bloody Sunday really was an attack on an intimate community. You couldn't walk down the town in Derry on a Saturday without meeting someone who was connected, maybe who was wounded or lost their loved ones. Then of course thousands of ordinary Derry citizens were there on the Bloody Sunday march. There was a whole support mechanism and in Derry you are never more than fifteen minutes away from the furthermost outreaches; it was much easier to call meetings. When the bombs went off in Dublin, it happened in a large capital. The casualties were spread out all over the city, all over the nation and indeed all over Europe. That was a big problem. If it hadn't been for someone like Margaret Urwin who kept the threads together, they could easily have unravelled. Along with Nora Comiskey, she had the foresight to see the importance nationally. I know for a fact there were times Margaret could easily have given up.

I began to look at it from the perspective of helping the campaign and writing a book. But what was important to me was that I didn't want to be accused of pushing my own or anybody else's agenda. For me, central to all this was what the families wanted. I began to meet the families and encounter the human face of this tragedy that had been swept under the carpet for nearly a quarter of a century. One could sense their scepticism, anger, disillusionment and loss of faith in the institutions of this state. I think in dealing with me in the early days, understandably they were very cautious but as with the Bloody Sunday families, I began to gain their confidence.

I attended the first meeting of the families and Margaret with the Victims' Commissioner, John Wilson. My role in that, although I spoke briefly, was to be a listener and the one thing that encouraged me was the anger directed at Mr Wilson. I must say he handled it with great dignity but I was glad to hear it coming out, for where there is anger there is energy and it's energy that can be directed. I realised that these people do want this resolved and they are very committed and what we see now is that the campaign is actually gathering a momentum. One of the most important things I felt—and again I learned this from the Bloody Sunday Campaign—was that when you had a large group of people, they are going to be coming with their own personal and political baggage. If that is not addressed at an early stage, it can create confusion and rifts and I think that was what actually happened in the early stages of the campaign. What I thought was absolutely imperative was to agree a statement with the relatives and wounded, in terms of what it was they wanted and what are the demands of the campaign. So I drafted this and worked with the lawyers on it and came up with one statement, basically saying we wanted closure to this and the only way to get closure is when the Irish political and police authorities deal honestly with us and tell the truth and nothing but the truth in relation to Dublin/Monaghan. The best way we believe to get closure is by the holding of an public tribunal of inquiry. In September of last year [1998] this statement was presented to the families and ratified by them. The great thing is that now the statement becomes the touchstone for all the meetings, so it's clear in everyone's head this is what we are about. You leave all your baggage outside and the one objective of this group is to get a public tribunal in order to get the truth. From then on, the meetings were far more focused.

I said to Margaret, 'Margaret, I'm not happy going to meetings where there are no families. I want to see the families becoming more and more central to this. I want to see the families taking more of a public face in terms of this whole issue. This is their campaign. I only want to be involved if they want me to be and I only want to work on it if I have their confidence.' I worked on the same principle on the Bloody Sunday Campaign as well. In both cases I have their confidence and they are beginning to take more and more responsibility. For example, we wrote out to all the members of the Oireachtas but I made sure that all the families got involved, folding the letters into the envelopes, licking the stamps and posting them—just a sense of them doing something.

We have a major international postcard campaign and we hope between now and the anniversary to get several thousand postcards shifted to the Taoiseach so it will become clear that this is really becoming a serious campaign. I know there is incredible support out there. You just talk to anyone who is a native of the city and ask them if they remember the Dublin/Monaghan bombs, most people would say they were very lucky that day, they had gone down the street an hour beforehand or whatever. Everybody in the city has a story. There also is a sense that these people have been abandoned, particularly when you compare it to Omagh. When you talk to the families, they don't begrudge the people of Omagh but they feel, 'We are just as innocent and what is wrong with us? We are being treated like lepers'. Sadly that sense of abandonment by their own state and people has actually intensified their suffering.

The bombs were part of a concerted plan to wreck the Sunningdale Agreement. It was basically a very clear warning from members of the RUC, people in the UDR and British military Intelligence to the Irish government: back off or you can expect more of this. I think it put the fear of God into the political authorities down here and achieved its objective. For a long time there was a sense of denial. According to the families, people like Gay Byrne said to the families when they wanted to do programme on Dublin/Monaghan, 'Let sleeping dogs lie'. That is a very interesting insight in terms of the mindset that if you attracted too much attention, you might have another attack. So people preferred to go into denial, turn away and leave these people alone.

The reluctance now of the authorities to open this up and the reticence of the Guards is incredible. Why the reluctance? My sense of it is, the Monaghan Garda Station can rightly be described as the hub of Garda contact with British military intelligence. We know a detective up there called Detective John McCoy, nicknamed 'Badger', had extensive contact with British military intelligence. I have spoken with Captain Fred Holroyd and he confirmed he met him on a regular basis when he reported to MI6. Holroyd told me that McCoy was the tip of the ice-berg and that a lot of Guards were involved.

British military Intelligence were involved in masterminding and carrying out the attack. I think part of the reason why the Gardai and authorities are reluctant to open this up is because it will begin to unravel the layers and layers of their involvement with British Intelligence operatives. They don't want this to be known. But the question is: do they have the right to do this and to condemn innocent families to another quarter of a century of doubt and pain? I contributed to a book recently which was published by Saint Vincent de Paul called *To Act Justly*. Fifty people from various sectors of Dublin society were asked to write a reflection. One of these was the Garda Commissioner Pat Byrne. We all had to start off with a quotation and the quotation he used was, 'Let justice be done, even if the heavens fall'. In the case of Dublin/Monaghan, it is a good opportunity for him to practice what he is preaching.

One of the things that has intrigued me was, not only was there a national dimension but also an international dimension. I have been trying to develop that. I would be conscious of my work in AFrI (Action from Ireland) that governments are sensitive to international opinion; therefore I'm deliberately developing that in relation to the Irish government. There were two French women caught up in the bombs. One was a young woman called Simone Chetrit. Simone Chetrit was born on the 2nd September 1943; there is a great significance in that. She was Jewish, born during the holocaust into a France which was occupied by Nazi Germany. I have written elsewhere, 'To conceive and bring forth a child during the holocaust is an extraordinary act of faith and hope. Such a child was not only a gift to the Jewish community but a gift to all humanity and was therefore entitled to live long and be well loved'. She spent a very happy month in Ireland. Helena Gunn, who hosted her, said to me, 'The only comfort I have is that I know that Simone's last month on earth was very happy'. Just to think that she came and was murdered in this bomb is appalling. I have made contact with the Jewish community in Paris and I have got them involved. The Irish Embassy in Paris should be receiving several hundred postcards sent by the Jewish community in relation to Simone Chetrit. I'm hoping the French media will take this up as well as we approach the anniversary. What intrigued me was the French papers of the time did mention the bombings, but there is little mention of French casualties and I wondered why. Then I realised; the weekend it happened there was a major French Presidential election involving Francois Mitterand and Giscard d'Estagne, which was a cliff-hanger. Amongst the hype, the two young women were lost.

The other foreign person was Antonio Magliocco. Antonio belonged to the Italian community in Ireland and was working lawfully in the Republic. I actually visited his grave and met his widow and three children there. There is a valley called Valle di Corino and a few little villages, one of which is called Casalattico, another called Casalvieri, close to Atina, south of Rome. They are situated in a beautiful region within the Appennine Mountains, not too far from Monte Casino, famous from the second World War. There is a tradition of people travelling from this valley to Ireland. In fact, most of those who own the fish and chip shops in Ireland will tell you they come from this region. They actually celebrate Saint Patrick's Day. As I drove into Casalattico, there were a few tell-tale signs which hit me. One was 'La

Piccola Dublino—Fish and Chips'. Then there was a billboard with the Italian and Irish flags on it where Casalattico had been twinned with Naas in County Kildare. But there is a sense of a great hurt in that valley, that one of their sons went to Ireland and was murdered. What compounded that hurt was that Antonio had cashed a cheque that morning and the money was never returned to the family. Antonio's widow was abandoned. The only income she has now is the rent she gets from their fish and chip shop in Dublin. She never got a pension; the Irish authorities said it was Italian responsibility and the Italian authorities are saying it's Irish responsibility because he died in Ireland. So the poor widow has been left in the situation where she has to cope with her three children. I have ensured that the Victims' Commissioner, John Wilson, is aware of her situation.

So we have got a postcard campaign from the French/Jewish community. The Italian campaign is due to start very soon. I also have a lot of contacts in the States and I travel there occasionally. I have enlisted the help of people who belong to the US Italian and the wider Irish communities. I have also been in touch with the *Irish Echo* and the *Irish Voice* and been asked to write an article on the French/Jewish connection by the *Jewish Weekly* newspaper.

As regards Bloody Sunday, I worked out the theory of a sniper killing people from the walls. I asked Robert Breglio from the United States to come and do a field study. His conclusion was that shots had come from the Derry walls. Building from that experience in relation to Dublin/Monaghan, I went to Congressman Joe Crowley and I said I needed a bomb expert. Sometimes in order to ask the right questions you need to have a fair amount of experience and if you don't have it you have to find people to help. Congressman Crowley put me in contact with a former member of the NYPD's bomb disposal squad, Ken Dudonis, who is now working in security with Fox Television, and he was very helpful. He pointed out that it was a murder case and asked where the bomb debris was and could the Irish police establish a chain of custody of the bomb debris. I'm a great believer that in order to get the right answers you have to ask the right questions. He looked at the meticulous execution of this operation, the way it was planned, the fact that in Dublin the three bombs went off in the space of ninety seconds. The chemical mix of the explosions were such that they exploded with one hundred percent efficiency. These were very professional operators. He told me that he was actually the wrong person, that I needed a military bomb expert and he has now put me in touch with retired Sergeant Major Ed Komac. Komac has put together a team of military experts who are prepared to act as international advisers for the campaign. They have also agreed to give their services free apart for out of pocket expenses. The team is made up of people drawn from the US Army and Navy. If they are given access to the debris, they are going to try and reconstruct the whole thing. From the debris they will be able to interpret a lot of what was going on—if the debris is still there.

On the 22nd of April, Congressman Ben Gilman is holding meetings on the RUC and I asked him to have Dublin/Monaghan as part of these hearings because there are clearly RUC connections here. I talked to the lawyer and maybe we'll bring one of the families to Capitol Hill and internationalise this. I'm only interested in the families of the dead and the wounded and in the truth. The truth is always in the interest of the health of democracy. Why should we fear the truth? If the forces of a supposedly friendly state were involved in a covert operation to kill and maim innocent human beings, then it's not only in the interest if our state to know what was happening but also in the interest of the British state to know that there were people within their forces who actually did this and to weed them out. I think what we are doing is making a contribution to democracy.

4

SEAMUS LUDLOW
1 May 1976

Killed by loyalists/UDR

The body of Seamus Ludlow, a 47 year old forestry worker from Thistle Cross, Mountpleasant, County Louth, was found on the afternoon of 2 May 1976 by two walkers. It was lying in a ditch beside a road near his home. A subsequent post-mortem by the state pathologist, John Harbinson, revealed that he had 21 bullet wounds in his heart, lung and liver. The fatal shot had passed through his left hand—which he had clearly raised to defend himself—his heart and his left lung before lodging in muscles to the right of his spine. On 5 May, two and a half thousand people turned up for Seamus Ludlow's funeral, the largest such gathering ever seen in the area. Seamus Ludlow was an inoffensive bachelor who lived with his mother, his sister and her children. The high point of his week was to go drinking on a Saturday afternoon and evening in Dundalk. There was no apparent reason for anyone to kill him.

Gardai mounted a major operation to investigate the murder. Two thousand people were questioned, 1,700 homes searched and 1,000 vehicles stopped at checkpoints in the four weeks following. Then abruptly, the investigation ceased. No explanation was officially given to the family. Unofficially they were told that the murder was the work of the IRA, the implication being that Seamus Ludlow had been an informer. Some family members were even told that other members of the extended family had known about his activities. Neither of these stories was true, but they served to suppress the truth—and in the process divide the family—for the next two decades.

In the mid-1990s, a journalist from the North, John Ellis, spoke with some of the family and informed them categorically that the murder of Seamus Ludlow was the work of loyalists, not the IRA. This was confirmed by Detective Sergeant Owen Corrigan who had worked on the case but was by then retired. As a result of this information, two of Seamus Ludlow's nephews, Michael Donegan and Jimmy Sharkey, began a campaign for the truth about their uncle's death. They called a press conference in Dublin's Buswell's Hotel on 2 May 1996 and two weeks later had the first of a number of meetings with the Gardai. A Garda inquiry by Chief Superintendent Ted Murphy commenced, while in the North, RUC Chief Superintendent Jim Molloy was assigned to investigate the case. As a result, on 17 February 1998, four suspects were arrested—three in North Down, and the fourth, who had originally lived in the area, in Staffordshire, England. The four were questioned for four days and released without charge; however, a file was forwarded to the Director of Public Prosecutions in Belfast.

On 8 March 1998 journalist Ed Moloney carried the story of one of the four suspects, Paul Hoskings, in the *Sunday Tribune*. Hoskings claimed that on Saturday 1 May 1976, when he was 19 years old, he had been drinking in a bar called the First and Last in Comber, County Down. There he fell in with three other men, R.D, a captain in the Ulster Defence Regiment (UDR), J.F, also an officer in the UDR, and a loyalist known as Mambo. All three were members of the Red Hand Commando, an offshoot of the Ulster Volunteer Force. They took off in a car together—a yellow Datsun—and eventually ended up drinking in a bar in Omeath. The loyalists were armed. They left the bar at closing time. But instead of returning immediately to the North, J.F. drove towards Dundalk. On the outskirts of the town they saw a man thumbing a lift and stopped to pick him up. The man was Seamus Ludlow.

Seamus Ludlow had left the Lisdoo Arms in Dundalk at closing time and began to hitch a lift to his home, about two miles north. He climbed into the car with the four loyalists and shortly afterwards directed them to the road to his house. At this point, Hoskings claims he got out to urinate and heard loud bangs coming from the car. He looked back and saw Mambo shooting. Seamus Ludlow was dead. As the post-mortem confirmed, he was shot in a sitting position from a distance of no more than two feet. His body was dumped in the ditch; the fact that there was no mud on his shoes confirmed that he had been shot elsewhere.

Hoskings had been a rank and file member of the Ulster Defence Association in 1974, but claims that he was not only uninvolved in Seamus Ludlow's murder but was horrified by what happened. The others warned him in the days following that he would be killed if he reported what he had witnessed. Two years later, he left to live in Scotland and got married. The marriage later broke up and in 1986, he returned to live in Comber. Shortly afterwards he was at a family funeral when a relative who was in the RUC told him that the RUC Special Branch wanted to talk to him. He arranged to meet the Special Branch in a pub in Newtownards in January or February 1987 and told the story that he would tell again to Ed Moloney eleven years later. His recollection was that the Special Branch man 'seemed to know all the story' already. Hoskings' revelations came as no surprise to the Special Branch man because the Gardai and RUC had known the facts of the case for many years. A detailed RUC file had been handed over to two senior Garda detectives at RUC headquarters in Belfast in 1979. Although this file was passed to Chief Superintendent John Courtney, now retired, it was never acted upon. (Mambo received a two and a half year prison sentence in England in March 2000 for assaulting a man in a bar.)

In July 1999, former Tanaiste John Wilson produced his report on behalf of the Victims' Commission. In it, he called for a private inquiry into the case. 'To avoid compromising any criminal prosecution, this inquiry should not publish its report until any prosecution has finished, unless no prosecution has been initiated before the completion of the inquiry or within twelve months, whichever is the later.' Two months later, Taoiseach Bertie Ahern announced that such an inquiry would take place. Although the campaigners were very dissatisfied by such restrictions on an inquiry, they had little possibility of countering the decision while the file on the four loyalists remained under consideration by the North's Director of Public Prosecutions. However, on 20 October 1999, the DPP announced that there would be no prosecutions, thus removing the logic behind the Republic's decision to have a private inquiry whose report would not be published. On this basis, the immediate aim of campaigners was to have a public inquiry.

The story of Seamus Ludlow's death and its aftermath is told by his nephews Michael Donegan and Jimmy Sharkey.

Michael Donegan and Jimmy Sharkey

It wasn't just a story about a cover up by the Gardai or the RUC; it's a story of a family who was abused, seriously abused by the authorities who should have been investigating the murder.

Michael Donegan: Seamus Ludlow was a 47 year old bachelor who lived with his elderly infirm mother in his life-long home in a place called Thistle Cross, Mountpleasant. He worked with his brother-in-law, the late Tommy Fox, for Danny Phillips, a local timber merchant, in Ravensdale Forest. He was murdered on the night of the 1st of May 1976. He was a man of very simple tastes. He was unmarried and his life centred around his mother, whom he idolised, and all his numerous nephews and nieces. His social enjoyment was found in local pubs along the border. Although he didn't drink very much, he did drink; it was one of his few vices. He has a fairly large circle of friends in the Border Inn and in the Ballymascanlon Hotel. There wasn't anything complicated about the man's life. He wasn't a Republican; he had no opinions about the north; he wasn't involved in the political situation in the north. He wasn't in the IRA; he wasn't an informer. He was a member of Fine Gael, the party which had traditional support with his family, coming down from his father, and was on close personal terms with several prominent members of the party. He was an inoffensive man who would never hurt a fly. He had no enemies in the world.

On the first of May 1976, which was a Saturday, he went to work as usual that morning with his brother-in-law Tommy Fox. He quit work about one o'clock and arrived back home. His married sister Nan Sharkey, who is Jimmy's mother, made him something to eat. After a while Seamus cleaned himself up and went into Dundalk as he was often wont to do. He was known to have spent time that evening in several pubs in the Lisdoo and Bridge Street areas of Dundalk. He was apparently last seen in the Lisdoo Arms late at night. Around half past eleven he was apparently seen thumbing a lift outside Smiths Garage, which is just outside Dundalk. The next time he was seen he was found dead lying on top of a ditch down a lane off a road which is known locally as the Bog Road, a by-road which connects the Newry-Belfast Road with the Carlingford Road, roughly 150 yards from the back of the Ballymascanlon Hotel. His body was found the next afternoon by two holiday makers from the north who were walking a dog and they raised the alarm. Sometime afterwards his two brothers, Kevin Ludlow who is still alive and still lives in County Cavan, and Paddy Ludlow who sadly is dead, came upon the scene.

That morning, when it was discovered that he hadn't come home, my aunt Nan Sharkey raised the alarm, for it was very unusual for Seamus not to come home at night. Auntie Nan obviously knew something was wrong. She contacted her brothers who went to look for him. After some time they came upon a Garda road check on the Bog Road, found white tape across the road. A Guard was standing. When they asked what had happened, they were told a body had been found. Kevin Ludlow told the Garda that they were out looking for their brother who had been missing all night. A few minutes later he was taken to the lane and he there identified the body of his brother. With that a so-called criminal murder investigation began, which of course went nowhere.

The family was in mourning and their grief was trampled upon by the Gardai, who had no sensitivity or sense of respect for the family grief. Apparently there was a post-mortem held in Dundalk in Louth Hospital by the state pathologist, Dr John Harbinson. The family have only gained access to the pathologist's report in the past year, along with depositions from the subsequent inquest. Apparently the State Pathologist concluded that Seamus Ludlow had been shot three times. There was a bullet in the liver; another went through the heart and lodged in a muscle in the back; a powder burn in his left hand showed that he had put up his hand to fend off a bullet. A third bullet was found in his clothing; this clearly went through his body. The report makes no mention of the calibre of weapon or type of bullet which was used.

An inquest was held on the 19th of August 1976, without the knowledge of the family. The family had to read the brief reports of the inquest in the *Dundalk Democrat* the following week. We are aware in other cases that families were given good notice in advance of an inquest to ensure that they and their legal representatives were there to ask questions. All we know is that my uncle Kevin Ludlow was phoned three quarters of an hour before the inquest began. He was already away to work in Newry and couldn't be contacted, but even so, there was no time to get himself there let alone to contact or brief a solicitor. The family was denied any access to the inquest and denied any opportunity to ask pertinent questions which needed to be asked. What kind of weapon was used? What time did Seamus Ludlow actually die? What forensic evidence was gathered from the scene to point to the identity of the killers? What was extraordinary was that the man who actually identified the body—my uncle Kevin—wasn't even there. We are told a Garda, Sergeant Gannon, who had been at the scene where the body was found, represented himself at the inquest as the representative of the family. He falsely represented himself, with no authority from the family. The Gardai were attempting to keep the family away from the process with clearly something to hide.

Seamus Ludlow was buried two days afterwards at Calvary Cemetery in Ravensdale; it was one of the biggest turnouts in this area for many years, such was the respect that the man was held in. Yet, even though Seamus was a member of Fine Gael, there were no Fine Gael TDs present, no Dublin ministers present. This was a law-and-order government, an anti-republican government, which said that he was killed by the IRA, yet they weren't taking advantage of this for their own propaganda purposes. Clearly they didn't even believe the lies.

In the months that followed, it was obvious that the family were being kept in the dark. My late father, who had taken it upon himself to go and see the Gardai in Dundalk on a regular basis to see if any progress was being made, was told that, 'the IRA did it', but even more disgustingly that some members of the family had also been involved. The words he told me still stick in my craw: 'A family affair'. Yet no member of the family was ever arrested nor no member of the IRA was ever arrested for the crime. It was pure logic that they didn't even believe their own lies.

Jimmy Sharkey: My father had been a delivery man and his work brought him into close contact with the Gardai. He knew a lot of them and would have been friendly with them. After Seamus was killed, they wouldn't talk to him. He, like Kevin, would have been from the 'Old School'—if the police said anything, they were telling the truth. The IRA must have been behind it. So for twenty years it was put on a shelf. It definitely wasn't forgotten about, but we had never anything to go on.

Michael: We of course are not only critical of the Garda handling of the case. In the north my mother was visited two days after the murder by the British army. She was questioned about her dead brother. They made all sorts of insulting remarks about him. They said, 'He must have been a bad man. Surely the IRA wouldn't do that for nothing'. They claimed they were there on behalf of the RUC. My father told them that it had nothing to do with them; they were not police and it didn't even happen in this jurisdiction. He then got on his bike and cycled to Forkhill Barracks to demand an explanation from the RUC. But when he got there, there were no RUC back in those days; it was an army installation. He was put into a British military helicopter, lifted to Bessbrook where he was questioned about what line of inquiry the Gardai were taking in their investigation. We saw this a further evidence of the British army covering up their own involvement by trying to see what was known.

As I said, the army had told my mother and father that day that the RUC had sent them, but from that day to this, the RUC has never troubled us about the murder of Seamus Ludlow. What was interesting was that the British army were able to connect my mother, whose name was not Ludlow, with Seamus. They clearly had gone to a lot of trouble to establish who my mother was.

We know that nothing more was done with the investigation north or south. We have been told in recent years that the investigation was actually suspended after three weeks. We don't know where the orders came from, but we understand that it was from a very high level, not in the Gardai but probably also the Department of Justice. The whole investigation was suspended. Once Seamus was buried, the whole investigation was buried with him. There was nothing to suggest that the RUC were looking for his killers. Even though he was an alleged informer who had been killed by the IRA, the RUC or the Gardai weren't arresting people. There was no real investigation, just a pretence.

Seamus Ludlow was blackened, branded an informer who had been murdered by the IRA. Of course, if he was an informer, a word in Irish society which carries all kinds of connotations, no one gives a damn if his murder is ever solved. And of course, because he was a single man, unmarried, no children, no worldly possessions, he was easy meat. He was an ideal victim for a cover-up; he was unimportant in the state he lived in, expendable, a nonentity in their eyes.

Jimmy: We now know that Paul Hoskings was one of those who was in the car the day that Seamus was murdered. He got married and went to Scotland just after Seamus was murdered. The marriage broke up and he came back to Ireland around 1986. Around January or February 1987 he was attending the funeral of a relative. His brother-in-law, who was a Special Branch detective, approached him and told him that the RUC wanted to talk to him about something serious. He said he knew what it was, so he went to a pub and an RUC man did the interview. Hoskings told the RUC man he wanted to talk to him about the murder of Seamus Ludlow in 1976. The RUC man said, 'We know you were there; we want to hear your story'. Hoskings asked him, 'What happens now?' He was told to forget about it, it was political.

A reporter from Northern Ireland, John Ellis, came to my mother's home in Thistle Cross in 1985. He was investigating a lot of the murders around the border area and had come across Seamus's case. My mother didn't want to entertain him; she chased him. He came back again around September 1995. My mother contacted me and I met him in Dundalk. He asked me, 'Who do you think murdered Seamus Ludlow?' I told him I didn't think it was the IRA, that I thought it was the SAS. He told me he knew who had murdered Seamus and asked if we wanted to do anything about it. I said 'Yes'.

In March 1996 we wrote to the then Garda Commissioner, Patrick Mulligan, and asked for the case to be reinvestigated—not reopened, for it was never closed. We set up a meeting and it was fairly heated. That was the 16th of May 1996. They never told us what they had; they were obviously sussing out the family to see what we knew. Over the next twelve months other meetings were held. The Gardai thought that by setting up meetings with us they would keep us happy. Chief Superintendent Murphy met us. I knew what his game was before I even met him. He was trying to suss me out. He told me that I had the wrong names. Then eventually the police told us there were four fellows involved in the murder.

These boys were arrested on the 17th of February 1998. One of them lives in Staffordshire. This boy is known as Mambo to his associates. They were all connected to the Red Hand Commandos. Two of them had been in the UDR, at least one of them a captain. Mambo wasn't in the UDR, but quite possibly was an agent.

They were all released without charge. I have to say that I was a bit taken aback for I had been told that the evidence was so strong.

Then myself and Kevin Ludlow had a meeting with Ed Moloney in my house. He told me that one of the boys in the car that day—Paul Hoskings—had given him his story and he wanted to publish it. I told him that he couldn't for it would jeopardise any court case that may follow. He asked me if I realised that these boys weren't going to be charged. He told me that this was our last hope and it was true. So I started to tell him this story. Kevin broke down and had to leave the room. On the 8th of March 1998 he published the story, giving the details we now know about Paul Hoskings, Mambo and the UDR.

Michael: When we opened the paper we were stunned. For my mother it was an awful thing to see in the paper a report about her brother. Here was the murder described in such clinical terms; she wasn't prepared for it. The first thing I thought was I am going to see that man Moloney. I phoned him the next day and told him I wanted to talk to him. He came to see us. What we wanted to know was what more was there. We knew in our guts that he had more, for no journalist like him would put his reputation on the line. We wanted to know was Hoskings serious; I suspected he was. Moloney spent three hours with us and told us a lot more than what is actually in the paper. We told him everything that had been done or said to us over the years, by the Gardai and the RUC, the British army, etc.—stuff that had never been in print before. It wasn't just a story about a cover up by the Gardai or the RUC; it's a story of a family who was abused, seriously abused by the authorities who should have been investigating the murder. This allowed us a chance, almost therapeutic, to unburden ourselves of a lot of bitterness which had built up over the years. A lot of it had been internalised and I suppose that is what the Gardai wanted. They were looking to separate and divide the family, turning one against the other.

Believe me, there was a lot of shit that had happened between us before that. We weren't on talking terms. But the appearance of that report in the *Sunday Tribune* on the 8th of March had an unexpected result; it brought us together again.

Jimmy: After that, I may have done a lot of the donkey work but Michael went about approaching all the people whom we have asked for help. I wouldn't have had a clue that these places and people existed.

Michael: Living in the north and having a political mind, I knew of the existence of these people. I wrote letters to various organisations. I wrote to British Irish Rights Watch on the Monday morning. On the Tuesday evening when I came home from work, I was told that Jane Winter had called. Next morning I spoke with her on the phone. She was fascinated by the case and told me she would do whatever she could to help.

Similarly I wrote a letter to the Pat Finucane Centre and Paul O'Connor phoned back. He told me they knew about the case, but they didn't get involved unless the family invited them to. Once we asked them they were more than happy to help us. Furthermore they adapted my letter and placed it on their web site and they have updated it with more stuff.

I have also corresponded with the Irish Council for Civil Liberties in Dublin. They have written to the Taoiseach on our behalf, calling for a public inquiry.

Jane Winter gave us respectability because we are not just a family anymore crying for justice. We are a family whose demands are recognisably validated by a legitimate and respected human rights activist who is known around the world. And we cannot praise ICCL enough for all they have done for us. They have opened doors for us. A family can easily be fobbed off, but when the family has big guns like that in their closet, then they have to listen.

We have also had remarkable amount of support from Monsignor Murray. He actually referred to our case in his book, *The SAS in Ireland*, in which he mentioned my father being taken away by the British army. And the funny thing about that was that we had never contacted Monsignor Murray. I don't know how he found out. This is a story that we are telling publicly only in the last year and here it has been in print for ten years.

On the 18th of February we held a press conference in a hotel in Dublin, Buswell's Hotel, just facing Leinster House in Dublin. We invited along a number of TDs, various press, tv and media to be present. Members of the ICCL turned up. ITV and TV 3 were there; RTE wasn't. It was a very well attended press conference. We returned to Dundalk that evening for a very successful and well attended public meeting in the town hall. Jane Winter was on the panel again. Also Michael O'Donnell, chairman of Louth County Council, and Seamus Byrne, chairman of Dundalk Council. Almost every branch of the family was there.

I always think that at the end of the day we would feel better if someone said, 'Sorry'. That little word hasn't been said by the RUC, the Gardai, the coroner in Dundalk, the British army. What they are doing is holding their corner, protecting themselves from us because they know we can do them harm. They are not prepared to admit and apologise for the harm they have done.

The RUC asked Jimmy to supply a list of questions before they would agree to a meeting with the Chief Constable. Jimmy sent them the list of questions. They then wrote back and said, 'Thank you for your list of questions but it would not be appropriate for a meeting to take place at this time'. It was an attempt to probe us and to see where we were going.

Jimmy: I have a personal feeling that the Gardai felt that they were about to be hung out to dry over this. I think that they have been told to stay away from the family.

In 1979 the Chief Superintendent of the Garda Siochana, John Courtney, travelled to Belfast with another detective. I think that it was the time when the Pope was coming to Ireland and they were looking for a lot of security from the RUC. I don't think they were down in Belfast with anything specifically to do with Seamus's case. While they were there, they were given the names of four suspects and all the information they had to do with the case. It was brought back to Dublin and someone told Courtney to put it into a file marked 'Classified'.

We went to see Courtney about September of last year; we drove to Dublin to see him. After about a half an hour, he came out to see us. He's a man of about seventy. He asked us what we wanted. I showed him my driving licence and, with my name being Sharkey, he looked at it and said, 'I don't know you'. Then Kevin showed him his and when he saw 'Ludlow', his face changed colour. 'Oh, that's right. I know you. What do you want?' I asked him did he have the file in 1979. He started to use abusive language towards us and threatened us with the Gardai. I asked him why he would do that when we were only asking him a question. Kevin couldn't believe his reaction. I asked him what did he expect; a leopard doesn't change its spots.

We want to know when did the Garda know the identity of these bastards? Was it a day, a week, a month, a year after the killing? We believe it to be closer to the day than the year, but that is beside the point. We want to know had they made arrangements to allow people across the border. Had the roads been made clear? Was the checkpoint taken away from the Lisdoo Arms to allow them in? Was the road through Carlingford and Omeath cleared to allow them to cross the border? Had the Gardai prior knowledge? Did they deliberately blacken the good name of the dead man, the innocent victim, to allow a cover up to take place? Who was responsible for the abandonment of the original Gardai investigation after only three weeks? Who stopped the inquiry which took place in 1979? Was it the Garda Commissioner, who may or who may not have been an MI5 spy? Was it his assistant who had the file on his desk? Was it the five Superintendents who had it on their desks? Was it the Minister for Justice? Was it the Cabinet?

Michael: You have to ask, who were they protecting by covering it up? Were they protecting the killer, who may or may not have been an agent of the RUC Special Branch or British military Intelligence? Was he so important that he could be allowed to get away with that? Were they protecting the two gentlemen who were in the UDR, one of whom was a captain? Or were they protecting somebody in Dublin? It may well have been that protecting the killer was a means to an end. He may have been a very small cog in the bigger wheel. What was going on? It was incredible that he was able to kill a Catholic down here and the Garda knew about it. They certainly knew about it in 1979; I would say they knew about it in 1976.

Two of the men were in the UDR and they could legitimately carry firearms for their own protection. The killer wasn't in the UDR but could have used one of their guns to carry out the killing. So the question arises: did the Gardai send the ballistic reports to the RUC? Clearly within a short time they would have traced those guns right back. We know from recent reports that the Gardai sent material from the Dublin bombings to the forensic laboratory in Belfast which has subsequently disappeared with no trace. You have to ask yourself did they do the same in our case. Has it disappeared too?

There are lots of things about uncle Seamus's death. In the weeks that followed there were reports in the papers that his clothes had been partially removed. There was this rumour that he had allegedly been taken in mistake for somebody else, a known republican. This republican, who I may say is known to me pretty well, is a former British soldier who deserted the army. He was a paratrooper who ended up with the IRA in Dundalk. He apparently has tattoos on his left arm. There were reports in the press, that weren't mentioned in the pathologist's report, that Seamus's coat and shirt were pulled off as though someone was trying to see what he had on his arm.

Jimmy: I went to see this man with Kevin Ludlow. I asked him did he think it was mistaken identity and he said, 'Yes'. I asked, 'How do you know that?' and he said, 'The Special Branch in Dundalk told me that'.

Ten days after uncle Seamus was buried, eight SAS soldiers were captured by the Irish army trying to cross the border at Omeath, armed to the teeth. There were several instances of people being kidnapped from this area along the border. We know of the exploits of the Jackal and Robert Nairac along the border. That they crossed that border to kidnap, kill and spy on people is not in dispute. But the Gardai were looking only in one direction as regards Seamus's murder, blaming it on the IRA. It could well be that they knew all along who did it but weren't prepared to do anything about it.

The one thing that we are all determined to get is truth for a man who never hurt a fly, who was loved by us all. That's why we object to the government's proposal for a private inquiry. We want a public inquiry. We want to be at this inquiry. We want our lawyers to be there. We want them to ask the questions, to subpoena witnesses and to ask the questions that we want answered, not the questions that they want us to ask. We want Joe Soap to be able to walk in there and to hear everything that is going on. We want it reported in the *Irish Independent*, the *Irish Times* the next day.

The one over-arching motive for everybody here in our family, six branches of it, is to get truth and justice. This basically was a good man and nobody should ever get away with scandalising his good name. That man was worth it; that man was not the person they portrayed him.

5

GARY ENGLISH
19 April 1981

Killed when run over by a British army Land Rover

On Easter Sunday, 19 April 1981, there were street disturbances in Derry. Given the anniversary of the 1916 Easter Rising and the fact that Bobby Sands' hunger strike was entering a crucial phase, a confrontation between local youths and the British army was unexceptional.

A crowd of between 60 and 100 youths was stoning British army vehicles at the junction of Creggan Road/Creggan Street and Marlborough Terrace/Infirmary Road. At one point the army vehicles in Infirmary Road withdrew a short distance, thus drawing the crowd into the middle of the crossroads. Shortly afterwards, two British army Land Rovers drove at speed down Creggan Road—an extremely steep hill. None of the witnesses saw any sign of attempts to slow or brake as the crowd in the centre of the crossroads scattered. The leading Land Rover struck three youths. One was not seriously injured. Another, James Brown, aged 18, was thrown a distance of approximately 60 yards by the impact. A third youth, Gary English, aged 19, was hit a more glancing blow and fell close to where he had been hit. The Land Rovers continued to speed past his body and across the road junction, after which they braked and stopped. As they reversed, the second Land Rover, which had not been the one which struck the youths, ran over Gary English and then stopped. The soldiers inside emerged, lifted Gary English into the vehicle and drove back up the hill to Rosemount RUC station. There Gary English was examined by an army medic who could find no visible signs of life. He was then driven in an army ambulance to Altnagelvin Hospital

55

where he was pronounced dead on arrival. James Brown, meanwhile, had also arrived at Altnagelvin in a civilian ambulance and died shortly after his arrival.

The RUC issued a short statement to the effect that 'two youths died as a result of a road accident', but eyewitnesses questioned the British army actions. One eyewitness quoted in the press stated, 'You could hardly call driving at speed the wrong way along a one-way street into a crowd an accident'. Bishop Edward Daly called it 'a stupid and cruel deed', and Fergus McAteer of the Irish Independence Party talked of 'another all too bloody Sunday'. Factories throughout Derry closed to allow workers to attend the funerals at which the priest called for an examination in particular of the circumstances of the death of Gary English.

The immediate point of contention related to the cause of Gary English's death; did it result from the initial impact or from having been reversed over by the Land Rover? If the latter, as Tony Gifford later put it, 'Gary English may at least have had a chance of survival if he had not been crushed by the weight of the second vehicle'. Either way, the whole incident raised a number of questions, in particular relating to the purpose and intentions of the army actions. The British army claim, as it later emerged, was that the Land Rovers constituted a quick reaction force whose purpose was to block off the entrance to Infirmary Road, thus trapping the rioters between themselves and the military vehicles already in Infirmary Road. Arrests would then be made. Why then did the Land Rovers overshoot the junction with Infirmary Road? The only possible explanations were that they did not intend to stop, but sought to injure or kill people in the junction, or that they were travelling at such high speed that they were unable to stop.

A transcript of radio messages monitored by a local man could be taken as possible support for the former explanation; at least it provides little evidence of the shock and remorse which might be expected to follow after a fatal accident. The 'hotel' references are to army code names.

> Hotel 33: The crowd is thick in the middle of the road.
> Hotel 29: Are you sure?
> Hotel 33: Yes, across to Middlette Stores.
> Hotel 29 (to Charlie 34): Go, go, go!'

And shortly afterwards:

> Charlie 34: We have doggo*, we have doggo.
> Hotel 29: Good. Well done.

*'Doggo' is army slang for 'corpse'.

The following August the driver of the lead Land Rover which had struck the youths, Lance Corporal Stephen Neville Buzzard, aged 23, was charged with causing death by reckless driving. His commanding officer, Colour Sergeant Hugh Dalton Smith, aged 33, who had sat beside him in the front passenger seat, was charged with aiding and abetting. The driver of the other Land Rover which had reversed over Gary English was not charged.

The trial took place between 14 and 20 January 1982 with Judge Hutton presiding. The evidence of Buzzard and Smith was substantially different from that of the civilian eyewitnesses. Smith claimed to be driving at no more than 30 mph as he came down the hill and to have braked before reaching the crossroads. Buzzard, his commanding officer, declined to estimate the speed of the vehicle. Buzzard was certain, but Smith less so, that there were no people actually in their path as they crossed the road junction. Smith stated that a number of youths came suddenly from the left and 'got in the way of the vehicle'. Much of the second day of the trial was taken up with discussion of the admissability of Smith's original statement to the RUC when it emerged that he had been interviewed as a witness, not as a suspect, and that he had not been advised of his rights.

From the start it appeared that the case was skewed towards the defence rather than the prosecution. Buzzard's professionalism was stressed, in particular the fact that it was his fifth tour of duty in Northern Ireland. The judge ruled out any implication that the vehicles had deliberately been driven at the crowd in order to injure or kill. Indeed, the judge seemed to be at pains to support the defence case. He advised the jury 'to consider whether you think that perhaps unconsciously some of the witnesses called for the Crown had a tendency somewhat to strengthen their evidence against the Army'. And he suggested that the driving, while reckless, might not have been unreasonable in the circumstances, given the rioting and the purpose of the mission being the apprehension of rioters. Certainly it appeared that the Crown lawyers gave up the fight at an early stage. Senior counsel Mr McCollum withdrew from the case before the defence started; no explanation was given to the jury. Cross examination and summing up was left to junior counsel, Mr O'Reilly.

After three hours deliberation, the jury found the two soldiers not guilty by a majority verdict of ten to two. There was vociferous objection from some of the public present, with women in the gallery shouting 'murdering bastards'. The father of Gary English, Michael, was quoted as vowing to continue to fight on in relation to the death of his son. He did so, and managed to obtain an inquest. This was an unusual development as the initial response of the authorities was that an inquest could not add to what had already been brought into the public domain through the trial.

The inquest into the deaths of Gary English and James Brown took place on 3 and 4 May 1983 with Ronald O'Doherty the coroner. Much of it centred on the cause of Gary English's death. Six of the seven British soldiers who appeared as witnesses offered little to the proceedings; they said that they had not seen anyone being hit by the leading Land Rover, nor were they aware of anyone having being reversed over by a Land Rover. The seventh soldier testified that one Land Rover had reversed over a body but that he did not think it had actually touched the body.

The expert state witnesses—Professor Marshall, the State Pathologist, and John Taggart of the Northern Ireland Forensic Laboratory—concluded that Gary English had most likely died as a result of the initial impact and not from any subsequent crushing by a vehicle. John Taggart, for example, stated that he saw no evidence from Gary English's clothing that he had been driven over by a Land Rover. Thomas Cahill, counsel for the English family, drew his attention to Gary English's shirt which showed clear signs of a tyre mark. Taggart was at a loss to explain this contradiction, stating that it was possible that he had examined the wrong shirt.

The English family obtained the services of a traffic accident expert from Denmark, Professor Jorgen Dalgaard, who stated that the most probable cause of death was crushing by a vehicle, not impact. Some of Gary English's injuries, such as the broken thigh bone, resulted from an impact, but the cause of death—a ruptured aorta—was in Dalgaard's view caused by crushing.

The jury found that both Gary English and James Brown had died as a result of being struck by a Land Rover. They concluded that one Land Rover had indeed reversed over Gary, but that this had not been the cause of death. They gave no credence to the attempt by RUC photographers at the inquest to prove that a masked rioter they had photographed was in fact Gary English—as if this somehow justified his death. On the basis of this partial vindication of his argument, Michael English called on the DPP to reopen the file on the two soldiers who had been acquitted. This did not occur.

Michael English has continued to fight in the intervening years to prove that his son was killed when the Land Rover reversed. He now tells the story of his struggle.

Mickey English

I knew I wasn't going to get justice, but what I could do was get the truth, and let people know what happened, that he wasn't killed as a result of an accident, but he was deliberately driven over.

My son Gary, who was then 19 and a half years of age, died on Easter Sunday 1981 as the result of having been first of all struck by a British army Land Rover and then subsequently, as he lay on the ground unconscious, driven over as the vehicle reversed over his body. Within the family circle we knew him as a quiet, respectable young man who held a position as a bar steward in a pro-unionist establishment called the Northern Counties Club, which was frequented by barristers, judges and solicitors.

He had, as the rest of the family on that day, gone to the commemoration of those who died in the struggle for the freedom of Ireland. Immediately afterwards, himself and a group of four young men went to a local park to have a game of soccer. In the course of playing the soccer, it became quite clear to them that there was trouble at a junction called Creggan crossroads which was just opposite the park. Being curious, they stopped playing their soccer match and went over to see exactly what was happening. From the position they were standing, they couldn't very well see because the confrontation was taking place at Windsor Terrace, and to get a good view, you had to stand exactly in the middle of the crossroads.

There was a group of about thirty or forty people standing observing a group of youths who were rioting against the British army and the RUC. As they were doing that, there was a cry went out, 'They're coming! They're coming!' It was two Land Rovers coming from the barracks in Rosemount, which was about 500 yards above where the confrontation was taking place. It was a steep incline. The Land Rovers were coming down somewhere between 50 and 70 miles an hour. There was little time for the people gathered in the middle of the road to get out of the path of the jeeps. My son made an attempt, and another young man called Jim Brown. They turned and ran to what they thought was safety down Creggan Road, but as they ran, the leading Land Rover was deliberately driven in such a fashion that it struck Jim Brown and my son. Jim Brown was thrown some 60 feet in the air and his body came to rest against a lamp post some 60 yards further down the street. My son was struck by the passenger side of the Land Rover and his body came to rest almost at the spot where he was struck. The two Land Rovers then proceeded down towards the body of Jim Brown. The leader of the unit, Colour Sergeant Smith, jumped from the lead vehicle, looked out and said, 'Don't bother, chaps; he's dead'. He jumped back into the Land Rover and proceeded to reverse. My son's body lay prostrate on the ground in the middle of the street. There were no cars on either side of the road way, there was no vision barrier to the people who were driving the Land Rover; they could quite clearly see my son lying in the middle of the road. Paying no regard for his life, they reversed over his body. At that point in time, my son died.

We didn't know exactly at the time what had happened our son. We didn't know why our son. Could it have been avoided? Could his body have been picked up? Would he have been still alive if he had been given first aid?

I was invited to join a group called Silent Too Long. It was a very elite club, an unenviable club. Its membership consisted solely of the relatives of the victims of violence. I was vice-chairman of Silent Too Long in this area. It gave us an outlet; we could talk to one another; we could raise questions about the circumstances in which our loved ones died. Was it necessary? Was it avoidable? Were we being told the truth by the authorities? There was a lot of questions we wanted to ask, but as individuals, we felt we wouldn't get a hearing; as a group, possibly there was a much better chance. The group was the brainchild of Father Denis Faul and Father Murray and was supported by the Catholic hierarchy in respect of funding. As time went on, it became more like a coffee morning group; we would talk to each other, but we didn't seem to be talking to people that mattered. There were no legal people involved; we weren't getting the right kind of advice about how to go about things, and we felt that, in our vulnerability, we were being used. It became a struggle between the Catholic church and the republican element in Silent Too Long. They were wanting to make it more political, which was the right way to go. It was through that aspect of Silent Too Long that I got contacts that were to help me in the future. Three of us went on a speaking tour at the invitation of the Troops Out Movement in London, rather than as a result of anything put forward by Silent Too Long itself.

I left Silent Too Long and began to work on my own, not in total isolation, but with the help of people in the medical profession, the legal profession.

The trial was truly amazing. The prosecuting barrister took himself off the case after a day and a half, and gave no excuses to the court why, and the rest of the case was left to a junior barrister to run. This was a trial where two people were charged with reckless driving and causing two deaths. On the second day of the trial the judge became aware when the first defendant, Lance Corporal Buzzard, was called to give evidence, he was giving evidence in his initial statement as a witness, not as a person who had been charged. He was not read his rights at the initial interview by the RUC. The defendant had every right to have the case dismissed and thrown out of court. But rather than let that happen, they took the unique position of dismissing the jury. While the jury was dismissed, Buzzard and Smith were read their rights as they stood in the witness box. Then the jury was recalled. It was explained to them by the judge that they were dismissed because of a technicality and it was a matter of a legal debate between the prosecution and defence as to whether the trial should go any further but it was agreed that the case could go on.

People have a concept of the mechanisms of the justice system in the court and how it operates. You have the prosecution whose job it is to prosecute somebody that they have charged with a crime and to make sure that they pay society for that criminal act. On the other hand you have the defence who are there to defend somebody, pronounce their innocence. That's how I saw a court case before I walked into that court in Belfast in January 1982. But what actually happened was that you had a prosecution who called witnesses who were RUC members, British army members who were in the patrol along with the two defendants, the expert testimony of Professor Marshall [state pathologist] and Mr Taggart [forensic expert]. All the evidence that they presented as prosecution witnesses was in actual fact reinforcing the case for the defence who were proclaiming that they did not actually run over my son, that my son ran across the path of the jeep as it came down the hill and they had no option only to keep going. It was not their fault; it was my son's fault. How could you prosecute somebody with the prosecution witnesses rubber stamping the defence case?

The forensic expert's evidence in particular was a tissue of lies. The best that I could say about Professor Marshall was that his evidence was half-truth, hiding and obscuring the facts. I couldn't accuse him of telling lies. It was the things he was not saying that were crucial and would have secured the prosecution. But he elected not to divulge those facts to the court.

The way that the law stands, there is a great well in the middle where people like ourselves fall down into the middle of it. We are forgotten. These two soldiers were passed through the system as quickly as possible, and were taken hand in hand by the prosecution through each stage of it, and they were assured from point A to point B that they would not do a minute of time in jail, that they would be found not guilty. There is no appeal against that. We can't go back and say, 'Look, that finding is wrong'. There has to be some way in law that allows us to say, 'Right, they were charged with reckless driving and causing two deaths, but was it not the case that the indictment should have been murder or at least manslaughter?' And while they are not guilty of reckless driving, we're saying that they were guilty of murder or manslaughter and they should be re-charged and tried on that basis.

Initially there was no intention of prosecution in Gary's case. What leads me to that inescapable fact was that neither Buzzard or Smith were read their rights; you only read the rights to someone whom you have a view to prosecute. The statements that were taken off them at that initial point in time were only witness statements. It wasn't until I started the campaign through Silent Too Long. The other person who did a great deal of work with respect to Gary's case was Lord Tony Gifford. He wrote a pamphlet called *Death on the Streets* about the case of Gary and Jim Brown, and another young man killed by a plastic bullet, Paul Withers. One of the very first voices to come in support of an investigation into their deaths was Bishop Mehaffy of Derry and Raphoe.

Gary and Jim Brown died on the 19th of April 1981 and I don't think the prosecutions began to be considered until October 1981 when a date was then set and it was quite clear that two soldiers were going to be charged—a combination of pressure from myself, from the local media and national media. The intention wasn't to prosecute, but it was forced upon them.

We pushed from day one to get an inquest. The family felt that we would have a hands-on input into an inquest which we didn't have in the court case, because it wasn't actually until we had purchased the transcripts of the trial and I had come across mortuary photographs that we saw that, in the case of my son's death, two and two were not making four. We had the autopsy reports from both my son and Jim Brown and we found a great discrepancy. We actually had in black and white from the transcripts of the trial the statements of the state pathologist, Professor Marshall, and the expert from the Northern Ireland forensics department, Mr Taggart. While Professor Marshall's findings were calculating two and two as five, Mr Taggart's were making two and two 44. I decided that what we needed for the inquest was someone who could put all these things in perspective and through the contacts I made through the Troops Out Movement, I got in touch with Professor Jorgen Dalgaard, a recognised international expert in traffic pathology from Denmark. When I presented to Professor Dalgaard what I wanted done, he said that Professor Marshall was a highly respected, dedicated pathologist, and if he said that my son died as a result of the findings that he had, then I could rest assured that, in all probability, that was why my son died. So I asked Professor Dalgaard if he would look in any case at the autopsy report produced by Professor Marshall, the medical photographs from the mortuary, and the evidence given by Mr Taggart. He said that he would read them, but he didn't expect to find anything. I sent them off. Exactly five days later, I got a telephone call. It was Professor Dalgaard. He was utterly shocked, amazed, and he said what happened my son bore no respect to the forensic report or the pathology report. He said that what was said to have happened on the day was quite impossible and that if I still needed him to do a full report, he was available. And he said furthermore, if I felt it was necessary for him to fly to Derry for the inquest, he would do so. And if I would pay his fare and put him up, he would come at 24 hours notice.

In a letter I had received from the Lord Chancellor's Office, it said that, as a court case had taken place, it was not deemed necessary to have an inquest. There would be no reason to pay taxpayers' money to establish the 'how', the 'why' and the 'when', when this was already established. And the next thing was, out of the blue I got a letter, again from the Lord Chancellor's Office, to say that an inquest had been scheduled. The next move was down to me; what do I do? I've got what I've been calling for, so where do I go from here? I've got all these legal people together, but at the end of the day it came down to expenses. I knew that I was in some way being compensated for Gary's death, so I borrowed all that I could, I begged all that I could beg in respect to that, and whatever recompense I would get for his death, I would pay for the truth. I knew I wasn't going to get justice, but what I could do was get the truth, and let people know what happened, that he wasn't killed as a result of an accident, but he was deliberately driven over; he was cold-bloodedly murdered as he lay unconscious on the street.

There was a date set for the inquest initially. The two main players that I was keeping as a last minute surprise were two eminent barristers from England, Helena Kennedy and Michael Mansfield. Both had agreed that they would do the inquest and share the cross-examination between them; all they wanted was their air fare and they could stay with the family or friends. We indicated this at the last minute to the Northern Ireland Bar Association. I got a call from my solicitor, Brendan Kearney, to say that there was an awful uproar and that neither Mike Mansfield or Helena Kennedy could represent the family at the inquest in Derry. The explanation he was given was that they had not passed the Bar Association exams for Northern Ireland and therefore they weren't eligible to act in an inquest in Northern Ireland. Helena Kennedy said, 'Look, there's a way of overcoming this. We can be introduced to the inquest as friends of the family and cross-examine on that basis.' Brendan Kearney phoned Hugh Kennedy, the chairperson of the Bar Association and outlined what I had told him. His response was that Helena Kennedy and Mike Mansfield were both high-profile barristers in the Old Bailey, they would be recognised as such, and there was no way they could cross-examine as friends of the family. We had to postpone the inquest because of this setback.

The funny thing is, when we went to the court that day, of the twelve jurors for the inquest, I knew at least eleven. There were a lot of friendly faces. When the inquest finally got under way some two months later, I looked at the jury; it was entirely different. Of the twelve people, eleven were from North Tyrone. Only one person in the jury came from the city of Derry, and that person came from the Waterside. There was nobody from the west bank of the Foyle. I couldn't understand why I knew eleven of the first twelve jurors when the RUC and the Ministry of Defence were not expecting a high-profile inquest and on the second time round, the jury should consist of names like Winston McC-, Dallas E-, Lucinda S-. You have to bear in mind that juries are not independently called as people sometimes think. The coroner has no control over who is called to do jury duty. It's not the coroner's office; it's actually the RUC who subpoena people from a list to sit on a jury. The foreman of the jury was a man called Winston McC-, who was a former member of the UDR.

We went through the inquest. Mr Cahill, the barrister, who only had a matter of weeks to go through the legal papers, totally discredited Mr Taggart. Mr Cahill put him under such stress that he actually had to leave the dock; he just wasn't capable of answering any more questions. The coroner, Mr O'Doherty, said he couldn't understand why Mr Taggart as a forensic expert could look through a microscope at minuscule pieces of paint but missed a tyre mark across the shirt of the victim, my son Gary.

The cross-examination of Professor Marshall threw up quite a new thing as far as I was concerned, but it was too late. It wasn't until I actually read through the inquest notes at a later date that I came across this discrepancy. When trying to arrive at a suitable explanation of how my son died Professor Marshall said that he died as a result of the impact, having a severe rapid blow to the chest, which severed the aorta valve. At the inquest, when he was asked did he not think, bearing in mind Gary's injuries—where he had the heart extruded from the heart sac, all fourteen ribs crushed, lungs crushed, spleen, kidneys extruded from their sac, all upper body injuries that you would expect from somebody being crushed or run over by a heavy vehicle—did he not think that this would be more likely the cause of death since none of these injuries occurred in the other victim, Jim Brown, where it was mostly spinal and head injuries. Jim Brown's aorta was totally intact. He said that in his experience, if the aorta had been crushed by being passed over by a vehicle, you would expect more than one laceration. But he had forgotten than in his autopsy report you can find that the aorta had two major lacerations, one which completely dissected the aorta, and the other one was a tear two centimetres long along the wall of the aorta. Now, if one bears in mind that the aorta at any give point is only three centimetres thick, a two centimetre tear means that there is only one centimetre left and it's hanging by a thread. If Mr Marshall was right, that if the aorta was severed as a result of crushing or a heavy weight passing over the body there should be more than one injury to the aorta, then how could he actually say that my son died as a result of a severe rapid blow to the chest and only one injury?

Professor Dalgaard said that Gary was knocked forward in such a way that his body actually did a 90-degree turn and he fell back down practically on the spot where he had been struck. Mr Taggart's evidence was that he was struck, pushed forward, fell underneath the front of the jeep and his body then became entangled underneath the jeep as it went forward. So you have this vision of my son underneath the jeep, face downwards, being pushed along as the jeep kept its forward momentum, and then, as the jeep stopped, reversed back, leaving the body in front of the jeep at all times. But this was an impossibility, even by the evidence that was given by the soldiers who were travelling in the back of the jeep. They said that, when the jeep came to a halt, as they looked out the back door, they could see a body some 30 to 40 yards back up the street. He also stated that the scrapings that he took from the headlight housing on the front of the jeep were found to be human hair which matched the hair of James Gary English. The point is, if a Land Rover hit you with such a force on the head, embedding your hair in chrome work of the headlight, you would expect to find some major damage to the head; my son didn't have any head damage; he didn't have a fractured skull, he lost no teeth. It was all upper torso.

Still, the verdict was very healthy for an inquest in Northern Ireland. They found that James Gary English had been struck, not at the junction, but some way into Creggan Street, as he had been running with his back towards the Land Rover in question, he had been struck in the back and at a point of time some time after, the body had then been reversed over by the Land Rover. But it was felt that he was already dead at this point, that he had died as a result of the initial impact. That threw the whole direction of the judge to the jury [at the initial trial] out the window, because he directed them to find that Mr English must have been a leading protagonist and been struck as he ran from Windsor Terrace across the junction. The whole ethos of their case was that he had been struck in the junction.

There's always a hidden agenda. In my son's case there was probably a hidden agenda which nobody knew about at the time. If you think about it: April 19th 1981, some 20 days before Bobby Sands died. The last thing they wanted was street demonstrations and they wanted to reinforce in people the dangers of going out onto the street in protest. And what better way than to kill two people on the street? I don't really know. But I know that my son and Jim Brown were deliberately murdered but more so my son, because Jim Brown did die on impact. My son could have been lifted off the ground that day, received hospitalisation and would have been alive. The minute they stopped, the only action they took was to dismount, look at Jim Brown's body, get back in and immediately reverse over the top of my son's body. What they were doing was making absolutely sure that both people were dead.

In 1985, my second son, Charles, died while he was on active service as a member of the Provisional movement. I felt the family had been victimised all over again. We had buried Gary, he was now dead four years; we had accepted his death; we would go to the grave every Sunday; on his birthday we were up, and his anniversary. He's dead, but he's still part of the family. There's an acceptance there. There has never been an acceptance of what passed for justice. That still hurts, that still remains. And in 1985, that was further compounded when I lost my second son. And it is my conviction that I would not have lost a second son had justice operated for us in the first place over the death of my first son, because my second son went down the line with me in respect of my pursuit, my obsession with obtaining the truth and justice. He supported me fully. And when that was denied at every turn, it framed in his mind that you cannot get anything from the state. If you want something from the state, you've got to be prepared to take it from them through force of arms, because force is the only concept that the state can understand. I could never say to my son, 'You're wrong; there are other ways'. I lost my son, and that would never have happened had justice been served.

That has been my family's story. It is not a unique story. It is a story that is shared by a lot of people in the course of Irish history, particularly in the last 30 years. We have become victims through the deaths of our loved ones and those of us who expected truth and justice after the death became further victimised by the state.

From the point in time when Gary died till the point when I'm put in a box myself, I will give interviews and I will talk to people and I will show people in black and white what happened my son, and the more people I talk to, somewhere along the line, the truth will be, not just there, but accepted by everybody. Everybody will know exactly how my son died and will know the corruption of the state that we're asked to live in and they'll understand why people want to change the state.

It was just something I felt I had to do. It probably had become an obsession, a compulsion with me at the time. I just wanted to scream out: 'Do you really know what happened to my son? Do you really know that because of what happened to my son, I lost another son?' I don't want to lose any other sons. And I'm now in a position where I have grandsons, and I don't want to lose any grandsons. I want it to be over, and I want to know exactly what happened my son. I'm no different from somebody else whose son or daughter or loved one has died in the circumstances of Northern Ireland. We should have a truth commission. You'll never get justice but you can let people know the truth.

I don't expect anything off them. I can't see them sending me a letter some day, saying, 'Look, these two people who murdered your son did so in the uniform and in the service of the British government and in that respect we are sending you this letter of apology.' I'm never going to get that. I don't necessarily want that.

At the end of the day, I'm probably not going to get anything except self-satisfaction that I have let people who didn't know my son, who didn't know the circumstances under which he died, how he died, who he was, and the kind of state that we live in that could corrupt itself, and corrupt people who would see themselves having no relation to violence at all, such as professors and doctors—how this state corrupts everybody.

6

CAROL ANN KELLY
22 May 1981

Plastic bullet victim

Carol Ann Kelly, aged 12, lived in the Twinbrook area of West Belfast. During the evening of 19 May 1981, she was playing near her home when a neighbour asked her to run to the shop for a pint of milk. As she returned with some friends at about 9.30p.m., a number of British army Land Rovers drove past. Two plastic bullets were fired, one of which hit Carol Ann on the head. She collapsed instantly, still clutching the milk she had bought. She was taken to the Royal Victoria Hospital unconscious, where she died two days later on 22 May 1981 as a result of her extensive head injuries.

The period was one of widespread tension. Bobby Sands, the first republican hunger striker, had died earlier in the month, and two other hunger strikers, Patsy O'Hara and Raymond McCreesh, died one day before Carol Ann Kelly. Throughout the period plastic bullets were used continuously and with lethal effect by the RUC and British army. In the month Carol Ann was killed, May 1981, 16,656 plastic bullets were fired, causing three fatalities. Henry Duffy, a 44 year old widower and father of seven, was hit by a plastic bullet as he walked along a street in the Creggan, Derry on the day Carol Ann died; he died shortly afterwards in hospital. Julie Livingstone, a 14 year old from Stewartstown Road, not much more than a mile away from Twinbrook where Carol Ann lived, died on 13 May, one day after having been hit by a plastic bullet. In fact, since Easter that year, 15 people had been seriously injured by plastic bullets, in addition to the three fatalities mentioned.

Fathers Denis Faul and Raymond Murray issued a statement on 21 May condemning the aggressive use of plastic bullets by the RUC. Their use, they said, was 'an attempt to terrorise local people and prevent them from exercising their political right to peaceful picket'. Jack Hermon, RUC Chief Constable, was belligerent in his reply: 'The critics demand "'Ban the plastic bullet", but do they demand "Ban the petrol bomb" or "Hold an inquiry into nail bomb or rocket"?' Plastic bullets were, he said, 'a minimum force weapon not designed to kill ... The security forces do not fire plastic bullet rounds without reason. Their use can be stopped immediately—if violence stops immediately'. In a reference which seemed to cast doubt on the innocence of victims such as Carol Ann Kelly, he added:

> Let parents exercise their responsibility over their children ... in order to avoid a repetition of the tragedies which have already occurred. That is the real answer.

The uncritical reader could be forgiven for believing that there is no such thing as an innocent plastic bullet victim—a point made even less subtly by the *News Letter* the day after Carol Ann Kelly's death. Their account of her death has all the detail and clarity of an eyewitness, but given that their own reporters were not on the spot, the hand of the British army press machine is evident, not least in the barbed final sentence. Because of rioting at a local school being used as a polling station,

> A quick reaction force of troops was sent to back up colleagues guarding the polling station. On the way to it they were attacked with stones and petrol bombs. One of the Army vehicles became separated from the rest of the force and the crew fired a single plastic bullet to repel rioters pelting them with stones and bottles. The plastic bullet hit the ground, bounced and hit the girl on the head. According to one source, she had a bag full of empty bottles.

The family of Julie Livingstone, killed in similar circumstances less than two weeks earlier, had experienced the same phenomenon of guilt by press innuendo. Julie's brother Robin recounts their experience.

> My sister Julie was 14 when she was killed by a British army plastic bullet in 1981... As you can imagine, my mother took it hard—it's not a natural thing for your youngest child to go before you do. But what made it a thousand times harder for her was to watch as the sights of the media—local and British—were turned on her dead child. The next day's *Belfast Telegraph* quoted army sources to the effect that a full-scale riot was in progress at the time. I should add that the inquest later found that the area was quiet at the time and that Julie was an innocent victim. That wasn't enough for the *Telegraph*, however. The same report also helpfully pointed out that it was believed that she was from a leading republican family. Most of the hate mail my mother received was of the 'wee republican rioters deserve all they get' kind. My mother telephoned the *Telegraph* and asked to speak to the editor, but she couldn't get through. She jumped in a black taxi and went to the *Telegraph* offices in Royal Avenue. She told the

receptionist that she wanted to speak to the editor and was going to sit there until he came down or the office closed. The editor didn't appear, the office closed and my mother went home... *The Sunday Times* went one better, though. Chris Ryder, a well-known journalist, reported that doctors had found that the child had an abnormally thin skull and that the plastic bullet impact wouldn't have killed a normal child... Already traumatised by the murder of her child, the reporting of it and the hate mail that it brought, my mother retreated into an armchair in the corner of the living room under a large framed picture of Julie and quietly knitted until she died.

The inquest into the death of Carol Ann Kelly opened on 7 May 1982, the day before what would have been her 13th birthday, and was adjourned until 21 May 1981. The verdict was reached on the latter date, one day less than a year after she had died. The Coroner, James Elliott, sat alone without a jury and refused the request of the Kelly family's solicitor, Oliver Kelly, for an adjournment to allow for the appointment of a jury.

The British army version of events was that soldiers had been guarding St Luke's school, which was to be used as a polling station in the local government elections the following day. They had come under attack from rioters and had called for reinforcements. As two Land Rovers arrived, they too came under attack, the leading vehicle sustaining a broken windscreen. Two plastic bullets were fired, one from each Land Rover; the second hit Carol Ann Kelly.

There were a number of discrepancies in the British army version, not least the claim that Carol Ann was shot in the vicinity of the school, which is in fact a quarter of a mile from where she fell, just outside her home. In addition, local people insisted that there was no rioting in the area until after Carol Ann's death. There had been trouble in Twinbrook, as in many other nationalist areas, at various times in the two weeks previously following the death of local man Bobby Sands. However, local people stated that there was no trouble that evening. But earlier in the day five British soldiers had been killed in an IRA land mine explosion near Bessbrook, County Armagh.

As the Land Rovers approached Carol Ann and her friends, one of the friends with her heard a soldier shouting, 'We will get one of you for our five mates today'. Two plastic bullets were fired, the second of which hit Carol Ann in the head. As her mother watched from an upstairs window, Carol Ann collapsed. A British soldier ran up shouting, 'It's only a little girl', and at Mrs Kelly's insistence, was allowed through by the crowd to attempt to administer first aid. He was reprimanded by his commanding officer for leaving down his weapon to attend to Carol Ann.

The Coroner accepted the British army version of events, with one slight qualification. He referred to 'technical rioting', that is, at least three people gathered together and stoning the soldiers. There was not, he concluded, by any stretch of the imagination a large crowd present. That said, the Land Rovers were attacked and the occupants had fired plastic bullets in order to extricate themselves. Needless to say, there was uproar in the court, with neighbours accusing the soldiers of murder.

Coroner James Elliott found that Carol Ann Kelly 'was innocently returning home from a nearby shop and happened to be in the wrong place at the wrong time'. Carol Ann's mother, Eileen, later stated:

> My child was shot outside her own front door. If that's the wrong place at the wrong time, then what are we to do? Take our children in and lock them away when the jeeps come round?

Eileen Kelly, Carol Ann's sister, tells the story.

Eileen Kelly

An acknowledgement would be something, but it wouldn't be enough. Again we get back to that sentiment that murder is murder and it didn't apply in our case nor in any of the other plastic bullet cases.

I always remember the first time I was told. I had gone looking for Carol Ann who had gone to the shop. My friend Briege had asked me to sit with her wee one while she went to see if she could find Carol Ann. I told her to be quick, for the word had gotten out that one of the hunger strikers had died and I was worried about trouble starting. So Briege went down the street and I was sitting in the flat with Martine. The next thing I heard the footsteps coming up her steps and the door being banged and Tracey Burke was standing there. She said, 'Oh Eileen, come quickly, come quickly; your Carol Ann has been shot.' I can't remember thinking anything. I just remember running down the street. I got down to where she was lying on the ground and there was a good few people about, just people from the houses up and down the street, probably about twenty, plus members of the British army, standing around. One was kneeling on the ground beside her, shouting. I remember looking down and seeing nothing only Carol Ann. I never saw any blood. She had long hair and it was fanned out behind her. I remember the soldier taking out this white cotton pack and positioning it where the wound obviously was and it was then that I knew it was her head. There was another soldier standing there with two guns in his hand. Obviously the one who was kneeling on the floor owned the other gun. I just lashed out; I hit him. He had really red carrot hair. Someone said, 'Take her away; she is pregnant'. So I was taken into the woman's house next door to my mummy's and the ambulance was sent for. Outside was so calm. I mean shouting had broken out, but now it was calm.

From where my mum's house is you could see right to the top of Twinbrook; you would see an ambulance coming in. The ambulance was seen coming round and then it didn't appear; then it was seen going back out again a couple of minutes later. That's when people did get very angry; there was screaming and yelling and this one woman, I think it was Mrs Convery, went in and phoned again. They told her the ambulance was sent away because it was a false alarm. She explained the situation and the ambulance was sent back again. The army told the ambulance driver again it was a false alarm, but the ambulance driver replied that they were told to investigate the matter because the calls had come through again.

Carol Ann was put into the ambulance very quickly. They couldn't work on her in the street. My mum and Mrs Robinson got into the ambulance; they wouldn't let me in, as they said they needed to work on her. By this stage, someone had gone over to the priest's house. Afterwards people said that Carol Ann's blood was everywhere. I didn't see that; part of my mind just blanked. But the people realised just how bad she was and the priest was got. He came over to give her the last rites.

I went to the hospital. Initially we were left in Casualty and then brought into a side room. A doctor and a nurse came over and said that Carol Ann was in the operating theatre and that they were only doing exploratory surgery to see the extent of the damage and if there was anything they could do and that it could take quite a long time. I left the hospital to go and contact other family members. When I came back, Carol Ann was still in theatre. I left the hospital to go home and look after my other brothers and sisters. I went out to the Falls Road to get a black taxi and, lo and behold, there were no taxis going to Twinbrook. I knew that trouble had broken out and I started to panic, for I was worried about the other kids. One of the taxi drivers, when he realised what had happened, said that he would take me as far as he could. The estate was under siege; soldiers were lying across the street like snipers, pointing guns with live rounds. The driver left me at the complete opposite end of the estate from where I lived and I had to go through the estate. It was like Beirut, for the lights were all out. There was shooting, petrol bombs and people screaming; it was awful. I got home and got my brothers and sisters home and put them to bed. I can't remember if I slept or not.

That was Tuesday. On Wednesday, things were just the same; she was on a life support machine. I never went back to the hospital after that; I just didn't want to look at her. I have to admit even now, I used the excuse of looking after the others to keep from going back to the hospital. Wednesday night was much the same; as soon as darkness fell, trouble began. Thursday was the same; by this time the army was getting cocky again. Carol Ann had survived the shooting and they were using plastic bullets again very frequently, to the extent that the back of our house had three plastic bullets shot through the upper bedroom window where the kids were in bed. We spent that night underneath the stairs, petrified. It was the next night, Friday, that Carol Ann died. Mrs Robinson came to tell me. She just said it was all over, she had gone. I'll never forget those words: it was all over. That was the last thing I wanted it to be.

Carol Ann died on a Friday and wasn't buried until the Tuesday. She had been hit behind the ear and there was a lot of bleeding in her head and her face was extremely badly bruised. It looked as if someone was playing football with her; the swelling of the brain and the shaved head—she didn't look anything like herself. When I saw her, I got extremely upset for I thought they had brought the wrong body. I thought it was a wee boy. I hadn't seen her since she had been lying on the ground and she didn't look like that.

There was never a proper investigation into Carol Ann's death. They didn't do any measurements or take statements from witnesses. A lot of the local people went to Woodburn Barracks to give statements and they were told it wasn't necessary. That there never was any proper investigation into her death became very obvious in the coroner's court, a year later, on the anniversary of her death. Carol Ann was killed when she was twelve years and two weeks old and the inquest came up exactly one year later, as if it was planned that way. When we went to the court as a family, the soldiers who had been on patrol and fired the shots were there. They read from prepared statements, which is not common practice; even though the coroner's court is not a court of law, this is not common practice. You are entitled to look over your statement beforehand but not to go into the court with it in your hand. But because the police had made no inquiry, they made major miscalculations. They said that Carol Ann had been shot in the school because at the time the soldiers had been in the school for it was to be used as a polling station the next day. Our solicitor immediately asked if the army had developed a new weapon which could fire round corners. They were a bit taken aback; then they said that is where they had initially been stationed, but they had to go out in their jeeps. They had contradicted themselves and when our solicitor tried to pin them down, one of the soldiers became very anxious and upset. He looked as though he was about to tell all. The coroner stepped in and said that the questions had already been asked and answered. That saved him. The coroner was right; the questions had been asked and answered, but not necessarily in a satisfactory way. It was James Elliot who was the coroner and it was Private xxxxxxxx who shot her.

The bit that got me and still does to this day, the bit that sickens me to the absolute core of my being was the fact of the mistakes they made and the lies they told. It's not because they got away with it, but that whoever made up the story knew it didn't matter what they put in because they were going to get away with it. It didn't matter how many mistakes they made.

The law states in Northern Ireland that three or more people constitutes a riot and this was supposedly Carol Ann and her two friends walking down the street. Elliot believed that there was no rioting at the time she was shot and that the debris which was in the street was due to rioting after her death. He recommended that we as a family should prosecute in a civil action; that is impossible for us; it was far too expensive. He knew in his heart that she had been murdered and as far as I'm concerned he was just as much a part of the whole cover-up. What went on in that coroner's court that day is a disgrace to the so-called British justice system in general. One soldier asked my sister did she want to go out for a date and I had a sexual innuendo made to me. When my sister objected to this, we were told we would be forcibly removed from the court. Soldiers sat across from us and laughed the whole way through it, along with an RUC official standing at the back of the court. They disgust me. I have to work with the police as part of my job, but I have absolutely no respect for them as a force. I would not trust them. As far as I am concerned, they are the scum of the earth.

Not long before Carol Ann was shot, Margaret Thatcher had made a statement saying 'Murder is murder is murder'. So my mother wrote to ask why was it not murder in the case of her daughter. She replied. She totally ignored the fact that the rules governing the use of plastic bullets had been pushed aside. It was shot from a moving vehicle, which is not allowed. Also, it was developed as a means of crowd control, and should be fired at the ground so as to cause minimal damage, not at people's heads. Worst of all, there was evidence to show that the bullet that Carol Ann was shot with was doctored. There were grooves cut into the bullet to make it spin and, according to the doctor, when it hit her, it was like a drill going into a wall. The damage was such that, if she had lived, she would have been a complete vegetable. Thatcher totally ignored that; she just wrote back more or less saying that Carol Ann was a casualty of war and God help these poor soldiers.

It suits the British system to call the Irish situation a war when it is good enough for them, but it is a conflict between two religious factions at most other times. A system which boasts of being the best in the world and they say they are proud of it! They should be proud; they have learned how to manipulate it to absolute perfection. It is the best-manipulated system in the world. I am very angry about that.

There had been a couple of very young people shot [with rubber and plastic bullets] before Carol Ann. So it was really concerned families who got together and said that this needed to be kept in the public eye; these children cannot become statistics. When we became involved in the campaign, initially I thought it was just general stuff: doing a couple of talks, writing to different MPs. It very quickly became bigger than the original idea. There was a lot of money collected for members of the group to go to England and America to talk about the campaign. My mum did a tour of America. England was the place which was visited most— England, Scotland and Wales. We went to the factory in Scotland which actually produced plastic bullets. You can imagine; it was the middle of winter and all we saw was the wee security man on the gate, who was very nice, but that was it. We saw Charles Haughey in Dublin, who was very sympathetic to our case and recognised that there were some illegal things going on and he would make his concerns known to the British government; but again, it was pointless.

We were well received. People in other countries did want to know what was happening here and there was sympathy, but there was an element of disbelief.

What I found was, when I went to England, a lot of the talks took place in universities, for students are very much into human rights and civil liberties. In quite a large part, however, I would say that English students were not interested in the Irish situation and some were extremely insensitive to the point of being hateful in some of the things that were said. I remember one university. It was a huge hall. I went into this hall and thought, 'Oh my God!' I am generally quite a shy person and I was there on my own. There was a group of lads who came in and sat at the end of the hall and shouted up that we were nothing but Irish bastards; so what if she was only twelve? I was telling them what I just told you and this was only a year after her death. I was in shock, for I couldn't believe that people could be so evil. Although saying that, I had the exact same attitude in this country last year. In the lead-up to the July holidays there was a bit of rioting between Catholics and Protestants and there was a Catholic shot with a plastic bullet; he wasn't killed. This person said, 'Yes and I suppose they were carrying a pint of milk'. It was two days after Carol Ann's anniversary. Another person said to me—now this person was very young, maybe about twenty—in all seriousness, 'Oh yes, they'll say they were carrying a pint of milk or using a paint brush on a wall'. Now she didn't know who I was, so I explained it to her. She had actually been brought up to believe that Catholics said these things to try to secure more sympathy for the deaths of their children. I don't know why they should try to secure more sympathy for the deaths of their children; you cannot justify someone in the so-called armed forces taking a gun and shooting a child. There is no justification for it.

There was a lot of us over in England one time, Archie Livingstone [father of another teenage plastic bullet victim, Julie] included. We all met up at the Liverpool ferry coming back and the next thing, the English police arrested Archie. Now Archie at that time was old and he wasn't very well; he was weak and they knew that. They took him off that boat and held him under the Prevention of Terrorism Act. He was the one who was being terrorised. We were the ones who had experienced the terrorism through the British system and the British forces and he was being arrested under the Prevention of Terrorism Act. It's so hypocritical. He was taken away and the boat was delayed for an hour, but it turned out they kept him and we had to go on. It was a way to intimidate us. I am really, really terrified of them. There were other arrests, but I have to say I was quite fortunate. The one person they could have stopped was me and thank God, they never did. I think that is perhaps because I was quite young; I was only seventeen or eighteen. Maybe they were worried about adverse publicity if they arrested me.

There was a monument put up to Carol Ann just outside my mum's house. I have to say that it is the God's honest truth that the monument has probably had more visits from the British army than anyone else. Every time a new regiment came in, there was a visit to that monument late at night. You would have heard them making some awful remarks: 'Wee Irish bitch', things like that. There was one night we had to get out and stand in front of the monument because they threatened to run over it. These soldiers were drunk. My mother had to go out, for when my brother tried to go out, they said to him, 'Mick, if you move, you will join your sister'. Now nobody had said our Michael's name. One of our next door neighbour's wee boys was taken away and told he would end up like Carol Ann Kelly if he didn't stay off the streets. There were other times I was stopped on my own in the dark by a foot patrol. The army would stop in the street and point their guns and look through their sights at you. For me it was: 'Is this boy going to lose it and pull that trigger?' I don't think that that was something they did particularly to families who had lost someone through plastic bullets. I think it was just something they did by way of intimidation.

I met Bob Harker the first time when I was doing a talk for the Peace People here. He was in the British army and he told us he had been ordered to use plastic bullets. He told us how they are told that we are the enemy, scum. They basically dehumanise us during their training. This obviously makes it easy for a young soldier to pull that trigger and to think nothing of it. He became very involved in the campaign to ban plastic bullets and he attached himself to our family in particular.

The whole case of plastic bullets is being pushed in Strasbourg on the basis that they have been used in this country in an illegal fashion and that the force of these bullets is excessive for what they are supposed to be used for, which is crowd control. They are using Carol Ann's case as an example because of the open verdict in the coroner's court. That takes money and a lot of legal wangling. I don't know how you actually take a case to Europe because I am not involved with the campaign any longer. If I was asked to speak, I would do so, but I have moved on for my own emotional survival. You can only bang your head against a proverbial brick wall for so long before becoming exhausted.

There was a lot of media coverage of Carol Ann's death. Even while she was in the hospital, the press, local and national, came to the door asking for photos or information on her. There were a lot of photographs of Carol Ann which we give the press that were never given back.

Quite a lot of the media reports at the time of Carol Ann's death were very favourable; there wasn't a lot of negativity around our family or what Carol Ann was doing at the time of the shooting. There were suggestions that rioting was going on at the time of the shooting, but what I always say is, 'Regardless if there was rioting going on at the time or not, the bullet that she was killed with was doctored. It was used in an illegal fashion by someone who was supposedly there to uphold the law. It was used to kill when it is supposed to be a crowd control bullet. It was used to commit murder.' So I don't care if people think she was rioting or not; it was used to commit murder. It seemed to be accepted that the people who were killed with plastic bullets were rioting and it was their fault. It would have been very different if these people had have been killed with lead bullets because they are not supposed to use live rounds, or even plastic bullets on the streets of England—but that is a nonsense. Death is death. But it was a very good way of fooling the people, fooling the public.

I think there is part of me that, even though I know the system to be so corrupt, I want to believe in the system. I need something to believe in. It is a very confusing way to live. I have to sit here and tell people about the law, about reporting and how they will be treated and about what happens, and I have to have some faith in that and I don't have much; it is such a confusing way to live. But when I say it, I genuinely believe it and I hope they get justice.

An acknowledgement would be something, but it wouldn't be enough. Again we get back to that sentiment that murder is murder is murder and it didn't apply in our case nor in any of the other plastic bullet cases. I would like someone to have to stand trial. I would like an explanation as to why that soldier felt that he was going to get something out of killing a young girl. What was in his head when he pulled that trigger and what way did he feel when he knew? He didn't create the cover-up, for that was more than one person. He may have been told to shut up and not tell the truth. Or did he go along with it and think, 'Great, I've killed one of them'? We don't know; he was never actually in the court. He never was called; it was just the other ones. I didn't know what he looked like. His statement was read out. He wasn't in the country anymore; he had been posted out of the country. His whole regiment was in the country at the time of the court case, but not him.

At the time, I didn't have my child; I was pregnant. Now I have two children and a grandson and I would die for my kids. Has he got older and got kids? Does he realise what it must have been like?

We spoke to people all over the world and the people said, 'We believe you; that is terrible and these bullets shouldn't be used. They are obviously being used in an illegal fashion'. But at the end of the day, it was allowed to continue. Nobody did anything about what was going on in this country. I dare say five or ten years down the line they'll all say, 'That was awful; they allowed those children to be murdered'. But they are all guilty, for they allowed it to go on.

I got a lot out of it. I didn't play the British state's game. Carol Ann was not shot during a riot and, as long as I could tell as many people as I could, the campaign gave me the opportunity to do that. She is not forgotten and never will be forgotten.

They haven't stopped using them, but they have never used them to the extent which they did at that time. I think because of us doing what we did, we have saved other lives. If they were allowed to do what they had been doing, a lot more people would be dead. I don't regret getting into the campaign for a minute. I got to give people in other parts of the world a truer picture of how the British government so-called 'keep the peace'; they terrorise people into silence with these guns.

For me and my mummy, because there was never anything done about Carol Ann's death, it's like it's not over yet. We are coming towards Carol Ann's eighteenth anniversary and it's like there is no end and that grieving process has never ever stopped. On two occasions very recently I had to stop and try to explain to people that when someone has been killed by a firearm in an illegal way, it is murder. They can shrug their shoulders and say it was an accident, but these people were murdered. We as the family members shouldn't have to keep telling people this. It's not our job to educate these people; it's not our responsibility. It is the responsibility of those who committed the crime and the government for allowing them to commit the cover-up and for playing a part in the cover-up with them.

7

Nora McCabe
9 July 1981

Plastic bullet victim

Nora McCabe is one of 17 people who have been killed in the North of Ireland as the result of injuries from rubber and plastic bullets fired by the British army and RUC. Eight of these victims have been children. The worst year for their use was 1981, the year of the republican hunger strikes. In May 1981 alone, the month in which hunger striker Bobby Sands died, 16,656 plastic bullets were fired. Casualties were inevitable. Julie Livingstone, aged 14, was killed on May 13, and Henry Duffy, aged 45, on May 22.

On July 8 1981, the fifth hunger striker, Joe McDonnell, died. Word of the death spread through the Lower Falls in Belfast early in the morning. Around 7.45a.m. Nora McCabe, aged 33, left her home in Linden Street to walk the short distance to the Falls Road to buy cigarettes. At the same time two RUC Land Rovers came up the Falls Road and, as they drew level with the corner of Linden Street, one plastic bullet was fired. It hit Nora McCabe on the back of the head from a range of ten feet or less. She died the following day in the nearby Royal Victoria Hospital from skull and brain injuries. The RUC have never acknowledged firing the bullet which killed her, nor even halting their Land Rovers at the corner of Linden Street and the Falls Road. The most they have conceded is—in agreeing to pay damages to her family in November 1984—that she died of injuries 'consistent with having been hit by a plastic bullet'.

The inquest into her death opened on 19 November 1982. It was immediately clear that there was no consistency between the evidence of RUC witnesses on

75

the one hand and civilian eyewitnesses on the other. One civilian eyewitness, Jean Mooney, said that she went out onto the street as bin lids announced the death of Joe McDonnell. There she joined 15 other women in saying the rosary, after which she walked towards the Falls Road. She saw an RUC Land Rover turn into Linden Street and stop. As it did so, she heard a bang, saw sparks coming from the Land Rover and saw Nora McCabe fall. Nora McCabe was no more than ten feet from the Land Rover. There was, maintained Jean Mooney, no evidence of rioting at the time.

For their part, the RUC witnesses maintained that they had not pulled into Linden Street, nor fired any plastic bullets into that street. They had, they insisted, fired plastic bullets only at identified rioting youths at the corner of Clonard Street and the Falls Road, approximately 30 yards away from Linden Street. The RUC witnesses were identified only by letters, with one exception—Chief Superintendent James Crutchley, who was in charge of the patrol, had been in the first Land Rover and had given the orders to fire plastic bullets.

At the inquest, solicitors for Nora McCabe's family introduced footage taken by a Canadian film crew as evidence. Coroner James Elliott adjourned the inquest to allow the authenticity of the footage to be checked. Subsequently, the DPP appointed RUC Superintendent Entwhistle to examine the film. He also travelled to Montreal to interview the film makers, Jean Pierre Plouffe and Jean Guy Pervost.

When the inquest resumed a year later, on 5 November 1983, Superintendent Entwhistle confirmed that the film was authentic. The film was then shown to the court. It showed the two Land Rovers in question travelling up the Falls Road. One turned into Linden Street and as it did so, a bang was heard and smoke was clearly visible emerging from a black object sticking out of the side of the vehicle. Superintendent Entwhistle agreed that there was no evidence of any petrol bombs being thrown at the Land Rover. He reported on an interview with Jean Guy Prevost that stones and bottles had been thrown, but no petrol bombs. The RUC continued to insist that they were under fire from petrol bombers, that they had fired plastic bullets only at identified targets, and that no plastic bullets had been fired into Linden Street.

The jury, while agreeing partially with the RUC version of events, found that Nora McCabe was an innocent bystander. 'At the mouth of Linden Street, the leading vehicle in the RUC patrol turned sharply to the right and stopped briefly, at which time a baton round was discharged from an offside porthole. There is no clear evidence to suggest that there was a legitimate target to be fired at in that street. Neither is there evidence to suggest that the deceased was other than an innocent party.'

At the inquest it was announced that the DPP, having also viewed the film, had concluded that there would be no prosecutions against the RUC over Nora McCabe's death. This spurred a reaction from various groups and politicians. Seventy Labour MPs signed an Early Day Motion calling on Home Secretary

Douglas Hurd to have a public inquiry. John Hume and many people urged the DPP to reconsider his conclusion on non-prosecution of the RUC. And Yorkshire Television broadcast a 'First Tuesday' documentary on 4 December 1984, in which the Canadian film footage was shown. All of this was to no avail.

On the day following Nora McCabe's death, Sinn Féin issued a statement calling it a murder 'for which, we confidently say now, no RUC man will ever be convicted'. Three and a half years later, on 21 December 1984, Labour MP Joan Maynard asked Douglas Hurd about the RUC men in the patrol which had killed Nora McCabe. Hurd replied: 'The 11 police officers involved in the patrol are still serving in the Royal Ulster Constabulary. Three have since been promoted: one to Assistant Chief Constable, one to Chief Inspector and one to Sergeant'. The Assistant Chief Constable was James Crutchley.

During the week Nora McCabe died there was widespread civil disorder in Toxteth, Liverpool. For the first time, CS gas—which had been used in cities in the North of Ireland since 1969—was used in a British city. On the day Nora McCabe died, Home Secretary William Whitelaw informed parliament that the police would not rule out any means, including plastic bullets, of restoring order. However, plastic bullets have yet to be used in cases of civil disorder in Britain.

Jim McCabe, husband of Nora, takes up the story.

Jim McCabe

We as the victims of state violence were ignored by the state from the day and hour it happened. We became victims of the state.

On the 8th of July 1981, Nora was living with my kids in Linden Street. I was in my mother's. We'd had a short separation—nothing serious, just one of those things. At about half eight or nine o'clock, someone came to my mother's door. She answered it and I heard someone say, 'That man's wife has been hit by a plastic bullet'. Even though I was the only other person in the house, I never connected it with me. My mummy came in and said, 'Jim, you better get down; Nora has been hit with a plastic bullet'. I just said, 'Right, okay'. It never dawned on me for one moment it was serious. I never envisaged anything serious happening to any of our family, even though in 1981 people were being shot dead by plastic bullets, lead bullets, dying on hunger strike; you never dream it will come to your door. Myself and my sister walked down from Locan Street to Linden Street and when we got there, a friend of mine, Billy O'Hare, said, 'Jim, it's serious; she has been taken to the hospital'. I said, 'Where are my kids?' One of Nora's family had taken them to her mother's.

Things start going a bit fuzzy, but I remember going to the hospital to enquire about Nora and being shown into a cubicle. Nora was lying on a stretcher. I can't even tell you what she looked like. I remember the doctor coming and telling me she was being taken away and they were going to operate. I remember meeting her sister and her father in the hospital. I asked if we should stay. I was told it would take a long time, so I decided to go and find the kids. I brought them to my mother's, then I returned to the hospital. I think I had been told at that time that it looked bleak because it was an extensive head injury and that these types of injuries were usually fatal. But still, we had hope. She went through seven hours in the theatre and she was taken from there to the Intensive Care Unit. It's all sort of vague. I think I went home and told my mother that things didn't look good, that I didn't think Nora was going to pull through. I remember saying to my sister,' 'She is not going to live'. She replied that God was good and my reply was, 'Not that good; he should not have let her be shot in the first place'.

The following day—I'm not sure whether it was two o'clock or one—I was sitting talking to Nora's brother and someone came out and said, 'Jim, you better come; Nora has died.' The staff in the hospital were excellent but to me they were cold. We had to leave the Intensive Care Unit; we had to leave Nora with them until they would hand her over to us for burial. I went back to my mother's house.

No RUC men had approached me for any information in the hospital. I was only in the house a half an hour when a phone call came from the RUC asking for me. I don't know how they knew I was there. The RUC man asked me did I know what happened and I think I said, 'One of your fellows shot her with a plastic bullet'. 'Have you any witnesses?' 'I don't know if there are any witnesses'. 'Well if you get any witnesses, would you please refer them to us?' What I said as a result wasn't very nice. I slammed down the phone and that was the first and last contact I had with the RUC.

We were requested to go to the Royal Victoria Hospital so Nora's remains could be released for burial. My mother and my sister's husband went, for at this time I was in a daze. Nothing was real and anyone who said anything to me, I just said 'Yes'. Nora's remains were then taken to her mother's house for burial. She died on the Thursday and was buried on the Saturday.

After that, I returned home to my mother's house with my children and we lived there. Gradually the story came out through different people. What had happened was she had left the house to go to the shop and when she was returning, the Land Rover pulled up, a plastic bullet gun was produced and Nora was hit in the back of the head.

Things sort of quietened down. Friends of mine who were in the Order of St John of God came up and visited me and I went and stayed with them for a few days. Whilst I was away, my child had been outside his grandmother's in Iveagh Street, playing on a lorry. An army Land Rover came up and, whether it was a catapult or stones, he was hit in the face. He was left with a huge bruising around his eye. His aunt brought him to the hospital; thankfully he was alright, but this seemed to me to be a continuation of the whole thing and caused a sense of guilt in me. I wasn't with Nora when she was killed and I wasn't there when Jim was injured.

The next stepping stone was when I went to see the solicitor about taking action. The solicitor was Pat Finucane, who wasn't only a solicitor but who became a very good friend. He handled the case with understanding and it was he who located the video and it was he who employed the barristers and did the legal things. And I was doing nothing. At the same time, my mother was looking after my children, and I was doing nothing. I felt useless on top of the guilt. I left work. I had been employed in the bookies for about thirteen years, all my married life, and adored it. There I was now doing absolutely nothing and through all this, everyday life was going on around me. I had nobody to talk to. I thought it would be selfish to talk about my problems. But to me, everyone was looking at me strangely and in a different way; to my mind it was either out of pity or in an accusing way. I started drinking more than I should. My saviour came when Jim got enrolled in the local nursery school and I got involved in the school for quite a few years afterwards, about ten years, long after Jim had left it, even after Áine left it. That was the only activity in my life—the kids and the nursery school.

In the meantime, I had moved into Elswick Street, a new house, new area and nobody knew me. I was thirty three when Nora died and when I moved house, I would have been maybe thirty four. I was a young man with three young children, with no wife or no partner, so obviously people were curious. Those who didn't know the circumstances eventually found out from those who did and it started all over again. When I went to the shop, people were looking at you. They looked at you in the street, the pub. So for about two years I didn't go out, didn't drink. I just went to the nursery school with the kids and when I did socialise, it was with the staff from the nursery school.

According to Pat Finucane, the only means of getting to the truth was to take a civil action. It was left to the RUC as to whether charges were to be brought against the guilty person. But what I wanted to do was to take direct action: to sue the chief constable and James Crutchley and this is what Pat was engaged in as well as handling the inquest.

At the inquest we had James Crutchley, at that time a chief superintendent in the RUC, the officer in charge of the RUC in West Belfast. There were about seven or eight RUC officers who sat two rows behind myself and Nora's family, the only civilian eyewitness and my mother, who had to be there because she identified Nora's body. On the first morning, James Crutchley took the stand and stated under oath that no plastic bullets were fired in Linden Street. The only plastic bullets were fired in Clonard Street, the next street down. They were fired because his patrol of two Land Rovers had come under attack from petrol bombs. His words were, 'The Falls Road was strewn with rubble, bricks, beer barrels, etc, and there were burning vehicles in the area at that time'. He had given the order to fire a plastic bullet at a petrol bomber. Crutchley claimed he didn't know until five o'clock in the afternoon that someone had been seriously injured. Nora was injured at seven forty five in the morning and admitted to the Royal Victoria Hospital and yet James Crutchley, the most senior member of the RUC, was unaware anyone had been injured!

The other members of the patrol took the stand, gave evidence and told similar stories. The only member of the patrol who was not there was the person who fired the plastic bullet because, under Northern Ireland law he was not required to be there. His statement was just read out in court. It seemed peculiar to me because, if the RUC was as innocent as they claimed and they didn't fire a plastic bullet at Nora, then why did the person who had fired the plastic bullet in Clonard Street not volunteer to go in there if he had a clear conscience? Then the only civilian eyewitness—a girl called Jeannie Mooney—took the stand and told them how she had heard the Land Rover coming into the street, turned and saw the Land Rover stop, saw the plastic bullet gun being produced, saw it being fired and saw a woman who had had her back to it, who had turned away from it towards the wall as if to protect herself, slowly slide down the wall. She didn't know who Nora was. She then said she saw the Land Rovers withdraw from Linden Street and drive on up the Falls Road. Jeannie Mooney said she had felt like a liar because those guys were so convincing. How did the jury feel? Their stories were so good that had I not been so closely involved, I would have been inclined to believe their stories too. There was nothing here to put them in the picture or in any way to blame.

There was then a lunch break. After lunch, Charlie Hill, the barrister, decided to produce the video. When it was suggested there was video evidence, the RUC's attitudes changed; they became quiet and concerned. I looked directly at Mr Crutchley and he was not enjoying this at all. Their counsel did not want it submitted as evidence. The Coroner suggested that the video be handed over to the RUC. Eventually the video was handed over to the DPP. And he then handed it to the RUC for investigation to see if it was authentic. They put a guy called Superintendent Entwhistle on to this. He went to Canada to interview the Canadian film crew. He took still photos, measurements, etc in order to find out if the video was authentic or not.

Almost exactly twelve months later the inquest was reconvened. In the meantime I had settled the civil case against the RUC, Sir John Hermon the chief constable and James Crutchley in the high court and I accepted compensation. I have to say I regret doing so because of the feeling of guilt in accepting money for my wife's death, of profiting in some way from Nora's death. As a result, I found out later, this stopped me from taking further action, for example, the European Court. I was not told that. I discovered this myself. I never forced them into court to tell me why because it was settled out of court. It was a case of the carrot being dangled in front of you. The amount of money I received was not huge. Under the terms, I am not publicly allowed to disclose it; at the same time, it didn't make a rich person out of me. It didn't matter how much the amount was; it could never compensate. I accepted this amount of money and walked away with the knowledge that the RUC were not going to explain their actions. I went away with mixed feelings—disappointment that it was like a damp squib, but with the knowledge that I had money which was paid into court on behalf of my children, which meant that, at least when they were eighteen, they had a few quid coming to them; that I could afford to take them on holiday and give them a comfortable home and buy them things they wanted without having to put them through any more grief, sort of trying to convince myself that I had done the right thing but knowing that I really hadn't. Also, I had planned to bring a private prosecution and perhaps use that money, but that was on down the line. I discussed this with Pat Finucane and he passed on my feelings to Charlie Hill who was against it and advised me not to take it because I wasn't guaranteed it would be successful and had I gone ahead with it, the Director of Public Prosecutions could have taken over and it would have been out of my hands. They advised against it and even though I wanted to press on, nothing more came of it.

That was after the inquest had been reconvened. At the reconvened inquest Superintendent Entwhistle was put on the stand and asked for the results of the investigation. He said he believed this was an authentic video. This came as a surprise to me that the RUC had done something honest. The video was shown to the jury who were then sent away to decide what their statement would be. Their statement when they returned was that Nora was an innocent victim, there was no rioting in Linden Street, no evidence of any rioting in the area at the time and, I think a very important one and one that displeased the coroner, that there was no legitimate target to be fired on at that time in Linden Street. The RUC got up and stormed out and I went with hopes up a bit, given this statement the jury had made, that the DPP would reopen the case and something would be done. But I was told then that the case was closed. The DPP had decided not to prosecute anyone. There was no one to be prosecuted. They point blank denied any knowledge of Nora's death. Here we had a person who died under mysterious circumstances, who died from injuries consistent with that of plastic bullet injuries. We had a video of a plastic bullet being fired in Linden Street at the time of Nora's death. We also had the evidence of Superintendent Entwhistle that the video was authentic. We had eyewitness evidence of a plastic bullet being fired at Nora, hitting her on the back of the head and her falling down injured. Yet the RUC had no knowledge of this, despite the investigations. That was the last I heard. As far as everybody except myself was concerned, that was the end of it.

I was involved with Yorkshire Television in the making of a documentary into Nora's death. It was made for the 'First Tuesday' series. That was shown in December 1984, a month after the inquest. As a result, I think upwards of eighty members of Parliament signed a petition to have the case reopened; even that was ineffective. From then on the interest in the case was gone and it was back to picking up the pieces of your life.

In August 1984 John Downes was killed and out of John's death the United Campaign Against Plastic Bullets was formed. I didn't get involved in that until quite a few months after it had been founded. I had gone into my shell, concentrated on my family. I'm not a publicity seeker. I am not the type of person who would campaign or do things on my own. I'm the kind of person who has to be led, shoved or pushed into doing something. I was approached by Clara Reilly to go and picket the fireworks factory in Dumfries because they manufactured plastic bullets. I went on the picket and started to become involved in the campaign. The thing kind of snowballed from there. I'll never forget that first night, for as I said, I had gone into myself and it was like a night out for me. I went and I met these people for the first time. These people were active, they were concerned; they were selfless and they talked in a way I understood. They weren't barristers or politicians; they were ordinary people like myself who had been thrown into the situation they didn't want to be in and I drew parallels with them. My life was the same as theirs in some ways. For the first time, I could sit down and talk of my fears and concerns and put forward suggestions to make it better for all of us. You weren't looked down on or looked up to. You weren't different. For once you were a piece of a jigsaw that fitted in; you weren't a square peg in a round hole anymore. I was excited; I felt as though I was moving forward. A comment which was made by a very good friend was, 'What do you hope to achieve? You know they won't ban plastic bullets'. That brought me down to earth. But my attitude was, just because that stone is too big or too heavy doesn't mean to say that I can't at least try and move it; you will not get anywhere by not trying. You can sit in the house and feel sorry for yourself. You can sit at home and look after your kids and be quite justified in doing so and no one could blame you. You can sit and shout at the television when the RUC come on and call them murderers, but alone you will not be able to do anything. With these people you will be able to do something.

I did not realise how much work was involved. I think I was chucked in at the deep end. They sent me over to England for a full week—a different city every day, maybe two different meetings every day—at times frightening, harrowing, exhausting but all the time exciting in that here I was being given an opportunity to speak. I spoke to trade union groups, political groups, people like Ken Livingstone and the GLC. The Labour Committee on Ireland organised public meetings. It was frightening, for in no way was I a public speaker. At the same time, I had confidence in myself in that I didn't have to remember or read from a script; all I had to do was to tell the truth. I did not need to prove what I said was true because it was. I did not need to cover up or worry that at the next meeting I might say something different because it was always the same, it was always true. This gave me the confidence and it wasn't as if I was going to forget my lines or be contradicted because it was fact.

I think the most difficult thing was when it came to the question of why the RUC would want to shoot an innocent person? I can't answer that question. I can give an answer like: they try to intimidate people of the streets, so they shoot innocent people. They try to intimidate a community, so they pick on the weakest within that community; they shoot mothers and children. Why use plastic bullets? To control the population, to scare them. I can give all these reasons but they are not necessarily acceptable or true, not real reasons. The only people who can answer that question are the RUC and up to now they have given no explanation. They have given no apology. They have not charged, prosecuted or brought to court anybody. They have not even disciplined internally anyone within the force. What they have done is promote. They promoted James Crutchley to assistant chief constable, and he was then awarded an OBE or MBE or something by the Queen. As have so many other people involved in these things, they have all been promoted and rewarded for the activities here. These are the types of things I explain to people who on the whole are quite ignorant and surprised for they were only educated through the British media and the British media had its own version of events. That is what I saw the remit as, to go and educate people.

I don't see myself as an activist in an individual sort of way. I don't go around looking for things to campaign for week in and week out. I'd be guided by what the campaign's activities are and thankfully our activities within the past years have not been called upon because of the lesser use of plastic bullets. The RUC and the British army do not use them in the indiscriminate way in which they used to. They used to fire them at children playing football in the street. They used to fire them at a couple of drunks walking up the street. They used them in pub fights, at a drop of a hat and for no reason at all. They used to use them without regard to the law or without fear of anyone criticising their use. I believe that we have publicised and internationalised it so much. Myself and Brenda [Downes] were invited to put a submission before the Senate in Washington; I wasn't able to go but Brenda went. That was very successful. We've had meetings with Amnesty International and Helsinki Watch, the European Court and the European Community. The European parliament have come out and condemned the British government for the use of plastic bullets. This week a human rights hearing in Geneva condemned the use of plastic bullets. All this stems from our campaign. A plastic bullet was shown to the members of the Canadian parliament and because of that, Margaret Thatcher stated that the United Campaign Against Plastic Bullets was nothing more than a front for the Irish Republican Army. This is a great compliment to us! No way were we connected to the IRA, but this was recognition that we were doing some damage. Close friends say, 'Do you not think you are wasting your time, for they haven't banned them?' Okay, but I do believe they now think twice before they use them. Having said that, I know they used them in Derry and in Drumcree and, as one person in Derry said, they were like confetti. But we do not get the other incidents where an RUC Land Rover is driven down the street and all of a sudden a plastic bullet is fired for no reason. We do not get incidents where they are fired into people's houses for no reasons at all. Hopefully we will get to the stage where they will stop using them.

I believed we should meet everybody irrespective of who or what they were, for we were telling the truth. Even the sceptics you have to meet. I think the fact that we were a single issue campaign made us strong. We could avoid other issues and not be distracted. The politicians only spoke out about plastic bullets when someone was killed and the next day they moved on. We formed to concentrate all of our time and energy on this issue. That made us a strong and a close-knit group. Many times people have attempted to sideline us but we will not be sidelined. I believe we are a successful watchdog, self-appointed, but nevertheless a watchdog. It doesn't matter who they fire them at, whether it is a loyalist, republican or just an ordinary person who is involved in a street fight. If they fire a plastic bullet to cause serious injury or death, we will be on them as we have been in the past. We will pounce and let the world know how they use them.

We met the Patten Commission. You had myself who lost a wife, Kathleen Stewart who lost a son, Kathleen Duffy who lost a son, Brenda Downes who lost a husband, Clara Reilly who lost a brother and another girl, Rosaleen Shannon whose daughter was injured by a plastic bullet. It was important that they be heard, that their reasons for wanting the RUC disbanded be heard. But the impression I got from the Commissioners was one of disinterest; in other words, 'We are only here because we have to be seen to be listening to you people'. We were kept waiting for nearly an hour before the meeting started. Part of that time we were standing in a corridor with no seats. And remember, Kathleen Stewart was dying; she had got out of her sick bed to come to the meeting. When we eventually got into the meeting, I believe there were only two questions asked after we had finished: one from a lady member who asked to see a plastic bullet because she had never seen one; and one from the ex-Metropolitan policeman who asked us what the alternative to the plastic bullets would be. That was the type of question they asked, which I felt insulting and irrelevant. They didn't give a stuff about our opinion. We all agreed afterwards it was a waste of time; it achieved nothing except that when they do publish their findings, at least we can say we went and put forward our opinions about the RUC.

It's a different situation to the Victims Commission. We were not invited to give evidence nor were we mentioned in their findings. We as the victims of state violence were ignored by the state from the day and hour it happened. We became victims of the state and, as I have said all along, 'When you become a victim of the state, you became an enemy of the state and you are treated in that way whether or not you wanted to be'. I consider myself lucky in that I have experienced little harassment, unlike the Livingstone family, unlike Emma Groves whose sons were arrested and whose house was raided.

When you look at the other side of the coin, they go out of their way to accommodate other victims. Only a short while ago we had the victims of the Omagh bombing; I make no complaint about that, because those people are victims and should be looked upon as victims. They were taken away by the Free State government and looked after in Dublin. You are treated different. It is hurtful and a double victimisation. It is your fault you are a victim of the state; it's not their fault. You are made to feel guilty for being a victim by those people ignoring you; you don't exist. In Nora's case in particular this seems to have gone the whole way along the road. In the first place, she wasn't killed. In the second place, successive government bodies, secretaries of state and Taioieachs have ignored the fact that there are victims like Nora McCabe. We continuously lobbied the Irish government. We got loads of sympathy but that's all. Other victims—and I do not begrudge them that—actually do much better. Some of the members of our group did meet the previous president, Mary Robinson. But that was amongst other people, not us as victims of the state. We have never ever met with members of the British government. We did meet with members of the Labour Party before they came to power and they did write in their manifesto that when they came to power, they would ban plastic bullets; but yet they won't even meet with us. The Secretary of State and no member of the British government will meet us. This is not a failure of the campaign but it is the failure of the British government to recognise us as victims. The campaign has in no way failed. The stone is heavy and we will continue to try and move it.

It has gone beyond the point of revenge, beyond the point of seeing someone being punished for Nora's death. It is difficult to say what I would be satisfied with; it is what my children would be satisfied with. My campaigning has interfered with their growing up. It has kept the issue of their mother's death to the fore; it has spoiled their childhood. How do I make up for that? It's a situation of the devil and the deep blue sea, because on the one hand I could have stayed at home and ignored the feelings I had in regard to trying to achieve justice; but at the end of the day I would have felt guilt because I did not do enough. In a way I still feel guilty because I did not do enough. Maybe I should have tried the private prosecution; maybe I should not have accepted compensation and would have been able to go to the European Court. Delving into the realms of fantasy here, say out of the blue some RUC man comes along and confesses that he murdered Nora. I can't see myself getting a lot of satisfaction. There is no sense of satisfaction to maybe sit in a court one day and see some guy be sentenced to life imprisonment for Nora's murder. There would be an emptiness—not that it is ever going to happen. Even an apology from the RUC or the British government would be an insult at this stage. If the British government said they were going to ban plastic bullets, that would be less empty for there you would have something good coming out of something negative. You would know that never again would anyone go through what I am going through, never again would any child go through what my children went through because of this particular weapon. This would be much better that someone getting sentenced for Nora's murder and plastic bullets still being used, harassment still going on, cover-ups and the lack of justice still going on.

When the first cease fire was called I had mixed feelings. I watched the people batter the hell out of the RUC Land Rovers. I watched them paint a 'for sale' sign on the barracks, climbing up and planting a tricolour in the spy post and I didn't know whether to celebrate or cry. We walked to the Springfield Road barracks and some people were already coming away from it. Tom Hartley was one of them. He must have read my thoughts, saw the disbelief in my face. He approached me and said, 'Jim, it is a very sad day'. I said, 'Yes Tom, it is'—not because I wanted war to continue. It was the feeling that if things go back to normal, will we all be forgotten? Will those who died in the troubles be forgotten like those who died in the past troubles and be just a name in a history book where only those directly involved will remember and visit the graves?

My life has been affected in so many ways. I'm fifty one years of age. My daughter will be eighteen next March. My oldest son left the country five years ago. The son upstairs will settle down and get a job. I have no relationship to fall back on. I'm too old to go out seeking a relationship. Even when I did have a relationship, my campaigning activities affected that. To retrain for employment, I just don't feel able for it. Because of what happened, my life has taken that path rather than me taking the path.

Between 1981 and 1984 I was alone. The formation of Relatives for Justice was the oasis in the desert I had been looking for. I was part of a group who were setting out to do something. A high point was the making of the video, 'Plastic Bullets: the Deadly Truth'. On one occasion a couple of us met with some Germans who watched the video. I watched grown men cry. That has to be a high point if you succeed in getting your message across to someone. There were many times I thought about saying, 'To hell with it; get on with your life'. My kids at one point asked if it had to always be me who would go to the meetings when we were not getting anywhere. Through sheer exhaustion, you ask the same; then just around the corner there is a high point. Someone comes along to do an interview. They might ask a certain question and all of a sudden they light the fire inside you again and you start all over again.

About two weeks ago I went to that pub on the corner, the first time I ever was in it. A friend's wife was celebrating her birthday. I was introduced to this man and he said, 'Jim McCabe? I know you; och yes, you're the plastic bullet man'. I'll continue on as long as there is an issue to be pursued—maybe not as actively as before, but I will continue.

8

GERVAISE MCKERR, SEAN BURNS AND EUGENE TOMAN
11 November 1982

MICHAEL TIGHE
24 November 1982

SEAMUS GREW AND RODDY CARROLL
12 December 1982

All victims of RUC shoot-to-kill operations

Towards the end of 1982, a number of killings by the RUC in north Armagh led to a long-running and explosive dispute over the issue of shoot-to-kill. On the evening of 11 November, 1982, three IRA members—Eugene Toman (aged 21), Sean Burns (21) and Gervaise McKerr (31)—were shot dead at Tullygally East Road, near Lurgan. Almost two weeks later, on 24 November, Michael Tighe (aged 17) was shot dead in a hay shed on Ballynerry Road North, Lurgan. He was not involved in any paramilitary organisation, although his companion, Martin McCauley (19), seriously wounded in the same incident, was later charged. Finally, on 12 December 1982, two INLA members—Seamus Grew (aged 30) and Roddy Carroll (21)—were shot dead at Mullacreevie Park, Armagh.

All the killings were the work of the RUC, specifically of a specially trained undercover unit known as the Headquarters Mobile Support Unit (HMSU). The legal and political repercussions of the three incidents were to reverberate for the next 12 years.

On 5 October 1983, the Armagh Coroner Gerry Curran opened and immediately suspended the inquest into the deaths of the six men because of the pending trials of four RUC men and of Martin McCauley. 'All evidence and statements of persons present when the deaths took place would have to be excluded at such inquests if the subsequent trial of the persons charged would be prejudiced by the publication of evidence.'

The first such trial to occur was that of RUC Constable John Robinson, a former British soldier. He was charged with the murder of Seamus Grew. Robinson's defence was that Grew and Carroll were under surveillance on the day of the incident because it was believed that they were about to ferry INLA chief Dominic McGlinchey into the North. A road block had been set up to intercept Grew's car, but it had crashed through the road block. Robinson claimed that he then went to Mullacreevie Park, where Grew lived, where he spotted the car and its occupants. Robinson said he recognised Grew and waved his policeman's cap out of the window to identify himself to the INLA men. He claimed that he then emerged from his car, put on the RUC cap and approached Grew's car. As he did so, the passenger door opened and there was a loud bang from inside the car. He stated that he had shouted a warning but that Grew's car began to reverse. At this point he opened fire. 'I fired to kill because I believed they were trying to kill me.'

In point of fact, not only was Dominic McGlinchey not in the car, but Grew and Carroll were unarmed. The prosecution case was that Robinson first shot Carroll from a distance of six to ten feet, emptying the magazine of his Smith and Wesson pistol in the process. He had time to reload, walk around the front of the car and then shoot Grew from a distance of 30 to 35 inches as Grew emerged from the passenger side of the car. This, said the prosecution, was incompatible with Robinson's claim that he believed that his life was in danger. 'At such a range, it must have been simple for the accused to decide whether the type of force needed to deal with the situation that had arisen would require the shooting of Carroll.' And as regards Grew: 'It is inescapable that this was a deliberate shooting carried out in circumstances which must have made it clear that the deceased was not using a weapon'.

On the other hand, the prosecution seems to have been less hostile to Robinson than these statements imply. As it emerged during the trial, they had shown him crucial forensic evidence and had given him the opportunity to change his statement. In addition, some of what they had to say would not have been out of place coming from defence lawyers:

> It is expected that they are facing a potential armed enemy whose whole aim and object is to shoot police officers when the opportunity presents itself. Any police officer might have to take a split-second decision on which his life depends.

Also during the trial it emerged that the original RUC account of the killing was wrong on a number of significant points. It was revealed that an RUC Special Branch inspector had been following Grew and Carroll all that day, in the Republic as well as the North. No contact with Dominic McGlinchey was made, but he continued to follow them as they approached the HMSU road block set up to intercept them. However, there was a collision between vehicles driven by the British army and HMSU at the road block. In the confusion after the collision, the car containing Grew and Carroll drove through undetected. The Special Branch inspector following stopped and picked up one of the armed HMSU members, Robinson, and continued in pursuit of the INLA car. The other members of the HMSU patrol meanwhile made a bogus radio call to the effect that the INLA car had crashed through a police road block. After the shooting of Grew and Carroll, the Special Branch inspector immediately left the scene and his presence was hidden from detectives investigating the incident, a fact revealed for the first time at the trial. In addition, Robinson revealed that, immediately after the shooting, he was debriefed by the RUC Special Branch who had concocted some elements of his story and suppressed others. He was then ordered under the Official Secrets Act to present the doctored version of events to investigating detectives.

On 3 April 1984, Constable John Robinson was cleared of the charge of murder. The RUC announced that he was free to return to normal duties.

Later that same year, three RUC men—Sergeant William Montgomery, and Constables David Brannigan and Frederick Robinson—were charged with the murder of Eugene Toman. The prosecution accepted the RUC version of events, that the car containing the three IRA members had crashed through a police roadblock, after which the RUC opened fire. However, the case against the RUC men was that Toman was alive when the car finally came to a stop and that he was shot while getting out of or fully out of the car. This was supported by forensic evidence from State Pathologist Professor Thomas Marshall to the effect that Toman had been shot in the back.

The RUC men's defence was that they were trailing the IRA men that night on the grounds of intelligence that they were en route to kill a member of the security forces in Portadown. In addition, the RUC suspected Toman and Burns of having killed three RUC members—Sean Quinn, Alan McCloy and Paul Hamilton—in an IRA landmine explosion at Oxford Island, near Lurgan, on 27 October 1982. The HMSU, it was claimed, had set up a road block through which the IRA car had broken, endangering the life of an RUC man. Consequently, the HMSU members opened fire. One bullet, they said, caused a flash when it struck the metal of the car, leading them to believe that they themselves were under fire. So they continued firing until all three IRA men were dead.

The shooting of Toman and the others was therefore justifiable; these were dangerous men on a murder mission; there was no time for niceties. As Deputy Chief Constable Michael McAtamney testified, the three defendants were part of a special unit given special training for undercover operations. As such, they worked on the principle that 'if you decide to fire, you shoot to take out your assailant'— 'permanently', he added when asked to elaborate. In the past, said McAtamney, RUC men had hesitated in such situations and suffered the consequences. No hesitation was possible. The judge agreed; it would be unrealistic to ask the RUC to hesitate before firing at a dangerous suspect because they might face a possible murder charge.

As in the previous trial of Constable John Robinson, it emerged during this trial that the Official Secrets Act had been invoked. Specifically, the three defendants did not initially reveal that they were operating undercover when questioned by detectives.

On 5 June 1984, Lord Justice Gibson found the three RUC men not guilty. He launched a scathing attack on the DPP for bringing the case on the basis of such 'tenuous evidence'. The defendants knew of the suspicion that the three were on their way to commit murder, of the probability that they were armed (although they were not in fact) and that 'both were dangerous terrorists who had let it be known that they would not be arrested alive'. He added: 'There never was the slimmest chance that the Crown could have hoped to secure a conviction'. All that the trial had done, in his view, was to expose three members of an undercover police unit unnecessarily.

Gibson went on to commend the three RUC men:

> I wish to make it clear that, having heard the entire Crown case, I regard each of the accused as absolutely blameless in this matter. That finding should be put on their record along with my own commendation as to their courage and determination for bringing the three deceased men to justice, in this case, to the final court of justice.

As Malachy Toman, brother of Eugene, later stated, 'He virtually said that my brother and his friends were better in the graveyard than in jail'. But not everyone was as unhappy with the verdict. Alan Wright of the Police Federation said that it proved that when the police were involved in such incidents there was not a shoot-to-kill policy, but rather a shoot-to-live policy.

One of the three acquitted RUC men later committed suicide. The judge, Maurice Gibson, and his wife Cecily were killed in an IRA landmine explosion near the border on 25 April 1987.

No one was charged with murder in relation to the remaining shoot-to-kill incident, the killing of Michael Tighe. However Martin McCauley was charged with possession of weapons. The testimony of HMSU officers at his trial was that they had been on routine patrol and had seen a man with a gun at the hay shed. They then heard muffled voices from inside the hay shed, as well as the sound of weapons being cocked. They ordered the people inside to surrender but got no reply. Instead, they saw McCauley pointing a rifle at them and they opened fire in response. Further shots were fired at Tighe who appeared a few seconds later, also pointing a rifle at them. Eventually McCauley was dragged out of the hay shed, close to death, and the body of Tighe was discovered inside. Three old Mauser rifles were found, but no ammunition.

Under cross-examination, the HMSU personnel admitted they had lied about the nature of their patrol; they had not been on routine patrol, nor was the sighting of the supposed gunman what drew them to the hay shed. The rest of their story, they insisted, was correct. They had, they said, been ordered to lie by Special Branch under the Official Secrets Act.

Martin McCauley's defence presented a markedly different account of what happened. He said that he and Tighe had climbed in an open window in the hay shed out of curiosity and had seen the rifles. Without warning they were shot at and Michael Tighe died instantly. Only then was there an order to come out. When McCauley tried to do so, he was hit. Unable to move and losing a lot of blood, he was dragged from the barn.

On 15 February 1985, Martin McCauley was found guilty of possession of the weapons and given a suspended sentence of two years.

After the first of these trials—that of Constable John Robinson—official disquiet about the revelations of cross-border excursions by the HMSU and of Special Branch doctoring the evidence led to the decision to appoint a senior police officer from outside the North to investigate the six shoot-to-kill deaths. John Stalker, Deputy Chief Constable of the Greater Manchester Police, took on the task. He quickly discovered that what he termed 'the common denominator' in all three incidents, which had not emerged properly during any of the trials, was their connection to the 1982 IRA explosion at Oxford Island in which three RUC men had died. Stalker discovered that an explosives dump had been under police surveillance; despite that, the IRA had managed to remove explosives undetected which were used in the bomb which killed the RUC men. Afterwards, an informant gave names to the RUC of the people allegedly responsible for the bomb attack. Within six weeks of that information being delivered, three of those named—Toman, Burns and McKerr—were dead and one, McCauley, was injured. It was difficult to avoid the conclusion that the RUC were out to even the score.

Even more dramatically, Stalker discovered that, unknown to the HMSU personnel, MI5 had placed a bugging device inside the hay shed where Tighe and McCauley had been shot and had recorded the encounter between the HMSU and the two victims of their shooting. Stalker sought to gain access to this tape, but was repeatedly blocked by Chief Constable John Hermon.

In fact, from the start Stalker faced opposition, in particular from the RUC Chief Constable and Special Branch. Hermon made it clear that he saw Stalker's investigation as a relatively low key affair rather than the full-bodied one envisaged by Stalker himself. In addition, Stalker recounts a remarkably bizarre incident during his first meeting with Hermon when the Chief Constable produced Stalker's family tree drawn out on a flattened out cigarette packet. The family tree did not chart his father's branch, Protestants from Liverpool, but only his mother's side, Catholics from the Republic. It traced the family back to 1900, mentioning cousins Stalker himself had never even heard of!

By September 1985, Stalker had completed his investigations of the killing of Grew, Carroll, McKerr, Toman and Burns, but was unable to finish that of Tighe because of failure to access the MI5 tape. He thus produced an interim report and delivered it to the DPP. He concluded that, in relation to the three shoot-to-kill incidents, senior RUC officers had concocted lies and ordered subordinates to repeat them in court. There was, said Stalker, clear evidence of an RUC attempt to pervert the course of justice. He concluded that Grew, Carroll, McKerr, Burns, Toman, and Tighe had all been killed unlawfully and that in one case at least—that of Michael Tighe—there were grounds for charges of conspiracy to murder.

Stalker concluded:

> The Special Branch targeted the suspected terrorists, they briefed the officers, and after the shootings they removed the men, cars and guns for a private de-briefing before CID officers were allowed access to these crucial matters. They provided the cover stories, and they decided at what point the CID were to be allowed to commence the official investigation of what occurred. The Special Branch interpreted the information and decided what was, or was not, evidence; they attached labels—whether a man was 'wanted' for an offence, for instance or whether he was an 'on-the-run terrorist'. I have never experienced, nor had any of my team, such an influence over an entire police force by one small section.

And as for the RUC investigation of the six deaths:

> The files were little more than a collection of statements, apparently prepared for a coroner's inquiry. They bore no resemblance to my idea of a murder prosecution file. Even on the most cursory of readings I could see why the prosecutions [of the four RUC men] had failed.

Apart from accessing the MI5 tape, Stalker had one final outstanding task: to formally interview the Chief Constable, the Deputy Chief Constable and at least one Assistant Chief Constable of the RUC because he had grounds to believe that one or more had committed criminal offences in relation to the shoot-to-kill deaths. The first of these formal interviews was arranged with John Hermon for 2 June 1985. On 29 May, Stalker was informed that he was himself under investigation, possibly facing disciplinary charges in relation to his alleged association with criminals in Manchester. His name was linked to that of Manchester businessman Kevin Taylor who was also being investigated. Stalker was removed from the shoot-to-kill investigation and the policeman in charge of investigating him—Colin Sampson, Chief Constable of West Yorkshire—was also put in charge of completing what had started out as the Stalker inquiry. Sampson completed his report in March 1987. It is unlikely that it added anything of substance to Stalker's interim report.

By that time, the Police Committee in Manchester had dismissed all allegations against Stalker and reinstated him as Deputy Chief Constable. His reputation severely dented, Stalker left the police in March 1987. Kevin Taylor was charged with fraud. In January 1990, after a 16-week trial, the prosecution withdrew the case and advised the judge to ask the jury to acquit Taylor, which they did. Taylor's businesses, in the meantime, had collapsed.

In 1988 Attorney General Patrick Mayhew stated that there would be no further prosecutions of any police or MI5 officers on the grounds of national security.

However, in an apparent attempt to dispel continuing public disquiet over the matter of shoot-to-kill, Secretary of State Tom King announced a further two inquiries in February 1988. The first, by the Northern Ireland Police Authority, examined whether there was need for disciplinary charges against any of the top ranks of the RUC. The second, under Charles Kelly, Chief Constable of Staffordshire, looked at possible disciplinary charges against those of the rank of chief superintendent and below. In March 1989, Kelly recommended disciplinary proceedings against 20 junior RUC officers. One officer was cautioned, charges against another were dropped, and in 18 cases, officers were reprimanded. It is believed that all the charges related to obstructing Stalker in his investigation.

Because of the trials of RUC men which had already taken place in relation to two of the incidents, normal practice would have been that no subsequent inquest would occur. Inquests in Northern Ireland are unable to do more than establish the basic facts of death, facts which, it is claimed, would already have been revealed as a result of trials. But because of new evidence turned up by the Stalker and Sampson inquiries, a decision to reopen the suspended inquest was taken by Coroner James Elliot in 1988. One of Elliot's first decisions was to rule that the unsworn written statements of the RUC personnel involved in the killings were admissible without the RUC men having to attend the inquest or be subjected to cross-examination. This was challenged by Eleanor McKerr, widow of Gervaise. The Coroner refused to change his mind, so Eleanor McKerr and her legal counsel withdrew from the inquest. The inquest continued, with two police witnesses giving evidence from behind screens; both had been involved in command and briefing in relation to the incidents, but not in the actual killing. The families of Sean Burns and Eugene Toman withdrew from the inquest at this point, objecting to the admission of hearsay evidence which was designed to protect the police and discredit the deceased. Other policemen then gave evidence, including two who had accompanied the three unnamed officers who had carried out the actual killing, but were not present in court. Solicitor Pat Finucane, acting for Eleanor McKerr, returned asking for an adjournment on the grounds that leave for a judicial review had been granted by the High Court in Belfast. The Coroner refused to adjourn on those grounds, but had to halt proceedings anyhow in order to prepare for the judicial review.

In the High Court in Belfast, Lord Justice Carswell eventually ruled that Elliot's decision to allow the RUC statements was valid, but that he was wrong not to have granted an adjournment pending the judicial review. Eleanor McKerr appealed Carswell's judgement on the grounds that the failure of the coroner's court to compel a person who had caused a death to attend the inquest was ultra vires, i.e. this rule of the coroner's court clearly contradicted a principle of statutory law. The appeal was upheld, thus apparently requiring the RUC men to attend the inquest and to testify in person. However, the government in turn appealed this decision to the House of

Lords where, in March 1990, the judgement was reversed; the Coroner's original ruling was upheld, that the RUC men were not compellable witnesses.

A year before, on 12 February 1989, Eleanor McKerr's lawyer, Pat Finucane, was murdered by loyalists in Belfast.

These and other legal wranglings rumbled on for years, holding up not just the inquests of the six victims from north Armagh, but also a number of other inquests in relation to state killings where similar legal arguments were raging.

Eventually, the shoot-to-kill inquest reopened on 5 May 1992. Coroner James Leckey stated in his opening remarks that he had read the Stalker and Sampson reports. Despite the fact that parts had been deleted in the version he was given as a result of a Public Interest Immunity Certificate issued originally in November 1988, Leckey said that the statements taken by the Stalker inquiry were valuable in relation to the inquest. Because of their potential to present a fuller account of the incidents, the Coroner concluded that holding an inquest would be in the public interest. 'The statements they took have been made available to me and the public has a proper interest in knowing whether any further evidence came to light. For that reason and that reason alone, I am holding Inquests.'

Eleanor McKerr sought another judicial review in June 1992, objecting to the selection of the inquest jury. The mechanism for selection involved a computer choosing several thousand names at random, from which 20 people were then chosen and called to attend the inquest. However, the method of choosing the final 20 was not made clear. Moreover, the first 11 to arrive constituted the jury; no challenge of jurors by lawyers representing the families was possible. The eligibility of jurors was not checked. In addition, there was no check that the same anonymous jurors turned up each day.

The inquest reopened for the last time in 1994. Members of the Greater Manchester Police Inquiry team stated that they could not confidently give evidence without re-examining the Stalker reports or their own working papers from the time. The latter were by this point in the hands of the RUC. However, the potential Manchester police witnesses were refused access to both their own working papers and the Stalker report by the RUC.

In addition, Coroner Leckey had served writs on the Chief Constable of the RUC to produce the Stalker report. The RUC refused to comply and sought a judicial review of the Coroner's demand. On 11 July 1994, Justice Nicholson judged that the RUC did not have to comply with the writs. This left the Coroner's hands totally tied. He had reopened an inquest on the basis of exploring possible valuable new evidence, but was refused access to the Report in which that evidence appeared and to evidence from the police personnel from Manchester who had collected the information used in the Report. Consequently he abandoned the inquest. 'In the light of the judgment of Mr Justice Nicholson, I have decided not to resume the Inquests but instead to proceed to register the deaths... my aim in deciding to hold Inquests for the reasons I expressed when I opened the Inquests into the deaths of Toman, Burns and McKerr is no longer achievable' (8 September 1994). Leckey had been the fifth coroner involved in this long-running inquest.

In April 2000 the European Court of Human Rights heard evidence in relation to the killing of Gervaise McKerr. Three other cases were considered at the same time: the deaths of IRA members Patrick Kelly at Loughgall in 1987 and Pearse Jordan in 1992, and the killing by loyalists, in collusion with the RUC, of Sinn Féin member Patrick Shanaghan in Castlederg, County Tyrone in August 1991. The argument of lawyers was that the British government had failed to uphold Article 2 of the European Convention on Human Rights, the right to life. The Court found that the British government had a case to answer in relation to all the deaths concerned. It is not known, as of the time of writing, whether the judges will move to a full hearing or reach a judgement without such a hearing, as they are entitled to do.

Two of the people centrally involved in the struggle to achieve truth and justice through the inquests are now dead—Pat Finucane, murdered by loyalists in 1989, and Eleanor McKerr, the widow of Gervaise, who died of cancer on 31 October 1996. Before her death, Eleanor wrote a personal account of her struggle for an anthology of women writers; that account is reproduced below. Part of the complex story of shoot-to-kill in North Armagh is also told by Eleanor McKerr's twin sister Mary Green, and by the Carroll family.

Eleanor McKerr

Thursday 11th November 1982 started for me as just another day, but before that dreadful day was over, my life had been changed drastically. Nine years have now passed, with many people talking and writing about what happened that day. I feel it is now time for me to write the personal side of my story.

I sit and watch my two sons talk and laugh, watching them proudly. I think to myself, if only Gervaise would have lived to see this day. David my youngest is now 12 years of age, a chubby boy, fair hair, the picture of his grandfather Mat, his build, his looks and sometimes his ways—a good child, very thoughtful, but sometimes he is so huffy and moody.

Then I looked at Jonathan. My, he is turning into a fine young man, I thought. He is now 17 years of age, in a few months time 18 years old, an important age in life—tall for his age and mature; you would take him for older. Jonathan is a quiet child, a thinker just like his father. He is a good child, thoughtful also. They chat happily together as if life to them was as normal as the kids round the block. But it wasn't the same for them, I thought, and thinking what would life be like for them today if Gervaise wasn't dead—to have a father to play with, to talk to, to tell their problems to. I watch them chat and my mind wanders back to my age of 16.

That was the age I met Gervaise. We met at a local youth club at the skating; we were young and carefree, not a care in the world. We started going out together and things developed from there.

It was at that time crowds of people assembled in every town in the six counties asking for their civil rights. Gervaise and I were two of the crowd that assembled in Lurgan. Even in those far-off days I was very conscious of the great love Gervaise and I had for justice. It seemed such a little thing to ask then, for one vote. But I remember clearly how adamant we all were. The struggle of people for civil rights has developed a long way from 'one man, one vote' and has been well documented in many ways and I don't intend to go into it.

In the year 1972 Gervaise and I were married. Like many young couples of that time, we had great hopes for the future. Gervaise finished his apprenticeship and was now a joiner by trade and I, like many of the Lurgan girls, was a stitcher in a local factory. We moved into our home shortly after our marriage. We were looking forward to the birth of our first child. Jonathan was born in January 1973. I recall it clearly how proud Gervaise was to have a son.

Our son was still a baby when the first of our personal troubles came. Gervaise's uncle by marriage was shot dead in a sectarian murder. His death was a great loss to all the family and we were all deeply saddened by it. The next death to affect us personally was that of our neighbour John Green.

When Jonathan was four years old, we went to visit Gervaise's brother Damian and his family in Canada. It was a lovely holiday and so far removed from Ireland! We toyed with the idea of starting a home in Canada and in many ways, looking back, I can't help wondering how different life would have been had we gone to Canada.

In 1979 our second son David was born. The years seemed to be passing quickly. There were times when we thought the trouble would soon come to an end, but it didn't. 1981 we saw the start of the hunger strike. There were protest marches nearly every night in Lurgan and we both attended most of them. The terrible tragedy of Bobby Sands' death, as far as I am concerned, rests completely with England. Gervaise and I attended Bobby Sands' funeral as we did for the others.

July 1982 was perhaps one of the most memorable times of our lives. With our American friends we saw parts of Ireland that we had never seen before. After our American visitors left, Gervaise, myself, Christine, our baby sitter, and the children went off to Blackpool for our summer holidays. We spent a most enjoyable week there doing things a family would do. Gervaise believed in having a holiday every year. 'We both worked hard and we deserved it,' he would say.

July we had finished finalising plans to buy our home. Gervaise spent a lot of time improving our home. He was a hard worker and very good with his hands.

Many times throughout the years Gervaise was stopped by the RUC and UDR, his car searched and the usual questions asked. That was until the 11th November.

That evening I travelled home from work with my sister Mary. We usually got back home up around 10.45. On that particular night, when we reached our house, I remarked to Mary that Gervaise's car was not there. I thought nothing of it really at the time. When I went into my home, a young friend was baby sitting. She told me Gervaise had gone on an errand and would be home shortly. He had been in the proceeds of tiling a new shower room and he left everything sitting, so I knew he had intended finishing the job when he came home.

Shortly after arriving home, a friend came to my home and told me that there had been someone shot in the Craigavon area. They said that roadblocks had been set up. As time went on and Gervaise had not returned, I assumed he could not get home with the roadblocks. But as time got on, I worried where he was. The babysitter was still with me and the neighbour that had called, when my front door knocked. When I opened the door, to my surprise it was the police. They said they had come to search my home. I did ask them, 'What for?' I also asked them had they a warrant to search. I don't think I ever got a reply to my questions.

Jonathan and David were both sleeping. I was ordered to waken them up and bring them down the stairs. When I awakened them, naturally they both cried. They were frightened of what they saw—policemen with guns and police dogs. I was in a daze; what is going on, why are you doing this? Nobody spoke. They just kept on searching my home, going through my cupboards, all my personal belongings. At one point my phone rang and I went to answer it. The police woman took the receiver out of my hand. The same police woman continuously questioned my son Jonathan about where his daddy was.

All the time during the search I was hoping Gervaise would come home. There was not one place on my house that the police did not search. I kept asking them what they were looking for; it seemed so pointless, as I knew there was nothing in my home that could possibly be illegal.

At 2.45 they left my home with not a word. I still didn't know what was going on. But looking back now, the policemen who came to my home deliberately concealed the death from me and were apparently looking for evidence to support the theory that they had shot a terrorist in action.

After the RUC left, our local priest came. His words will always remain with me. 'Mrs Kerr, there has been an accident. Your husband has been shot dead.' What happened in the next few hours remains a blank. As the hours passed, I was aware of a lot of people around me. At one point I heard on a news bulletin that three terrorists had been shot dead, naming Eugene Toman, Sean Burns and Gervaise. It was only then that I realised that Sean and Eugene were also dead.

On Friday evening the 12th November, my husband's body was brought home. The coffin remained closed with the flag of our country draping over it. I could not believe that in this box was my husband. Had I been able to it least see his body, it might have been easier to contemplate him being dead. People came for far and near to pay their last respects. Many floral tributes came, telegrams, phone calls and mass cards too numerous to count.

Saturday morning I awakened after another sleepless night. The first thing that came to mind—Gervaise was dead. Was it a dream? The emptiness, the pain was awful. How can I face another day? How I got through those days I don't know; I suppose I was deeply in shock. People came, people went, it still didn't occur to me Gervaise was dead. 'It's not true', I kept saying to myself.

Sunday 14th November. My husband, Eugene and Sean were laid to rest in St Coleman's cemetery after Mass in St Peter's Church. They received a republican funeral; a large number of people attended the funeral.

For a few weeks I still had plenty of people calling, but gradually they drifted away. My father stayed with me at night because I was terrified of being on my own. I continually kept asking questions to anyone who would listen. Why if Gervaise had been suspected by the RUC of being a terrorist, had they not arrested him at home? All sorts of questions were going through my head. I couldn't make sense of anything that had happened—sometimes not really believing that Gervaise was dead. It was like living a nightmare.

At this stage my feelings were not helped in any way by the awful sinister phone calls I was receiving at all times of the day and night. In the end I had my phone number changed. The awful letters also came and there was nothing I could do to have them stopped.

On Wednesday night, November 25th, I was again deeply saddened when I heard the tragic news of yet another young man in the Lurgan area being shot dead and his friend being wounded, coming barely two weeks after my husband's death.

It was around this time that [the Association for] Legal Justice started to hold an inquiry into Gervaise, Eugene and Sean's death. I was of little help myself but was happy that at least someone was trying to find out the truth. By now, and not realising it at the time, I was feeling very low. I know I felt I had to do something about the injustice that had been going on around me, but I felt so helpless.

Then it came on the news again that two more men had been murdered in Armagh: 'shot dead at a checkpoint, car didn't stop, suspected terrorists, so RUC opened up, firing at the car, killing terrorists outright', is what the papers said. Just the same thing all over again, I thought, just as Gervaise died. I cried, 'Something has to be done. I must try and do something'.

At this stage I was not physically able to go to the homes of the men who had been killed, but I did write to the families and expressed my sympathy at their loss. After what had happened, we the families of those who had been shot got together. We had many meetings in the days to come. We decided to call on the public to help us. In doing so, we arranged for a demonstration to take place in Lurgan. We stressed that this demonstration was non-political and was organised solely by the relatives of the six murdered men. The march took place. It was a great success. Thousands turned out for it. All we wanted was the truth of how our loved ones had died and justice seen to be done.

We kept on going, collected signatures, writing to governments, to newspapers, to anyone who would listen to us. The continuing stress and pressure I was now under began to take its toll on my health and by the end of February, I was mentally and physically exhausted. My sister Mary had been asking me for some time to see a doctor, but I refused, thinking to myself that I would fight it off. Eventually my family called a doctor for me. On his advice I was admitted to hospital. I was on the verge of a breakdown. My health had deteriorated. I was now down to six stone in weight. I couldn't eat or sleep. I was smoking about 60 cigarettes a day. I just didn't care what was going on around me and my poor children, I didn't even know what was happening to them. I just wanted to die. It was awful. I was in a wee world of my own. I hope to God I never end up like that again.

Luckily I had my sister Mary. Without her to this day I just couldn't have managed or got through life without her. She saw to the children while I stayed in hospital. After weeks with complete rest and treatment, I began to feel a lot stronger. I had gained weight and had come to terms and accepted Gervaise's death more.

By now various people and politicians were calling for a full inquiry into the circumstances of their deaths. Mr John Stalker, a chief constable from Manchester, was sent over to undertake an inquiry into their deaths. John Stalker arrived to carry out an inquiry into all the deaths in the Armagh area and was obstructed at every turn as has been well documented. And when it became obvious that he meant to tell the truth, he was removed from his job, suspended while an inquiry went on which found him innocent, but by that time they had replaced him on the inquiry.

When the inquiry was completed in 1987 by Mr Stalker's successor, a Mr Sampson, it concluded that a number of policemen had conspired to subvert the course of justice. The British government prohibited the publication of its findings and determined that no policemen would be prosecuted in the interests of national security and public interest.

Eight years have passed by and I'm still fighting on for the truth to be known and for justice. Sometimes I felt like giving up, but someone else would be killed in similar circumstances, so I was determined to carry on for justice.

November 1988, a date was set once again for the inquest. The inquest had been adjourned nine times before that. What with dates getting set back and coroners resigning, the situation was being reduced to a case of rent-a-coroner. Eight years had elapsed since my husband was murdered and I still hadn't received a death certificate. My solicitor Pat Finucane and I went to Craigavon courthouse to the coroner's court. Mr Elliott was the coroner. In spite of all its shortcomings, the coroner's court is the only place that there is the slightest chance of getting to the truth. So when the coroner stated that he was not going to call the policemen who had actually killed my husband to the inquest, even though they would have been behind the screens, I instructed my solicitor to fight this particular ruling. We left the court that morning and my solicitor applied to the High Court in Belfast to seek a judicial review. Belfast High Court upheld the coroner's decision, so I lost the High Court case, but we appealed it and won on appeal. Then the DPP lodged a further appeal with the House of Lords, so that meant the inquest was stopped once again.

It is with great sadness that I recall the killing of my solicitor Pat Finucane. Pat was shot in his home on February 13th, 1989 in front of his wife and children. His wife was also wounded. A loyalist group claimed responsibility for his killing. I will never forget Pat. He understood the true meaning of justice and it was his desire for justice which made him take on my case when others thought it was a waste of time. But sadly his determination for justice and also his success rate cost him his life.

January 1990 I travelled to London to attend the hearing in the House of Lords. Sadly I lost again. I was very disappointed at the outcome, particularly for my legal representatives who put up a very good case on my behalf. But at the end of the day I still believe the policemen involved in the killing should be required to give evidence.

It is with great sadness that I recall the Christmas of 1982. I had made a conscious effort to try and make it enjoyable for my children. With my sister Mary's help we put our Christmas tree up and arrange our presents. On Christmas Day we went to my parents' home and spent the rest of the Christmas holiday there. I visited Gervaise's family home. His mother, father and brothers were very deep in mourning and had given little thought to Christmas that year.

Now I sit here watching my children with Christmas 1991 approaching very quickly. In a few days time Gervaise will be nine years dead. I feel very sad. In a few years' time, hopefully Jonathan will be away to university, David will still be attending school, and what will the future have in store for me? Will the inquest be over by then? Will I put the past behind me and make a new life for myself? Life's hard, life's lonely, but life must go on.

Mary Green

She used to say, 'At least they will think twice before they do this again'. I think that she was right because after that, there was less shoot-to-kill. In its place there was collusion; they just got somebody to do the shooting for them. I'd like to think she made an impact.

On the evening of 11 November 1982, my sister Eleanor and I went to our work as usual. When we returned home later than night, about 10.45 p.m., Eleanor said to me that Gervaise's car was not there. She thought nothing of this and went into the house. I went home myself. About 3 a.m. I was awakened by a knock on the door. When I opened, a friend told me to go to Eleanor's house as she needed me; they said Gervaise may have been murdered.

When I arrived at my sister's house, she told me that the RUC had just left the house after raiding it. The search had lasted a few hours. Her two young sons were taken from their beds and made to sit through this ordeal. During the search my sister kept asking why her house was being raided; had they arrested her husband? They said nothing. A police woman was looking though one of Eleanor's photo albums continually and asked her son Jonathan to point to his daddy in the photographs. The RUC found nothing. As they were leaving, my sister asked the person in charge had Gervaise been arrested and if so, which barracks he was in. The RUC man stared at her, turned his back and left without saying a word.

At about 3.30 a.m., I was called into the kitchen as a priest had arrived and asked to speak to Eleanor. We brought him into a room where he told Eleanor that Gervaise had been murdered, along with two other people. Eleanor screamed, 'The bastards have murdered him'. A short time later I left to inform Gervaise's family and my own family about his death. One of Gervaise's brothers then went to identify the body.

When Gervaise's body arrived home, the lid of the coffin had to be kept on and this made it harder for my sister to accept his death. A few months later she suffered a nervous breakdown. Once she regained her health, she decided to seek the truth about her husband's murder through the courts.

Although Eleanor wanted to fight, she was worried where she was going to get the money to pay for the legal battle. Gervaise was dead; she had no job, two small children and little money to live on. I told her they couldn't get blood from a stone; if she hadn't got it, they couldn't take it from her.

Three RUC men—Montgomery, Robinson and Brannigan—were charged with the death of Eugene Toman, one of the others murdered along with Gervaise. Nothing came out of that court case. The RUC men were acquitted. At that time the judge, Gibson, said the RUC had brought Gervaise, Eugene and Sean [Burns] to the final court of justice. Eleanor didn't go to hear the verdict that day. In fact, she only went to the court for a couple of days. She couldn't listen to the lies.

During the trial the RUC said they had followed two of the men (one of whom was Gervaise's cousin) to Eleanor's house that night before they later shot them. Eleanor said if they knew all these things, then why didn't they come to the house and lift them? She said the police should be charged, for there should not be one rule for the police and another for everyone else. The truth was the most important thing, the truth and then justice.

The next stage was to get an inquest. Eleanor's solicitor told us he would get a date for the inquest, but, as far as we could gather, all he wanted was to get the inquest over as quickly as possible. Eleanor told him no way was she going into the court house and not putting up a fight. She decided to get another solicitor. We spoke to Councillor Brendan Curran and he said he would look for another solicitor for us. Pat Finucane was introduced to us and he became Eleanor's solicitor. When he got all the details from us, he said: 'I am your solicitor. I'll do all I can for you. You tell me what to do and what you want and I'll do it. Whatever you don't know, I will guide you.'

This course of action led to a legal battle which lasted 12 years and numerous court appearances. Eleanor went from the coroner's court to the High Court, the House of Lords, back and forth. Always at her side was her solicitor, Pat Finucane, who was brutally murdered while the case was going on. At each appearance in court, especially the coroner's court, the heavy RUC presence was intimidating; but this, and even the murder of her solicitor, could not deter my sister from her fight for truth and justice.

During this time, Stalker, a top policeman from England, was brought in to investigate these murders and the murders of three other men in the north Armagh area at the same time. Stalker and other members of his team visited Eleanor. She listened to them and answered a few questions. She told him that there had been a court case and that the policemen had been acquitted. They told her that if she had got new evidence, she could bring the policemen back to court. But she told them they didn't understand where they were. This is Northern Ireland, not England; it's like beating your head off a brick wall in this country.

It was the end of 1994 when the inquest finally ended. The RUC blocked access to documents, so the Coroner, Mr Leckey, decided that the inquest couldn't get any further. In the end, he just issued death certificates.

While my sister's legal battle was going on, her house was raided by the RUC and British army on many occasions. During one of the raids, they suggested to her that she should go to America to live. She was followed by the RUC and any car she was travelling in was stopped. Over the 12 years of legal action my sister continually asked the RUC for the return of her husband's car, the contents of the car and his clothes. All she received was a wallet and wedding ring. We believe everything else has been destroyed.

My sister believed in what she was fighting for until the day she died. She was a really strong person. She used to say, 'At least they will think twice before they do this again'. I think that she was right because after that, there was less shoot-to-kill. In its place there was collusion; they just got somebody to do the shooting for them. I'd like to think she made an impact. She might not have seemed to have got justice but she achieved a hell of a lot. That was her way of keeping going. In her mind she had to do something. First of all, Gervaise was a good husband and she really loved him. And she also thought why should the police not be prosecuted like everyone else. There shouldn't be one rule for the RUC and one for everyone else.

The Carrolls

No policeman goes out to shoot anybody hoping that in retrospect it will all be ratified; you can't do that. In this system, you know that when you pull the trigger, it's okayed before you do that. You are protected.

Mrs Carroll: We were just home from my father's funeral that night. We were only in the house an hour when Adrian phoned to tell us that there was shooting at Mullacreavie. Some of them here in the house decided to go over to Mullacreavie to see. The police had it all blocked off. We wanted to go on down but the police wouldn't let us. Then somebody said it was Seamus Grew. We came back home then; it was nearly three o'clock in the morning. At three o'clock the police came then to tell us what had happened. They said there had been an accident over at Mullacreavie; there was a road block and they didn't stop—that's what they said.

The funeral was on the Thursday. After the funeral was over, Father Murray came. He went around asking people what they had seen, taking statements. Stalker got the statements. There was an RUC man charged with the murder.

Tommy: They had come up with this story that they had pulled in front of them and waved an RUC cap out the window in order to stop them. We presume that Roddy had already been shot. Seamie Grew got out of the car, put his hands in the air and one of his fingers was shot off. I think that was why they charged Robinson; the fact that Seamie had got out of the car didn't hold up the story of two men bursting through a road block.

I was in Long Kesh when Roddy was shot and the screws came down to the hut window probably about one o'clock in the morning and asked for the hut OC. I was called over. The screw shouted through the window, 'Your brother has been shot'. That is the way I was told.

Mrs Carroll: The inquest was set. The night before, it was announced that the policeman was being charged with the murder and that was it stopped.

Tommy: Robinson was charged with the murder of Seamus Grew. The whole thing burst open when Robinson panicked. He thought that the trial was for real and that he was going to get done. He said that after the shooting they had all been brought back up to Gough Barracks. Assistant Chief Constable McAtamney was there and they concocted this story that they were to give to the investigating officers.

Mrs Carroll: What came out at the trial was this. My father was buried away at Desertmartin and they had got home before us. Irene lived in Monaghan at the time and they brought her home to Monaghan. They were tailed to Monaghan and down to Castleblaney.

Tommy: There was a man in 'Blaney called [X...] whose house they called at that night. When they left the house, [X...] phoned the RUC. The RUC followed them from the South. In the meantime, back in Armagh the RUC had already planned to murder them but they had to get them into the right position. They had a hit squad sitting in Armagh. When they got the phone call, they left the barracks and a road block was set up at Girvan's Bridge, about three miles outside Armagh city. Roddy and Seamie came down through the road block, but the hit squad who were supposed to shoot them crashed the car. Roddy and Seamie drove past the people who were meant to shoot them at Girvan's Bridge, not even realising what was going on. But the RUC commandeered someone else's car and drove after them towards Mullacreavie. The RUC contacted [X...] and he got a taxi up to Keady Barracks, ran inside it and never was seen since. The RUC knew that when they left [X...] home they were not armed.

Mrs Carroll: Robinson got off; he was acquitted. He said he thought that his life was in danger and that is why he shot.

Tommy: I applied for parole when my grandfather died and to this day I often wonder if they used that knowledge, knowing that the Carroll family were going to be in the one place, to start tailing. I think the gardai were aware that the RUC were in the 26 counties although it was claimed that they were not carrying weapons. When Stalker came he was specifically told not to investigate the role of the garda or anything over the border. They were tailed to Monaghan, through Enniskee and we were supposed to believe that the gardai were unaware of it.

Stalker was brought in because of what happened in that trial. When he was brought in to investigate, he took statements from people up in the parochial house. Harry McBride, an ex-RUC sergeant, said he heard a barrage of shots; he thought he was under fire and dove under the settee. When he realised that there were no bullets coming through the window, he got up and to this day he would tell you that he witnessed murder.

Mrs Carroll: He thought that his house was under fire, that it was the IRA shooting at him, so he and his wife got down on the ground. When he realised that it wasn't at him, he got up. He said that he heard two single shots long after the attack.

Tommy: I remember it was literally hours before Hermon was about to be interviewed that Stalker was suspended. In 1989, Patrick Mayhew, who was then the British Attorney General, said that in the national interest the eleven RUC men who perverted the course of justice would not be prosecuted. When you look at the whole thing, they actually sat down and planned how they would murder people and then swing an operation in to make it all plausible.

Tommy: We are always being told, 'It's in the past. We can't open old sores. It's too long ago to investigate'. This week someone from the Second World War has been charged under English law with murdering four Jews in Belarus fifty years ago. You tend to become cynical about the whole thing.

Mrs Carroll: At every juncture they were signing public immunity certificates. You had Mr Leckey conducting it all like it was perfectly normal. You just have total disgust for the whole lot of them. They talk about the thugs and killers in our community but what they have is well-dressed, well-educated, well-spoken murderers. In my mind that is simply what they are.

Tommy: If you take the case of Toman, it was the same scenario—'Drove through a road block at high speed'. Toman got out of the car too. But the handle is on the inside of the door; you couldn't fall on it to open it; you had to specifically put your hand on it and pull it out to open it. How could a dead man do that? The people who investigated the scene of the crime didn't even notice that.

Mrs Carroll: I never knew Eleanor [McKerr] beforehand. She contacted me to see what we could do. We had meetings and organised protests. She went to England a lot—Troops Out meetings, protests and things like that.

Tommy: The RUC stage-managed looking along the roadside for arms that they knew weren't there. So that is all part and parcel of the imagery that they build in people's minds.

I think it was 12 years before they issued the death certificate. And all the magnificent, majestic law had to offer us was that they were dead. When you look back on it all—from the shooting, the lies that were issued and the RUC men looking for guns on the road, the inquest, the murder trial, the Attorney General issuing the immunity certificate—you realise that the state can dispose of you and then can set the wheels in motion to make it all look legal.

Public Immunity in the national interest was used all down the line. The national interest is something that would be used in the case of a high powered spy. My brother Roddy was twenty two years of age and had never left Armagh. They were using these big sledgehammers to contain something that was in the local area.

Mrs Carroll:: He was harassed every time he went out. He never had a day's peace, up and down the town with the police and army. He was lifted more times.

[On Eleanor McKerr] She went on her own. The Tomans and Burnses didn't go. She made up her mind that she would never give up; she went on to the end.

Tommy: But you saw the futility of it all. You had all the respectable people in Ireland, it was acceptable to them all. You had bishops and nuns taking the RUC into the schools. The nationalist establishment offered tuts about it, but it didn't really bother them; it didn't impinge on their lives.

Mrs Carroll: We met Stalker up at Father Murray's. I thought it was a whitewash. I gave the statements and went along but when you are dealing with the police you know you are going to get nowhere.

Tommy: When they went to destroy Stalker, there was an English businessman called Kevin Taylor; they destroyed him too. So they were prepared to destroy everything to protect themselves. That is how you know it went right up to cabinet level. No policeman goes out to shoot anybody hoping that in retrospect it will all be ratified; you can't do that. In this system, you know that when you pull the trigger, it's okayed before you do that. You are protected.

In the case of the Lurgan ones, the judge, Gibson, actually congratulated the RUC on good shooting. When you look back, you can see things. They were trying to introduce an Ulsterisation policy. They had decided they were going to wipe people out. They thought the RUC could do it and get away with it, but the RUC were not able to do it and get away with it. That is why the SAS came in to do it. The SAS came in to do the shooting and the lawyers made sure they were debriefed. The RUC were seen as too partisan; they had all the baggage of their unionist, loyalist backgrounds. They couldn't shoot people while pretending to be an impartial service; it just wouldn't wash. They learned out of those six killings that it wasn't going to work. They knew they were going to have to get rid of certain people here so they needed another method. So they just brought the SAS in accompanied with lawyers.

I wouldn't want anybody to go to jail, for they were agents of the Crown carrying out the orders of the Crown. But that it all didn't happen in vain is for the people who sent them, those in the suits and the ermine robes, to apologise to the people of Ireland for what they had done—then for them to leave Ireland in a situation whereby nothing like this could ever happen again.

You hear the politicians talking about 'real victims'. Anyone on the Irish nationalist side is not a real victim in my opinion. Mo Mowlam can spout off her huggy wuggy and kissy wissy, but she is not really sincere. Everything that happened here happened because they wanted it to happen and it was carried out for a specific purpose. We are not considered to be real victims; we are miscreants and deserve what we get.

Mrs Carroll: Because of the campaigns, they couldn't get away with them. They sort of called a halt to them. They might have had more lined up to wipe out.

9

JOHN DOWNES
12 August 1984

Killed by plastic bullet fired by RUC

On 12 August 1984 the 13th annual commemoration of the introduction of internment took place. As usual, this involved a large march and rally on the Falls Road in West Belfast. What was unusual was that it was widely expected that Martin Galvin would address the rally at Sinn Féin's Connolly House in Andersonstown. Galvin, a lawyer, was the director of NORAID, Sinn Féin's U.S. support organisation. He was the subject of an exclusion order banning him from entering Northern Ireland.

As the march made its way up the Falls Road, there was a large police presence evident. However, there was little trouble; even the RUC later acknowledged only three brief and minor incidents of stone-throwing. At Connolly House the rally was addressed by Gerry Adams, President of Sinn Féin. At about 3.30 p.m. the crowd in front of the platform was asked to sit on the road and at that point Martin Galvin appeared on the platform. As he took the microphone to speak, he was greeted loudly and enthusiastically by the crowd. But he did not get the opportunity to speak. The RUC immediately closed in to arrest him. Plastic bullets were fired—31 according to the RUC, more than that according to media reports. Men, women and children were batoned; 20 were admitted to hospital afterwards. Despite an extensive search of the house and grounds, Galvin escaped.

During the incident, 22 year old John Downes from nearby Slievegallion Drive, was seen at the edge of the crowd, brandishing a thin stick and running at two

106

RUC men who were involved in the police action. The RUC men had their backs to him. Another RUC officer spotted him approaching and fired a plastic bullet at his chest from a range of approximately ten feet. In full view of the cameras, John Downes died on the road as attempts were made to resuscitate him.

After a lengthy six and a half hour delay, the RUC issued a statement in which they referred to stone-throwers and concerted attempts by the crowd to obstruct the police intention to arrest Galvin. They added that an unnamed 22 year old man, 'who has been identified as a rioter', was hit by a ricochet plastic bullet and was dead on arrival at the Royal Victoria Hospital. Plastic bullets, they claimed, were fired in the air and not into the crowd.

Most of the claims in the RUC statement were rejected by eyewitnesses, including those from the mass media who had, unusually, been at the receiving end of the police action. Eyewitnesses contended that:

- there was no riot before the police moved in; if anything, it was the RUC's behaviour which constituted a riot;
- any stone-throwing which did occur was brief and ended 45 minutes before the police moved in to arrest Galvin;
- plastic bullets were fired into the crowd;
- the plastic bullet which killed John Downes was fired at him from point blank range; it did not ricochet.

Many media commentators said the RUC ran 'berserk'. The *New Statesman* went further and called the RUC action 'cold-blooded and official state terrorism against a peaceful and unarmed crowd'.

On 12 April 1985 Reserve Constable Nigel Hegarty (aged 27) appeared in court charged with the unlawful killing of John Downes. He was remanded in custody, but later that day was granted bail of £200 with two sureties of £1000 each. Subsequently he was suspended from duty pending the outcome of the trial. His trial for manslaughter began in Belfast on 15 September 1986. He was the first—and to date only—RUC man to be charged as a result of a death caused by plastic bullet.

Much of the prosecution's case rested on the video evidence of the incident. John Downes is clearly shown running at the two RUC men whose backs are turned towards him; they are wearing flak jackets and riot helmets. He appears to be intent on hitting them with a thin stick he is carrying. Nigel Hegarty fired at the upper part of John Downes' body from a distance of about 10 feet, not the 20-25 yards he had claimed originally, the minimum distance officially recommended for their use. The prosecution argued that Hegarty could have found an alternative way of protecting his colleagues—such as shouting a warning, or intercepting Downes—and that the amount of force he used was therefore unreasonable.

Hegarty's defence was that he had fired at the lower part of John Downes' body and that he had only done so to protect his fellow officers whom he believed to be in danger. Two days into the trial, the defence moved for dismissal on the grounds that there was no case to answer. Mr Justice Hutton refused. The defence responded by offering no evidence and the trial moved quickly to a conclusion. On 24 September 1984 Nigel Hegarty was acquitted. Hutton rejected the suggestion that he could have acted differently to stop John Downes. He accepted that Hegarty had acted 'probably almost instinctively' to defend his colleagues and that, given 'the stress of the moment and the obvious determination of the deceased' to attack the two RUC men, Hegarty's response was not unreasonable.

On the wider issue of the use of plastic bullets, Hutton noted that their use in most instances does not lead to serious injury or death. 'It is not the function of the court trying an accused who has fired a baton round to seek expressly, or by implication, to lay down guidelines as to the circumstances in which it is or is not a criminal offence to fire a baton round and to do so would not be practicable.'

Nigel Hegarty's suspension from duty was immediately lifted. A suggestion that he might face disciplinary action was rejected the following day by the RUC.

Because there had been a trial, the coroner concluded that there was no need for an inquest. Brenda Downes, John's widow, challenged the coroner's decision, seeking a judicial review in the High Court in April 1988. Justice Carswell upheld the coroner's decision. Four months later a public inquiry conducted by Father Des Wilson and Springhill Community House took evidence from over 70 eyewitnesses to the killing of John Downes, and called for an official independent inquiry into the events. No such inquiry was instituted.

On 30 November 1989, Brenda Downes was awarded undisclosed damages. She stated afterwards: 'They got away very cheaply... Although I have received compensation, I have been denied justice. No one has been convicted of murdering my husband who was shot in full view of the world's media.'

The story of the death of John Downes and the subsequent campaign is told by his wife, Brenda Downes.

Brenda Downes

Anyone looking at that video would have seen that it was a police riot... They had guns and the crowd was in a sheer panic, lying on the ground. The police were not under attack. John could have been arrested but the reason they did not arrest him was because they obviously had the power to do what they wanted.

On the day of the march we assembled at Dunville Park. John and I waited until most of the marchers were past and then walked up the road to Andersonstown at the very end of the march. The place was black with RUC men on every corner and there was a very bad atmosphere. When we got to Andersonstown, the speeches were already started. We couldn't really hear what was being said. We had our daughter with us, so I didn't want to push forward. I asked John to move closer to listen to what was being said. I waited outside the chapel. As I said, the atmosphere was heavy; there were cops on top of Land Rovers and on the shop roofs. I was getting very nervous. So I decided to walk round the street behind the chapel to get to the other side of Connolly House where the speeches were being made; I thought I might be able to see John then. When I got to the hill at the bottom of Slievegallion Drive, the shooting had started. A woman pulled me and my daughter into her house. I kept saying, 'My husband's down there'. But she said, 'You can't go down there with that child'. I must have waited about an hour. Then I decided to go on home to see if John had arrived there. There was no sign of him. I called at his Aunt Kathleen's, but he wasn't there either, so I went back home. Then two friends came to tell me he was in hospital. I asked why, and they said he had been hit by a plastic bullet. I thought that maybe he had been hit in the leg or the arm; for some reason I didn't think it was anything too serious.

When I got to the hospital, they couldn't tell me whether he had been admitted or not because there were so many casualties. Some of the injured had been sent to Musgrave Park Hospital. I started to panic. I asked a nurse if I could have a look round before heading off to check at Musgrave. She told me to wait. She came back and asked me for a description of what John had been wearing. I told her, and they went away again. Then she came back again and asked me if he had any tatoos. I told her he had one on his arm. By this point I knew something was up. The nurse said to me, 'The doctor would like to talk to you'. The doctor came out and told me he had very bad news for me, that my husband was dead. There had been cops standing in the hall the whole while this was happening, and my first reaction was to run to get them and take it out on them. But they were gone. They asked me to identify the body, but I wouldn't. In fact, I wouldn't believe them that he was dead and I thought that what would happen was that I would have to go in and look at someone else's dead body. I contacted my father-in-law and he came down and identified the body. It was John.

Realistically, from start to finish it was a public execution. The simple fact was that they had the whole run that day to do what they wanted; they didn't care who got in their way. They went in to beat all around them; cameramen and journalists were batoned. They drove Land Rovers into women and children, knowing that they wouldn't suffer any consequences from doing so. The statement that came out from John Hermon said that it was a ricochet bullet that hit John that day. What he wasn't aware of was that the whole incident had been videoed. So, to me, they concocted their whole story to cover up what they'd done. They also said that John had an iron bar and had been running towards the police. But anyone looking at that video would have seen that it was a police riot in full riot gear. They had guns and the crowd was in a sheer panic, lying on the ground. The police were not under attack. John could have been arrested but the reason they did not arrest him was because they obviously had the power to do what they wanted.

I was actually surprised about what a number of newspapers reported the next day—that it was indeed a police riot. The reason for these reports, I feel, was because they too were on the receiving end; reporters and cameramen were also batoned and shot at. Everybody was getting 'done' that day regardless of who or what they were. The RUC went in that day to look for Martin Galvin and he walked right past them. Had they been able to get him, he would have been put on a plane and that would have been it. Getting him was their excuse; they had every intention of causing as much harm as they could. John was the person who died but there were loads of casualties.

I remember seeing the coverage on television and watching the actual murder happening. It was very frustrating because I saw the policeman and all who were involved and yet nothing was being done about it. This went on for months afterwards. John's murder was blatant, black and white, but there was no mention of the person who murdered him being charged; it was like he was dead, it was over, forget about it. It nearly drove me nuts. One night, I felt like going to Andersonstown Police Barracks and chaining myself to the railings. I thought maybe I would get some movement or get some publicity to get things moving. I never did it but when I look back, I wonder if it would have been better for me—although people would have thought that I had definitely gone off my head!

Jim McCabe and Clara Reilly had been talking and apparently Pat Finucane expressed a keen interest in taking on the case, since he had dealt with Nora McCabe's case. Finally, I thought that here was someone who was eager and interested. I then went to see Pat Finucane and handed the case over to him. He took the case on but, unfortunately, he never was able to finish it because he himself was killed.

Pat said that if ever there was to be a prosecution in a plastic bullet case, it ought to have been in relation to Nora McCabe. There was such strong evidence, especially the video. But the only prosecution ever was in relation to John's death. It was obvious why they picked this one. It was a foregone conclusion that any policeman charged would just have to say that he was acting in self-defence to protect himself and his colleagues. There was never going to be a conviction. Yet they could turn round later and claim that they had done something to guarantee justice.

And that's the way it turned out. It was about six months after John's death that the RUC man, Nigel Hegarty, was charged with his murder and another six months before that farce of a trial took place. He was first charged with murder and then it was reduced to manslaughter. I wasn't informed that the court case was taking place. I was on holiday with my mummy, daddy and my child. I came back to find that the whole thing was over, but a friend of mine had heard that this was happening and she felt she should go to the court. Apparently, there were only police witnesses, no other people who were there that day—just police. They sat in the courtroom with typewritten statements and they read from these statements. There was a statement read out on behalf of Nigel Hegarty. He didn't appear in the witness box. Then the case was dropped because it was believed that he acted in self-defence, in that the life of his colleagues was in danger. He was acquitted.

There was no inquest into John's case. I did receive a letter to go and register his death. I had some knowledge of the proceedings from other relatives and their legal cases, so I thought there should have been an inquest first before the death certificate could be issued. I took the letter to Pat Finucane and he said that under no circumstances should I register the death, that we would have to get an inquest. This was our turn now. They had taken the prosecution, set up the evidence—that was their turn, and now it was ours. The questions that we needed answered would come out in the inquest. But they refused to hold an inquest because there had been a trial and my commonsense told me 'what trial?' We then appealed and during that time, Pat Finucane was shot dead. The appeal was turned down. To this date, there has been no inquest and I haven't taken this any further. I haven't pursued a private prosecution because you cannot charge a person twice with the same crime. No matter what I do, I have no other way of getting justice because as far as they are concerned, it is over and done with.

Some time after, I was invited to attend the Plastic Bullets Campaign meetings. My brother-in-law, Gerard, often went to different meetings and travelled to England to campaign against plastic bullets but it was a number of months before I became involved. I found it a good support and it did help me through. For the first time I realised that I wasn't the only one who had suffered. I met Emma Groves. The fact that Emma had lost her eyes and the life she had after that, rearing her whole family; and Jim McCabe who had lost his wife and what he had gone through; and other relatives and what they had come through—looking at all of these people, I realised I wasn't the only one. This gave me strength to go on. It took many years before I began to feel stronger.

I went to England and spoke to students in universities. If anyone offered you a platform to talk, you just went. The location didn't really matter; it was the fact that you were given a chance to tell the truth, just how it was and not what had been written in the papers about ricochet bullets and iron bars and that John was a rioter. It was more important to be able to go and tell the truth and I found consolation in that because I felt that I was doing something; you were achieving something by getting out and telling what really happened.

The Campaign had been invited by Donald Payne to make a statement to Congress in Washington and I was invited along. The fact that Congress was listening to us and agreeing to help us and put pressure on the British government was a brilliant experience—to be actually able to talk, produce evidence, statements and facts and to have it recognised. There was a panel of Congressmen sitting and listening to testimonies and I remember, when it came my turn to speak, I just broke down after speaking for about five minutes. I was overwhelmed by emotion. In fact, I had to leave. They were very patient and I honestly believe that people were taken aback with what was said. I was able to return and finish the testimony after the next speaker.

I felt great being able to talk to Congress, but after returning home, there was Drumcree where the same abuses were taking place, with plastic bullets still being fired in Derry. Nothing had changed. It was still the same old story. You can go to one part of the world and get such a warm reception and the assurances that things would be done and then you return to Belfast and nothing has changed.

Emma Groves in the earlier days also went to America. A company in the USA were making these bullets and we campaigned and lobbied and the company stopped making them. So this did have an impact, which was excellent. You were campaigning, doing something about it and then you saw action. It might not have seemed that anything was being changed, but the fact that you were out there and you were speaking out against it made me feel better about myself also. I felt an obligation to the person who was dead. You couldn't just sit back and do nothing; there was plenty to be done. It was a voice for them to know their life was not taken in vain. I remember there was talk about the banning of plastic bullets after John's death. I thought maybe something good would come out of this and I remember thinking that if John had given his life for that price, then there would be a positive angle to it.

Unfortunately, the banning did not happen. Even when Hegarty was charged, I kept hoping and praying that this time something would be done, but again, you were just let down. They didn't do anything about it. You just hope against hope and sadly, you were again let down. I was so disappointed.

I remember Emma and I would be popping a valium inside of us before talking in front of a crowd because we were so nervous, but we had to do it. I felt compelled to speak because of the fact that this terrible wrong had been done and the people responsible were not going to get away with it as easy as they would have liked. I swore that as long as I had breath in my body I would keep campaigning. There are times when you just want to go away and forget about it. You sometimes waken up and say, 'This did not really happen to me'. Even at meetings, when you have to talk, it can be very hard, but there is something inside which says you have to do it.

I have become known to people as John Downes' widow, which in a way takes away my identity. I mean no disrespect, but people are not seeing me as a person in my own right. It made me feel as if I was being subject to a victim role. I have never wanted to be classed as a victim and have never wanted pity. I would wish to be taken seriously for who I am, not the widow of John Downes.

Looking back, if I have any regrets about the Campaign, I think there could have been more done—more follow-up, more pressure. The British, in the way they plan and the money they have to spend, were definitely way ahead of us. There were times when you wish you could have challenged that, to have had the opportunity to switch off from everything else and sit down and build a movement in direct agitation against them. But it is hard to do all that and live a life as well. Returning to study, going through the whole education process, finding a job and keeping bread and butter on the table was a hard struggle.

For a time after John was murdered, I was informed by my neighbours that, when the RUC passed my house, they shouted abuse, although personally I didn't hear it. After a couple of years, I had put John's mass cards in the shed in a small case and again, I was informed by the neighbours that they had seen the police taking the mass cards out and scattering them over the garden. Another time, they came to search the flat and asked me where my husband was, to which I replied that they should know where he was. This was just rubbing salt in the wounds.

I have been harassed by them when I was stopped as I was going to Queen's University and asked to open my bag. I was told that they were going to search me, to which I replied that they would have to get a police woman because I wouldn't let them. I was informed that they could keep me all day if they wanted and even though I had a lecture to go to, I replied that that was okay because I had all day. I enjoyed Queen's; it was like another world. But I couldn't help looking at other students and thinking, 'Do they have all this going on in their lives?' What I had to go through to get to a lecture!

I remember during the time of the West Belfast Festival when I was leaving Culturlaan to get a taxi when the taxi depot was surrounded by police and I was singled out to be searched. I remember feeling humiliated, as if I had been robbed of everything and didn't know the reason. I had had a good night and just wanted to get home, but the thought of that police woman placing her hands all over my body was a terrible thing and I will never forget it. When I eventually was in the taxi and away from the police, all I could do was cry. It was August and that month was a very sensitive time for me because of John's death.

Before that, I remember walking with Claire, who was about eight years old at the time, and again being stopped and searched. To be stopped and searched in front of your child is very degrading. Even before I moved to Gransha and lived in the flat, the RUC would come in and say things like, 'You are a right propagandist, aren't you?' They ruined everything; nothing was left untouched. I didn't have the privacy of my own home, where it was supposed to be my safe place. My personal things were read, torn apart, turned over.

Early one morning they came, but they were cute. There were no jeeps. They were just dropped in and then the others cleared off and returned when they were finished. They brought in Alsatian dogs, which climbed all over my child's bed. I was not allowed to go and wake her. They let the dogs jump all over her. How the child didn't wake up I will never know. I just thank God that she didn't. How would the child have coped? She would have been hysterical. They wrecked the place—holes in the floors, holes in the walls, holes everywhere. I was unable to take legal action. The only thing I could do was to apply for compensation for the damage that was caused.

This never put me off campaigning. Looking back, there was nothing more they could have done to me; they had done it all and that was the final straw, so to speak. It was hard on Claire. I wanted her to grow up without hatred, but she was seeing all these things happening around her.

I come from a community that has been tormented, beaten by the RUC. In 1998, some members of that community wanted to have a game of football with the RUC. I found that soul-destroying. It wasn't about the sport, it was the principle of the matter—especially what the RUC represented and how they have brutalised the community over all these years. And because there is a peace process and people see things in a different light, all of a sudden the RUC become part of it. The RUC have never been held accountable for the acts of violence they have carried out on this community. The thought that some members of this community would want to play a football match with them was very disheartening, almost like a betrayal.

The fact that Hegarty was acquitted gave the RUC the right to say that they could do what they wanted and they were not going to be held responsible for their actions. Up to now no one has been made accountable for John's murder, but maybe one day we will have a truth commission and someone will be made accountable. For the British government to put their hands up and say, 'Yes, these people were murdered by us' would not be enough; there would need to be more. That policeman, Hegarty, is out there somewhere and he has a wife and child and is living some kind of life. He has never been made accountable. He has torn my life apart and probably is unaware of the consequences as to what my life has been afterwards.

Whilst Hegarty pulled the trigger, the others that were with him and the one who gave the orders should also be held responsible for what they did. Then there was the bigger agenda—Heseltine and the ban on Martin Galvin. Overall, a lot of people have to pay a price because my life has been torn apart. Sometimes I wonder what it would have been like to live somewhere else, not being brought up here and not having these experiences. What type of person would I have been? What would I be doing now? The things that happened in my life I didn't have any control over. It was almost like a film and I was part of the scene.

How do I get back the years that have been stolen?—the years I had without John, the loneliness, the frustration and the anger of watching more injustices and abuses. How do I even begin to start to heal? The healing process has never started for me. There were times, even nights, I would go to the cemetery. People would say I was cuckoo, but there is something which compels me, something inside and I just have to do it. I could be fine for months and there are times when I just have to be at John's graveside. If John had died in different circumstances, I might have got over it by now, but I find that there are times I relive it all again—like when meeting with the Patten Commission; or you might be watching TV and something would remind you of that day and you relive it all over again.

But the fight goes on. The truth of what happened that day should be known, regardless of what the RUC says. And at the end of the day it's not about Hegarty or any other individual cop; they were carrying out orders. The whole British regime is at fault. What I want is an end to that regime and for them to admit their mistakes, to say they were wrong.

10

CHARLES BRESLIN, MICHAEL DEVINE AND DAVID DEVINE
23 February 1985

Shot by British army undercover squad in Strabane, County Tyrone

In the early hours of 23 February 1985, a five-strong IRA unit took weapons from a dump in Strabane, apparently with the intention of attacking a passing RUC patrol. Having made no contact, they went to return the weapons to the dump. The SAS were lying in wait near the arms dump and opened fire, killing three of the IRA unit—Charles Breslin (aged 20), Michael Devine (20) and David Devine (16). The two other members of the unit—Declan Crossan and Damien McCrory—escaped.

The initial RUC explanation of the incident was that a routine British army patrol had encountered a group of armed men and had opened fire on them. Three rifles, two grenade launchers and home-made grenades had been found in a follow-up search. Later the RUC claimed that forensic tests showed that one of the rifles had been used in the murder of a UDR man, Robert Elliott, in Castlederg on 1 January 1985. There was no evidence that the grenade launchers had ever been used.

From the start, there was widespread suspicion that the patrol was far from routine and that the IRA men had been trapped in an SAS stake-out. This was confirmed by later revelations at the inquest.

The funerals of the three IRA members took place on 27 February 1985 amidst an unprecedented security operation mounted by the RUC. In effect, the families and mourners had to battle with the police to bury the dead, in particular Charles Breslin who received a military funeral.

On 29 March 1985, Declan Crossan was charged with conspiracy to murder on the basis of the unsuccessful attempt to attack the RUC patrol in February. A year later, on 3 March 1986, he was found guilty and sentenced to 20 years imprisonment. Judge Andrew Donaldson said Crossan was lucky not to have died along with the others. 'They that take the sword perish by the sword', he added.

Meanwhile, on 7 October 1985, the IRA executed Damien McCrory, the fifth member of the IRA unit. In their statement they stated that he had been working as an RUC informer since September 1984. On the night of the killing of Breslin and the Devines, he had, they said, informed the RUC of the location of the arms dump, as a result of which the stake-out and killing occurred. He was, said the IRA statement, paid £400 for the information.

There seemed to be little impetus on the part of the RUC to investigate the incident. The families were not approached and key witnesses were not interviewed. In December 1985 the Director of Public Prosecutions announced that no criminal prosecutions of the soldiers would take place. And in December 1986 the *Irish Press* identified and interviewed six key witnesses who had not been interviewed by the RUC.

Any chance of disclosure now seemed to rest solely with the inquest. No less than the funerals, the inquest turned into a battlefield. It opened on 3 February 1987. None of the jury selected was from the Strabane area. In his opening statement, the Coroner, Ronnie O'Doherty, reminded the jury that their job was not to apportion blame but to reach a verdict as to how the three men died, where and when.

Statements from the three anonymous soldiers who had fired 117 rounds of ammunition in killing the three IRA members were read to the court. None of the three soldiers was present, on the grounds that, as the Coroner put it, 'they are persons suspected of causing the deaths of three young men and as such they are not compellable witnesses'. In fact, the Major in charge of the operation later revealed under questioning that the three soldiers had not even been informed that the inquest was taking place. The statements repeated the claim that a routine British army patrol had encountered the IRA unit, and when the IRA men had levelled their weapons at the soldiers, the soldiers, believing their lives were in danger and having no time to shout a warning as required by their Yellow Card instructions, opened fire. No shots were returned by the three IRA men.

David Devine was hit five times, Charles Breslin at least 13 times and Michael Devine at least 28 times. Dr Thomas Marshall, Northern Ireland State Pathologist, said that most of the bullets which hit Michael Devine did so as he lay on the ground. Marshall, had 'rarely if ever' seen such extensive injuries to a victim. He added that each of the three dead men had received a single gunshot wound to the head, fuelling suspicion that the British army had administered a *coup de grace* in each case.

Solicitors for the Breslin and Devine families insisted from the first day of the inquest that a covert shoot-to-kill operation had taken place and found support for this argument on the basis of evidence known beforehand and information which emerged at the inquest.

- British army representatives consistently refused to confirm that the SAS was involved and any attempt to question them on this refusal was blocked by the MOD solicitors and the coroner himself.
- The number of British army personnel in the area—at least 50—was too large to be termed a 'routine patrol'.

- The entire Headquarters Mobile Support Unit (HMSU) of the RUC—about 30 officers—normally stationed in Derry, had been moved to Strabane on the night before the incident.
- There had been a preliminary briefing of army and police personnel in Strabane Barracks the night before the incident.
- One member of the HMSU stated that he had been wakened at 5.10 a.m. and told that Charles Breslin was dead, even though the shooting did not cease until 5.15 a.m. and identification of the bodies did not take place until later still.
- One RUC member of the Quick Reaction Force (QRF) based in Strabane barracks stated that they were called to the scene and arrived just before the shooting started.
- Another RUC member of the QRF said that, as he travelled by car to the scene with a soldier, the soldier told him that rockets had been found, yet the rockets were not found until a follow-up search took place after the shooting.
- A forensic scientist questioned revealed that, although rifles found near the three dead IRA men were loaded, two had their safety catches on and none had been fired. He also stated that the three men were shot mostly in the back from a range of about 20 feet, even though the British army evidence was that they had been shot as they walked towards the patrol.

There were many angry exchanges between the solicitors for the families and the MOD solicitors and the Coroner. The families' solicitors sought to establish that the question of SAS involvement was relevant, while the MOD objected to questions about SAS involvement. For the most part, the Coroner backed the MOD by ruling out such questions as being outside the scope of an inquest and therefore inadmissible. For example, on the seventh day of the inquest, the Devines' solicitor asked an RUC witness was he aware that it was an SAS operation. The Coroner ruled the question out of order. The solicitor replied that it was relevant in terms of establishing how the men met their death. The Coroner stated, 'The particular units of the army—I don't find that relevant', to which the solicitor replied, 'You must be closing your eyes to matters which are blatantly obvious'. Even when the soldiers refused to reveal their rank, the Coroner agreed that, while they must give their occupation, they did not have to elaborate and that it was outside his authority to require them to do so.

During the first week, the Breslins' solicitor was physically abused in the court by the RUC who accused him of trying to remove photographs. He had asked repeatedly to be allowed to take the photographs away overnight in order to study them—a privilege granted to the RUC and MOD solicitors—but had consistently been refused by the Coroner. Later, he complained to the Coroner of being harassed outside the court by the RUC. The Coroner replied that, while he was not unsympathetic to the solicitor's plight, he was not responsible for the conduct of the RUC outside the court.

On the fifteenth day of the inquest the solicitors for both families withdrew after heated exchanges with the Coroner. In particular, they protested at the Coroner's failure to keep order—jurors were leaving the court room without the Coroner's permission during the proceedings—and at the proposed adjournment for a week. They also cited the RUC intimidation of civilian witnesses, including Mark Tinney, who arrived in court limping. He had been assaulted by the RUC the previous weekend and suffered a bruised eye and dislocated knee. He stated that he no longer wished to participate in the inquest.

On 22 April 1987 the jury found that the three IRA men died of gunshot wounds. At that point, the Devines' solicitor approached the High Court in Belfast seeking to have the verdict quashed on the grounds that it did not deal adequately with the issue of how the men had died, and called for a new inquest. The High Court hearing did not occur until April 1988. The families' case was that the original inquest was contrary to both the coroners' rules and natural justice. Eight objections were cited.

- The repeated adjournments meant that the jury had difficulty retaining the facts of the case.
- The families' solicitors were not allowed to take away maps, photographs and statements, even though the MOD and RUC counsel were allowed.
- Contrary to the coroners' rules (number 10), the soldiers responsible for the killing were not informed that the inquest was taking place.
- The Coroner did not keep order in the court; in particular, jurors were allowed to leave unsupervised.
- The soldiers' statements were ruled to be unchallengeable.
- Members of the public were refused entry, even though two rows of seats were reserved for RUC personnel who did not turn up.
- The Coroner did not permit questions about the occupations of the soldiers, in particular, whether or not they were in the SAS.
- The post-mortem did not follow procedures; in particular, the families' doctors were not present.

Mr Justice Carswell responded that, if he were to quash the verdict, it would be unlikely that a new inquest would come up with a different verdict. The 'where', 'when' and 'how' of death had been established. On that basis, on 9 September 1988, he concluded that, despite some 'errors of judgement' on the part of the Coroner—in particular, the post-mortem irregularity, the failure to keep order in court, and the refusal to allow the families' solicitors equal access to photographs and documents—there was not sufficient reason to quash the original verdict and grant a new inquest. The families appealed the decision, but in December 1990, Judge Sir Brian Hutton agreed with Carswell.

A subsequent attempt by the families to appeal to the House of Lords also failed, as did an attempt to bring the case before the European Court of Human Rights. The only other legal route left open to the families would be to take a private action which would enable them to call soldiers A, B and C to give evidence and to be cross-examined. That private prosecution is likely to occur in the year 2000.

The story is now told by the Breslin and Devine families.

The Breslin Family

Charlie was what he was and for that we make no apologies. The British army and the RUC are forces of law and order. What were they doing in covert operations shooting down people who they could have very easily arrested through superior man and gun power? What message does that give out? It's not law and order; it's a war. And if it's a war, then call it a war.

Corina: I was doing homework up to about half one. I was doing my O Levels. Charlie had come in earlier on and left about nine o'clock. My brother [Joseph] lived next door; he was getting married; his girlfriend was pregnant. We had gone on to bed about half one, two o'clock. The noise woke us up then about five to five. We woke up with the massive explosions; we didn't know what was going on.

Mrs Breslin: I said, 'That couldn't be shooting; that is like explosions all over the town'.

Corina: Massive explosions; they sounded really loud—you know how things always sound louder at night. The first gunfire was really heavy, like explosions, really scary. The second was like sustained automatic fire, semi-automatic fire, heavy as well but of a different kind. The third was like, one, two, three, four in quick succession; there were two at the end. Mickey Devine had two close-range wounds.

Mr Breslin: Michael was shot on the nose and they couldn't understand why the bullet hole didn't go through the balaclava, because they said he had his balaclava down but there was no hole in it. So the only way they could have done that is by lifting his balaclava before shooting him.

Corina: Or else he hadn't got the balaclava down at all. It was accepted that the safety catches were still on the guns; the guns weren't ready to be used. There was none of them that could have been used at that stage.

Their case was that there were three ordinary soldiers lying up in the hedgerow there and that these three figures, without any warning, came across the field and they were silhouetted against the dark. They heard the noise and realising it was soldiers, they were going to shoot. Now these guys were out in the open and they were going to shoot at somebody lying in the hedgerow, according to the soldiers' story. This didn't make sense. Not that any of it made sense. They claimed to be three ordinary soldiers and yet they had the most massive back-up squad ever. They were all long-serving members of the British army, with the shortest serving twelve years, whereas the normal squaddie would only be on his first or second tour of duty, three or four years in the army. There wasn't any of those guys under thirty and the major was in charge. How many ordinary serving Brits on the streets would have a major being in command of a six man unit?

At ten past seven they raided our house and they raided the Devines'. They raided another house of someone else whom they suspected had got away. Now they knew what houses they wanted to raid and the fellow of the other house they raided subsequently was sentenced to twenty years; he confessed that he was involved. So they knew exactly who they were looking for. They knew before the guys left the house who would be there and what they would be doing when they got there.

Mr Breslin: Sergeant Buchanan said he was wakened at ten past five and he was told Charlie Breslin was dead.

Corina: The coroner asked him twice. The coroner actually said, 'Now Sergeant Buchanan, are you saying that you were woken at ten past five and told?' He was giving him an opt out. He said, 'Yes, that is right'. The shooting didn't end to a quarter past five or twenty past five.

It came out at the inquest that there were three QRF [Quick Reaction Force] units in Strabane ready to back up this one military patrol which was patrolling at five o'clock in the morning. They weren't in uniform. The QRF are specifically there to mop up after military contact and there were three of them in the barracks that night ready to go. This is how quick it happened. The shooting began approaching five to five, and the QRF agreed that they were on the scene within two minutes. Now it takes me five minutes getting from Barrack Street to the house with the child from school; granted that is during the day, but you wouldn't even get up there in two minutes if you were driving at full speed.

They came and raided our house at a quarter past seven. We didn't know what to think. My mum went to make sure the boys were in bed sleeping and neither of them were, but then Joe was with the girlfriend for she was near her time. There was no indication at all. At half eight the postman came and Linda my baby sister had got her eleven plus results. We were delighted for we didn't expect it for she was such a happy-go-lucky child. She had got the top grade, so we were running around bumping her up in front of them. They stood and smirked at us. As the police were going out the door, the priest came in; it was Father McCloskey. My mum was upstairs and I was in the hall. I saw the priest first and I thought, 'Oh my God!' I knew then. There wasn't even a question whether it was Joe or Charlie; I knew Charlie was dead and don't ask me why, for I didn't even know that Charlie was involved. The priest said to my father, 'I want to see a photograph of Charlie'. I couldn't help myself, I started to cry. My father's hands were shaking when he started to look through the photo album for a photograph of Charlie. It's a funny thing too, we couldn't find a photo of Charlie. There were about two thousand of Joe for Joe loved himself, but Charlie was a lot shyer. I remember his hands were trembling and he got out a photograph of Charlie. It was at the kitchen table and he said to you, 'I'm ninety nine percent sure that the boy up the field is not Charlie'. My mum came down stairs and asked what the priest wanted. My dad told her that the priest thought it was Charlie but that it wasn't. She started to go into hysteria and I knew, I just knew. My mum turned round and said, 'If everything is alright, then why is she crying?' I turned my head away for I was giving the game away. Then the priest came back in and said, 'Mary, I'm awful sorry, I'm awful sorry'.

Mr Breslin: The RUC did the exact same with the Devines. They tormented them. I mind Billy, God rest him. They said to him about the trophies, 'He was a good snooker player, wasn't he?'

Corina: That was Charlie and the two Devines dead. The two Devines were very friendly with our family; they never left our house. So it was like a triple shock. Mickey Devine, God love him, took the most bullets. He took twenty seven bullets. David had five and Charlie had thirteen. There were multiple entry wounds with the automatic fire. They kept using the words, 'At least'.

Mrs Breslin: Mark Tinney lives in that row of houses just up here. They were having a party and they could hear the boys shouting, 'Don't shoot, don't shoot'. At that they heard the English voice saying, 'Too fucking late, mate'. They could hear all the English voices and Mark said the field was saturated, there was so many of them.

Corina: In order to explain this, 'Don't shoot, don't shoot', the RUC came up with this thing at the inquest that it was a Mr Kelly from Plumbridge. Now Plumbridge is just a small village a couple of miles from Strabane and everybody knows everybody there. There are a couple of Kellys there but none of them fitting this description. Mr Kelly in a red car drove through the shooting. The shooting had been going on for about ten minutes by this time; the shooting would have been heard all over the town. He was stopped by the RUC, made to lie and the ground and shouted, 'Don't shoot'. He was allowed back into his car and sent on without the registration being taken. They went to Plumbridge and surprisingly couldn't find Mr Kelly. They actually got into the stand and said that, and the coroner sat seriously writing his notes and not a blink.

Mr Breslin: There was a woman, Rosie McCorrigale, saw one of the boys being dragged down the field. The bodies were actually dragged and lain together. I never realised it until McCartney the barrister said to me, 'Do you see how they laid them out in the shape of a cross?' There was a person seen running across the park and the soldier shouted, 'Let him go'.

Corina: Someone shouted, 'Contact', as if he was going to shoot him and the other guy said, 'No, let him go'. That was the informer who, we are led to believe, watched the proceedings from this side of the road.

They were shot in the early hours of the Saturday morning and they didn't release the bodies until the early hours of the Monday morning. It was one o'clock on the Monday morning before those bodies were released out of the morgue in Derry and we had been there from about eight o'clock in the evening for they were supposed to be released then. There was dozens of cars that came down from Strabane. We were scared of loyalists for we would have to go through loyalist areas to get back. They wouldn't let the three hearses come up together; they split our hearse from the Devines. People were harassed coming to and from the wakes; they were tortured. Some of the comments they made were really awful. They were keeping an eye on the Devines but they were really anxious about ours for they knew that Charlie had his military honours in the house, so they were waiting for someone to turn up. The Land Rovers went round and round the house and every time they passed, they were backfiring. Every time we heard the slightest bang, I was choking, I couldn't breathe. If someone slammed a door, I was jumping. It was no accident; they were backfiring to scare the mourners and to scare us.

The morning of the funeral, from the bottom of the street outside our house right up as far as you can go, the Land Rovers were bumper to bumper. The same up the Greyfair Road and the same up the town. Having said that, Charlie got his volley of shots in the back garden and they weren't able to stop it. The RUC sent for the parish priest and told him they suspected it was to be a paramilitary-style funeral. They sent the parish priest up to tell us to tell the IRA to go away and we told the parish priest to go on.

Mr Breslin: He said, 'This house is going to be swamped with the RUC.' I said, 'I don't care'. He was threatening us with the RUC. He left and banged the door.

Corina: He was right about one thing: the RUC did their damnedest. It was the largest deployment of British soldiers and RUC since the large protest outside the city hall after the signing of the Anglo-Irish Agreement. It was in the papers at the time that the security operation for Charlie Breslin's funeral was the biggest since Bobby Sands' in Belfast. A hundred thousand attended it and Strabane is a hell of a lot smaller than Belfast.

The funerals were the battle zone at that time and that is why we wouldn't give in, for it would be like saying his death was okay. There was three or four deep of young lads from Strabane and three or four deep of RUC and every one of them had their riot gear. I dropped a flower from my hand; when I bent down to pick it up, out of the corner of my eye I saw a rifle butt being shoved into the boys' feet and legs. But they had their arms locked and they wouldn't let them near the coffin.

Everyone seemed to be going mad around us and we seemed above it all, like a dream and yet, now I can remember every detail. Down on the road about one hundred yards from the house they stopped us dead. They wouldn't let us go any further unless we took off the beret, gloves and the flag. My sisters were saying, 'Let them, let them; my mother isn't well'. I said, 'No way are they getting that flag'. A compromise was reached; my mother would be able to carry the gloves and beret and the flag would be allowed to stay on the coffin. At that stage we put the coffin into the hearse. Joe came back up and said, 'My da has collapsed'. I thought he was dead. I just said to myself, 'I'll deal with that later. Let's just bury Charlie first'.

Mr Breslin: I think even Billy Devine was sorry after it that he didn't have a military funeral. He didn't see the significance of it. He was in the Royal Navy during the war, but he was just treated the same as the rest of us.

Corina: Even the inquest—what Billy expected from it and what we all expected from it was different. I think in the end it killed Billy; it killed his spirit for he realised that all the things he took as sacred weren't there at all.

Mrs Breslin: They raided our house a month to the day after it, the 23rd of March. They arrested Joseph. And when he was inside, they kept throwing the photos of the bodies, you know, of all the bullet wounds. No matter what policeman, they would have shouted to me, 'Charlie's a Tetley tea bag'. That went on for long enough.

Mr Breslin: Sure, you remember you were walking down the street one day and they shouted after you—that was exactly a week after the funeral—'Mrs Breslin, there is a terrible smell of death from you'.

Corina: It would have been a week or ten days after the funeral, I went back to school. I was doing exams. This all started then. Whenever I'd be walking to school every morning, the RUC decided to bring a Land Rover up the Grove. It would be up there when I'd go by at the top or whenever I'd go in, it would come in after me and drive up. Sometimes it would backfire and other times it would just sit there and do nothing. I think it was to frighten me, but it didn't at that stage. I was past caring.

Linda was still at primary school and one day they stopped and shouted to her, 'Linda, run up quick; we have shot Joe too. Run quick.' The child took to her heels and ran, for she believed it. We had to go and get Joe just to prove to her that it wasn't true.

Mrs Breslin: During the inquest they'd say to Marie, 'Your old girl and old boy aren't looking too good; there's not much left in them'. When Marie was coming in to her job at night, they'd stop her and keep her at the searches knowing she'd be late for her work.

Corina: And then all the letters. My sister who was over from England gave me a letter and told me to put it up into her handbag. I went up, but curiosity got the better of me. It was an obscene letter, written in big blue scrawly letters, and it said, 'Charlie won't get his egg this Easter'. They knew his name and address and the address hadn't been published in the newspapers; but our address was well known to the police for we had been raided often enough. The things they were saying, it was as if they knew him.

I was arrested twice. I am one of the very few solicitors from Northern Ireland who once spent the night in custody! There had been a rocket attack that had really overshot the mark and myself and my husband left our house and went to his mum's for you could get a really good view from there. I went up home again about nine o'clock. The area was cordoned off. I went under the white tape and two Brits held their guns at my chest level and told me I wasn't going up. I told them I was sorry, but I had to go for my mother was waiting on me. The RUC came, dragged me by my hair, with my arm up my back and arrested me. That was the one time I had a really vivid recollection of them slagging me about Charlie's death. They said to me, 'You know what is wrong with you, pet. You want to be like your brother; you want to be lying dead like a tea bag in the field'. And they all started laughing. It was like a crowd of bullies around me, but these were grown men and I was seventeen. I couldn't believe that grown men would taunt a seventeen year old about her brother who had only died two years before. A lot of times I chose to forget most of it for my own sake. But that night I was so scared; I had never been in a Land Rover in my life.

They cautioned me about assault at four o'clock in the morning. At eight o'clock that morning they released me. They arrested me for refusing to give my date of birth. I took them to the high court over that one—whether under the EPA you are required to give you date of birth. You are not; my high court case hit that one on the head.

That time when they were taking me to the barracks, they petrol bombed the Land Rover I was in. I heard my mother shouting, 'More power to your elbow, boys'. Little did she know that her daughter was stuck in the back choking!

But to get back to the shooting—nobody came to get a statement from us. I mean, it was a fatal shooting and there was no investigation. Not that we expected it, for we knew the score. But sitting now and looking at the Stephen Lawrence case, why the hell wouldn't we expect it? Why wouldn't we be expected to be interviewed and to be asked was there anything suspicious about all this? We just took it as par for the course.

Then Gerry Moriarty from the *Irish Press* came up. All the attention was now on the shoot-to-kill policy and about the Armagh shootings in 1982. Gerry Moriarty came to do an exposé on the Strabane shootings—the fact that there was no inquest and that none of the witnesses who had really relevant evidence to give had even been questioned. The article appeared in January. We got a letter the following week saying that the inquest was set for February the 3rd at Strabane courthouse.

We knew we weren't going to get to the truth at the inquest, but one thing I wanted was to try to get some of Charlie's belongings back. He had a special jacket, the grey and black jacket he'd bought in a club book. He never had much for he never had full-time work but this was his pride and joy and he had been wearing it that night. They said the clothes were destroyed for 'health reasons' and the coroner accepted it.

The inquest lasted in total seventeen days. It ran from the 3rd of February and closed on the 23rd of April. From the 3rd of February, it ran almost solid and then the coroner started to get really aggravated with the solicitors. There were two sets of solicitors involved. John Fahey for us and Frank Collins for the Devine family. The inquest isn't legal aided and the two solicitors did it as a favour. So they thought it was going to be a half day affair. All credit to the two firms, they dug their heels in, minutely cross-examined every witness. They had me and a whole lot of other people sitting taking shorthand notes. The RUC stopped me taking notes; at one stage they tried to seize my notebook. At one time they suspected that John Fahey was smuggling photographs of the deceased out of the court. They attacked him, knocked him to the ground, landed on top of him and pinned him to the ground using their knee on his neck. And that was in the court. This was what they did to our solicitor and we were supposed to have faith in the system.

Mr Breslin: The only depositions our solicitors were allowed to see were the ones from the British army—A, B, C, D. They weren't allowed to see any other depositions and there were over 60 witnesses. And all you heard was, 'I don't recall'. I counted one particular person saying three hundred times, 'I don't recall'. At what point does 'I don't recall' become perjury?

With them not getting the depositions, Collins would keep the witness on the stand for maybe an hour to allow John Fahey to read the depositions. That was the only way they could work it. They were sort of a double act. Collins—everybody thought he was slow, but he took his time to allow Fahey to look at the depositions.

Corina: It just went on and on. It was ironic that the police accused of colluding in these deaths were coming up and giving evidence and then doing court security. The stick we were getting going in and out of that court was awful. The things that were said to us walking up the steps of that courthouse in clear earshot of senior police officers, who would turn round and laugh, joining in with it as well!

Around the 27th of February they broke up for a week's adjournment and then there was another one for a fortnight. Basically what was happening was that the coroner wasn't allowing any questions of any of the witnesses apart from these: what wounds caused death?; when?—we knew that; we were there and we heard it; where?—we knew that. And we knew how—it was obvious they were killed by gunshot wounds. When witnesses tried to elaborate on their answers, they were stopped by the coroner. So at that stage it became a farce. The solicitors took us outside and told us we could carry on or walk out and tell them where to stick their inquest. We were going to walk out after a certain date, but we judicial reviewed it instead because they weren't allowing certain questioning. So the coroner sort of calmed down a bit, for the judicial review was pending in the high court. He knew the high court was watching.

Tom Marshall was the Northern Ireland pathologist who examined the three bodies down in Derry morgue. He wasn't able to come to any conclusion about the timing of the different gunshots. He was very careful not to give any view. He was asked about the gunshot wound to Davy's head. He replied that gunshot wounds to the head are very hard to predict in terms of trajectory because the head is such a pivotal part of the body. He refused to give a conclusive answer about the gunshot wound to Davy's head.

We then smuggled the pathologist's report and the photographs out of the court. But it had nothing to do with John Fahey and it was long before John was pushed to the ground. They were gone the first day. Myself and a friend drove with this bundle of papers to meet a man whom I don't know in Dublin. He took the papers off us. Harbinson, the pathologist in the Irish Republic, examined the evidence. He concluded that nearly all the bullet wounds were done while they were in a prone position, leaning forward, either falling or on the ground. In Davy's case, it was uncontradictable that the wound he got to the head was at very short range, no more than two and a half to three feet and that whenever administered, there was already a blow to the base of the spine which would have incapacitated him. From that he concluded without any shadow of a doubt, unlike Tom Marshall, that Davy was still living when he was shot in the head, God bless him.

Mr Breslin: What we wanted to do with Harbinson's report was to bring Marshall back. If he was faced with Harbinson's report, you could have told him Davy was actually shot while he was still alive and wounded and he wasn't going anywhere.

Corina: Montgomery, the crown forensic expert, told the inquest that his investigation was hampered by the RUC for he was not allowed to return to the field. He made the point that this was extraordinary that he, a forensic scientist, could not be trusted to go back into the field. He wasn't allowed to explore the other half of the field. He only explored the area of the field where the bodies were. If he had been allowed to explore the rest of the field, it is possible he could have found evidence of the use of the gimpy [general purpose machine gun] for it would have been totally different bullets.

They always denied there was a general purpose machine gun up there. In fact Frank Collins and John Fahey even tried to talk us out of arguing that because they said it was a red herring. We were sure of the type of gunfire for my brother is in the Irish Army and the weekend that Seamus McElwaine was shot dead, April 1996, we were in the Curragh in Kildare. We could hear the gimpy fire. It was the first time we heard that noise since the shooting. When we asked what it was, my brother told us it was a general purpose machine gun, a gimpy.

John's closing statement was that he had received instructions from his clients that they could have no confidence in the inquest. There were so many things that were done wrong. There were so many questions asked and not answered. As far as he was concerned, the coroner's conduct, the conduct of the police and the military witnesses was such that made the inquest nothing more than a rubber stamp on a state killing.

So we took the judicial review. We went to the high court, the court of appeal and the House of Lords, and we were turned down. We then were refused admissibility in Europe. This case has been trundling on; the boys are dead now fourteen years; the inquest was about twelve years ago; the legal proceedings ended about '93, '94, when it became unstuck in Europe. But we have one other legal avenue that we can use to cause trouble for them, a civil action.

We highlighted the case through the courts but not through the media. We didn't really trust the media because of the morning of the shooting. Up until then I wanted to be a journalist. But the morning of the shooting a guy from the *Daily Mirror* shouted over, 'Mrs Breslin, how do you feel now knowing that your son was a terrorist?' I just slammed the door and took my mum into the living room. After that I said to myself, 'I couldn't do that to any family. I don't care if they are the worst bastards in the world—some mother who's after getting word about the death of a son.' That was my career in journalism very quickly ended.

The 'Panorama' team came and told us they were doing an exposé on shoot-to-kill. It would have been about '87, '88, post-inquest, whenever we were pursuing the case through the courts. They came to do an exposé on the SAS in Ireland. When the programme came out, it was a glorification of the SAS. We should have smelt a rat. They wanted us to act out as if we were asking advice from our solicitor. We went over to the solicitor's house and acted as if we were asking advice about where the case was going. If you are not a trained actor, you can't act something out. We should have known then. There is a republican band from the Head of the Town and I brought them up, to get some footage of them in military uniform. So naïve! The older guy was an animal, a true British colonialist, but the younger one seemed interested in what was going on. He said to me, 'Corina, you class your brother as a soldier and he had a gun in his hand the night he died'. I said, 'Yes, he had'. He asked me if I wasn't trying to get the best of both worlds. 'You're crying "foul" when he is shot dead, yet he would have shot the guy who shot him'. I said, 'Surely it's you who is trying to get the best of both worlds. You call him a terrorist and he's lying dead only a few yards from his home. The guy who shot him was hundreds of miles from his home and had no business in my country'. Charlie was what he was and for that we make no apologies. The British army and the RUC are forces of law and order. What were they doing in covert operations shooting down people who they could have very easily arrested through superior man and gun power? What message does that give out? It's not law and order; it's a war. And if it's a war, then call it a war.

I changed to law after I'd seen John Fahey in action. Gerry Moriarty was lovely; he came back to see if I had gone into law. He asked me if I was still a republican and I said, 'Yes, nothing has changed in this country and so nothing had changed in me'. He asked if my work dispelled some of the myths I had been brought up with and I said, 'No, it just confirmed them'. Some of them don't have the same culpability, but where do you draw the line? We had some nice wee British soldiers reading the Bobby Sands book and their CO came in and chased them.

Mr Breslin: A year after the shooting they were raiding and they were in her room. One of them was an arrogant blond boy. The other one was under the bed and he said to me, 'Mister Breslin, is this her stuff? She is very republican'. I told him we were all very republican and we made no apologies about it. The voice came from under the bed, 'You are darn right, mate'.

The Devine family

We are trying to get some answers as to why they were killed and not taken prisoner. They had no reason to let them go by and then shoot them, for the guns they had were all dismantled.

Cathy: I was living here at the time with my husband George and the two weans; it happened my house was getting renovated. That morning, mummy came down the stairs and switched on the radio. It was about eight o'clock and she was getting ready for work. I heard her coming back up the stairs and she said to my father, 'There were three boys shot in a field in Strabane last night'. He told her to go into the room to see if the boys were in. Davy or Michael weren't in, so she went on to her work.

About nine o'clock there was a knock at the door. My father opened it and it was the RUC. The RUC man said, 'Mister Devine, we are here to raid your house'. My father said, 'What for?' He told him he didn't know. I went up the stairs and I saw a black figure going past me and I thought it looked like Father McCloskey. I listened at the door and I heard Father McCloskey telling my father that Davy was one of them but that he didn't know who the other one was. He said he'd go back up to the field with one of the local fellows to try and identify him. He came out of the room and I said to him, 'Father McCloskey, what is wrong?' He told me Davy and Charlie Breslin had been shot. Our Sheila started to squeal and he told me, 'Cathy, don't be letting them boys down the stairs get to you. Keep her quiet'.

It went on to eleven o'clock and the neighbours tried to get in and they wouldn't let them. The RUC looked out in the kitchen and the snooker trophies were all up in the kitchen and they said, 'There was a quare snooker player in here'.

Mrs Devine: That morning I was going to my work over the bridge and I met a fellow and girl who worked with me. I asked them if they knew who was dead and they didn't, but the fellow said to me, 'Mrs Devine, all we heard was the terrible roaring and shouting: "Don't shoot, don't shoot".' He said, 'Look up there'. I never saw Land Rovers and police like it.

Liam: Me and Antoinette lived at the other side of the town, and we got the telephone call from George to say that Davy had been shot. So we said we'd go up to the Head of the Town to get Michael in his girlfriend's. We went and asked if Michael was there and she said he had gone out last night and didn't come back. From her house you can just look over to the field and you could still see the bodies in the field. I realised he had been shot and I said to her; she started to cry.

I came down here to Billy [Mr Devine] and I didn't want to tell him that Michael too had been shot. Then the priest came in and broke the word that Michael had been shot. After that, Billy and I went down to the morgue to identify them. Looking at that man after having to identify them, for their bodies were all riddled—he was wrecked.

Antoinette: When we came down we found it hard to get into the house; the RUC were everywhere and they were laughing. They were pulling out the presses in the kitchen. The tea pot was on and my mother was sitting there crying.

Mrs Devine: Father McCloskey said, 'Calm yourself down, Billy; don't let them get to you at all.' And Billy said, 'I was with the Navy for thirty years and I never saw anything like those weans got—terrible!'

Cathy: They said that Father McCloskey had a nervous breakdown after that for he said he'd never seen a sight like it. And a couple of weeks later he had to go to identify his own cousin who was shot and left on the side of the road.

Mrs Devine: Our Michael had thirty three bullets in his body. Davy had five. Our Michael was buried with bullets in his body; the surgeon couldn't get them out. Another thing, too—they lifted the hats off their heads and shot them. They couldn't get the bullet out of Michael's nose. Bad animals! We never got their clothes, boots or nothing. Never once did they mention it. Never once did they come since the boys were murdered.

Antoinette: Two years after the boys were killed, we got an inquest. One of the police pathologists said that they were shot from behind, that they were let go past and then shot. One thing got to them, when the forensic man said that he hadn't been allowed to back into the field for to take any more tests.

Liam: In the court, one of the RUC officers threw a cigarette and it hit Billy and burned his trousers. One of them shouted, 'I must go now for a game of snooker'.

Antoinette: When they were showing the photos round the court, even the jurors were sitting laughing at them. It was breaking our hearts. But I think they started to panic when it was going on for so long; they expected it to be over in a day. The solicitors put their heads together and went into every detail. The finding was just that it was death by gunshots. We weren't happy with the findings, so the solicitors took it on. We went over to the House of Lords. We wanted the verdict overturned. We got nothing there. We are just waiting on the private prosecution coming up in Belfast. We are trying to get the soldiers into the court, to bring them back again as witnesses. We are trying to get some answers as to why they were killed and not taken prisoner. They had no reason to let them go by and then shoot them, for the guns they had were all dismantled.

Cathy: It was actually my father who wanted to take it further. He told Fahey and Collins that he wanted that inquest scrapped because it wasn't the truth and he wanted to take it further. My father was very smart and Joe Breslin is very smart. He would always confide in Billy and the two of them would talk it out. Joe Breslin and my father said they were going to push it for they weren't going to let it rest like this. My father said, 'No amount of money would be any use to me at my day and age. I would rather get to the truth.'

Mrs Devine: Billy failed every day from that. It killed him. That morning, it was Antoinette came down. He wasn't well and she rang the clinic and the doctor said nothing was killing your father only a broken heart; it wasn't anything else.

11

Patrick Kelly
8 May, 1987

Killed in SAS ambush

During the mid-1980s, the East Tyrone brigade of the IRA engaged in a high profile bombing campaign against RUC stations. For example, in Ballygawley on 7 December 1985, they raked the local RUC station with gunfire, killing two police officers—Reserve Constable William Clements and Constable George Gilliland. Three other RUC members escaped out the back door. The IRA unit then ransacked the station, taking documents and guns, and left a bomb which wrecked the building. In another attack, on the Birches RUC station near Portadown on 11 August 1986, they drove a mechanical digger containing a bomb up to the building and demolished it. There were no RUC casualties in this attack as the station was only staffed on a part-time basis and was empty at the time of the IRA operation.

At approximately 7.30 on the evening of Friday 8 May 1987, a unit of IRA men mounted an attack on the RUC barracks in Loughgall, County Armagh. This would seem to have been intended as a carbon copy of the attack at the Birches the previous year. The barracks was normally staffed on a part-time basis only, between the hours of 9 a.m. and 11 a.m. and from 5 p.m. to 7 p.m. It ought to have been empty at the time of the attack; as Mark Urban puts it, 'it seems that their aim was not to kill but to destroy police stations'. However, from 2 o'clock that morning, at least 24 members of the SAS and additional RUC personnel were lying hidden, having been forewarned of the attack. Although the majority of the

129

soldiers and police were outside the barracks, there were two SAS members, including the commanding officer, and three RUC personnel inside.

Five of the members of the IRA unit arrived in a hijacked blue Toyota van. Three others were on a hijacked mechanical digger which contained a bomb. As two armed IRA men stepped from the van and raised their rifles in the direction of the barracks, the SAS opened fire. Those on the digger managed to set off the bomb, badly damaging the barracks. When the shooting ceased, eight IRA men were dead. A number had been shot as they lay wounded. Two had been killed 150 yards from the Toyota van; both were unarmed. Six of the IRA men were killed in or beside the van, the body work of which had 125 bullet holes. Some estimates are that over 1200 shots were fired by the SAS in an attack which lasted about ten minutes.

As there were no roadblocks in the vicinity, a number of civilians were caught in the onslaught. Two brothers, Anthony and Oliver Hughes, were returning from work. Their Citroen car sustained 34 bullet holes. Anthony, the driver (aged 36), was shot 15 times and died instantly, still strapped in his seat belt. Despite having been hit 11 times, Oliver attempted to get out of the car; as he did so, he was shot three times in the head from point blank range with high-velocity bullets. Remarkably, he survived.

The dead IRA men were Patrick Kelly (32), Declan Arthurs (21), Seamus Donnelly (19), Michael Gormley (25), Eugene Kelly (25), James Lynagh (32), Patrick McKearney (32) and Gerard O'Callaghan (29). One of the most successful IRA units had been 'taken out' in one major undercover operation. It was the largest single loss of IRA personnel since the 1920s.

The killing occurred only 48 hours after an NIO announcement of increased security in the wake of the IRA killing of Judge Maurice Gibson and his wife Cecily in a car bomb explosion at the border on 25 April. Gibson had been the judge who, in dismissing a case against three RUC men accused of the shoot-to-kill murder of Eugene Toman in North Armagh in November 1982, had commended the RUC men for bringing Toman and his two republican comrades 'to the final court of justice'.

In 1988, the DPP concluded that there was no evidence to warrant any prosecutions against the soldiers or police involved in the Loughgall operation.

There was not a great deal of sympathy in official quarters at the plight of the IRA men. James Molyneaux, leader of the Ulster Unionist Party, stated at the time: 'I hope we are not going to have any accusations of a shoot-to-kill policy. The answer is that the terrorists should not be driving a bomb into an RUC station'. Secretary of State for Northern Ireland Tom King echoed these sentiments: 'Those who launch such attacks have to face the consequences'. And Belfast's Lord Mayor Sammy Wilson of the Democratic Unionist Party congratulated the security forces on giving the IRA 'a dose of their own medicine'. Even nationalist criticism was muted. Seamus Mallon pointed to a major difference between the shoot-to-kill incidents in North Armagh in 1982 and the Loughgall operation. The former had involved the shooting of unarmed people who were under surveillance for some time and could have been arrested with minimum force, while the latter involved an obvious confrontation between two armed groups.

In this atmosphere, there were few voices of dissent. Apart from republicans, Father Denis Faul was almost alone in stating that the IRA unit could have been arrested. And Mary Holland made a perceptive point in the *Irish Times*: 'Is the IRA to be treated in future as an armed enemy, to be ambushed and shot on sight? If so, it would seem that the British government has now acceded to the IRA's view that what is happening in the North is war...If not...there are serious questions to be answered about whether the security forces acted within the law...'

The most consistent source of criticism from nationalist and Labour Party MPs surrounded the death of Anthony Hughes. Many asked why, in such a well-organised operation, it was not possible to prevent the Hughes brothers' car and at least two other civilian cars from driving into the ambush. Despite such criticism, there were a number of veiled insinuations in the press that perhaps the brothers were not so innocent after all. The RUC contributed to this atmosphere of suspicion by repeatedly visiting Anthony's widow Brigid, even during the wake, demanding to know what he had been doing in the vicinity. Under pressure from the likes of Seamus Mallon, the RUC finally released a statement two weeks after the incident attesting to the innocence of Anthony and Oliver Hughes. In July Oliver Hughes was released from hospital after major brain surgery.

The inquest into the nine deaths began on 30 May 1995. The coroner was Henry Rogers and the jury consisted of five men and five women. On the first day Oliver Hughes gave evidence, as did another civilian caught up in the ambush, Francis Tennyson. He had driven into the ambush and had taken refuge in a nearby alley, having been unable to get into any of the adjacent houses. It transpired that this was because the occupants had been removed by the British army and RUC before the IRA arrived. After the shooting stopped, Francis Tennyson was made to lie on the ground, tied hand and foot, and only released after questioning. Detective Inspector McLaughlin also gave evidence on the first day of the inquest and revealed that the British army unit involved was SAS—the HQ39 Infantry Brigade.

On the second day of the inquest, the relatives and legal counsel of the IRA dead walked out because of the coroner's ruling that they could not consult witness statements in advance. They announced their intention to seek a judicial review of the coroner's ruling. The inquest continued without them, despite their request for an adjournment. The RUC detective who had interviewed the 24 undercover soldiers involved in the operation read out their statements. One told how he shot an injured man in the back of the van because 'he made a sudden move'. Another, Soldier B, stated that he shot a man after the order to cease fire because the victim 'made a sudden movement as if to get a weapon which was lying nearby.' Paul Mageean of the Committee on the Administration of Justice summed up the frustration of many in response to these statements.

> None of the soldiers responsible... gave oral evidence. They were not compellable. They were helicoptered from the scene and not interviewed

until they had a chance to consult with their army lawyers. These lawyers were also present when each soldier dictated a statement to the police justifying their actions, statements which were at one in asserting that the victims at Loughgall shared with others killed by the SAS the rather surprising alacrity to move threateningly when faced with armed soldiers.

Details of the fire-power involved in the operation were revealed on the third day of the inquest, 1 June 1995. The SAS had used 23 weapons, including 18 SLRs, 3 M16s and 2 General Purpose Machine Guns. At least 600 bullets were fired by the SAS, including tracer bullets which fragmented inside the victims' bodies. Professor Jack Crane, the State Pathologist, singled out the case of Seamus Donnelly who had died as a result of a shot delivered from merely a few feet away, probably as he lay on the ground. For their part, the IRA had 6 SLRs, a Magnum revolver, a pistol and a semi-automatic shotgun, the last two of which were not used, and were said to have fired 78 shots.

On 3 June 1995, the jury found that all nine had died as the result of gunshot wounds.

The previous day in the Belfast High Court Lord Justice Kerr had refused an application to adjourn the inquest pending the outcome of a judicial review of the coroner's ruling. The judicial review itself went ahead. Almost a year later, on 25 May 1996, Lord Justice McCollum rejected the application for judicial review and upheld the Coroner's ruling. Although McCollum's judgment ran to 16 pages, copies were merely handed out in court and the judge made a very brief statement. Mairead Kelly, sister of dead IRA man Patrick, responded: 'We have waited eight years for these documents and this hearing was over in a minute'.

Mairead Kelly formed the Loughgall Truth and Justice Campaign in June 1995 in the aftermath of the frustrating inquest experience. The Campaign insisted that 'the nine men were deliberately murdered in a premeditated act by the SAS. We firmly believe that this was a plan sanctioned at the highest level of the British establishment'. Having failed to achieve satisfaction through the domestic legal system, the plan was to seek an independent public inquiry as well as to bring the case to the European Court of Human Rights.

Ten years after the killing, an independent public inquiry took place at Pace University Law School in White Plains, New York. Sponsored by the Gaelic Law Society at Pace University Law School and the Hibernian Civil Rights Coalition, a group working for the civil rights of people of Irish heritage in the US, the mock trial examined the evidence, including depositions and forensic photographs, from the inquest, and questioned independent experts in pathology and police tactics. The inquiry concluded 'without a doubt that the agenda of the British security services that night ... was not one of prevention but instead of murder'.

From the start the Campaign has had to work in the face of presumptions that there are no issues of truth or justice involved in relation to eight of the nine dead. Thus, in the atmosphere of concern about victims in the aftermath of the Good Friday Agreement, they had difficulty establishing their right to equal treatment.

In January 1999, members of the Campaign finally met with Victims' Minister Adam Ingram at Stormont. They had to run the gauntlet of DUP politicians and members of loyalist victims' support groups outside the building. Brian McConnell, spokesperson for the South Armagh-based Families Acting for Innocent Relatives (FAIR) said: 'We feel that justice was served that night, but we are still waiting for our justice'. Another member of FAIR, William Fraser, stated: 'It's an insult to be classed in the same category as these people'.

In April 2000 the European Court of Human Rights heard evidence in relation to the Loughgall killings. Three other cases were considered at the same time: the deaths of IRA members Gervaise McKerr in 1982 and Pearse Jordan in 1992, and the killing by loyalists, in collusion with the RUC, of Sinn Féin member Patrick Shanaghan in Castlederg, County Tyrone in August 1991. The argument of lawyers in all the cases was that the British government had failed to uphold Article 2 of the European Convention on Human Rights, the right to life. The Court found that the British government had a case to answer in relation to all the deaths concerned, in itself a major victory for the campaigners. As of the time of writing, it is not known whether the judges will move to a full hearing of evidence or if they will reach a judgement without such a hearing.

Mairead Kelly, sister of Patrick Kelly, tells the story of the Loughgall incident and the subsequent campaign.

Mairead Kelly

In our case the opening sentence is always that, 'On the eighth of May, eight IRA men and one civilian were killed by the SAS'. The fact it's eight IRA men, it's immediately a shut door. Nobody wants to know. We have never hidden the fact that these people were on active service; you couldn't have hidden that if you wanted to. What we were campaigning for was that civil rights were for everybody or for nobody.

My brother's wife was expecting their fourth child and it was due in a couple of days. My brother was to be home at half ten and he hadn't come home, so she phoned her father. Her father went out to my mother's house and said that he was a bit worried because he had heard the news. My mother went with him to sit with my brother's wife. They thought that if it had been him, someone would have come to tell them. My mother went to a couple of friends in the estate and asked them if they knew anything. They knew people had been killed, but they didn't know who. Two of Patrick's neighbours came then to the house and told my mother that it was him. We have never had any official notice of it. In the very early hours of that morning, Saturday the ninth of May, there was a UDR patrol came up the estate and they had a wee banner saying, 'Eight nil'. I think basically that was the way all the families were told. The only one different was the Hughes family. A detective came to them to tell them that Anthony had been killed and that the brother was in the hospital. I know that Mrs Lynagh, whose son Jim was killed, didn't actually hear until the next morning. When she came back from mass, there was a crowd of neighbours at her house who told her. He had been dead about twelve hours before she found out.

I first heard about it on the ninth of May at 5.45 in the morning. I was living in Dublin. My aunt and uncle came to the house to tell me. I had heard about the incident on the news the night before. I had no phone at home, so my aunt and uncle had been told and they waited until morning to come because they wanted me to have a sleep. On the way up, I have to say we were not stopped at all. I know a lot of people that were travelling that day were stopped on the roads. Myself, my husband and the kids went up. There was a lot of people in the house. The solicitor had come and said that he needed two people down to identify the body at the morgue. My mother wanted my sister and myself to go rather than my father, so myself and one of my sisters went down. We got a lot of abuse on the way down. Just on the road here outside, two RUC cars passed us and tooted the horn and flashed the lights. Then they would go up the road a bit, turn and come back and do the same on the other side, because we were in my brother's car. We got a bit of abuse at one of the check points outside the morgue. When we got there, they told us we were too early because they had not finished the autopsy and we had to come back. We went back. The people inside the morgue did not give us any hassle. On the way home, we had the same carry-on; we had the same two cars follow us there and back.

What came out was that an IRA unit had attacked the Loughgall Barracks. They said it was a gun battle between the two sides. There was suspicion that the Hughes brothers were part of the IRA unit, but that was quickly taken back; they said they were caught in the crossfire.

We were in shock and we didn't know what to do. Nobody came to advise us; we never had one person to advise us what to do. It could have been a fault on our side; we sort of accepted what had happened; they were on active service, well eight of them anyhow. They were bombing a barracks. What avenue did you pursue?

We got notification that there was to be an inquest in 1991. There was a hold-up over the fact that the inquest of Gervaise McKerr was held up because they wanted to bring the soldiers that were responsible for their murders and the soldiers didn't want to come in. One of the solicitors involved in our inquest wanted to see the outcome of that, so that is why it took so long. In May '95 we got notification that the inquest was going to be held at the end of the month. We got a barrister to represent six of the people. We had had no contact with the Hughes until the day of the inquest. One of the families vaguely knew them, but there was also a fear of contacting them in case they would have been implicated as being part of it. Ten days before the inquest we were given the autopsy reports of each of the nine people. The solicitor asked for the depositions and a list of the witnesses. We got a list of the witnesses, but we weren't allowed the depositions.

The inquest started on the 30th of May. The barrister asked for a copy of the depositions. The Coroner, Rogers, wouldn't give them; he said that, as each witness read out his statement, he would give our barrister a copy of it. The barrister said, 'I can't possibly question anything before I have actually read it. I am getting fresh information on the spot'. He told us that he would keep asking for them. He tried that and he couldn't get anywhere.

The first witness was the scenes of crime officer, Detective McLaughlin. He was detailing what his role was that night. Our barrister said to him, 'Who was the unit that was brought in that night?' He told him it was the HQ39 Infantry Brigade, or something like that. He asked if that was the SAS and he said 'Yes'. That was the first time that we had officially been told it was the SAS. There was a lot of outcry from the MOD counsel. The RUC counsel stood up and demanded it be struck off from the jury. They objected to the jury hearing that and they said it was irrelevant to the inquest. But that was the first bit of information we had got. We couldn't believe that they actually admitted this.

Throughout the day, the different depositions had been read out. When it got to the deposition of one of the RUC men from some elite unit, he said that he had volunteered to man the RUC barracks that day, for it was only a part-time barracks manned at certain hours. So we thought, here is another piece of information; the barracks would have been empty by the time the IRA arrived. Normally it would have been empty and the only reason that night that anybody was in it was so the elite unit of the RUC—three of them volunteered, along with six SAS men—could use that information to say that their lives were in danger. 'They were planting a bomb and we were right to retaliate.' Otherwise, they wouldn't have been in the barracks and there would have been no justification, for their lives wouldn't have been at risk.

The soldiers didn't appear; their statements were just read out. We didn't hear any of them; we read them in the paper.

When Oliver Hughes, the civilian injured, went to the stand, he said that somebody was telling lies about what had happened. The MOD counsel, the RUC counsel and the Crown counsel more or less told him that, because of his injuries, he was mistaken about what he was saying. The newspaper reports and the state at the time tried to put out that Anthony Hughes and his brother Oliver had been reversing away from the scene at high speed and that they were very erratic. This had caused the soldiers on the ground to believe that they were part of it, trying to escape. The fact that Oliver was wearing an overall similar to the IRA was justification for shooting at them. Oliver was trying to make the point, and he still maintains, that they didn't reverse away. What happened was they were going home from work. The bomb had gone off when they had come over the hill and there was a lot of rubble on the road. Oliver said to Anthony that they wouldn't get through this way. Anthony was driving and, when he started to reverse, he was hit. Oliver tried to get out of the car; he was hit fourteen times altogether. After the eleventh shot he opened the car door and there was a soldier standing right beside him. The soldier told him not to move, but he was panicking or it could have been a reflex. The soldier said that he thought Oliver was trying to get something, so he shot him three times in the head. They claimed that they did try to administer first aid to him when they realised he was a civilian. But they didn't actually administer first aid until an RUC man arrived on the scene. It was only then, after they had walked up and down the road, did they administer first aid to Oliver. They probably thought he wouldn't have survived anyhow. He survived and is actually doing very well. The only thing is that he has no recollection from the time he was shot until he woke up in the hospital six weeks later.

At the inquest they really badgered him. They were saying his statement wasn't accurate and that they both were wearing overalls. Anthony wasn't wearing overalls at all; he never wore overalls in the car; they were in the boot of the car. It was after that we decided that we were going to have to get more information before we could go any further into the inquest. The coroner said that he wasn't going to adjourn the inquest for us, but that we could take a high court hearing. So we left and the coroner said the inquest would carry on; if the families didn't want to be represented, that was their decision.

We took the decision that there was no point in us sitting there because we weren't getting a fair hearing. We weren't going to get anything from it. There were three objectives: 'who' the people were, which everybody knew; 'how' they were killed, by gunshot or whatever; and 'where' they were killed, and everybody knew that. Even if we got the papers before the soldiers' statements were read out, we could maybe make something of them. But they wouldn't give them to us. The inquest finished on the second of June '95 and the high court hearing was in September. The judge said he would reserve the judgement. We had to wait until the following May for the judge to say he wouldn't grant an adjournment, but sure, the inquest was over. He wouldn't grant us a new inquest, for he said that it was at the coroner's discretion whether he gave out the papers or not.

There was an interesting point made in the high court by Justice McCollum. He said that, if we really wanted to know what had happened, we should have taken a civil case, for in a civil case you can get the discovery notes. The discovery notes compel the other side to give you the details. He quickly added that, even if we did go for a civil case, we could end up with PIICs being issued [Public Interest Immunity Certificates]; they are not compelled to disclose the information on the grounds that it would act against security. We hadn't had any of these at the inquest. Unlike other inquests, we didn't push for the soldiers to be brought in, which we would have done had we got a new inquest.

During the inquest we had had an opportunity to view the photographs. That was the turning point for me and some of the other family members. Until then, you didn't actually know the extent of what had happened. We did identify Patrick in the morgue, but we only saw his head. The injuries we have now seen in his autopsy reports weren't even reflected because the undertaker did such a good job. Our Patrick had thirty four bullet wounds on him. He had a very large wound to his brain which meant that he was shot at very close range. Seamus Donnelly was only nineteen. He hadn't got a gun near him when he was shot. His hood was lifted by one of the soldiers who were coming down the road, the ones who had actually shot the Hughes brothers. He had a close range gunshot wound in his neck. He was possibly still alive at that point; although he had severe gunshot wounds, that was probably the final injury.

So, when we saw the photographs, I know that I said on the way back in the car, 'It is wrong what has happened. I'm not going to let it go at that.' The others asked what was the point; what was I going to do? I said I didn't know, but that I didn't feel it was right to let people kill people and not be accountable for it. A lot of people said I was mad, that I was going on an uphill struggle. We put our heads together and said, 'What can we do?' I thought we should write to the Irish government; they should be representing their own people. No matter what people thought of it, they were still Irish citizens. We went down to the CAJ in Belfast for they had been at the inquest taking minutes. There are no minutes at an inquest and because we weren't there, we didn't know what was being said. We asked if there was anything we could do. They said it was a deliberate killing, well planned and there were people killed when they shouldn't have been killed. They thought that we had a case to the European Courts.

We got all the nine families involved and we asked them did they agree if we should go individually or as a group. I would have liked everybody to go as a group, but I was going anyhow. So, in June 1995, we got together and formed a campaign. We went through the inquest papers, which had to be bought at a pound a page. We could get a copy of the photographs at a pound each too. When we got the papers together, we did a summary of the case. We highlighted the fact that the security forces and the ministers of the time knew that this attack was going to take place. It wasn't speculation; they had information. Where they got that information from still is a point that hasn't been pursued. But they got their information and they set out a plan to wipe out a unit which Jack Hermon has claimed was a very troublesome unit of the IRA. It was very successful blowing up barracks and they weren't able to do anything about it. He claims that what happened that night was justified on the principle that the IRA opened fire first.

At the inquest, the soldiers and the RUC said that they were told about this attack the night before. Now there was a lot of speculation that they knew weeks before, but the only thing we have in writing is that in their depositions they said they knew about it the night before. The soldiers were flown in the night before and they all had their briefing at eight o'clock. They did an outline of what way they were going to approach the situation to ensure that no one was going to get out of it. They had a circle around the barracks so that once the shooting started, they all moved in towards the barracks. This meant that anyone who was there wasn't going to get out alive.

There were officially twenty four SAS soldiers, six inside the barracks; their commander was inside the barracks with them. Three RUC officers were inside the barracks and the rest of them were outside. Loughgall, where the barracks is, is on the centre part of a hill. At the top of the hill there was an undercover unit sitting and at the bottom of the hill there was another unit. Any car which would have passed that area that day would have been radioed in and checked. When we went through the papers, we discovered that the IRA had passed this area of the barracks. I think at six o'clock that Friday the unit started radioing in that the blue van which was hijacked early in the day had passed by their location, passed the barracks and up past the last location of the soldiers at the top of the hill. At that stage the SAS would have been on full alert. The digger that had the bomb was spotted going up and down past, so there was certainty among them that this was going to go any minute. The two soldiers on either side of the barracks had been issued with caltropes to put across the road that would have allowed them to stop the vehicle and to have arrested them. The objective of the caltropes is to put them across the road and the spikes puncture the tyres. One of them claimed he tried to put them down and they didn't work. They wanted the bomb to take place, for they wanted justification for opening fire on the IRA unit.

During that day the Hughes brothers had passed the area twice, so I'd say the chances of their car being radioed through was very high. The SAS soldiers who shot them—soldiers S, T,U and V; we were only given letters of the alphabet—claimed they believed the Hugheses to be a part of the IRA unit. The car was shot thirty four times; Oliver was shot fourteen and Anthony was shot fifteen times. The newspapers tried to put out that they had been caught in crossfire, but they were shot by soldiers who were just ten yards away from them, behind a wall. There were other civilians in the area. There was a woman and her daughter going to a fete in the church hall. She lay down on top of her daughter. One of the soldiers came over to her and asked her if she was all right and directed her out of the area. She drove past the Hugheses who had been shot something like three yards away from her. There was another civilian, Francis Tennyson, who was going to work. He stopped his car outside the barracks, for he saw four masked men getting out of the van and stand in the middle of the road with their guns pointing towards the barracks. He ran down the side alley and one of the soldiers told him to get into the house. He tried to get into the houses, but none of the people were in at the time. We think that they were actually taken out of their houses, but no one will actually say that. It was very suspicious that not one single person was in the houses at that time.

There were six hundred and fifty shots fired by the SAS. The IRA fired something like seventy two shots. All these shots were directed at the barracks and nowhere else, and a lot of them actually hit the perimeter fence. They hadn't actually been firing at anybody, only the building. I think it was a three hundred pound bomb. Now, I'm not up to date on these things, but the bomb apparently had an impact that went in rather than out. There were houses within twenty feet of the barracks which didn't even have a window smashed.

We moved on the principle that the people were killed unnecessarily and that there was a predetermined plan to kill them and nobody had been held accountable. We wanted a full public inquiry and we were asking people to support us.

I wrote to every single TD. The only ones who agreed to meet us were Eamon Ó Cuiv, Caoimhghín Ó Caoláin and Dick Roche. Bertie Ahern did write back but he wasn't Taoiseach; he was the leader of Fianna Fail. He said that he did believe strongly when people are killed by the use of lethal force that they should be held accountable. He didn't say he would do anything.

Amnesty International wrote back to us. It was their belief that it was a case of summary execution. The British Irish Rights Watch gave us backing and Justice, another human rights group in England. None of the other human rights groups in England wrote back to us. The CAJ of course, they are representing us in Europe. I wrote to the ICCL in Dublin, who said that, because it happened out of their jurisdiction, it was nothing to do with them. I had a letter back from David Norris from Seanad Eireann, a great campaigner for civil and human rights. He started off by saying that he sympathised with me on the death of my brother. Then he went on to say how callous the IRA were, how they carried out the most horrendous acts, and if there was a hierarchy of sympathy, the IRA would be at the bottom of it.

In our case the opening sentence is always that, 'On the eighth of May, eight IRA men and one civilian were killed by the SAS'. The fact it's eight IRA men, it's immediately a shut door. Nobody wants to know.

We have never hidden the fact that these people were on active service; you couldn't have hidden that if you wanted to. What we were campaigning for was that civil rights were for everybody or for nobody. I think that the eight IRA men had the same rights as everybody else. Even if you take that limited approach, there was a civilian killed and nobody gives a damn about Anthony Hughes. The government, its ministers and the SAS made it quite clear at the inquest that he was shot intentionally because they thought he was part of the unit. Yet none of them went to Bridget Hughes or Oliver Hughes and said that they were sorry.

A lot of people thought that when we started we were looking for money. A lot of people say it helps, but how could it help me? I have no objection to people taking it if they have been left financially insecure. We are not rich by any means, but the money wouldn't serve us. It's not going to tell us what happened. The whole issue is to establish why they were killed in the first place.

I got a phone call one day from this American civil rights lawyer called Denis Lynch. He said he had heard about the case and would be interested in doing something to help us. So, he had a group of young trainees at the university do a mock court case based on the inquest paper. The mock trial took place in 1997; there were six family members who attended—the Callaghans, Oliver Hughes, myself and Roisin [Kelly] and Seamus Donnelly's brother. It was only a mock trial, but we had a real judge and students acting out the different parts. There was a jury of lawyers and based on the evidence they heard, they decided if the British government was guilty or not.

We got a Japanese pathologist to look at the photographs and the autopsy reports. He was totally independent and had no Irish connections whatsoever. His findings were that excessive force was used on the nine people. There were classic cases in six of the nine that they were shot at close range. Some of them probably could have survived apart from the close range shots. In his opinion there was an overwhelming desire on the part of the people who were carrying it out to kill because they had gone in and shot as much as they could. Patrick had thirty four bullets; Anthony Hughes had fifteen. But the thing we noticed was that ninety nine point nine percent of the wounds were above waist level; there wasn't any attempt to stop them by shooting them in the leg. Gerard O'Callaghan and Declan Arthurs weren't armed at the time; they weren't even near the digger when they were shot. Anthony Hughes was a civilian; he wasn't even told to stop and his car was just shot at.

The other independent guy we got was Kenneth Cummings. He was a member of the Seal Unit; that would be the equivalent of the SAS. He was actually trained by the SAS. He made a very damning report on them saying that from the reading of their depositions and from the layout of their operations and in his experience from being trained by them, the operation was never one to prevent an attack or arrest people. It was one in which they ensured that all people would be dead. He was critical of the fact that they had taken no precautions to prevent civilians from coming into the area. He also made a significant remark about the fact that our Patrick had an eye tooth missing. My mother and his wife saw him at half two that day. If he had an eye tooth missing, it would have been very noticeable. In his autopsy report it said that his eye tooth had been 'torn out'. The tooth hadn't been shot out because there would have been fragments of it in his mouth. A couple of people we spoke to told us that maybe his tooth had been taken as a souvenir. The independent guy said it was customary for the SAS, when they had been involved in an operation against what they classed as a group of terrorists, take as a trophy something belonging to the so-called leader of that unit. Because Patrick was supposed to have been the leader of that unit, in his opinion that was the trophy.

We got the final reports there at the end of May [1998]. I wrote to the Irish government telling them I had new evidence that would warrant an opening of the case. I wrote to the British government, to Adam Ingram, minister of security. I told him I had new evidence that would support an investigation into the Loughgall killings. He said I had to send it to the RUC or the DPP. I opted to send it to the DPP, for I don't believe the RUC is impartial and I don't believe they will do anything. I'm still waiting on word back from the DPP and that's since June. The Irish government agreed to allow one of their senior officials from the Department of Foreign Affairs to meet with us. We asked them to take a more active role. They have taken the line over these last three years that they can't be involved because we are taking a case in Europe. I think they were trying to claim that it could lead to sub judice if they interfered in a case which was going to court. But we are not stupid; we knew they didn't want to be seen taking an active role.

We gave the findings from the mock trial to the media and the media just refused to take an interest in them. The general opinion was that it was so long ago that nobody cares and that eight of the people were on active service and they were going out to kill, which I'd argue very strongly against. They were going out to blow up what should have been an unmanned barracks and the risk to lives would have been minimum or none at all. Because of the times we are in, no one cares; the evidence is damming but nobody cares.

We have had a lot of trouble with the RUC trying to obtain the clothing and personal belongings of the families. It's eleven years and there are still some families who haven't had the personal belongings returned. In Patrick's case, we did get his watch, medal and rosary beads, but there are still some families who didn't get that. What we wanted was his clothing, not for any morbid reason, but to get the clothes analysed by our own forensic person. In 1996 I wrote and said that I wanted my brother's clothing and shoes returned. They wrote back and told us that the coroner had requested that the clothing would be kept until the outcome of the judicial review. That meant they still had them. So, after we lost the judicial review, I wrote and asked if I could have them. In March this year [1998] they wrote back and said they had been incinerated. I wrote and asked them on whose authority they had done this, for the coroner had said that we were entitled to them. They wrote back and said they had done this in the interest of public safety and health. They said that the clothes were blood-stained and that they were a public health risk.

I think we have a good case in Europe. I don't know whether we will win on lethal force because they can always argue that there were people armed that night. I think we can argue that it was planned and it failed to uphold what they call their law. They went out that night to kill; they didn't go out to try to arrest.

Last March, in the light of prisoner releases, they appointed Adam Ingram as minister for victims. At the start we thought this would be a problem, for as the minister for security he never wanted anything to do with us. We got this meeting with the Victims' Liaison Unit in Belfast. It was a very civil meeting, but you still get the prejudice. Our submission to them was that we can't move forward until we can put the past to rest and we can't do that until we find out what exactly happened. That mainly centres around the issue of truth. All the people killed that night, if they had been arrested, would have been released now, not under the Good Friday Agreement, but they would have had their time done. Also, there were eight children left behind and we thought they should have been included in any of these packages that they were setting up—counselling, education and that. We also thought it was important that all the families and friends who lost someone could write down their story and have it recorded in history. I know our story is well known, but it is well known by what the British and media put out. There are very few people who know about the facts of that night. And there are an awful lot of people whose story isn't told. We thought maybe a cultural centre where people could go in, record their story and maybe even talk about it—a counselling session or an information meeting—would be a good idea. What we got back that day from the two people we met was that we would have to look at truth all round. We said we wanted that. Billy Stephenson [of the Victims' Liaison Unit] said that the IRA had to tell the truth. I told him that they had never hidden what they were going to do that night. I also told him that we are only families. We have no ties to anybody. Who would we approach to find out any information? We don't have any connections. People assume that because of who our families were we have a direct line to somebody; we don't.

There are nine families with different political persuasions; we don't campaign on a political agenda. The case may be political but the campaign isn't.

We are now waiting on a meeting with Adam Ingram as victims minister. At the end of the day we are still victims. I mean, I hate the word 'victim'. I don't know what you would call us. The people who are left behind are more survivors. That is basically where we are now.

When we started out people said we were crazy. But you will always get somebody, even if it is only one person here or there, to listen. You get a letter back from someone who will say, 'I didn't know that happened'. The few TDs that wrote back said it never came across like that; it always came across as a battle between two sections and those with the upper hand won. We got the opportunity to go to America and got to do an interview on one of the American stations. We got a lot of feed back from people who didn't realise what had happened. Before they had said, 'What is their problem? Their family members went out to do something that night and got killed before they got doing it.' Even wee things, radio interviews, you can always get a chance to say your bit. The main thing that we can say we have achieved now is that we have made a lot of people, even the families, aware that it was not just a straightforward case of people being shot. If you tell someone a person was shot, they think of one or two bullets. But if you can actually detail how many times a person was shot and where they were shot, the fact they have been shot at close range, it's such a turning point for people. Up until then you just accepted it.

I think there should be some sort of a system where the state is made responsible; I mean, the state is supposed to uphold the law. It's ridiculous; they say its peace time now and you have to put the past behind you. But I think that the past will always be repeated if it's not resolved. I couldn't accept anything less than the truth of what happened, why it happened, and I think people should be held accountable. Whether people would ever be sent to jail or not, I don't believe that would happen. But I would like them to say that these soldiers were following orders and I would go as far as to say these orders came from Margaret Thatcher herself. She and her ministers should be held responsible for the war crimes. They should be made to say in a public way, 'Yes, we did go out that night to kill them. What did you want us to do? We couldn't get these people into court so we went out to kill them.' Then, based on that, I would like to see them held accountable. I would like to see them indicted for murder, whether they would ever serve a sentence for it. I don't think that would ever happen, but the satisfaction of seeing them charged with it, to me that would be a start.

12

AIDAN McANESPIE
21 February 1988

Shot by British soldier

A idan McAnespie, a 24 year old from Aughnacloy, County Tyrone, was shot dead at a border checkpoint on 21 February 1988. He had been at a wake at his aunt's house half a mile south of the border and left to go to a local GAA football match. The football pitch was just north of the border, situated between the border and the British army checkpoint. Aidan parked his car in a little housing estate next to the checkpoint and walked back through the army checkpoint towards the football pitch. As he did so, a soldier at the checkpoint fired a General Purpose Machine Gun, killing Aidan instantly.

An initial statement made by Secretary of State Tom King in the House of Commons reflected the British army explanation of the incident. 'I understand that the police have confirmed that three rounds were discharged; that they all hit the road and the deceased was killed by a ricochet.'

This bland announcement was immediately challenged by the McAnespie family and a number of eyewitnesses. There were initial reports that only one shot had been fired; that a man dressed in a tracksuit was driven away from the scene in a British army Land Rover—he may or may not have been the off-duty army medic later acknowledged by the authorities to have been at the scene.

But most disturbing of all was the fact that Aidan McAnespie had been subject to a five year campaign of harassment by British state forces. He lived in the north and worked in the south, in Monaghan town. He was frequently harassed during his twice-daily trips across the border. In an interview he gave to the *Sunday World* (22

143

February 1987) a year before his death, he noted that during one 11-day period he had been stopped ten times. Although he had worked as an election worker for Sinn Féin in 1983, and his sister had stood as a Sinn Féin candidate in local government elections in 1985, there was never, before or since, any suggestion that Aidan was linked to the IRA and had as a result drawn the British army's attention. He was prominent in the GAA locally and this alone could have been enough to ensure he was singled out. As SDLP councillor Austin Currie put it on the day of Aidan's funeral: 'The security force personnel based in Aughnacloy are infamous throughout the South Tyrone area ... The hostility towards Gaelic footballers is particularly intense'.

The death occurred at a time of intense debate over the accountability of the state forces in the north. A decision had just been taken not to prosecute the RUC officers involved in shoot-to-kill operations in Armagh in 1982. On the day of Aidan's funeral, Private Ian Thain, jailed for the murder of Thomas 'Kidso' Reilly in West Belfast in August 1983, was released after less than four years in prison and rejoined his regiment. At the funeral of Aidan McAnespie, Cardinal Ó Fiaich, who had returned from the US specifically for the occasion, stated: 'One could hardly be surprised that many people are asking, are the British forces above the law?'

Two days after the funeral, on 24 February, 18 year old Private David Jonathan Holden of the Grenadier Guards was charged with the manslaughter of Aidan McAnespie. At a brief hearing in Cookstown Magistrate's court, he denied the charge and was remanded in custody. His custodial experience was brief. The following day, he appeared in Belfast's High Court. He stated that he had been on duty at the permanent vehicle checkpoint from 8 a.m. on the day of the incident, which occurred at around 3 p.m. In the sanger at the border checkpoint, he said, there was a General Purpose Machine Gun, loaded at all times with a belt of 50 rounds. He had cleaned and oiled the gun, which was then reloaded and replaced 'by someone else'. Holden said he noticed that the gun was facing away from its normal position, namely towards nearby high ground from which any IRA attacks might come; he decided to move it to the correct position. As he did so, his finger slipped and hit the trigger. His hands were still wet from cleaning the gun, it was an automatic weapon and 'if it is touched even slightly, it goes off'. He concluded that he had been horrified to discover that he had hit a civilian passing through the checkpoint, and denied that he had aimed the gun at anyone, even in jest. He was remanded into military custody with bail set at £100 and two sureties of £500.

His next appearance in court was on 27 September 1988. In a statement lasting less than one minute, it was announced that the DPP had decided there was not enough evidence to continue with the prosecution. Charges were dropped and David Holden walked free. In June 1989 it became known that he was back on duty with his regiment, having been fined an undisclosed amount by the British army for negligence.

In the meantime, the issue of Aidan McAnespie's death had continued to be a cause of widespread concern and indeed inter-governmental friction. The British authorities continued to maintain that the death was an accident, caused by a ricochet bullet. At the funeral, Cardinal Ó Fiaich had called the death 'murder'. At the same event, Austin Currie had summed up the feeling of many: 'Was it a mere coincidence that the one person well known to the security forces and whose complaints of harassment by them on him were well documented should be the victim of a stray, random ricochet accidentally discharged at a distance of 200 yards?' The Irish government entered the debate in two practical ways: firstly by arranging for a second postmortem, additional to that carried out by the North's state pathologist; and secondly, by establishing its own police inquiry under Eugene Crowley, Garda Deputy Commissioner.

The second postmortem took place on 28 February 1988 after Aidan McAnespie's body had been exhumed. It was carried out by the Republic's State Pathologist, Dr John Harbinson. On 4 March, Dublin government sources indicated that preliminary findings seemed to cast some doubt on the official explanation that Aidan McAnespie was killed by a ricochet and that he had been shot in the chest, not the back. However, seven weeks later, there was a volte face, with Dublin sources now subscribing to the ricochet theory. That has been their official stance since.

The Garda inquiry took evidence from many witnesses—including one ex-British soldier who testified to the regular harassment Aidan had experienced at the checkpoint—who were unwilling to give evidence to the RUC. In September 1988 press reports indicated that Crowley's findings were that the death of Aidan McAnespie had most probably been caused by a ricochet bullet. The report was not published because, as Irish Justice Minister Gerry Collins put it, it would be difficult to do so without revealing the identities of the witnesses who had given evidence in confidence. When John Wilson, chair of the South's Victims' Commission, issued his report in July 1999, he expressed the opinion that the report of Crowley's investigation should be made public. To date, this has not happened.

The inquest into Aidan McAnespie's death opened on 28 November 1988 and was immediately postponed indefinitely. Like a number of other inquests, it was held up pending the outcome of legal proceedings in another case, that of Gervaise McKerr and other victims of the RUC shoot-to-kill policy in Armagh in 1982. Eleanor McKerr, widow of Gervaise, had sought a judicial review of the coroner's decision not to call the RUC men responsible for the killings to the inquest. Pending the final legal outcome, any inquest where it was likely that there would be a demand that members of the British army or RUC be called to give evidence—such as that of Aidan McAnespie—were postponed. The final legal outcome was that those members of the state forces who had carried out killings were not compellable witnesses at an inquest. Consequently, five years after Aidan's death, an inquest was held. David Holden was not required to attend and a key witness, also a British soldier, failed to turn up. As a result, the family withdrew and the inquest carried on without them. The Coroner, Roger McLernon, stated that Aidan's death 'was avoidable and should have been avoided'. He repeated the RUC's belated acknowledgement that there was no suggestion whatsoever that Aidan had ever been involved in illegal activity.

Eilish McCabe, sister of Aidan McAnespie, tells the story of his death and the subsequent campaign.

————————————

Eilish McCabe

People who knew Aidan knew the truth; no one can take that away. They can never take the truth from us, but it's important that there is a public acknowledgement from them to say that they have done wrong.

Aidan was the youngest of a family of six. We live here in Aughnacloy— a very divided town, a very divided community. It wasn't a town where there was much work for anyone, particularly if you were a Catholic. Aidan wanted to stay home with mum and dad, so he found himself a job in a poultry processing factory in Monaghan town. To get to Monaghan—it's eleven miles from here—he had to travel in and out through the permanent border checkpoint every morning and evening. Every morning he was stopped and searched. Maybe he'd be stopped and his lunch box would be taken apart. Maybe the following morning they would take him into the search centre and keep him there for an hour. That went on in the evenings when he was coming home from work as well. A Sunday newspaper, the *Sunday World*, decided a year before the shooting that they would carry a story on him. The headlines of their newspaper article called him, 'Ireland's most harassed person'. The harassment got to a stage where he could hardly bear it; he went to the trade union at work, to the parish priest here in Aughnacloy. He went and made official complaints to the RUC. He made loads of complaints to solicitors. He asked for support from other people as well, but it just went on. So he saw the article this newspaper was doing—raggy and all as the newspaper was—it was still, for him, an outlet to get telling what was happening to him in the hope that maybe they would slow off and stop the harassment, allowing him to get to and from his work.

The harassment did ease off a bit, but gradually it just got back to where it had been. In fact, there was one evening he was coming home from work through the checkpoint and he was stopped at the middle where they had this hut. There were two or three soldiers and police in it. They stopped him, asked him to get out of the car and open his boot and bonnet. So he opened the boot and bonnet. Then they asked him to take off his coat and he said, 'I'm not taking my coat off, for it's bucketing with rain'. So they said, 'Take off your coat, shoes and socks'. He refused and the soldiers actually sat upon him. They pulled him to the ground; one grabbed him by the throat and forcibly held him on the ground while another soldier pulled off his shoes and socks. He came up here to me; he was completely soaked, but even worse were the marks on his neck. My husband said, 'Right, we are going to make an official complaint'. He went with Aidan and made an official complaint. He went to a solicitor as well. The next morning, when Aidan went through the checkpoint on his way to work, the soldiers wagged him on through. When he looked in his mirror, the soldiers were laughing at him. He drove straight on to where he worked in Monaghan and when he got there, the gardai were sitting waiting on him, the Special Branch. They arrested him and took him to the Garda station in Monaghan. One of his friends from work phoned me and told me he had been arrested in the South and I immediately went and got my mum and dad and went straight to the Garda station. We were there before 11a.m.; it would have been around quarter past eight when Aidan had been arrested. The gardai said, 'Yes, he is here and we will let him go now'. They let Aidan out. They never questioned him once. To this day my father has been challenging the gardai to see why they arrested him there. We know that it was in collaboration with the security forces in the North, that whenever the heat was put slightly on the soldiers for the way they had abused him on the side of the road that night, they decided to ease off for a while and asked the gardai to pick up where they couldn't go.

On the weekend of the shooting, my mother's sister's husband had died. The family all went out to the funeral. She didn't want to go back to the empty house, so she asked us all back for a meal. Aidan was sitting beside me at the table. All my mother's family were there, her brother, sisters and cousins; it was just like the last supper in a way. We finished the meal and Aidan said to me, 'I'm going to head down to the football match'. And I said, 'Right, Aidan, I'll see you in about an hour'. He just seemed to be out through the door about ten minutes when my husband Paul came in. He said, 'Eilish, you better come out here. There was an accident down at the checkpoint and it was Aidan. I think it's bad'. The checkpoint is only about a mile and a half from my aunt's house; she lives in the South. We drove down towards the football field; the football field is in the north, just inside. If you are going to the football field, you come to the football field, then the checkpoint. As we drove down to the football field, we noticed an awful crowd standing on the road. I could see an ambulance. I thought, 'Well, I'm on time; they are waiting on me'. I started to run towards the ambulance because there was a tape across the road where the car couldn't drive anymore. I ran right past a crowd of maybe two hundred people. The crowd opened up and made space. I saw there was a body on the road. There was a blanket over the body. There was a policeman standing right beside the body with a gun in his hand. I just walked over—all these people I knew, who are friends of mine, standing staring at me, no one speaking. It was just like the most natural thing in the world to lift the blanket. My worst nightmare had come true; under the blanket was Aidan and he was dead. The ambulance was sitting there because there was no point in taking Aidan anywhere; he was dead. The police told me I couldn't touch him because I wasn't allowed to move him. I wasn't allowed to embrace him. I could only hold his hand at the side of the road. I did embrace his body for a long time. The policeman stood beside me with his gun in his hand all the time.

Within about ten minutes my mum and dad came in another car. What I've described to you was heartbreaking, but, when you've seen your parents going over there to their son lying dead on the side of the road, they are scenes that never leave you. Aidan's body was removed from the road to the ambulance and dad and myself went with him in the ambulance to the morgue in Craigavon. Anthony McGonnell, an SDLP councillor was there. He immediately rang the Northern Ireland Office to see what was going on. The Northern Ireland Office, less than an hour after the shooting could tell him that it was an accident, before any investigation.

The first media reports were of a shooting and then, it was an accident. The accident was pumped in almost immediately. It's the first impression that sticks in people's minds. It was the way in which they were prepared and had their statements ready, so soon, less than an hour; it was all worked out. They were treating it as an isolated incident. They were not including the fact that Aidan had been harassed. My mother used to sit in the evenings waiting for Aidan coming home from work. He would phone from the filling station at the end of the town. He would park his car there and then mum would cycle down to meet him. The two of them would walk up through the checkpoint together. About six months before Aidan was shot, a soldier actually stood out on the road one day and said, 'Mrs McAnespie, are you trying to protect your son?' That was it. About two years before Aidan was shot, a patrol of soldiers stopped daddy one day in the car and asked for his ID. When he produced it, they asked if he was Aidan's father; he told them he was. They said, 'Will you tell Aidan we have one here for him?' There was nothing isolated about it; it was premeditated.

Aidan's body was released to us about half twelve on the Sunday night, and he was brought home again to the house.

We were told by the media that a soldier had been taken away after the shooting for questioning. We didn't have an awful lot of confidence or faith in that because of the way Aidan had been treated by them. Aidan was buried on the Tuesday, and on the Wednesday morning, about three minutes to ten, I got a phone call from the CID in Dungannon to say there was a soldier being charged with the unlawful killing of Aidan at Cookstown court house at ten o'clock. Now, to get from Aughnacloy to Cookstown takes twenty minutes. He was taken into army custody. He was allowed to leave army custody to go to England and then on holiday with his family for three weeks. After the three weeks were up, we heard this through the media—no one from the Northern Ireland Office came to tell us—the DPP said the charges were being dropped because of insufficient evidence.

There were people coming into our house all day to pay their respects—Aidan's friends from work in Monaghan and they were heartbroken. For a lot of them, this would have been the first time they were affected by the troubles. When Fergal Caraher was shot, my father said, 'I have to go down to Caraher's house. I have to go down to see Peter John'. Daddy and Peter John would have been acquaintances of one another through music sessions and football. We took dad down to the Caraher's. Peter John and daddy met in the door way and the two of them cried like babies. But you could see Peter John's face, you could see it helped having daddy come to him. Other people had suffered and came to offer support. We were the same in our house. I will never forget Mrs McKearney from Moy coming to us; she had buried two sons and since then she has buried her third son. There were other families who had suffered and they were taking time out to come to us and sympathised with us. They didn't have to say anything; just their presence coming into the room was a comfort.

The road was closed most of the day on the Sunday while the RUC were allegedly carrying out an investigation into what happened. On the Sunday evening, the road was reopened. On the Monday night, I was sitting in the room where the coffin was and someone came into me and said they wanted to speak to me outside. I went out and they said they had come in through the checkpoint and that the police were in the process of closing off the road again. This was about half seven at night, February time, which was pitch dark. I thought, 'What can they be doing, closing the road now?' I went with the person and, as we got out of his car, someone came over to us and said there had been three shots fired from the checkpoint, and there was a red light pointing to the spot where Aidan had been shot. The three shots was them trying to support this ricochet theory that they had created. They had to make the evidence. The police made a statement later to say that they had been fired on from the Monaghan road and they had returned fire. That was denied by the people living in the housing estate. Then the IRA made a statement as well saying there was no activity down round the border area. The RUC still held tight to their ground. On the next news they said they had been fired on from the Caledon Road. This was denied by locals also.

On the Monday night we were very unhappy with the way things were going, so I got a doctor and asked him if he could go and examine Aidan's body. He informed me we would be better getting a pathologist, for his word would never be taken anyway. The Irish government stepped in at this stage and said they were going to carry out an investigation. We decided to bury Aidan in the South; that's where my mum's from. We knew we would have to exhume the body at some stage. I had suggested to my dad that we would hold off the funeral on the Tuesday and get a second opinion. The undertaker, who was a personal friend of my father felt that it would be very unfair. It would be better to go ahead with the funeral as planned and to look at ways of having the body exhumed, so we went with that.

On the Sunday when he was going to the football field, Aidan drove right through the checkpoint. He parked his car on the northern side, down at the housing estate. The housing estate is called Coronation Park; despite this, it is mostly a nationalist community. Aidan had the keys when he was shot, so we didn't have access to the car. It was right underneath the nose of the sanger at the checkpoint, so we were happy enough to let the car sit there until after the funeral. But, whenever we came back in from the funeral on the Tuesday evening, one of the neighbours down in Coronation Park asked me what we had done with Aidan's car. I said, 'It's still sitting down there'. He said, 'Eilish, I hate to tell you this, but the car is gone'. So we immediately rang the RUC station in Aughnacloy and they said, 'We know nothing about your brother's car'. I phoned Eamon Mallie at Downtown Radio in Belfast and told him about the missing car. I also phoned the RUC and reported the car stolen. The RUC told Downtown that the CID in Dungannon had taken the car in for its own safety. They had gone to the morgue in Craigavon from Dungannon, took the keys of Aidan's car, waited til we were all out at the funeral and they had slipped in when they knew there was no-one in the houses at Coronation Park, because everyone had gone to the funeral, and stole the car without anyone's knowledge. As far as we are concerned, there are two reasons why they took the car: one was that they had Aidan's car bugged and they wanted to get the bugging devices out of it; or they were looking for some supporting theory to say why Aidan had been shot, to plant something or do something to blacken his name. The residents in the housing estate had foiled it by noticing that the car had gone missing.

On the Sunday night when dad and I came back to the house, there was a lot of media outside and I thought, 'What callous bastards!' Some of them walked over to ask if the family were going to talk to them. I just walked on up to the house past them. One of Aidan's friends stepped out and said, 'Eilish, who is going to tell Aidan's story?' That is when our campaign started. The parish priest that Aidan had made complaints to about the harassment and who had gone to the army on Aidan's behalf was in the house and I had to get him to tell the media that Aidan had been in touch with him about the harassment. I had to prove to them that Aidan has been harassed. The onus was on me to prove it, not on the security forces to own up and say why they had done it. It was for me to prove beyond a shred of a doubt that this harassment had taken place.

So, for us the campaign started on the very day that Aidan was shot. We had no time to stop and think of the loss of our brother, what Aidan felt in his last few seconds, what it was like for him to take his last breath of fresh air. You were thinking that these people were getting away with this. They are telling lies; they are denying Aidan justice; they are denying us a voice. So you just had to challenge it there and then; we didn't have a choice.

On the Wednesday a high-ranking member of the Garda was commissioned to go down to Monaghan Garda station and carry out an investigation there. There were a lot of people who had evidence that they didn't want to give to the security forces in the North. They had no confidence in the RUC or the legal system, so they said they would go up and give it to the commissioner in the South. The Irish government took all these statements from those people. My dad and I went down the week before Easter 1998 to meet them and we pleaded with them to hand us over the information in relation to Aidan's case, and they still haven't handed us anything.

On the following Saturday the Irish government rang and told our solicitor that they were granting our request to have Aidan's body exhumed for us to get our own independent doctor for a second autopsy. The state pathologist in the South, Dr Harbinson, would carry out the second autopsy in Monaghan hospital the next morning. We were glad that it was going to be quick rather that have to do it in a month or two.

I suppose one of the things I regret in the campaign is going ahead and allowing the state pathologist in the South to carry out the second autopsy on Aidan's body. When the pathologist was carrying out the autopsy, our solicitor stayed the whole time. We were allowed to have our own doctor there. The army's third statement said that a soldier had been cleaning a gun, the gun was loaded and the trigger accidentally slipped and discharged a round. One of the bullets hit the road, bounced up and hit Aidan in the back. Dr Harbinson carried out his autopsy and his report agreed that it wasn't a ricochet that hit Aidan—it was a straight entry and exit wound—and that Aidan had been walking away from the checkpoint but he wasn't shot in the back; he was shot in the chest and the exit wound was out through the back. To this day they argue with us that it was the other way around. We have gone through this time and time again. With Aidan that day there was practically no blood; it was a clean, pin-sharp wound right through and it exited at an angle going down to the lower part of the back. The exit wound was slightly more rugged and slightly more wide that what the entry wound was and the entry wound wasn't much bigger than a pin hole. We have been told that a ricochet bullet would have been tumbling at a fair rate. It would have torn through the body. There would have been a very big wound and the exit wound would have been even greater. But there wasn't that amount of damage done; it just went straight through Aidan's chest and killed him instantly. Our GP told me that Aidan didn't even breathe after the bullet hit him; he just went down instantly with it. That is something that I try to figure out in my head: how instant is instantly? Aidan was facing the checkpoint when he was hit, even though he was walking away from it, so we think someone must have called 'Aidan', or that something must have caught his attention and he turned round. They have denied that as well.

Dr Harbinson told us he could not be one hundred per cent conclusive; from the entry and exit wound he knew it wasn't a ricochet but he needed part of the rib cage to be conclusive. But that part of Aidan's ribcage was missing. They had actually taken part of Aidan's ribcage from the autopsy they had carried out in the North and retained it. Our solicitor wrote off immediately to the Northern Ireland Office to ask for the clothes that Aidan was wearing, the missing part of the ribcage and the photographs that were taken on the day.

We were told that the part of the ribcage had been destroyed. We then decided to bring in Keith Boer, a ballistics expert from England. The army closed ranks. He wasn't allowed to look at the gun, the sanger; they wouldn't allow him into the hut; they wouldn't allow him to take photographs of the vicinity. They did everything they could to prevent him from carrying out his own investigations. But one of the things he came up with was that it was possible that Aidan wasn't shot from the checkpoint at all, that he may have been shot from the hill overlooking the football field.

There was an awful lot of media coverage around the autopsy and Keith Boer's report. We started to campaign right away with the Irish government. We made contact with people in the US as well. We wrote letters to TDs, wrote letters to MPs. It's a big campaign for a family to take on. When you look back and think what you did accomplish at that time and what you were like psychologically at the time, you were going round like a zombie. But when I think of it now, nothing else mattered to me, Aidan's story had to be told and that was important; it's still important.

We demanded a meeting with Charlie Haughey. Brian Lenihan agreed to meet us in Iveagh House. He said he had news for us, that Dr Harbinson was invited down to meet Dr Carson in Belfast and that Dr Carson produced the missing ribcage. He said, 'I know that the pathologist's report seems conclusive, but he did change his mind when he saw the ribcage'. I went ballistic. I asked how could they do that without our solicitor or GP being told. How did he do that without any of us being there? How do we know what he showed him? One thing I regret was allowing Dr Harbinson to put his hands on Aidan's body. I'm sorry we didn't go for someone international. All we wanted was the truth, not lies or anything false. He changed his mind. I feel I let the family down on that one. Looking back on it now, the way they behaved over the harassment and the way Aidan was arrested in the South—when you look at what the Irish government have been involved in over the years, probably it wasn't the right thing to do.

I told Brian Lenihan that there was a high-ranking member of the Irish army driving through the checkpoint when the shooting happened. 'He made a statement to you. Could we have his statement and the other people's statements? Even if you don't want to give us names, give us a copy of their statements.' That was July 1988. They write about every four weeks to tell us they are still working on it. The whole thing was a big cosmetic exercise.

Aidan's friends in the poultry factory downed tools and stood outside the court house in Monaghan with placards asking, 'Why Aidan? Why our friend?' They were putting demands on the Irish government. Plus the GAA; because Aidan was going to a Gaelic football match, Dr McLoftus, the president of the GAA, came to Aidan's funeral and called it murder. The cardinal of Ireland, Cardinal Ó Fiaich came to the funeral and called it murder. There was pressure mounted on the Irish government, but I'm afraid it was a cosmetic exercise carried out by the Irish government to take them off the hook at the time and to give the appearance that they were doing something in response to public demand.

Five years after Aidan's death, we were told there was an inquest taking place. We were told that the soldier in question wasn't going to be present and that the only other soldier compelled to give evidence had gone absent without leave and was unavailable. We asked our solicitor to pull out and the inquest went on without us. I think five years on we had had enough cosmetic exercises without participating in any more. It was painful and hurtful.

One thing that did come out of the inquest was that the soldier in his statement said he had been cleaning the weapon. His fingers were wet because he had been washing the walls of the sanger ten minutes earlier. As he was putting the gun back on the stand, his finger slipped and hit the trigger. From our own ballistics it came out, for you to hit the trigger of a gun of that calibre it takes nine pounds of pressure to discharge the gun. What kind of soldier would be cleaning a loaded gun? What kind of training was that? He made another statement saying he had observed Aidan walking out through the checkpoint. Aidan was a Gaelic football player and he played for Aughaloo. Of course the media all hit on it, that Aidan was on his way to play a football match. But Aidan had a leg injury and he wasn't going to play that day. So the soldier in his statement said he had observed Aidan coming down that day, park his car, get out of his car, reach into the car and take out his football bag. He said he observed Aidan going across the checkpoint with his football bag in his hand. Aidan never had a football bag. He wasn't going to play; he was only going to watch the match that day. They were running with what the media said and sticking to this accidental theory. How could he have seen Aidan take a football bag out of the car? Hideous lies, ridiculous! We have never had him in a witness box.

Relatives for Justice was set up in 1991. It has been the one group that has been a great support to me and our family. Before it was formed, you were on your own. We carried on with Relatives for Justice, working and lobbying to change the inquest system. I went along with Mark Thompson and Martin Finucane to the United Nations in Geneva. We have lobbied practically every group who have come over here. We made a submission to the UN's special rapporteur.

In 1993 a policeman came to our house and said he wanted to speak to my husband and myself. He told both of us to upgrade our own personal security, for army files on both of us had turned up in a loyalist house in East Belfast the day before. How long the files were missing, we don't know. I told him I was then going to apply for a personal firearm for protection. They told me they didn't think I would get one, but that they would go down and get me a form. They said, 'Don't worry', because they would drive up and down past the house. I said, 'The more I would see you up and down past my house, the more scared I would be'. We have never had an inquiry into that. The content of the files they had on myself and my husband, we have never known, but we were told it was extensive, including car registration numbers. The army came and photographed the whole front and back of our house one day when we were out. I just came back in and went to the kitchen window and there was a soldier standing outside with a camera in his hand. That was about six to eight months before they came to tell us about the missing files.

One thing that came out of the campaigning was, the only access Aidan had to get to work in Monaghan was the main checkpoint here in Aughnacloy. We had roads that were blocked here for years and years. The community came out and asked, 'Why are we driving through that permanent checkpoint at Aughnacloy when all our roads are blocked here?' The Border Roads Campaign was set up after that. That was the one very positive thing that people could actually do and it was a brilliant campaign. Every Sunday, men, women and children went out with spades, a camera or a flask of tea, or they just went out to show support, or they went out with a digger and physically reopened the roads. It was defiance. People drove over these wee roads for weeks on end and it was private. Nobody watched over them and took notes of when they were coming or going. The community right along the border were involved in it, both sides of the border. I remember this town before the border roads were closed off and I remember people coming in from the south as part of their daily routine. It was a brilliant campaign. People were out there offering their tractors and earth moving equipment, very expensive, which could have been confiscated, and people were prepared to risk so much for a wee bit of freedom. When the road was opened, you made a point of using it; if we had come through the checkpoint, even with the hassle, we would have got through quicker, but it was the defiance. The community spirit: that's the one thing they never can break.

I never felt like stopping or giving in. I was always scared for my children that they would do something on them but I was lucky in that in the years that I was campaigning the children were not old enough to be away from my side.

When I think of Aidan, I always have to go there to him on the road before I can remember him elsewhere. It was like a fairytale relationship, our family with Aidan. He was like the good Samaritan in the family. He was the single one. He always had time for the nieces and nephews. He was the babysitter in the family, the person who would call in and take you out for a drink when he thought you were down. He was the character, the perfect brother. He was also a very close friend. He had a very close relationship with our parents. Their lives revolved around him. They had dinner with him in the evenings. He took mum shopping every week.

People who knew Aidan knew the truth; no one can take that away. They can never take the truth from us, but it's important that there is a public acknowledgement from them to say that they have done wrong.

What I am still looking for twelve years on is the truth. We are looking for the people responsible for the murder of my brother to be accountable. We are looking for an acknowledgement for the hurt, suffering, grief and pain that they have brought on our family and the community. It's not a lot for them to do to own up for their responsibilities and wrongs. I can't move on, move past from where I am now until there is an acknowledgement from them. I don't trust them. I have no confidence in the system, no confidence in the state, the legal system and no confidence in the RUC. The only way I am going to be able to move on is for them to come clean and tell the truth about their wrongs. I know at this stage you are not going to have anyone prosecuted for Aidan's murder; I know and can accept that; the family can accept that. At this stage I am looking for an acknowledgement and accountability and the whole truth surrounding this case to be told.

13

MAIRÉAD FARRELL, DANIEL McCANN AND SEÁN SAVAGE
6 March 1988

Shot by SAS soldiers in Gibraltar

Mairéad Farrell (aged 31), Daniel McCann (aged 30) and Sean Savage (aged 23) were three members of a larger IRA unit who travelled to Spain in March 1988 and from there to Gibraltar. Their intended mission seems to have been to explode a car bomb at the changing of the guard ceremony at Ince's Hall in Main Street, Gibraltar. The ceremony took place every Tuesday. On Sunday 6 March at 2.30 p.m. the three drove to near the Spanish border in a red Ford Fiesta. Farrell and McCann were seen by British Intelligence operatives as they crossed the border on foot. Savage drove a white Renault and parked it in the area where the military ceremony was to occur two days later. The three were seen in the vicinity of the car during the next hour. They then headed back towards the Spanish border on foot. After they had gone about a mile, Savage separated from the other two and turned back. Shortly afterwards a Gibraltar policeman sounded a siren on his car. As Farrell and McCann turned, two SAS men who had been following them closely opened fire, killing them instantly. Almost immediately, other SAS men fired on Savage. It was 3.42 p.m.

According to the post-mortem report, Mairéad Farrell was shot first in the face. As she fell, she twisted round and was then shot three times in the back from a distance of three to six feet. Her heart was cut to pieces and she died of internal haemorrhaging. Daniel McCann died from two gunshot wounds to the back and two to the head. Seán Savage was hit by 16 to 18 bullets, and had 27 wounds, five of which were in the back and five in the head. The cause of death was given as extensive brain damage. At the inquest, Professor Watson, who had carried out the post-mortem, agreed with the

155

lawyer for the IRA members' families, Paddy McGrory in his assessment of the death of Savage: 'Yes, I can concur. I do not like to use unscientific terms but it was like a frenzied attack I would say'.

The Gibraltar killings set off a chain of traumatic events during the following days. There was great difficulty arranging for the transport of the bodies of the three IRA people, but they were finally flown to Dublin on 13 March 1988. The funeral cortege was accompanied to the border by the Gardai and then handed over to the RUC. It was delayed as it travelled through the North, not least by harassment in loyalist areas it passed through. But finally the bodies were brought to their respective family homes for wakes. British troops patrolled near those homes. On the evening of 14 March, an IRA man—Kevin McCracken, aged 31—was preparing to open fire on British troops in the vicinity of the home of Seán Savage as the wake got underway. He was intercepted by British soldiers and shot dead.

The funeral of the three IRA members took place on 16 March. As the coffins were being lowered into the ground, a loyalist, Michael Stone, attacked with grenades and pistols. A crowd of mourners chased him towards the nearby motorway and as they did so, he killed three—Thomas McErlean (aged 20), John Murray (aged 26) and Kevin Brady (Caoimhin Mac Bradaigh, aged 30).

At the funeral of Kevin Brady on 19 September, two British army corporals—Derek Wood (aged 24) and David Howes (aged 23)—in plain clothes and driving a civilian car—drove at speed towards the hearse. Unaware at first that they were British soldiers, and fearing instead another Stone-type attack on a republican funeral, the mourners stopped the car and dragged the two armed occupants from it in full view of the media. The IRA arrived on the scene and concluded that the two British soldiers were SAS men. They drove the corporals to waste ground a few hundred yards away and shot them dead. Thirty four people were later charged with offences resulting from the incident, two of whom were jailed for life. None of those charged or sentenced was directly involved in the shooting of the soldiers.

All three IRA members killed in Gibraltar were from West Belfast. Mairéad Farrell had joined the IRA in the mid-1970s, on one occasion citing Bloody Sunday as a key influence on her decision. In October 1976 she was arrested following a bomb attack on a hotel in which another IRA man, Sean McDermott, was shot dead. A third member of the unit, Kieran Doherty, died on hunger strike in 1981. Mairéad Farrell received a 14 year sentence, the first woman to be jailed after the loss of political status which resulted from the criminalisation policy of the British government. Serving her sentence in Armagh Jail, she became the OC of the republican women prisoners there and later went on hunger strike in 1980 for 19 days seeking the reinstatement of political status. During the republican hunger strike by male prisoners in Long Kesh prison in 1981, she stood unsuccessfully as a candidate in the general election in the Republic. She was released in 1986 and was a student of Politics at Queen's University, Belfast at the time of her death.

Daniel McCann had joined the IRA as a teenager and had experienced a number of terms in prison. In 1979 he was sentenced to two years for possession of a detonator and participated in the 'no wash' protest in Long Kesh. In 1982 he was held on remand for a time on the word of a 'supergrass' (informer), but was released when the 'supergrass' retracted. Seán Savage had also been held for a month in 1982 on the basis of 'supergrass' evidence, but had no convictions. All three were clearly committed and able republican activists who were chosen for a highly important bombing mission.

It would appear that British intelligence became aware of the possibility of such a mission as early as November 1987. Co-ordination of the British counter-operation rested with the Joint Intelligence Committee of the Cabinet. That Committee had representation from all the agencies with a stake in the operation, including MI5, MI6, the Foreign Office, the Northern Ireland Office and the Ministry of Defence. Members of the IRA team—which may have numbered six or more members—were tailed on a number of reconnaissance trips to Spain and Gibraltar. Finally, in February 1988, when it became fully obvious what their plans were, a decision was taken by Prime Minister Margaret Thatcher, Foreign Secretary Geoffrey Howe and Defence Secretary George Younger to use the SAS against the IRA unit.

First reports were of 'a fierce gun battle' and the defusing of a 500 pound bomb. It soon became clear that the three were unarmed. Moreover, although there was indeed a car containing 140 pounds of semtex and 200 rounds of ammunition; it was later found in an underground garage in Marbella by Spanish police on 8 March. The parked car in Gibraltar was merely holding the space until closer to the time of the changing of the guard ceremony. Despite the revelation of these 'errors' in the initial official pronouncements, the British authorities continued to stick to the spirit of the defence of their actions. It was said that a brief examination of the parked car in Gibraltar led Intelligence operatives to believe that it did contain a bomb which was to be activated by one of a number of possible remote control devices carried by each of the IRA members. Once the move to apprehend them began, it was necessary to immobilise the IRA members as quickly as possible before they could detonate the bomb.

There was a certain plausibility in this explanation. On the other hand, there was a number of worrying questions which were soon raised by intelligent investigative journalists, including those working for the Thames Television series 'This Week'.

- Why did the examination of the parked car in Gibraltar by British Intelligence operatives only take two minutes?
- Why, despite such a cursory examination, was the word passed to the SAS that the car did in fact contain a bomb?
- Why did no one see, as any bomb disposal expert could have seen instantly, that a car containing 500 pounds of explosives would obviously have been loaded down with such a weight?
- Why, if these operatives believed that the car contained a bomb, was the area not cleared until 7 p.m., over three hours after the killing?

- Why did anyone with expert intelligence of bombs believe that a bomb in the car could have been detonated by remote control from a distance of one mile, despite the presence of a large number of buildings as obstacles?
- Why weren't the three—two of whom had been under unbroken surveillance by Spanish and then British and Gibraltarian forces since long before they crossed over from Spain—not arrested as they entered Gibraltar?
- Why was the operation to apprehend the IRA members signed over solely to the SAS, thereby being taken completely out of the hands of the local authorities?
- Why did the SAS men carry no handcuffs or other means of restraining three people they regarded as 'dangerous terrorists' whom they were supposedly about to arrest?
- Why was there no medical officer in the large pool of police and soldiers involved in the operation?
- Why, despite copious evidence of careful and intricate planning, was there no ambulance on standby in case of injuries?

The clear implication of all of this was that there was never any intention to arrest the three. Employing the services of the SAS was the clearest indication of that. As Paddy McGrory, the families' solicitor, put it during the inquest, the SAS 'is a highly-trained and motivated attack force which is wholly unsuited to arrest procedures'. Or as Jack Mitchell, father-in-law of Mairéad Farrell's brother Niall, put it in his epic poem, *Gib: A Modest Exposure*:

> *How do we know the intention was*
> *To shoot to kill? We know because*
> *The SAS, to put it straight,*
> *Is that intention incarnate.*

None of this came through in the MOD version of events which was the basis of Geoffrey Howe's cover-up in parliament. He said that when the three IRA people were challenged, 'they made movements which led the military personnel operating in support of the Gibraltar police to conclude that their own lives were under threat. In the light of this response, they were shot dead'. This was to remain the official explanation up to and including the inquest.

The possibility of disclosure of the truth was lessened by a number of other factors. The SAS operatives were flown out of Gibraltar before they could be interviewed by local police. They only made statements a few days later in England. The police investigation of the scene of the incident was far from professional. Many spent bullet cases went unaccounted, and key eye witnesses—such as Carmen Proetta—were not located by the police but by researchers for the Thames Television programme, 'Death on the Rock' (broadcast on 28 April 1988). The forensic evidence, the importance of which could prove crucial in the forthcoming inquest, was poorly put together. Professor Alan Watson, the crown pathologist, pointed out at the inquest that he was not allowed to see ballistic reports, nor even the results of the blood and urine tests he himself had sent for analysis; the clothes had been removed from the bodies before his examination, thus lessening his ability to make accurate judgements about bullet wounds.

Relatives of the three dead IRA people called for an independent inquiry—an option later supported after the inquest by groups such as Amnesty International, the International Association of Democratic Lawyers, Liberty, and Inquest—but this was was given short shrift by the British authorities. In the absence of an independent inquiry, the inquest became the only possible forum in which disclosure of the truth might possibly occur. However, the odds were stacked against the inquest being such a forum.

To begin with, the very culture of Gibraltar itself militated against a cool and objective consideration of the facts. It is a tight-knit, conservative colony in which few would have any sympathy for the fate that befell those who came to plant a bomb there. And yet it was from this community that the jurors were selected, senior civil servants among them. Local eye-witnesses had little room to hide in such a claustrophobic atmosphere. Carmen Proetta, who had told 'Death on the Rock' that she had seen Farrell and McCann raise their hands in either surprise or surrender before being shot, and who stuck to her position at the inquest, was the subject of a particularly virulent campaign of vilification which spread to the British press. She was titled 'The Tart of Gib' by the *Sun*, and in less emotive but equally malicious terms, the *Times* too 'revealed' that she was a prostitute. Proetta later won five libel actions against British papers. Kenneth Asquez, another eye-witness, told 'Death on the Rock' that he had seen a man, later revealed to be Seán Savage, injured on the ground; a soldier with a foot on Savage's chest fired into his body from point blank range. Asquez later retracted that most damning part of his evidence in court. His reason for doing so was directly connected to the threatening phone calls he received on his telephone with its ex-directory number.

At the inquest itself Public Interest Immunity Certificates were enforced. The effect of these was to prevent investigation of events before 4 March, as well as to curtail cross-examination of the seven SAS men who gave their evidence from behind screens. Witness statements were given in advance to the government lawyers but not to lawyers for the families of the dead. In addition, the Coroner, Felix Pizzarello, decided the order in which the witnesses appeared, thus further reducing the possibility of a coherent picture emerging. The important forensic evidence was reserved for late in the proceedings when its earlier revelation would undoubtedly have helped in questioning. Finally, the cost of the transcripts of the inquest was increased from 50 pence to £5 per page; the daily cost of acquiring a complete transcript amounted to between £500 and £700. Paddy McGrory, the lawyer representing the families of the dead, was handed the almost impossible task of questioning witnesses from such a disadvantaged position.

The SAS defence rested on a number of points.

- The three IRA people were not arrested as they entered Gibraltar because the Spanish police had lost sight of them temporarily at a crucial point; this was consistently denied by the Spanish.

– Because of this temporary loss of surveillance, it was not unreasonable to believe that the car driven by Savage contained a bomb.

– They were convinced that the bomb was to be detonated by a radio signal.

– They were also convinced that the three were armed.

When the siren from the Gibraltar police car was inexplicably sounded, the three 'dangerous and armed terrorists' were alerted. Quick and decisive action was therefore necessary before they could open fire or detonate the bomb. McCann, for example, according to Soldier A who shot him, 'moved aggressively... It looked as though he was definitely going for the button'.

For his part, Paddy McGrory's task was to question whether their alleged beliefs were indeed reasonable and also to introduce opposing factual evidence from eye-witnesses. He attempted to convince the jury that:

– Given the cursory examination of the car, it was not reasonable to conclude that it contained a bomb; the much more likely explanation was that it was a blocking car, left in place until the car with the bomb was brought in at a later date.

– There was no evidence to support the supposition that the alleged bomb would be detonated by remote control, a method unlikely to work in the built-up area of Gibraltar.

– There were no warnings given before the shooting began, or if there were, as Soldier B maintained, they were, in his words, 'probably useless'.

– As a number of civilian witnesses testified, Farrell and McCann had their hands in the air when shot.

– There was clear eye-witness evidence that Savage in particular was 'finished off' as he lay on the ground.

– Overall, there was no indication that the SAS had ever intended to arrest the suspects.

On the other hand, there was a question which remained unanswered: why kill them so publicly? One theory advanced was that the SAS were expecting the IRA unit on Tuesday. They had everything in place to trap the unit in the act of planting the bomb. They were caught off guard by the unexpected appearance of the three on Sunday—three members of an IRA unit and no bomb, only a blocking car in the place where the bomb was to be placed later. As the IRA members walked back towards the border, the realisation occurred that perhaps they would not return; perhaps they had sensed the extensive surveillance operation. As *Observer* journalist Ian Jack put it: 'An enormous effort, which had received the highest government sanction, would have been thrown away'. So the trap was sprung before they reached the border. Everything else—the bomb in the car, the button, the armed terrorists—was a smokescreen to hide the conspiracy.

On 30 September 1998, the 11-person jury deliberated for eight hours. For the first six of those hours three of the jury maintained that all three IRA members had been killed unlawfully. A fourth juror believed that Savage only had been killed unlawfully. Consequently, they returned to ask the Coroner's advice as regards returning an open verdict. Pizzarello urged them to avoid this, even though such a verdict was allowable. He also reprimanded them for the amount of time they were taking. During the next two hours, the juror who believed that Seán Savage had been killed unlawfully and one of the jurors who believed all three had been killed unlawfully changed their minds. Finally, a verdict of 9 to 2 in favour of lawful killing in all three cases was returned.

The families and their solicitors now turned their attention to the European Commission on Human Rights. Attempts to have the Irish government take a case on their behalf failed, so they moved independently. They argued that their domestic remedies had been exhausted—a precondition to consideration by the Commission—through the unsatisfactory inquest. Their claim was that Britain had contravened Article 2 of the European Convention on Human Rights, the right to life. On 6 September 1991, the Commission decided to investigate the shootings. It was 6 June 1994 before they released their conclusion: the British government had not contravened Article 2. On the other hand, the Commission chose to refer the case to the European Court of Human Rights for a final deliberation. Finally, on 27 September 1995, by a 10 to 9 majority, the smallest margin possible, the European Court found the British government guilty of contravening Article 2 of the Convention.

A statement from Downing Street concluded that the European Court judgement 'defied common sense'. Defence Secretary Michael Heseltine called it 'incomprehensible' and continued: 'If we were faced with similar circumstances as those in Gibraltar, I have not the slightest doubt that the same decisions would be taken again.' And the British press rushed to display jingoistic support for the Conservative government. The *Daily Express* called the judgement 'A verdict that insults us all', while the *Sun*, in its own inimitable fashion, punned: 'Off Eur Rockers'.

The Court exonerated the individual SAS men who had carried out the killings. It rejected the claim of the families' lawyers that the killings were premeditated. And, while agreeing to pay partial costs and expenses, it refused to pay compensation to the families. But there was no escaping the tremendous victory involved in the relatives winning support from the European Court of Human Rights, at least partially, for their interpretation of what happened in Gibraltar. It was the first time ever that a member country had been found guilty of violation of Article 2.

Niall Farrell, brother of Mairéad, now tells the story of his sister's death and the subsequent campaign.

Niall Farrell

*No one should be above the law, and that includes those who carried out
the killings and those who gave the orders. People think I'm daft when I
say Thatcher should be prosecuted for killing my sister, but why not? The
Spanish Minister of the Interior found himself in jail for a similar crime
and as we talk, Pinochet is in the dock. So why not Thatcher?*

On Sunday the sixth of March 1988 at 3.41 p.m. my sister Mairéad Farrell
and a companion Dan McCann were shot dead in Gibraltar. Seconds
later, Seán Savage, who was approximately 100 metres behind them, was
also gunned down. The killings were carried out by members of the British
Army's elite regiment the SAS.

While all three were on 'active service' for the IRA at the time of their deaths
they were all unarmed. They were in Gibraltar planning an attack against British
army personnel. Since November of the previous year, both the British and
Spanish authorities had been aware that such an attack was being planned. And
on March 6th the three had been closely followed by the Spanish police as they
travelled in two separate vehicles to Gibraltar from Marbella. The Spanish police
have stated since the killings that they informed their British counterparts that all
three were unarmed and were not in possession of any explosive devices.

At 12.30 p.m. Seán Savage drove into Gibraltar in a white Renault 5 car.
Indeed, he entered the colony using a passport in the name of Coyne, which was
known to the authorities. He parked the car in a parking area where, on the
following Tuesday, a British army band was to assemble. He did all this under the
watchful eye of the British military. My sister and Dan McCann crossed the
border at 2.30 p.m. and met Seán Savage near the parked car. They then set out
to return to Spain, with Dan McCann and Mairéad walking together. Seán Savage
who was following behind them, turned at a road junction and walked back again
in the direction of the town centre, away from the border.

As the pair passed a petrol station, a police siren sounded and they turned to see
at least two armed SAS soldiers in plain clothes approach them. According to one
of the principal independent witnesses, Carmen Proetta, who lives in a flat
overlooking the garage, both Dan and Mairéad raised their hands in surrender.
Despite that, the soldiers opened fire. Carmen Proetta was discovered not by the
police but by a researcher working for Thames Television which was making a
programme on the shootings entitled 'Death on the Rock'. Ms Proetta told
Thames TV that the soldiers opened fire without warning.

Another independent witness, Stephen Bullock, who was 150 yards from the
shooting, saw Dan McCann falling backwards with his hands at shoulder height.
The gunman was about four feet away. At the inquest into the killings Mr.
Bullock, a lawyer by profession, said that with one step the gunman could have
actually touched the person he was shooting.

Both Carmen Proetta and Stephen Bullock gave further evidence, along with a third witness, Josie Celecia, whose flat faces the petrol station, that the soldiers fired on Dan McCann and my sister as they lay on the ground.

The scientific evidence presented by the pathologist, Professor Alan Watson, at the inquest corroborated this evidence. Mairéad had been killed by three bullets fired into her back at a distance of a few feet; all of the wounds were within two and half inches of each other. The upward trajectory of the bullets meant that the gunman was either kneeling and shooting upwards or that my sister was on the ground or close to it when these shots were fired. Mairéad died from gunshot wounds to the heart and liver. She also had head wounds, but these were superficial. Professor Watson believed she had first been shot in the face and then in the back. In other words, even after being shot in the face, Mairéad was still alive and could have been arrested. In total she was shot eight times.

The pathologist further believed that Dan McCann had been first shot in the jaw. This had stunned him and then the lethal shots were fired when he was down or very far down. Dan had two entry bullet wounds in his back which were again close together. The trajectory of the bullets were also upward. He had an entry bullet wound at the top left back of his head, which also strongly suggests he was on the ground when this shot was fired.

At the time Mairéad and Dan were shot Seán Savage was walking in the opposite direction towards the town centre. He was being followed by two members of the SAS who said they were only five or six feet behind Seán when the shots that killed Mairéad and Dan rang out. According to the soldiers, Seán spun round at this point and one of the soldiers claimed to shout a warning and then proceeded to open fire; the second soldier then followed suit.

There were three independent witnesses to this shooting. Diana Treacy told the inquest that she saw two men running towards her. After she was passed by the first one, who was Seán Savage, the second man, who had a gun, opened fire. She saw this same gunman fire up to five shots into Seán as he lay on the ground.

Another independent witness was a British holiday-maker, Mr Robyn Mordue. In the commotion of the shooting he was knocked to the ground when a woman on a bicycle collided with him. He thought there was a madman on the rampage, as he saw a man who had been walking towards him being shot again and again. He got up and ran behind a car where he was sick. Mr. Mordue was a very nervous witness. He had reason to be. Before the inquest his identity was only known by the authorities. Nevertheless, in the weeks leading up to the inquest he received a number of threatening phone calls: 'Bastard... stay away'. Mr Mordue's telephone number is ex-directory.

Kenneth Asquez was the third witness to this killing. He had alleged in two statements to Thames TV—one hand-written and the other before a lawyer, but all unsigned in order to hide his identity—that he saw a man with his foot on Seán Savage's chest, firing at him at point blank range. At the inquest he decided to retract this statement. However, Asquez's retraction must be treated with scepticism. As the hand-written statement said, the man with his foot on Seán's chest was wearing a black beret and the shooting had been prefaced by the shout, 'Stop, it's okay; it's the police.' In fact, one of the soldiers who shot Seán had donned a black beret and the shooting had been prefaced with these words. But until the inquest these two facts had not been publicised. At the inquest many observers believed that Kenneth Asquez had also been put under pressure by those who feared the truth.

The scientific evidence produced by Professor Watson was damning. He believed that between 16 and 18 bullets had hit Seán. Seán had twenty nine wounds in what the pathologist described as 'a frenzied attack'. He had seven head wounds; five of them were presumed to be entry wounds. Our lawyer, Mr Paddy McGrory, showed Professor Watson at the inquest a photograph taken by the police of four circled strike marks within the outline of Seán's head. This was the first time the pathologist had seen this photograph. He was asked by our lawyer whether it seemed as though these four shots had been fired into Seán's head as he lay on the ground. Professor Watson replied: 'Yes, that would be reasonable.'

The role of the police in investigating these three killings must be questioned. In the case of Seán Savage's death the inquest was told that there were some thirty people who saw the shooting. However, there were only three independent witnesses found and two of them were discovered by the media. The same was true for witnesses to the shooting of my sister and Dan McCann. The police failed, for example, to set up the customary incident centres in the vicinity of the killings.

There is in police methodology a universal principle known as the preservation of the scene of the crime. It was applied sparingly in Gibraltar on that day. Within minutes of the killings, the police had ensured that it would be extremely difficult to reconstruct the killings. Spent cartridges were collected without first marking where they had been found. The bodies were removed without first photographing them in situ. The bodies of Mairéad and Dan McCann were not chalked around. And the killers were not interviewed by the police until two weeks afterwards.

The systematic disruption of routine procedures continued. The pathologist, Professor Watson, was not given the normal cooperation. The hospital had an X-ray machine, which he needed to trace the track of the bullets through the bodies, but it was not put at his disposal. The clothing had already been removed; torn fabric can help determine entry and exit wounds, while the spread of blood stains could indicate whether the three were upright or prone when they were shot. The photographs taken in the morgue were inadequate, the police photographer not being under Professor Watson's supervision at the time. He was not supplied with surgical assistance. Subsequently he was not given any copies of the ballistic and forensic reports, nor the reports on the blood samples he had submitted in London on his return to Britain.

The forensic scientist, David Pryor of the London Metropolitan Police, was also hampered in his work. The blood-soaked clothes had been sent to him in bags. He said that the clothing was in such a condition when he received it that accurate determination of which was an entry site and which an exit was very difficult.

March 6th was a Sunday. We'd been out that day and on returning home, I'd looked at the headlines on the teletext and noticed that there had supposedly been a shoot-out on Gibraltar. I wondered to myself what would ETA be doing there. Around 7 p.m. I got the answer. A call from my family in Belfast informed me that Mairéad had been shot dead. The next day I travelled from Galway to Belfast. Naturally we were all in a state of shock. But as little bits of the truth began to emerge, it was clear that they had been murdered.

It was going to take a long time before the bodies were to return to Ireland. They were murdered on the 6th and weren't buried until the 16th of March.

A brother of mine had to go over to identify the bodies along with Joe Austin of Sinn Féin. While there, my brother was arrested on a trumped-up charge of not having paid a hotel bill in Spain ten years previously. Eventually the charge was dropped. It was blatant harassment.

There were major difficulties getting the bodies back. No British Airways plane would take them and the airport staff were refusing to load their remains on to any plane. The republican movement tried to charter an aircraft, but Aer Lingus, Ryan Air and GPA refused. GPA, based in Shannon, would go to Ulan Bator for business, but not for three Irish dead in Gibraltar.

Eventually a plane was chartered from a non-Irish company to fly to Dublin, as we couldn't get permission to land at Aldergrove near Belfast. Seán Barrett of Fine Gael called on Haughey not to allow the remains to be flown into Dublin. I often wondered what he wanted to be done with the bodies—dropped in the ocean? Haughey ignored the ravings of the Blueshirt and the remains of the three arrived back in Dublin Airport from where they'd left on their fatal mission to Gibraltar.

I travelled with two aunts to meet the remains in Dublin. We then drove back to the border. All along the route the streets were lined with people. Garda even saluted the cortege as it passed; and to think that the Special Branch and C3 of the Garda were totally involved in the whole Gibraltar affair! It took hours to traverse Dundalk, as the coffins were carried through the streets of the town. The next leg of the journey from the border onwards was one we all faced with trepidation.

While we were making our slow journey North, something more chilling was to happen. The first of six to die on the streets of West Belfast in the aftermath of the Gib murders was killed. Kevin Mc Cracken, an IRA member, was shot dead by British soldiers.

Confrontation was awaiting the cortege at the border. The RUC demanded the tricolours be removed from the coffins. This caused problems for Jenny McGeever, a journalist working for RTE's 'Morning Ireland'. The next day she broadcast the voice of Martin McGuinness as he simply explained to journalists what the problem was. RTE's Section 31 prohibited the broadcasting of the voice of any member of Sinn Féin. For contravening RTE's most sacred of cows the journalist was dismissed. Naturally, her colleagues did not support her.

On crossing the border the hearses were surrounded by RUC Land Rovers. It meant the RUC could dictate the speed we travelled at. Every time we passed a loyalist protest, the cortege was reduced to a snail's pace, making us easy targets for the stone-throwing mobs.

At the M1 the RUC hijacked the hearses. The relatives were in three or four cars along with some of Sinn Féin's leaders. Of the convoy of cars, only these were allowed onto the motorway. There, blocked in by hundreds of RUC jeeps, we were held for a number of hours. The passengers in the other cars were subjected to extreme verbal abuse and threats. My aunts and myself, whether by accident or design, were virtually ignored. It was, nevertheless, a frightening experience.

Afterwards Mr Savage, who had been accompanied by Gerry Adams, expressed to me his shock at what had been said to him by the RUC. I wasn't unfamiliar with what passes for community policing in the North. A couple of days after the murders in Gibraltar Seamus Finucane—Mairéad's boyfriend—and I were stopped by the RUC outside Andersonstown barracks. The cop said to Seamus, 'Well, you won't be fucking Mairéad anymore'. All sorts of other vile comments were uttered. Afterwards, I made an official complaint, but as usual with the complaints procedure, nothing happened.

Even before the remains had returned to Ireland there were dire threats from the RUC of how they would physically prevent the display of any paramilitary trappings at the funeral; only the tricolour would be permitted. When the RUC returned the coffins to the three homes, there was no military presence around our house and not so much at the home of Seán. But Dan McCann's home was surrounded by soldiers and Saracens. Harassment was a feature of that family's life for years to come.

On the morning of the funeral we had expected a heavy RUC presence, just like at Larry Marley's funeral, but that wasn't the case. There was something uncanny about this. As the hearses moved three abreast down the road towards Milltown Cemetery, I kept expecting one of the parked cars we passed to explode. Then, as we literally buried our dead, that bigoted lunatic attacked. And those three young men were murdered and many more injured. The names of the dead should be remembered: Thomas McErlean, Caoimhin Mac Bradaigh and John Murray. Nor should the grief their families have suffered be forgotten either.

The attacker of the funeral must have had inside information. He knew there would be no RUC presence. There was a white Transit van parked on the motorway which borders the cemetery. As the killer made off in its direction, we all thought it was his getaway vehicle. In actual fact it was a heavily armed unit of the RUC and they did not intervene.

Days later the two soldiers were killed at Caoimhin Mac Bradaigh's funeral and three innocent men were convicted of a crime they did not commit.

The inquest was supposed to take place three months after the event but it was delayed for six months. There was some bizarre excuse that it would clash with some tiny festival on that week. The real reason for the postponement was that Margaret Thatcher wanted to travel to Spain to meet her Spanish counterpart Gonzales and get his agreement that the Spanish government wouldn't offer any evidence at the inquest. Thatcher had a bargaining chip. The Spanish government wanted to join the EU but didn't necessarily want to join NATO. Thatcher believed that to be in one, a government had to be in the other. But she softened her stance; the quid pro quo was that no representative of the Spanish state would give evidence at the inquest in Gibraltar.

Unbeknownst to the world at that time, Gonzales' own government had been waging a secret, deadly war against Basque separatists. The Ministry of the Interior had actually set up death squads to murder Basque opponents. In fact the Spanish Interior Minister was later to go to prison for this policy. So one can presume that Thatcher on her visit to Madrid did get a sympathetic ear.

By the time the inquest was held, the British government had prepared what they saw as a credible story. Despite having publicly praised in the House of Commons the role of the Spanish police in the surveillance of the three, the British authorities began to claim that the Spanish had lost track of the three on March 6th and that their appearance in Gibraltar took the British security forces by surprise. The British authorities believed, the story goes, that the Renault 5 driven into Gibraltar by Seán Savage—supposedly unnoticed—was packed with explosives. On top of that, the security forces were convinced that the bomb was to be detonated by remote control. The soldiers claimed that the movements of the three seemed to indicate that they were about to use a 'button job', as they described it in tabloid-speak, and therefore had to be shot to death.

To back up the claim that the Spanish police had lost the three, the Gibraltar police tried to present a copy of an alleged statement from a Spanish police inspector, Rayo Valenzuela, supporting this line. Our lawyer objected to its admissibility as the police inspector who supposedly made it would not be attending the inquest and therefore would not be available for cross-examination. It now transpires that this document was totally fraudulent. Not only was the statement unsworn, but the English translation delivered to the coroner was not even signed.

Any attempt by our solicitor, Paddy McGrory, to probe into the surveillance operation was made impossible with the issuing of a Public Interest Immunity Certificate by the British government. Nevertheless, when the head of Gibraltar's Special Branch, Detective Chief Inspector Joseph Ullger, gave evidence, he admitted that the authorities had deliberately allowed the three to enter Gibraltar in order to gather evidence for a subsequent trial. It also became apparent that on March 6th a member of the Gibraltar police was present on the Spanish side of passport control with the aliases and passport numbers of the three.

The British gave no real evidence to back-up their claim that the notional bomb in the white Renault would be detonated by remote control. The only fact presented by Mr O, a senior British intelligence officer, was that an alleged IRA arms cache had been uncovered in Belgium and it had contained a remote control device. This had supposedly led the authorities to believe that the Gibraltar bomb would also be detonated in such a way. This has since been shown to have been a lie, because what made the Belgian police believe they had discovered an IRA cache was the fact that the devices for detonating the semtex were not of a remote control variety. The remote control detonating theory totally contradicted what 'official sources' told the BBC on the evening of Sunday March 6th, when they referred to a bomb that was 'timed' to kill British army bandsmen on the Tuesday. The following day the Minister of State for the Armed Forces, Mr Ian Stewart, repeated this point on the BBC's 'Today' programme.

The other argument put forward by Mr O to explain the flawed remote control theory was that the IRA wanted to ensure that there was not a repeat of the Enniskillen bombing in which many civilians were killed. This argument contradicts what the SAS soldiers who carried out the killings told the inquest, that the three had to be killed quickly in order to prevent them using the remote control detonator suddenly. If the IRA did not want to incur civilian casualties why would they detonate this notional bomb in a car on a Sunday afternoon when only civilians would be injured? Besides, it was scientifically proven at the inquest that the three could never have detonated any bomb supposedly in the Renault from where they were killed. If the authorities were so certain that there was a bomb in the car, why then did it take them several hours to make the area 'safe'? The probable answer to this question is that they simply did not think there was a bomb at all.

Nevertheless, according to the four killers, these three people, who were unarmed, did not have a bomb or possess any detonating devices, made threatening movements when they were approached by armed men. Why should they do such a foolish thing? The true answer to this question is that they didn't make any threatening movements.

The inquest itself, by its very nature, was not equipped to determine the truth. The British authorities had access prior to the inquest and during it to the identities of witnesses, their statements or possible statements and were to some extent able, on grounds of availability, to dictate the order of calling some witnesses. In contrast, our legal advisers had virtually no information except one ballistics report and a pathologist's report.

Amnesty International in its report expressed its concern that our legal representative was significantly and unfairly disadvantaged in comparison with the British government. They rightly argued that the system was inherently weighted against us in preparing for cross-examination because Paddy McGrory received the other forensic reports after the inquest began. He did not receive any of the witnesses' statements in advance, and even during the inquest, he did not receive the statements made by security force personnel shortly after the incident. Without access to these statements in advance, he was not able to cross-examine witnesses on the basis of what other witnesses, who testified at a later stage, said about the same incident.

Our lawyer faced numerous obstacles, including the fact that the price of the court's daily transcripts was increased from 50p to £5 per page. Because the price was so prohibitive, our lawyer could not avail of them—not so the British Ministry of Defence, who along with the SAS had a huge legal team. It should be remembered that Paddy McGrory did our case for free.

The use by the British government of Public Immunity Certificates prevented Paddy inquiring into many matters such as the planning of the operation, including the role of the 'accessories before the fact'.

Finally there was the coroner's summing up of the evidence to the jury, in which he told them to avoid an open verdict. By doing this he unduly influenced these eleven men. After six hours of discussion, the jury was deadlocked, divided 7 to 4 in favour of a 'lawful killing' verdict. In normal circumstances an open verdict would have been a likely compromise, but this had been ruled out. The coroner then recalled the jury and gave them what seemed like an ultimatum to return a verdict. Two hours later they returned stating that they found, by 9 to 2— the smallest majority allowed—the killings lawful.

Already in the first few days after the murder, as we waited for the bodies to be returned, I began to think of how we must work to expose what had happened, how we must achieve justice. I had been a member, since the early 1970s, of the Communist Party of Ireland and NICRA. And I certainly was not going to ignore the fact that the Brits murdered Mairéad. So I arranged to meet together with a few friends and comrades of mine and we discussed in general what we felt needed to be done. Nothing definite was decided, but what came up in this first discussion was that a campaign should be developed to persuade the Irish government to take up the case on the families' behalf and bring it to the European Court of Human Rights.

It would be wrong to suggest that I was the only person who saw the need for a campaign. Over those ten very long days I met friends and relatives of Dan, Seán and Mairéad who were of a like mind. And from around the period of the inquest an active group of friends began to meet regularly at Mrs Savage's to plan fundraising efforts, as well as ways to give the campaign a high profile.

People respond to killings in different ways. I responded in a political, campaigning way. Others have got involved in military campaigns and see—or saw—that as the way forward. I don't. I've no doubt, however, that the Gibraltar killings and their aftermath resulted in many people joining the Provos in reaction to the appalling carnage instigated by the British.

At the beginning of May 1988 the three families held our first press conference in Buswells Hotel in Dublin. It was really the first time we spoke to the media about the murders. We called on the Irish government to take the case to the Strasbourg Court—the point being that if the Irish government had taken the case, it would have meant going directly to Strasbourg without first exhausting the so-called domestic remedies. It would also have been a warning to the British that their shoot-to-kill policy would no longer be tolerated.

We also revealed at the press conference that we had received information from a sympathetic source inside the Irish state that Mrs Thatcher had presided over a secret sub-committee that had planned the Gibraltar killings. The *Irish Times* scoffed at the idea, but it proved to be true.

In 1989 at one of the regular support meetings it was proposed by Mrs Savage that we start a petition calling on the Dublin government to take up our case. Relatives and friends travelled around the North, setting up stalls in search of signatures. For my parents—my da in his mid-70s and my mother in her late 60s—this was not a first time experience. They had been on the petition trail during the jail crisis of the early 1980s.

Signatures were collected at numerous events and towns throughout the country. Meetings were held in the hope of arousing awareness. Many politicians and trade unionists offered their support. In particular, a number of political figures from Galway, Michael D. Higgins, Eamon Ó Cuiv and Seosamh Ó Cuaig were always helpful. So too were Brendan Ryan and Tony Gregory, both of whom were very active on the Gibraltar case. Brendan O'Neill of Cork, Proinsias Mac Aonghusa and of course Raymond Murray were all very helpful. The Gibraltar murders was the beginning of a long history of working with Raymond.

The 50,000 signatures were presented to the Department of Foreign Affairs on the 2nd anniversary of the killings. A protest was held outside Iveagh House as the petition was handed in. No assistance, however, was forthcoming from Haughey's government. The Department of Foreign Affairs responded to our criticism by issuing sarcastic statements suggesting that if our case was so watertight we should take it ourselves. Of course, we did and when we won there were surely a few unhappy Britophiles in Iveagh House that day in September '95.

The support group that met in the Savage's family home came up with another idea of producing a video, just like the Plastic Bullet Campaign had so successfully done. Unfortunately, the person commissioned proved to be a charlatan and stole from our support fund.

As the third anniversary of the killings approached, the shoot-to-kill policy of the British was continuing unabated. I felt it was time to bring together other victims' families for a protest over the Irish government's inaction outside Government Buildings in Dublin. With the assistance of Raymond Murray and Martin Finucane I made contact with the McKerrs, the Carahers, the McAnespies and many others. On March 6th 1991 we held a demonstration outside Haughey's palatial Government Buildings to demand action. A month later in a hall in Dungannon we formed Relatives For Justice [RFJ]. We began meeting on a regular basis in Raymond Murray's residence in Armagh.

It was an important step that we joined together. We were the forgotten victims, because our relatives had been killed directly or indirectly by the British state. We needed to unite to strengthen our call for justice. On a personal level it was also beneficial. I met with a lot of courageous people from throughout the North, people like the late Eleanor McKerr—a very brave and tenacious woman.

Part of our work was to overcome our exclusion by the establishment North and South. One step we took was to seek a meeting with President Mary Robinson. She had met a myriad of groups, including victims of IRA violence. However, when we wrote seeking a meeting to discuss our campaign for justice, she refused, citing 'constitutional constraints of her office' as justification.

We continued to lobby for a meeting and began to highlight publicly her inconsistencies; on a trip to the North, she, quite coorectly, laid a wreath at the memorial in Enniskillen in memory of those killed in the 1987 IRA bombing, but adamantly refused to do the same at the Bloody Sunday memorial in Derry when she visited that city. On the famous occasion that she shook hands with Gerry Adams in Andersonstown, she insisted that no relatives of victims of state violence should be invited. To their shame the organisers agreed to this stipulation. It would seem even in our own community we and the murder of our loved ones were expendable in the cause of political expediency.

Eventually in February 1995, Robinson did meet a huge delegation of victims of state violence from throughout the Six Counties as well as relatives of the Dublin-Monaghan bombings. But it was only after the IRA called a ceasefire. Nevertheless, it gave us a certain recognition and exposed the lack of veracity contained in her previous refusals.

It was through RFJ's contact with the CAJ that we came to hear of Douwe Korff, a barrister who specialises in human rights law. Douwe came to speak at a conference organised by the CAJ and met Paddy McGrory. Not long after that he became part of our legal team.

In the absence of the Irish government pursuing our case, we first had to exhaust the domestic legal remedies, then the way would be open to take our case to Strasbourg. That meant taking a civil action seeking damages from the British for the killing of all three. The talk of compensation caused great annoyance to my parents—nothing could have compensated us for our loss. But this was the route we had to pursue to get to Strasbourg.

Statements of claim were lodged in Belfast's High Court on March 1st 1990, almost two years to the day of the murders. Two weeks later the British issued certificates barring the proceedings on the basis that the killings had occurred in Gibraltar, not in the so-called UK. Paddy McGrory then sought a judicial review to challenge the legitimacy of the certificates. Leave was granted in July 1990, but the government challenged that and our right to have a judicial review was withdrawn on 31st May '91. The legal advice we received stated that it would be pointless to appeal, so by August '91 the next hurdle was approached when we lodged an application with the European Commission of Human Rights in Strasbourg on the basis that our loved ones' right to life had been violated.

The European Commission's task was to weed through all the cases. It would decide whether a case had any validity to be considered first by it and after that by the European Court of Human Rights. An oral hearing was held in April '93 and by September the commission decided that they would consider it for admission and requested further observations from both sides. In March the next year they found by a majority of 11 votes to 6 that there had been no violation of Article 2 of the European Convention of Human Rights, which is the right to life. While the British were jubilant over this, they were a lot less pleased when the Commission, nevertheless, referred the case to the European Court.

During all this time Paddy McGrory's health had been failing. And although he didn't attend the Commission's hearing he nevertheless worked on the papers that Barra [McGrory] and Douwe presented in Strasbourg. He also prepared the case to be presented by Barra in February '95 to the European Court of Human Rights. Unfortunately, he died just before Christmas in 1994. And that was the great sadness for me associated with our victory the following September, when the European Court of Human Rights found that the British government had unlawfully killed Mairéad, Seán and Dan. Paddy had been the brains behind the case. The only evidence considered by the Court came from the inquest— evidence that Paddy, despite all the handicaps, had squeezed out of the killers and their accomplices.

With or without campaigning, we would have achieved absolutely nothing if it wasn't for Paddy McGrory. To have a committed and fearless lawyer on your side is priceless. I have often said that there were four families involved in the Gibraltar case—the fourth family was the McGrorys.

One criticism that must be made against the Court is that they failed to seek evidence relating to the planning of the killings, which the British, through the use of gagging orders, prevented from being presented at the inquest. This missing evidence would have given substance to our view that the killings were all part of a pre-planned conspiracy, that it was lynch law. They also failed to request the evidence from the authorities in Spain. This would have shown that the British had perjured themselves.

Nevertheless, it was the first time a signatory state to the European Convention of Human Rights had been found guilty of violating the right to life. It was an historic verdict.

The British response was also without precedent, when Heseltine, then the Deputy PM, said they would do the same again. The British government was showing contempt for the Court. They should have faced sanction at the Council of Ministers of the Council of Europe, but didn't. That body oversees the verdicts of the Court, but no sanction was imposed. The Irish government—Dick Spring was then the Minister for Foreign Affairs—should have been uncompromising. Again it failed us. It is worth remembering that at the time of the killings, Spring—then in opposition—had condemned them as murder. But once in government he began whistling a different tune.

A year after the verdict, almost on the anniversary, Heseltine's promise became reality with the shooting dead of Diarmuid O'Neill.

The media, however, excelled themselves. The *Independent* wheeled out Robert Kee who showed his true colours with a scurrilous article about the verdict and the relatives. RTE, seeing its opportunity to attack the judgment, gleefully referred to Kee's article on 'Morning Ireland' and Gay Byrne's show. To top it off, Kee was allowed on Pat Kenny's programme to slander us. The Irish media did us no favours throughout our seven and a half years campaigning for justice. It was, in fact, journalists in the British media who stuck their necks out.

The Catholic church didn't excel itself either. Bishop Eamonn Casey was the only bishop to sign our petition but the whole role of the church around the time of the funerals was anything but charitable. Bishop Daly, now Cardinal Daly, didn't make any comment on the killings—there were no words of condemnation. When my parents approached the parish priest about the month's mind [a memorial mass held one month after death], he told them that they could only have a mass if it wasn't publicised. He didn't want any riff raff attending his beloved church. To devout Catholics like my parents, who had just lost their only daughter, this was a real slap in the face. For me, it was just another example of the hypocritical humbug that is religion.

No one should be above the law, and that includes those who carried out the killings and those who gave the orders. People think I'm daft when I say Thatcher should be prosecuted for killing my sister, but why not? The Spanish Minister of the Interior found himself in jail for a similar crime and as we talk, Pinochet is in the dock. So why not Thatcher?

The armed conflict—thankfully—now appears to be coming to a close and there is a need for us to come to terms with the past. Most victims want to know the truth behind what happened to their relatives. I am no exception. I want to know the truth surrounding both the killings in Gibraltar and at the funerals. And this includes the whole truth from those who planned that IRA mission to Gibraltar.

But what really appals is that the British continue to live the lie that they are honest brokers in this conflict. They have no right to claim the moral high ground and it is only by establishing the truth can this situation be rectified. So the conflict has to be examined in the public forum in its broader historical context; the whys and the wherefores surrounding the creation and maintenance of the corrupt Northern statelet.

What also demands a public airing is the dirty war carried out by successive British governments, their use of a shoot-to-kill policy, of collusion to murder and terrorise the Catholic community and the many other criminal acts they carried out with impunity.

By establishing the truth one will level the political playing pitch and progress will surely be smoother. The hierarchy of victimhood, which has seen the victims of state violence marginalised, would vanish. It would also mean that the acts of criminality perfected by the British military during the conflict—tactics that were also employed against former colonies—are less likely to be used again particularly in Britain against what Mrs Thatcher termed 'the enemy within'.

Only when we establish the truth can we prevent such crimes being committed again.

14

PAT FINUCANE
12 February 1989

Killed by loyalists with assistance of British army and RUC

Pat Finucane (38) was sitting down to Sunday dinner with his wife Geraldine and family in their north Belfast home at 7.30 p.m. on 12 February 1989 when two loyalist killers sledge-hammered down their front door. The gunmen shot Pat Finucane once with an automatic rifle and 13 times with a 9mm Browning pistol. He was hit 14 times in the head and upper body. One of the bullets to his head was fired from a distance of 15 inches. Geraldine Finucane was also shot in the foot as she and their three children—aged 9, 13 and 17—watched. The pistol used had been one of 13 stolen from a British army base in 1987. A UDR soldier was later jailed for the theft of the weapons.

Pat Finucane was a successful lawyer. He was one of a handful of solicitors who had become proficient in the operation of criminal trials in the non-jury courts which operated under emergency law in Northern Ireland. He had been involved in a number of high profile cases, at one time defending Bobby Sands and other Long Kesh hunger strikers. At the time of his death he was involved in the protracted round of court cases surrounding the inquest into the deaths of Gervaise McKerr and others, shot dead by the RUC in North Armagh in 1982.

A number of Pat's brothers were active republicans—a connection that would surface from time to time in later arguments about his death. John Finucane died in a car crash in 1972 while on active service with the IRA. Dermot Finucane had escaped from Long Kesh prison in 1983 and was later extradited from the Republic to the North. And Seamus Finucane had served a sentence for firearms

175

offences and was the fiancé of Mairéad Farrell who was shot dead by the SAS in Gibraltar in 1988.

Pat Finucane's work meant he became a thorn in the side of those in the military and security establishment who had things to hide. The argument that he was a professional lawyer using the law legitimately to protect his clients cut little ice with those in RUC Special Branch and Military Intelligence who saw him— in the words of an RUC interrogator of one of Pat's clients in Castlereagh Holding Centre—as 'a thug in a suit'. His clients were frequently assured by RUC interrogators that their solicitor was to be targeted. Three weeks before Pat Finucane's death, prominent West Belfast UDA man Tommy Little was urged by his RUC interrogators to arrange Pat Finucane's death.

The vilification of Pat Finucane reached new levels when on 17 January 1989 Douglas Hogg MP, an under-secretary at the Home Office, returned from an RUC briefing in Belfast and announced in the House of Commons: 'I have to state as a fact, but with great regret, that there are in Northern Ireland a number of solicitors who are unduly sympathetic to the cause of the IRA'. He did not name any such solicitors. Less than a month later Pat Finucane was dead.

The UFF issued a statement claiming responsibility for his murder, stating that they had shot 'Pat Finucane, the Provisional IRA officer, not Pat Finucane the solicitor'. The allegations of his links to the IRA were denied by his family and friends, and this denial was underlined during the inquest in September 1990 when the RUC confirmed that there was no evidence whatsoever that he had been an IRA officer. The RUC also stated at the inquest that they had interviewed a number of suspected UFF men about the murder. Although they were certain that some of the perpetrators of the killing were among those questioned, they claimed to have no evidence on which to bring charges.

From the start the Finucane family alleged official involvement in the death of Pat Finucane, and cited the threats delivered to him from the RUC via his clients. Their suspicions were to be proven correct by the arrest in January 1990 of Brian Nelson. Nelson had been born in Belfast and had served in the British army for a time as a young man. In the early 1970s he had joined the UDA. But it was only in the 1980s that he rose to prominence in that organisation. He was recruited by British Military Intelligence, specifically by the Force Research Unit, one of a number of shadowy organisations active in the North before and since. The FRU had 50 officers and men and ran over 100 informers and agents.

The FRU ran Brian Nelson as a high level agent within the UDA. His role was clearly to refine the UDA's killing operations. Previously the loyalist group had operated an assassination campaign of 'any Catholic will do'. With Nelson in their ranks, FRU was able to turn this around to a policy of 'taking out republicans'. They provided Nelson with high grade information from RUC and British army files regarding republican activists, suspects and sympathisers. With such valuable information, Nelson quickly rose to be senior intelligence officer in the UDA. As such he accessed all the UDA's files, which he passed to the FRU for upgrading. This apparent reciprocal exchange of intelligence was in fact highly lopsided. Although FRU obtained detailed knowledge of UDA secrets, there is little evidence that they ever acted on this information to curtail the activities of loyalist killers. On the other hand, the UDA obtained invaluable intelligence which enabled them to perfect their killing. Nelson also visited South Africa in January 1988 to procure weaponry. Although his FRU handlers were aware at every stage of the operation, they claim to have 'lost track' of the arms consignment as it reached Northern Ireland. As a result, Nelson was able to procure for loyalist assassins 200 AK47 automatic rifles, 90 Browning 9mm pistols, 500 fragmentation grenades, 30,000 rounds of ammunition and 12 RPG7 rocket launchers.

The combination of high grade intelligence and high quality weaponry soon showed. In the six years before the arrival of the South African arms shipment— January 1982 to December 1987—loyalists killed 71 people, 49 of which were clearly sectarian/political murders. In the six years following the shipment— January 1988 to September 1994—they killed 229 people, 207 of which were sectarian/political murders. Nelson himself is believed to have been directly involved in 15 murders, 15 attempted murders and 62 conspiracies to murder. He was paid £28,000 per annum for his sterling work.

Nelson's role came to light as a result of a string of events which began in August 1989. On 25 August, the UFF/UDA murdered 28 year old Loughlin Maginn at his home in Rathfriland, County Down. They claimed he was a member of the IRA. To back up their claim, they made public RUC files on Maginn which were in their possession. Consequently, RUC Chief Constable Hugh Annesley asked the Chief Constable of Northumbria, John Stevens, to investigate possible collusion between the RUC/British army and loyalist paramilitary groups. Two UDR soldiers received life sentences in 1992 for passing on the files which led to the murder of Loughlin Maginn. But the Stevens investigation did not lead to the arrest of any RUC or British army personnel. Instead, 32 loyalists were arrested, among them Brian Nelson. The FRU protected their man for a time. They hid his files from the prying eyes of Stevens and his team and generally obstructed the investigation. On 11 January 1990, the evening before Nelson was to be arrested, he suddenly fled to England. On the same evening, a malicious fire at Carrickfergus RUC station destroyed much of the paperwork of the Stevens team. (In November 1999, the *Sunday Times* claimed that a secret British army unit, CME, the Covert Methods of Entry team, had been responsible for the arson attack.) Nelson was finally arrested and Colonel J, the commanding officer of FRU, finally cooperated with the Stevens investigators. He claimed the following logic for Nelson's work: the FRU gave Nelson information which allowed the UDA to target known individuals. When the UDA killing was set up, Nelson could inform FRU and the details could be passed to the RUC. In effect, Nelson's role was to save lives. Special Branch members assured the Stevens team that they could not name one individual whose life had been saved as a result of Nelson's work. This is despite the fact that FRU knew in advance on at least 92 occasions who the UDA was going to kill.

Nelson was charged with 35 offences, including murder. Eventually the 15 most serious charges were dropped. He pleaded guilty, which meant that little detail of the activities of FRU emerged in court. Colonel J provided an effusive character reference for Nelson, as did Tom King, British defence minister, and formerly Northern Ireland Secretary of State. Colonel J's reference was particularly revealing. Despite the fact that the FRU, as a result of Nelson's position, knew the names of UDA planners and activists, they allowed the organisation to continue killing with impunity. Yet Colonel J, without any sense of irony, stated of Nelson: 'His motivation was to make his community safer, to bring down the terrorist organisations'. It was clear that the term 'terrorist organisations' only applied to one side. Nelson received a number of concurrent sentences for possession of documents, possession of firearms and conspiracy to murder. He was sentenced to 10 years in prison and was released in 1996.

During all of this there was no direct connection made between Nelson's activities and the death of Pat Finucane. However, while in prison Nelson collaborated with journalist John Ware in the production of a BBC 'Panorama' programme, 'The Dirty War', broadcast in June 1992. Nelson admitted on the programme that he had provided the information which led to the targeting of Pat Finucane and that his FRU handlers had been kept aware of the UDA plans to kill the solicitor. In the spring of 1992, John Stevens was recalled to Northern Ireland. RUC Chief Constable Hugh Annesley stated that Stevens was merely following up on a few issues that had arisen in his previous investigation and that no arrests or prosecutions were foreseen. At the same time, it was widely expected that Nelson's new revelations would be part of Stevens' second investigation. Throughout the years following little was done to dispel this expectation. In fact, on 17 January 1995, Stevens stated: 'With regard to the murder of Pat Finucane, I can confirm that this matter was fully investigated during the initial and subsequent inquiry...' As late as 6 April 1999 Armed Forces Minister Doug Henderson stated in the House of Commons that Stevens had investigated Pat Finucane's murder. Yet amazingly, when Stevens returned for a third investigation in 1999, he stated, on 29 April, that at no time had he ever investigated the killing of Pat Finucane.

Stevens' third visit was triggered by a report into the death of Pat Finucane compiled by British Irish Rights Watch and submitted to the British and Irish governments in February 1999. The report, the contents of which have not been made public, produces irrefutable evidence of collusion and cover-up. It also names the RUC officers who allegedly procured Pat Finucane's murder. Names have been known to Stevens too. In 1995 he told the Law Society of England and Wales that he knew 'beyond a shadow of doubt' who was responsible for the murder of Pat Finucane. Possibly as a result of this knowledge, he lost little time acting on his third investigation. On 23 June 1999, William Stobie was charged with the solicitor's murder. This led to another set of revelations about official involvement in collusion and cover-up, this time pointing principally to the RUC.

Stobie had joined the UDA and UDR in the 1970s. In 1987 he received a suspended sentence for an arms offence. He seems to have left the UDR at this point. By 1989 he was quartermaster for the UDA in Glencairn, North Belfast, responsible for the supply and storage of weapons. He was at the same time working for RUC Special Branch. On 9 November 1987 he had supplied the weapons and getaway car used in the murder of a 19 year old Protestant, Adam Lambert, working in nearby Highfield estate. Lambert had been mistaken for a Catholic and was targeted in retaliation for the IRA bomb in Enniskillen the previous day which had killed 11 people. Stobie was interviewed by the RUC over his role in Adam Lambert's murder and was leaned on heavily by the Special Branch to become an informer. He agreed.

In February 1989, Stobie allegedly supplied the weapons which were used to kill Pat Finucane. Although he didn't know the exact identity of the target, he was able to inform his handlers that a 'top Provie' was to be hit, and the names of the team carrying out the operation. There was, he claimed, enough information there for the RUC to intervene. They did not.

After the murder of Pat Finucane, Stobie was compromised by the Special Branch. They asked him to deliver a cache of UDA guns to them, which he did. They returned them, but it was only when one failed on an operation that it became apparent that they had filed down the firing pins, making the guns unusable. Anxious to provide some insurance for himself, Stobie contacted a local newspaper, *Sunday Life*, and told the story of his involvement in Pat Finucane's murder to journalist Neil Mulholland. Stobie's intention was that if he was arrested in the future—and only then—Mulholland could print the story and reveal the RUC's involvement. However, Mulholland not only told his colleagues of Stobie's confession, but also went to the RUC and Special Branch. As a result, Stobie was brought in for questioning by the RUC between 13 and 20 September 1990. He asked repeatedly if he was going to be charged. Surprisingly, he was not. Later, the RUC claimed that Mulholland's reluctance to commit his statement to paper meant there was little they could do in terms of charging Stobie.

Around the same time Stobie went to another journalist, Ed Moloney of the *Sunday Tribune*, and repeated his story on the same condition. Unlike Mulholland, Moloney adhered to the condition of keeping Stobie's story secret.

The RUC almost had the last word, however. In November 1989 they raided Stobie's flat and found guns which, he claimed, they planted there. He was arrested and charged with possession. His trial began on 1 October 1990 and ended abruptly. Stobie informed the DPP that, unless he was found not guilty, he would reveal the RUC's inaction in relation to Pat Finucane's murder.

Subsequently an RUC detective made the elementary 'mistake' in court of referring to Stobie's previous conviction. The judge had no choice but to declare a mistrial. At the retrial in January 1991 the Crown offered no further evidence against Stobie and the DPP recommended a 'not guilty' verdict. The judge agreed. Stobie had taken on the Special Branch and won, at least for the moment.

By the time Stevens began his third investigation in 1999 Neil Mulholland was a press officer for the Northern Ireland Office. He supplied a 28 page statement, repeating Stobie's original confession and is to be the chief witness for the prosecution. As a result, Stobie was arrested. At this point, Ed Moloney was free to tell Stobie's story in the *Sunday Tribune*. The Stevens team then turned their attention on Moloney, demanding under the Prevention of Terrorism Act that he hand over his notes of the 1990 interview with Stobie. Moloney refused. It had been the position of the police and DPP from the start of the proceedings that, when interrogated in September 1990, Stobie had, in the words of Detective Inspector Turner, 'denied any involvement in the murder and was subsequently released without charge'. However, during cross-examination by Moloney's counsel, Turner remembered that Stobie had in fact confessed. It then came to light that there were in existence 120 or so pages of interview notes taken by the RUC when they interrogated Stobie. The significance of Moloney's 11 or so pages of contemporaneous notes to the Stevens investigation paled into insignificance in the light of this revelation. Equally important was the revelation that the DPP had decided on 16 January 1991 (seven days before the arms charges were dropped) not to charge Stobie with the murder of Pat Finucane, despite the existence of these notes and Stobie's confession.

As a result of these developments, Judge Hart granted Stobie bail. As the judge noted, this was unusual in a murder case, but was legitimate given Stobie's involvement in the 'murky and secret world of informers'. Later, on 3 May 2000, Stobie was charged with a further murder, that of Adam Lambert. Again, he was granted bail.

While Stevens and the courts were active there was a brief re-emergence of the vilification of Pat Finucane's name. On 30 April 1999, Ulster Unionist Ken Maginnis stated: 'It was also an open secret that Pat Finucane was inextricably linked to the IRA and committed to its objectives. No collusion was required to draw him to the attention of loyalist murderers'. Five days later, on 5 May, his fellow Ulster Unionist John Taylor stated in the House of Commons: 'Everyone in Northern Ireland knows the Finucane family is a strong republican family... What I am saying is that the family are one of the strongest republican families in Northern Ireland, who despise all police, whether they are RUC or English police'. And five days later again, on 10 May, former RUC Chief Constable Jack Hermon stated that Douglas Hogg's original slur on Pat Finucane, uttered in January 1989, 'was based on fact... Pat Finucane was associated with the IRA and he used his position as a lawyer to act as a contact between suspects in custody and republicans on the outside.'

For years the Finucane family have been calling for an independent investigation in relation to Pat's death. The independence, they argue, is clearly needed given the evidence of the involvement of the RUC, British army and MI5 at some point or other in:

- setting up the murder,

- failing to act on information provided prior to the murder,

- protecting some of those involved in planning and executing the murder,

- covering up the murder,

- obstructing police investigations,

- and withholding vital information from the courts.

The family's call has been supported by human rights organisations locally and internationally, including the New York-based Lawyers' Committee for Human Rights and Param Cumaraswamy, the United Nations Special Rapporteur. As of February 2000, the Irish government officially agreed to support their call, as previously did the Law Societies of the Republic of Ireland, Northern Ireland, and England and Wales. The British government's position until recently was that an inquiry was unnecessary; however, it now states that an inquiry is not ruled out, but that a decision must await the outcome of the Stevens investigation. For his part, Stevens has stated that it is unlikely that his report will be available until 2001.

In the meantime, there were periodic revelations of the Stevens investigation's operations, including its intention to question Douglas Hogg in relation to his House of Commons statement on Pat Finucane, and its attempts to find the ex-FRU operative who was continuing to pass information to the *Sunday Times* regarding the arson attack on Carrickfergus RUC station in January 1990. And on 24 January 2000, the *Independent* revealed that the Stevens team has passed the names of six UFF men to the DPP to be considered for prosecution. The six are believed to be the three men directly involved in the murder and a three man back-up squad. In response, John White of the UDA-affiliated Ulster Democratic Party stated : 'If any of these men, whether it's one of them or all six, are arrested and charged, then you can kiss goodbye to the peace process from our point of view'. But even the charging of the six men would still leave many questions unanswered. For example, how high up does the trail of guilt and negligence go? The FRU reported weekly to the Joint Intelligence Committee at 10 Downing Street, chaired personally by Prime Minister Margaret Thatcher.

Martin Finucane now tells the story of his brother's murder and of his own subsequent involvement in human rights campaigning.

Martin Finucane

It is now approaching eleven years since we embarked on this campaign.
We knew it was going to be a long and hard battle and we would encounter
many obstacles... We as a family only seek the truth. The memory of our
brother and the courage he displayed in doing the work that he did
deserves nothing less.

The events of 1969 dramatically changed the Finucane family's lives. As a young kid of eleven, just about to finish primary school, I was completely apolitical as any other young child. I can remember getting a beating in the street and being called a 'fenian bastard'. 'What's a "fenian"'?,' I asked my younger brother Dermot who was plumped down beside me. That explains how innocent I was.

Being burnt out in August 1969 changed our lives. We lived in Percy Street. It ran off the Falls Road at one end and the Shankill at the other. On the night of the troubles I spent the whole evening frightened under the bed with Dermot while loyalist thugs were outside along with the B Specials trying to kick the door down. It was a very terrifying night for my mother and father. I have no doubt in my mind that if the loyalists had gotten into our home they would have killed every one of us. Lucky enough, we survived.

We moved out of Percy Street in the early hours of the morning and stayed with family friends in Dermott Hill. Outside looked like a war scene. The remnants of a double-decker bus and a JCB truck that were positioned across the street opposite the mill were still smouldering. The small number of Catholic families that lived beside us and survived the frightening events of the night before quickly did the same as us and evacuated their homes, never to return.

I cannot recall how long we stayed in Dermott Hill but the Mackin family helped us out immensely. Moving further up the road to Andersonstown, life changed very much. Unlike the big house that we had in Percy Street, which suited the family numbers comfortably, ten of us, we were now squatting in a two-bedroom flat. It was absolutely hectic. It took several months before we got a new house. Like so many other nationalist families we were not alone in this situation, as the demand to house those refugees of the situation was enormous. I have been told that the number of Catholic families having to flee their homes in August '69 was the biggest exodus of people since World War II.

We eventually settled into our new home, a three-bedroom house in an estate that was quickly built to deal with the housing crisis. Some of the Catholic families who had lived in adjoining streets to us in Percy Street were now our neighbours.

Seeing British soldiers coming off the boat and marching on the streets of Belfast at the junction of Townsend and Hastings Street, everyone expected things to change. How wrong we were! Thinking that our nightmare ended in

Percy Street was premature as the situation was now on the verge of getting worse. With the political scene rapidly changing, the livelihood of many families dramatically deteriorated. Faulkner introduced internment and British guns were now being used against our people. Even before Faulkner's disastrous decision the family home was the brunt of continuous raids by the British army that resulted in older brothers being arrested. Our introduction to these foreigners was comical. We disliked these intruders to our home and despite the fact they were in to take one or two of his sons away, my father was prepared to make them tea. Unfortunately during another raid on the house some years later by the RUC my father took a heart attack and collapsed. The next day he died in hospital. Two of my brothers ended up being interned. Seamus at the age of 16 and still at school spent almost two years in Long Kesh. John was detained for a similar period. Within a few weeks of his release he was killed in a car crash. In terms of what we as a family were going through, many other families within our community were sharing the same. House raids, arrests, death—it was punishment in a communal sense by the British, never-ending.

Everything that was happening around you quickly made you analyse and categorise the developing situation. These developments and the politics of this struggle ended up taking over our lives. Call it what you want—losing your youth, growing up—to me it was simply the beginning of our own politicisation. We did not lose our youth, it was stolen from us and that makes a difference.

Belonging to a very close-knit community, as we did, on the Falls Road had its advantages where we now lived. The community bond that existed on the road quickly took its own roots and everyone soon became very much part of this new neighbourhood. Everyone was looking out for each other. Despite the hardships that we were all facing, our resolve as a family and a community was strong. The families that followed us up the road in similar circumstances began to make the area safe. Defending and protecting the community was paramount because it was a worrying time for Catholics. Loyalists, like today, were randomly killing Catholics and the British army needed to be reminded that they were not welcomed.

We became very much part of the community. Cutting our teeth in campaigning and lobbying issues that affected the estate was new ground but a good challenge. Setting up housing committees, getting ordinary people involved to improve their conditions and getting them to represent and make their own decisions were the first stages of the community developing its own voice.

Pat was a very good, young and innovative solicitor, one who did his best to help people, either innocent or guilty or whatever their religious or political affiliation. The law was his devotion, his life. He always came across as someone who personally cared about his clients—always there when needed and to many he was the best lawyer they could hope for. He and his partner Peter Madden set up Madden and Finucane in the late seventies and quickly gained a reputation in pioneering a good legal service. The firm has now expanded and has offices in Armagh, Downpatrick and Derry.

The firm began to deal with a whole range of cases and specialised in cases that were a result of emergency legislation introduced by the British government. Pat was successful in many of these cases in the courts and this was very embarrassing for the British government. As a result of the publicity these cases began to receive, Pat became more noticeable to the authorities. In effect he was holding up their own system to the world to be judged and when the rest of the world judged it, it was found to be wanting. It was an embarrassment and a very serious one.

He and Peter formed a good legal relationship that was winning cases and making inroads against oppressive laws. The agents of the state, primarily the RUC, took a dislike to the firm and to Pat in particular. They questioned his professionalism via his clients in holding centres, particularly Castlereagh and Gough Barracks. They disparaged his professionalism and character, right up to issuing personal death threats like: 'Get yourself another solicitor; yours isn't going to be around much longer'. They said other things, like that he was a 'fenian bastard' and that he would be 'shot dead' pretty soon. Five weeks before he was murdered, a client was told by an RUC officer that his solicitor was 'working for the IRA, and would meet his end also. He asked me to give Mr. Finucane a message from him. He told me to tell him that he is a thug in a suit, a person trying to let on he is doing his job, and that he, like every other fenian bastard, would meet his end.'

Very few solicitors took on criminal work and the few that did within the large number of law firms in the North were harassed and threatened by the RUC. As far back as May 1987, a number of solicitors issued a statement criticising the threatening tactics of the RUC. This call was issued from John Fahey's office in Omagh but fell on deaf ears. These threats continued unabated for many years so that many solicitors, my brother included, came to view them as an occupational hazard.

Pat also viewed them as part of the interrogation techniques used by the RUC to unsettle and frighten his clients. He documented these threats and made them known to various human rights groups. His concern at these threats took on a different consideration when Douglas Hogg made his disgraceful statement in the House of Commons at a Prevention of Terrorism debate in 1989. He said that some solicitors in Northern Ireland were 'unduly sympathetic' to the IRA. Hogg did not name these 'sympathetic' solicitors but it was obvious at whom Hogg's threats were directed—Pat Finucane.

Seamus Mallon MP immediately challenged him. He replied to Hogg saying, 'I have no doubt that there are lawyers walking the streets or driving on the roads of the North of Ireland who have become targets for assassins' bullets as a result of the statement that has been made tonight... Following [this] statement, people's lives are in grave danger.' Three weeks later Pat was dead. His death sent a veiled threat to lawyers and had a disturbing effect on the legal profession. People were shocked that it had happened, particularly to a defence lawyer.

I arrived back on the Saturday night from Dublin before Pat was killed. I had planned to go over to his home on Sunday for dinner with another brother. The following day the arrangements changed and I ate at home. Later that evening I received a phone call just after 7pm. It was the brother's father-in-law informing me that he had heard that a Finucane had been shot. He indicated that it might be Seamus. I was shocked to hear this and told him he must be wrong as he had just left the house. He replied that it might then be Pat. I was shaken by this news. I quickly pressed the buttons phoning Pat's home. My heart was racing a hundred miles an hour. A relative answered the phone. I asked was the news true and the reply was, 'Yes, he's dead'. I broke down. I banged the wall with my fist and screamed out in shock. The relative on the other side of the phone tried to calm me down and inquired where mum was and to get hold of her quickly to prevent her hearing this news from someone else or on the news. I knew where mum was and I ran quickly to the neighbour's house to inform her that her eldest son was dead. She was visiting a life-long friend from the Falls Road. As soon as I went through the threshold of Mrs. Gillen's house, mum knew right away that something was seriously wrong. She stood up on her feet and asked, 'Is it Seamus?' I moved closer to her and told her, 'No, mummy, it's Pat'. I had to wrap my two arms around her. I told her: 'They have killed Pat. He is dead'. Mum went into hysterics. Everyone in the house was in tears and deep in shock. Mum was asking for more information. All I could tell her was that Pat was shot dead in the kitchen of his home, Geraldine was injured and the kids were ok and had been taken out of the house to a neighbour's house. Telling mum that her son has just been shot dead in front of his family has been the most difficult thing I have ever done in my life. I took mum home and as the news of Pat's death began to break on the news and to become tomorrow's headline, the house soon filled with friends and neighbours offering their deepest sympathies. I was very concerned about mum and the family doctor was contacted.

Pat was shot 14 times. When he heard the front door being smashed in, he immediately stood up to investigate. As he opened the kitchen door two hooded loyalist gunmen from the pro-British death squad of the UFF were in the hallway. They instantly fired, hitting him twice in the stomach. They proceeded into the kitchen and stood over Pat and fired another 12 shots into his face, some from a range of 14 inches. A ricochet bullet hit Geraldine who was standing near the gunmen pinned to the wall with fright. The children who hid under the kitchen table witnessed everything and as they were being taken out of the house, had to step over the body of their dead father. One of the guns that murdered Pat belonged to the British army.

I had to try and contact other relatives and let them know about Pat. Dermot was in Portlaoise Gaol at the time. He was being held there facing extradition to the North. I had difficulty making the prison authorities realise the need to inform Dermot. I secured the intervention of Cardinal Tomas Ó Fiaich. I got his phone number from a very kind and respected woman in Derry called Kathleen Gallagher whom I knew to have worked all her life for the prisoners. My phone call to the Cardinal was successful. After offering his condolences to the family and telling me to keep my chin up he said to keep the line free, as he would make a phone call. Within 20 minutes Portlaoise was on the phone and I was able to speak to Dermot. He had already heard the news of Pat. Ironically at the time of hearing the news he was writing a letter to Pat's youngest son John.

I honestly cannot remember much about the funeral or waking Pat at the house. I do know that I spent a lot of time standing over his coffin in disbelief that I had lost my brother. Pat was a father figure to me. I was very close to him and when I needed his guidance and advice on something he was always there for me. The recent death of another solicitor, Rosemary Nelson, in circumstances hauntingly similar to those of Pat has brought some of the past memories back to me. Her death put an end to the career of another able advocate who like Pat was simply going about her work and doing her best for her clients. I was devastated by Rosemary's untimely death and I was not looking forward to going down to Lurgan to pay my last respects to this brave and wonderful woman. I remember as we got closer to her house I knew it was going to be difficult seeing her in a coffin. I was thinking of this moment the whole journey. Due to her horrific death, her coffin was closed and this robbed me of a final goodbye. However, my thoughts drifted back to the last time we met and what she has always given me returned to my face, a happy thought and a smile.

It was difficult for me and the family to deal with Pat's loss. We had no doubts that he was set up and that his death went further than the gunmen who killed him. It emerged at his inquest that he was killed by a gun that belonged to the British army. The revelation of the existence of a loyalist and British military intelligence officer, Brian Nelson, and his involvement in Pat's death confirmed the family's suspicions. Since then we have asked questions and have tirelessly worked to unearth the full circumstances which led to his death.

I moved to Derry shortly after Pat's death. I adjusted quickly in the city and took my time in making a decision of what to do with myself. Some people in the city from a number of backgrounds were at the initial stages of setting up a group around the Bloody Sunday killings. Its aim was to refocus national and international attention on this outstanding case and to gain as much support to have it reopened and finally redressed. It had a wider human rights remit than the Bloody Sunday case and this interested me. This group became known as the Bloody Sunday Initiative. It later changed its name to the Pat Finucane Centre in May 1992 after we brought the families of the Bloody Sunday dead and wounded together to form the Bloody Sunday Justice Campaign. Rather than confuse the general public with two Bloody Sunday groups, we acknowledged that the families should rightfully function with the Bloody Sunday title. Despite our name change we continued to work with the families and the change also allowed us to focus on many other cases and issues.

I am also a member of Relatives for Justice, a group that is primarily made up of relatives who have lost loved ones by loyalist death squads and the British state. I have been very much involved with both the Pat Finucane Centre and Relatives for Justice in highlighting abuses by the state and its agents. I have always viewed that these abuses and the corrupt nature of this state should and must be highlighted, as it was this combination that created and exacerbated this conflict that we are now trying to resolve. I got involved in this type of work to help others. It has been a challenge and one that has had its ups and downs over the years. At this present moment I am optimistic. I sincerely hope the peace process works for everyone. I know it is going to have its problems but they can be worked out if the political will exists. Making peace is not an easy task and finding solutions that will fulfil the hopes and expectations of everyone is everybody's responsibility. I acknowledge that there are some who are very much opposed to what has been accomplished. These people fear change, but no matter what they do to try and pull down this process they must not be allowed to succeed. The overwhelming majority of the people in this country voted for change and their vote gave all our politicians the mandate to find a solution that will create a better future. I respect this mandate and hope they make politics work.

My family has devoted itself to put closure on Pat's case. It is now approaching eleven years since we embarked on this campaign. We knew it was going to be a long and hard battle and we would encounter many obstacles. We are committed to this and we cannot give up now. It has been very gratifying to work with so many people over the years whose support we have gained and with their assistance to expose the lies; it has pushed our case forward and spurred us on towards our demand for an inquiry. I am very proud of my family, proud that we have stood by each other, our commitment to Pat's case and for not giving up.

The list is endless of the people I can thank for their help. The human rights organisations such as Amnesty, British Irish Rights Watch, Committee on the Administration of Justice, Relatives for Justice, the Pat Finucane Centre, the New York based Brehon Law Society, Human Rights Watch, Lawyers Alliance and the Lawyers Committee for Human Rights have all been the standard bearers in keeping this case to the fore.

Over the last ten years there has been a lot of information gathered in relation to the death of Pat. Based on many years of research the human rights group in London, British Irish Rights Watch, produced a detailed report called 'Deadly Intelligence'. This has been compiled by their director Jane Winter, a woman whom I greatly respect because of her tireless work on Pat's case and her devotion to many other human rights issues. It is a very detailed report and names many names. The report reveals shocking evidence and supports the family's call for an independent judicial inquiry. Some of the details reveal that Pat was under surveillance by British Military Intelligence for quite some time. His movements were followed and a photograph of him was passed on to the loyalist gang that murdered him. Other evidence strongly suggests that there was official collusion in his murder and that Military Intelligence and the RUC aided the assassins without hindrance. His case is rapidly becoming the tip of the collusion iceberg, an iceberg that shows a horrible, evil collusion machine that was put into place deliberately to pursue a policy of selective targeting. That policy was put in place before Pat was killed and remained since his death. The British government has known all these facts and has arrogantly dismissed them over the years.

The time has now come for the British government to announce an inquiry into the murder of Pat. Everything that has come to light points ever more sharply for this to happen. There is now only one honourable response to our demand for an inquiry and that is that the Prime Minister Tony Blair, who possesses all of the answers to the questions that we have raised, establish an independent judicial inquiry without any further delay or prevarication. The longer he and his government delays on this the more it makes itself a party to the shameful murders, lies and cover-ups that have been revealed so far.

The truth is never an easy thing to take. It is never an easy thing to swallow or to live with but you can learn to live with truth. You can't learn to live with lies and this is what we are asking for. Stop lying to us, stop telling us there was no collusion because there was. We as a family only seek the truth. The memory of our brother and the courage he displayed in doing the work that he did deserves nothing less.

15

SEAMUS DUFFY
9 August 1989

Plastic bullet victim

On 9 August 1971 internment was introduced in the North of Ireland. The anniversary of that event has been marked in subsequent years by marches and bonfires in nationalist areas. Often too it was an occasion for rioting between nationalist youths and the RUC and British army.

Rioting occurred on 9 August 1989 in the New Lodge area of North Belfast. During it, 15 year old Seamus Duffy from Ballycarry Street, off the Oldpark Road, was hit and killed by a plastic bullet, one of about 80 fired by the RUC that night. Seamus' father Brendan claimed that Seamus was an innocent bystander hit by a plastic bullet fired from an RUC Land Rover as he made his way back from an internment commemoration bonfire on the New Lodge Road. But the RUC's initial statement was that it was not certain that Seamus had died from a plastic bullet wound and that they would appoint a 'top policeman' to head the inquiry into the incident. A statement from Secretary of State Peter Brooke seemed to preempt the inquiry's findings regarding the use of plastic bullets: 'There are no grounds for suggesting their use last night was other than in accordance with the law'. As an RUC statement on the incident concluded, 'If there is no rioting, there will be no plastic baton rounds'.

The Independent Committee on Police Complaints, formed in 1988, was brought in to oversee the police investigation. It was the first time they had played such a role. With lawyer Brian Garrett as chair, the ICPC oversaw RUC interviews with almost 500 witnesses and others and produced a report 2000 pages long. Among those attracting the attention of the RUC investigators were the international journalists and photographers in town for the twentieth anniversary of the events of August 1969, from which the start of the conflict is often dated. A number of them were interviewed by the RUC and their photographs were perused for evidence about the rioting and Seamus Duffy's possible role in it. The RUC sought under the Police and Criminal Evidence Act to obtain film of an interview with Mark Brown, the friend who had been with Seamus Duffy when he was hit by the plastic bullet.

At the inquest, which took place on June 28 and 29, 1990, the RUC's position was that they had fired at an identified rioter from a distance of 43 metres. The pathologist, Dr John Press, said that it was likely that Seamus had been killed by a plastic bullet fired from a much shorter distance than that, namely nine or ten metres. Guidelines for the use of plastic bullets specified that they should not be fired from a range of less than 20 metres unless the officer's life was in danger. The plastic bullet crushed Seamus' heart and tore a four-inch laceration in his left lung. According to Press, Seamus Duffy was 'very drunk' at the time of his death, but this did not contribute in any way to his death.

Much of the RUC's case rested on video evidence showing a rioter wearing a Celtic Football Club supporter's shirt. However, this evidence was challenged on the grounds that the youth in the video was wearing an older version of the supporter's shirt than that worn on the night by Seamus. Amazingly, it emerged at the inquest that the written statements of two RUC men who had fired plastic bullets at rioters had been made after they had viewed this video.

The inquest jury concluded that Seamus had earlier been throwing stones at the RUC, but there was no evidence that he was actually involved in rioting at the point when he was fired on and hit by the plastic bullet. They discounted the RUC video evidence of the youth in the Celtic Football Club supporter's shirt. Seamus Duffy's father Brendan stated after the inquest that his son had been cleared and that he would now consider pursuing a civil case against the RUC.

The Coroner, James Elliott, said that the death was a tragedy and offered his sympathy to the family. At the same time, he sought to exonerate the RUC on the grounds that it was part of their difficult job to restore public order, thus echoing their own initial press release that there would be no deaths if there were no riots.

> It is a very tragic case that a young boy like this, at 15 years old, should have behaved in the way in which he behaved. It is a sad comment on the state of things in Belfast today that these things should take place. It seems this is the sort of tragedy which will continue to happen so long as people continue to act in this way.

No one was charged with Seamus's death. The DPP ruled that, while two RUC men admitted firing plastic bullets during the incident, it was impossible to establish which one of them had fired the fatal round. This was par for the course. Only one member of the state forces has ever been charged in relation to plastic bullet deaths, in the case of John Downes. By the time of Seamus Duffy's death, inquests or other legal proceedings had been held in relation to 17 plastic and rubber bullet deaths. In only four such cases was there a finding that the victim had been involved in any disturbance at the time of their death. Families of six of the dead had already received compensation, but the RUC had not admitted liability, even where legal proceedings had concluded that the victims were innocent.

Although plastic bullets continue to be used, no one has died as a result of their use since Seamus Duffy.

Kathleen Duffy, the mother of Seamus, had lost her brother, also called Seamus, earlier in the 'troubles'. Seamus Cassidy, a 22 year old IRA member, was shot by a British army sniper while sitting in a parked car outside the Starry Plough pub on the New Lodge Road on 27 July 1972. He died the following day.

Kathleen Duffy tells the story of her son's death and its aftermath.

Kathleen Duffy

I just cannot understand how we don't get recognition. It's the same hurt, the same as any other murder. I want the same recognition as everyone else. I don't want to be any different. I want to be on the same footing as any other mother whose son has been murdered. I think I have the right to that.

Dear God, I don't know what it was that day. This awful feeling came over me. I heard it on the news that night. First of all they said there was a fellow shot dead, a gunman with a Thompson sub-machine gun. I heard it and I never even thought. I went to my bed. I was wakened up in the early hours of the morning. There was a knock at the door and there was my da. 'Kathleen, I have bad news for you.' I never dreamt of my brother Seamus in a million years. My daddy told me our Seamus was dead.

The same feeling came over me the day my son Seamus died. That was the eighth of August and he had been in Dublin for two weeks. My brother had a shop there at the time, a mini-supermarket. It was coming up to the ninth of August and the bonfires and Seamus wouldn't stay; he wanted home. That day there was nothing unusual and I was going about my business, my housework and that. It was coming up to supper time and Seamus couldn't be found. So I took a wee dander down onto the Cliftonville Road. I just got a Chinese. I couldn't find the Seamus fellow anywhere. I knew he was out collecting bonfire wood, for they were up and down this street with the trolley putting bits of wood and what not on it. Lo and behold, he made an appearance. He took his Chinese and got ready. He bathed himself and I said to his daddy, 'There's a girl on the scene'. He had started taking a quare interest in himself and I knew there was a girl. He came down the stairs and I'll never forget his wee face. One of his mates called for him, Ciaran McKinney, and he went out the door. He had told me when he came in about the size of the bonfire on the New Lodge Road and he told me that the RUC had been giving them awful hassle because it was so big. Our bonfire would have been round here in the crickey [cricket field] and when he went out the door, just like any other mother in the times we live in, I just said to him, 'Seamus, I'm warning you; the crickey. You're not to let me hear tell of you being near the New Lodge Road'. Away he bounced out. He never walked—Seamus, God love him, had a bounce in his step. I was in the living room. He waved at me through the window and away he went.

I usually went up to the wee bingo but I didn't want to go. I just had this awful dread on me. I usually went with my sister-in-law, our Kevin's wife, and when he called and asked if I was going, I said, 'No, bonfire night'. We had the repetition of the same oul harassment, the RUC and the loyalists. Kevin just said, 'Well, sure, you know, if there is going to be anything, it will be later on and you and Susie will be well home by then'.

So I went. Coming back past the chippie, my Christine came along and she had Patrick all wrapped up in the buggy. She asked me where I was going and I told her I was going down to the crickey to keep an eye on Brendan and Seamus. She told me that is where they were going and I said, 'I'll tell you what, you go on down and keep an eye on them two and I'll go on round home with the child'. So I took the child on round to the house. Brendan was there and he went on to bed and I just sat there with the child. The next thing I heard was my next door neighbour shouting to me. I went out to the door and she said, 'Kathleen, our Thomas is only after phoning and your Seamus is only after being hit with a plastic bullet'. I came in the door and feel to my knees at the bottom of the stairs and I shouted, 'Holy Mother, don't, please, please'. I knew my Seamus was dead.

The next thing I remember is being at my sister's house. We went to the hospital. Going into the Mater Hospital is a blank to me, but apparently we were confronted by the RUC. My husband was already there with the child and that is how I know what happened. There is no point in me saying I remember that because I don't. But I was confronted by the RUC and I had a plastic bullet gun pushed into my stomach and they asked did I want to be next. The next thing, a wee nurse came on the scene and told them to back off. The nurse and other staff in the Mater Hospital told the RUC to go back into the room provided for them.

To cut a long story short, by the time we got there, my Seamus had been pronounced dead. You'd have thought he was sleeping. There was no blood, nothing, nothing to suggest that he had died such a violent death. But it sticks in my mind the wee nurse saying to me, 'He is spotless; his hands aren't even dirty. There is no trace of anything on him'. You know the way here the law is laid down that if you are a petrol bomber they have the right to shoot, but there was nothing on him. The girl asked us to take our Seamus's clothes before they doctored them. It was meant to be that we got Seamus's clothes and give them to our solicitors so that they could carry out their own private forensic tests, and that was done.

I never slept. All I can remember was the helicopter overhead constantly. The next day my husband found an envelope in the hall, before Seamus's body was even brought home, and it was a sympathy card from the RUC in Oldpark Barracks. They mediated with us was through our parish priest, Father Golden. The trouble we had trying to get my Seamus's body! Three times Brendan had to go to Forster Green [Mortuary], three times he had to go up to identify his son, until in the end the priest lost the head and asked them why they were putting us through this.

It ended up we got him home. They hadn't even washed his wee face. To me that was bigotry again that whoever it was up in that hospital hadn't even the decency to wash his face. We waked him here and buried him. The night he was buried, the RUC were going to arrest his father at the top of the street, only another peeler ran over and said, 'Do you not know who that is? Don't'; in other words, we are only after killing the son. It ended up that there was rioting on that road—not that I wanted it, but it was a penalty kick, for feelings were running high over Seamus being murdered.

The next thing is the RUC up and down outside the door, doing three point turns outside the door, pinning their headlights on the house, day and daily. That went on right up to December. We had cases of foot patrols asking Bronagh, his eleven year old sister, was Seamus coming out to play. The house next door to me was being raided one day and I was doing something at the window and there they were, pointing the guns up at me. I was coming out of the door one day and a peeler said, 'Cheer up, it may never happen, Mrs Duffy'. In saying that, I gave as good as I got, to be quite truthful.

My Brendan, his girlfriend used to live at the top of the Oldpark Road and to get to her house he had to pass the RUC barracks. The abuse that my Brendan took from them shouting out from the spy holes or passing jeeps: 'Do you want to be next, like your brother?' Of course he answered them back but to be quite truthful, he wasn't doing anything I wouldn't have done. He was walking up past the barracks; they came up, shouted something at him, Brendan shouted back. The jeep mounted the curb and pinned him in; they pushed their guns into his side. He was arrested for disorderly behaviour and the judge threw it out of court. Total harassment! This is your RUC, people who are supposed to be law enforcers. Our Mary was leaving here when Seamus's body was still in the house and they shouted at her, 'one nil'.

There was hate mail came here and he hid it from me until one day I was here on my own and I got it. By the way, the letters of sympathy outnumbered tenfold the hate mail. I say God help a sick person, anyone who would put pen to paper to write that to anybody: I wasn't a fit mother for Seamus should have been in bed—if he had been in his bed like her children who were tucked up tight and safe. To be honest, I think it came from an RUC man's wife. I was very happy to know that her wee children were tucked up in their beds for my wee children didn't ask to be born into this situation. The fact of the matter was that she was very lucky that her children were born into a fair world. My children had to fight to be recognised as human beings. My mind wasn't right at the time and I thought this was terrible, but thanks be to God, now I just feel sorry for them.

They tried to say our Seamus was doing this or that, but it came out at the inquest that our Seamus was found totally innocent. My Seamus and a wee boy called Mark Brown were making their way home when someone shouted, 'They are coming in', meaning the cops. Mark and Seamus were making their way up Sheridan Street when he said he heard the bang. When he turned round, my Seamus was on the ground. It was like a tropical rain storm, torrential rain and they said that the person rioting in the Celtic top was my Seamus. It was raining so hard that it was impossible to see. Brendan sat in that court for three hours and watched that video alone, more than what I could have done. The Celtic shirt my Seamus was wearing was a wee modern one and the one this person was wearing was an older one—you know the way they bring out a new football rig every year.

Seamus's inquest was apparently quicker than most of the other plastic bullet victims. Thanks be to God, Seamus was found totally innocent. The judge made out that the security forces couldn't be blamed because of the times we were living in and the measures that they had to take. Bad enough that they murdered Seamus, but to add insult to injury, to try and blacken his name!

They said that at the time Seamus was killed two police men shot plastic bullets at the same time. I know who they were; their names were given to us accidentally. I gave their names to those American lawyers who came here. I don't care because they murdered my child. I don't expect to get any justice, but I have to give the names of the people that killed my child, who are probably living a happy wee life now and are as carefree and little do they know the damage—not only to our lives, but my sisters' and brothers' lives. At the end of the day, they really don't care. I know they really don't care. A statistic—

that is it.

The RUC never came to my door; to this day the RUC nor the British army never came to this door. The only people who approached me was my parish priest, the United Campaign Against Plastic Bullets, and Relatives for Justice. Relatives for Justice are relatives of people who have been killed by the security forces. It was the same with that wee boy Keith White, the only Protestant killed by a plastic bullet; the Campaign approached him and apparently the woman wasn't in a position to join. She would then have been seen to be taking sides with nationalists. The woman's heart was broken because her child was killed just the same; God help that poor woman! She couldn't get out the hurt, the awful hurt that was inside her and she had no way of getting it out. That woman made them take her son's name off a loyalist mural; she said it was an insult. Only for the Campaign and our parish priest, Brian Feeney from the SDLP—it was him who told me how many plastic bullets were fired that day. The only other people who came to help me get some sort of appeasement were Sinn Féin. Every opportunity they get, they ring me to let me get the chance to tell my story. We haven't got the backing of the unionist politicians, Ian Paisley, Robert McCartney. I don't want people like that backing me anyway. I feel stronger being able to identify with people who have gone through and are still going through the same hurt as myself. People like myself don't need them for we have nothing to hide; we can only say what is in our hearts. We are telling the truth; there is nothing to fear from the truth. I wouldn't want a bigot behind me; the truth is stronger. I am an awful believer of 'long runs the fox'. Slowly and surely things are coming to the fore—like with Bloody Sunday. If they would admit to those people, just like myself, that they were murdered. They just want the word 'murder' mentioned. There is a peace process going on here but there is a hell of a lot to do to keep it on the right track—saying sorry or admitting and telling the truth, the right to truth, saying it happened, it shouldn't have happened.

Through the Campaign I met Emma Groves, Clara Reilly, Archie Livingstone and Jim McCabe—lovely people. These were people to give me support. They were the only people there for me for they had loved ones killed and injured with plastic bullets. Meeting these people was the only way that I could let people know what happened to my child. There was no other road I could turn; there was no other way I was going to get any sort of justice.

I got involved with the meetings and I went to England a few times with Troops Out to let people know the truth of what is going on. I take every opportunity to speak to the press. I feel that nothing can withstand the truth. It's my way of getting peace of mind, being able to tell my side of it, the truthful side of it. As with all the cases of plastic bullets, they are long drawn-out because the police are sitting piecing together their jigsaw puzzle, trying to fit it in to make up their own story. You see history repeating itself. What are the news reports? 'Riot situation.' That wee lad Stewart—there was no riot. The riot only occurred after that wee boy was killed. After Seamus was killed, the RUC appealed to the people of the New Lodge Road to come forward and give their account of what they had seen. They gave reassurances that no one would be charged with riotous behaviour because in most of the cases when people came forward and told what they had seen, they were charged and sentenced to six or eighteen months for being a part of it. Nobody would come forward and I didn't expect them to. What respect do the people in the New Lodge Road have for the RUC, when people are terrified and tortured? But if the people didn't go to the RUC, they came to my door to tell me it was murder.

Last November we had a private meeting with members of the Patten Commission. I had already been to the public one in a wee church up there. There is a wee group, Victims of Trauma, and I had been able to speak up there. I was quite up-front with Mr Patten. I pulled no punches. I told him that I hoped what I was saying was going to get somewhere, not another whitewash. We had got whitewashing and brushing under the carpet for too long. So we went to the private meeting with him. There was something like fourteen relations and they sent us out word that there was only to be ten. We decided among ourselves that it would be all or none of us. We were kept waiting for over an hour. Their excuse for keeping us waiting was that the room wasn't big enough and they needed more chairs. As someone said, they wondered did they keep the police widows waiting for an hour. This is what you are dealing with before the Commission's findings are published. As far as I'm concerned, the only way to change the RUC is to disband them. The ordinary police man on the street that murdered my son is accountable to his senior officers. So the way I look at it is that his fellow officers know the truth, the commanders know exactly what happened to my child. The rotten apples lie at the bottom and stretch right to the top as far as I'm concerned. It is common sense. You don't have to be educated to know that the lower rank answers to the higher rank and they are covering up what happened at the bottom.

As for Kenneth Bloomfield, the commissioner for victims, what a paragraph in a book! It was an insult! He would have been better leaving us out, totally ignoring us. That's what he really wanted to do. Nationalists at the end of the day have no other road to start off from other than campaigning for justice because we are just not recognised.

I just cannot understand how we don't get recognition. It's the same hurt, the same as any other murder. That wee boy must have been special when God gave him to me and my heart is torn asunder just like any other mother. That's what angers me; state killings just aren't recognised like any other murder. They have the right to take life because they are wearing a uniform. You have to sit and take it that this police man was doing his duty and they have broken rules and regulations and there is no disciplinary action—just swept to the side, forgotten about. You're supposed to sit and take that. No way; there has to be an end put to it.

When you say 'plastic', you think of a toy. Wrong name, wrong name! The right name for it is a bullet; plastic nothing, rubber nothing. You could hit yourself on the head with it and knock yourself out. The fact of the matter is that this is coming out of a gun at 130mph. It lacerated my child's heart; he probably didn't know what hit him. I don't know what killed Seamus; he could have drowned, for his lungs probably filled with water. The day that Seamus was killed a plastic bullet was found in a flat four storeys high. There were 108 plastic bullets fired within the space of an hour. They are lethal weapons and they are being fired at random with no control on them. There are rules and regulations governing the use of them. They are supposed to be fired below the waist and in every one of the deaths, they were hit from the waist up. If it wasn't head injuries, it was heart injuries. John Downes had the same mark, the same two rings on the chest—which proves that the cap which is supposed to fall away after it has been fired didn't. That proves that they were fired at point blank range.

I have no wish to see them used against anybody, but in the majority of cases it's the nationalist people. It is a weapon of oppression; in other words, if you kill someone, it's a way of putting the rest off the street. I've seen things like the riots at Strangeways Prison and the Poll Tax riots in England; they didn't see the need to use plastic bullets there. But at the drop of a hat, out they come to the nationalist people in the north of Ireland. It's as if we are a lesser people. I sat the other night and watched scenes on the television of an RUC jeep being turned over on its side by loyalists. If the shoe had have been on the other foot and that had happened on the New Lodge Road or on the Garvaghy Road, the plastic bullet guns would have been out.

Everybody is demanding that nationalists say they are sorry, for the IRA to say they are sorry. This wasn't a one-sided war. I would love someone to tell me they are sorry. Tell me it was an accident and I could accept that. My feelings are no different from the woman on the Shankill who lost her son. If it was a British soldier it is the same, someone's son. My brother was murdered by the British army but when there was a soldier shot on the Oldpark Road, my mummy knelt down and said an act of contrition into his ear. My mummy's words to me were, 'He is somebody's son'. I want the same recognition as everyone else. I don't want to be any different. I want to be on the same footing as any other mother whose son has been murdered. I think I have the right to that.

A year after Seamus was murdered, I watched the eleventh night [loyalist] bonfire celebrations and there were children running about, the same thing my fifteen year old was murdered for a year earlier. I wanted to know what the difference was that my child and any other nationalist children couldn't enjoy themselves at the bonfire. If the RUC hadn't shown their faces that night my child would be alive today. Their very presence is an aggravation of the situation for they are not acceptable to nationalists. They have murdered too many people, caused to much hurt. If they hadn't shown their faces, my child could have been living today, a big man of twenty five. At the end of the day they have to answer to God; He is the be-all and the end-all.

16

BRIAN ROBINSON
2 September 1989

Killed by British army undercover unit

B rian Robinson was a 27 year old member of the UVF in Belfast. On 2 September 1989, he was a passenger on a motor cycle driven by fellow UVF member David McCullough. They drove to the nationalist Ardoyne area of North Belfast. There, outside a shop, Robinson shot dead a 43 year old local Catholic, Patrick McKenna, 11 times in the neck and trunk of the body, killing him instantly.

According to journalist Nicholas Davies, Robinson and McCullough were being followed by an undercover unit of the British army for three days prior to the shooting. He claims that Robinson and McCullough were aware of the surveillance as they drove around looking for a target. On the other hand, it is impossible to verify this and many other aspects of Davies' account. Campaigners in the Robinson case are convinced that the killing was a set-up and that the British army undercover unit specifically targeted Robinson and McCullough because of prior information they had received about the UVF operation.

After killing Patrick McKenna, the UVF men took off on their motor bike; the British army unit gave chase. The vehicles sped down the Crumlin Road; shots were fired by the British soldiers and the leading car, an Astra, rammed the motor bike. Robinson was thrown a distance of about 40 feet; he lost his weapon in the process. At some point he was also shot in the back. As he lay on the ground unarmed, he was shot dead by one of the undercover soldiers.

Eyewitnesses claimed that the soldiers seemed determined to kill McCullough too, but were thwarted by the arrival of the eyewitnesses. The RUC were on the scene soon after. They arrested McCullough.

Patrick McKenna had been injured in February 1970 when loyalists had sent him a booby-trapped Valentine's Day card. After his murder, the UVF issued a statement that he was a member of the IRA. There is no evidence that he was.

On hearing of Brian Robinson's death, his mother, Margaret, died of a heart attack. Thus on 5 September, three funerals took place. At Patrick McKenna's, Bishop Cahal Daly called for an inquiry into the incident. Brian Robinson's funeral left the Glencairn estate and met up with that of his mother near her home in Crimea Street. Both were buried in Roselawn Cemetery.

The initial RUC statement on the incident stressed that the presence of the British army undercover unit was 'entirely coincidental' and not connected with the original shooting. There was a certain plausibility in this explanation given that undercover surveillance in nationalist areas was frequent. On the other hand, there were suspicions from the start among both nationalists and loyalists that the British army had been tipped off and were waiting for Robinson and McCullough. As McKittrick et al point out, the name of Colin Craig was later linked to Robinson's death. Craig was a UVF member and an informer who was killed by the INLA on 16 June 1994.

In April 1992, a joint inquest for Patrick McKenna and Brian Robinson was held, surely a very stressful experience for the McKenna family. The three undercover soldiers involved in the shooting of Robinson were not present. Their written statements were read to the jury. Coroner James Leckey said that this was a 'less than perfect' situation. He advised the jury that they were within their rights not to attach the same weight to the soldiers' statements as to evidence given by witnesses who appeared in person and could be cross-examined. 'You must treat such evidence with caution as it may be self-serving.'

Soldier A's statement was that this was not a planned operation. After the shooting in Ardoyne, the army followed the motor bike. The passenger, Robinson, was said to have turned and fired once at the soldiers' car. The car then hit the motor bike, throwing Robinson off. Soldier A said that Robinson then got up and came towards him, still holding the gun. He then 'appeared to trip'. As Robinson started to get up, Soldier A claimed, he feared for his own life and fired twice more.

This evidence was contradicted by forensic and eye-witness evidence. Robinson's gun was 55 feet away from his body. Civilian witnesses said they saw a soldier walk over to Robinson and fire several shots into his body from six or seven feet distance. Deputy State Pathologist Derek Carson concluded that the first bullet hit Robinson in the back when he was bent over or trying to crawl away. The second bullet hit him in the wrist. He died as a result of two bullets fired 'at fairly close range, possibly by someone standing over him'.

The jury concluded that Brian Robinson was wounded and unarmed when two fatal shots were fired into him at close proximity. The clear implication was that Brian Robinson could have been arrested.

At the same inquest, the RUC said that Patrick McKenna had been arrested twice and questioned in connection with IRA activities. Even though he was never charged with any offence, this may have been seen by some to lend credence to the UVF's justification for killing him. At the same time, it also created a suspicion of collusion; was it mere coincidence that both the RUC and the UVF believed in a connection between McKenna and the IRA in the absence of any supporting evidence?

On 19 February 1991, the driver of the UVF motor bike, David McCullough, went on trial. He was charged with 13 offences, including the murder of Patrick McKenna, and of James McCarthy, shot dead at the Orient Bar, Springfield Road, on 10 March 1989. He pleaded not guilty. The prosecution pointed out that, when arrested after the murder of Patrick McKenna, McCullough had made a statement admitting that he had gone with Robinson 'to kill an IRA man' in Ardoyne. McCullough's defence lawyers did not challenge this statement. The trial was brief. On 23 February 1991, David McCullough was jailed for life. Mr Justice Campbell accepted that he had been 'manipulated by particularly evil men', but that he had nonetheless carried out 'vile and sectarian' murders.

Neither Patrick McKenna nor Brian Robinson need have died if the British army had intervened earlier to arrest the UVF men. Why they did not do so is a matter of conjecture. Shortly before the incident, on 25 August 1989, a Catholic civilian, Loughlin Maginn, aged 28, had been murdered by the UFF in Rathfriland, County Down. In defence of their action, the UFF produced documentation acquired from security sources purportedly proving that Maginn was an IRA member—a fact consistently and strenuously denied by his family. This was one more case of collusion, the extent of which was about to be examined by the Stevens Inquiry. In this atmosphere, it is not far-fetched to conclude that the British army may have wanted to be seen to be even-handed and efficient in their pursuit of 'terrorists', whether loyalist or republican. A successful operation of 'taking out' some loyalist assassins may have been timely PR.

William Smith, a UVF ex-prisoner, set up a group, Justice for All, to campaign on behalf of Brian Robinson. The group was unusual, if not unique, in taking up the issue of shoot-to-kill directed against loyalists. Smith claims that there were approximately 20 such cases, including: Stephen Hamilton, aged 24, shot dead by the RUC as he drove a stolen car on the Ballygomartin Road, North Belfast, 19 October 1981; Ronnie Brennan, aged 22, shot dead by the RUC during an attempted robbery at Mallusk Post Office, near Belfast, 22 August 1982; and Billy Miller, 26 year old UVF member, shot during an RUC ambush on his stolen car, Elmwood Avenue, South Belfast, 16 March 1983. On the other hand, Sutton claims that overall only 13 members of loyalist paramilitary groups were killed by the British army and RUC, while McKittrick et al put the number at 15.

William Smith, now a member of the Progressive Unionist Party, tells the story of the campaign surrounding Brian Robinson.

William Smith

When IRA men were getting shot on active service or getting killed by the security forces, unionist politicians supported the security forces. But when loyalists were killed by the security forces, there was nobody in the unionist parties who would stand up and criticise the security forces. So

when Brian Robinson was shot dead, there wasn't one voice within
loyalism that condemned it. It was very difficult to gain support within the
wider Protestant community.

If you look at the political background of the time, it was just after the
Loughlin Maginn issue. When Loughlin Maginn was shot, people said he was
innocent and the UDA thought by releasing the montage of Loughlin Maginn,
that they could justify why they shot him because the montage and the details said
he was an IRA man. These details came from the security forces; that is what
initiated the Stephens inquiry later on. But at that particular time there was a whole
hue and cry; in that political background, the pressure was on to do something.

We set up an inquiry. We had a solicitor and a number of helpers. We went round
the community and brought down everybody who claimed to be eyewitnesses.
When we got all the statements, we were able to build up a picture of what
happened that particular day.

There were two people killed that day who didn't need to be killed. Those people could
have been arrested prior to the shooting, for the two [undercover] cars were already in
place. One was facing countrywards and the other facing citywards, so no matter what
way they went round the roundabout after the shooting, they had a car in place to follow
them right away. They already had information that there was going to be a shooting,
detailed information. It wasn't 'so-and-so may be shot'; they had actual information
about the time, location of the shooting, where they were coming from and the escape
route. They actually knew who was going to be shot and they allowed it to happen.

The car pursued them down the road. They were shooting out of the car. Brian
was on the back and as they were heading down the Crumlin Road pursued by this
car, the other car did a U-turn so that there were two cars pursuing them. Davy
slowed down to turn into Cambrai Street and that's when they rammed them. Brian
was hurled up into the air about 20 feet and landed on the footpath; he already had
been shot in the back. The gun that Brian had skidded down the road about 40 feet.
So he landed beside the bus shelter; the gun he had was now 40 feet away.

The two cars had now stopped. The car that rammed him, the people got out
and went over and shot him twice in the head. Davy had skidded on the
motorbike. The other car went after him; he was unconscious at that stage. What
saved him was that a taxi man who had two women in his car was just in front of
them. He had just come out of Cambrai Street, heading city-wards. He looked in
his mirror and saw the crash; he didn't know it was a shooting—he thought it was
a crash. He turned round to go back and help. When he turned round, that is when
the soldier went over to Davy with the gun. They would actually have shot Davy
only the car going back meant there were witnesses there so they couldn't do
anything and that is what saved Davy's life.

When IRA men were getting shot on active service or getting killed by the
security forces, unionist politicians supported the security forces. But when

loyalists were killed by the security forces, there was nobody in the unionist parties who would stand up and criticise the security forces. So when Brian Robinson was shot dead, there wasn't one voice within loyalism that condemned it. It was very difficult to gain support within the wider Protestant community and it was even more difficult to gain support from the nationalist community because a Catholic had been shot dead. There was no desire from anybody to take up the case. It was about two weeks later that I issued a statement to one of the newspapers asking for an inquiry because my investigation into it, especially with so many eye witnesses, suggested it was a public execution. This was a set-up. Brian was killed in cold murder, just as much as the Catholic was, when the security forces went over to him while he was lying on the ground and put another two bullets into his head.

First of all you had to convince people. You see, the security forces are supposed to support the people. There was a lot of shock and disbelief that something like that could really happen. There were people who I know that saw more than they told me, but they didn't want to get involved; they were just afraid. You are afraid of police harassment, that if you start talking about this you may be set up yourself, or you would be branded a traitor by saying the army did this or that. People are really bigoted; if a Loughgall happens, they say it's alright; they forget there was one innocent man killed there. Or any other incident where IRA men were shot dead, they think it's all right. But they are sacrificing a life for a political agenda, for that guy in Ardoyne could have been saved; they could have arrested them before on the way there. But that was not the political agenda. Through shooting a loyalist dead, they wanted to gain something politically out of it. Patrick McKenna and Brian Robinson were sacrificed that day.

There is nobody in the Protestant community or the unionist community who wanted to touch it with a barge pole. We had to go to the CAJ and Amnesty. We found that loyalists weren't confident with the CAJ or Amnesty, for they identified them with republicans. So we had to do something else. We set up Justice For All. I went up to see Alberta, Brian's wife, who was seven months pregnant. I didn't know the girl, but then I saw her on the road and told her that I had meant to see her before I had released the statement. She told me she was glad that I did it for not one politician had said a word. If you get the relatives onboard and they are prepared to do things, you can move on it. She wanted me to pursue it. So I called for an independent inquiry into the shooting because anyone who looked at it could immediately smell a rat.

Basically it was myself and the family. We started writing to MPs. But within the unionist community, you had nothing. There was not one unionist MP, the DUP, the Ulster Unionist Party, would listen to you or give you any type of support. You had to go to the CAJ and well-known lawyers in England who were fighting the Birmingham Six's case, Gareth Pierce and people like that. You had to depend on their advice.

Then of course we had to go to the UVF and ask them to shed light on it. But it was a shut-up shop as regards the police. We didn't get a death certificate for a year and a day, we couldn't glean any information or any statements and that is why Davy McCullough had to plead not guilty at his trial to get information. The trial was eighteen months later and you had nothing to go on, only what your eye witnesses are telling you and what you can produce yourself.

The inquest found in our favour. They found that Brian Robinson posed no threat because the gun was 40 feet away. The problem we had was that we couldn't get any soldiers to give evidence. You couldn't question or cross examine in an inquest. The inquest rules here are just basically cause of death. But for the first time ever in an inquest in Northern Ireland, they found that Brian Robinson posed no threat whatsoever as he lay on the ground because the gun was forty feet away. I was very surprised at that, for they don't usually do that.

Until the actual inquest you don't get the death certificate, so you don't know what actually happened. We didn't know until the inquest that he had been shot on the motor bike, for when you are driving a motor bike and trying to get away, you can't hear the shots, so even Davy, the guy who was driving the bike, didn't know. When we got the inquest and the papers stating the cause of death, that's when we found out he was shot in the back. The army denied ramming the bike but I had got the photo out of the *Telegraph* and it showed the damage. They denied it was a big impact, that he had just fallen off the bike.

The other thing we found out was that Brian had actually emptied his weapon. When a semi-automatic weapon's magazine is emptied it automatically locks back. If you are a trained soldier, you could see that it couldn't fire. They sat and watched them shooting a guy, get on the motor bike and once the motor bike took off, they followed it. If they were just in the area by chance why didn't they stop it, just get out in Ardoyne and save the fellow? It was all planned, choreographed; they waited until they moved off down the road to the part of the Crumlin Road where the peace line is and people don't walk up and down. It was pure luck that the taxi came down at the time.

There were other things: like the police, when they arrived on the scene, weren't panicking. They just came up and the soldiers lifted what we believe was their weapons out of the car and were driven in the Land Rover down to Tennent Street police station. There were a whole lot of things which weren't done which are normally done at the scene of a shooting. If you go to any scene of a shooting in Northern Ireland, you will see rings round bullet holes. You can look at the photos in the newspapers and you'll see nothing like that. The car was moved before forensics got near it. The police never asked for any witnesses. It was only when we raised the issue and we got the inquiry going, they actually raided my offices and took photographs that I had. It was about a week or two after we had the inquiry and I got an article into the *Sunday Life* newspaper. I got in touch with a reporter, showed her the evidence and said to her, 'Here are the witnesses'. So they did a two page spread on the story. When the RUC came to raid my offices, they wanted their names and I refused. When I asked them why they wanted them, they told me it was to interview them. I thought they should have done that on the day and I refused to give them the names.

We used Davy's trial and the inquest to get more information. Davy had to plead not guilty although all the evidence was against him, for us to get the facts. At Davy's trial we were able to glean the amount of weapons they had. They had two rifles, two machine guns, two hand guns and so many rounds of ammunition, all in the boot of the car.

Then we took a private case. What we had proved through the inquest and Davy's trial was that he had been shot dead while lying on the ground. As Alberta said at that time, she didn't want soldiers prosecuted; she just wanted the truth. One thing she would have liked was to say to the soldier, 'Why did you finish him off?' But because she was a loyalist and the pressure from within the community, we would not have got the support to prosecute, so she was content with what she got. To get to Europe, it would take another three years; we had no wish to do that. Nationalists or republicans on their side had the likes of McGrory who went to fight the Gibraltar case on his own time and his own expense. We had nobody on our side who was going to do that. You wouldn't have got the support from within the community to go as far as a prosecution. What it did prove was that there was a shoot to kill policy, within both communities.

The civil case was settled out of court. It took two years of Alberta's life to get to where we did. She had to get on with her life too. After two years she had two children; she had one when he was shot and the other was born just after he was shot. It was very brave of her. She came out of the inquest shattered, for that is when she realised he could have lived if they hadn't shot him in the head. In nationalist cases, they wanted soldiers to be there; we didn't want that. We got their statements. We weren't there to expose the security forces or to make a political issue out of it. We wanted the truth. On the nationalist side they wanted a political gain. We just wanted the truth and we got the truth, for the inquest agreed he was a threat to no one as he lay on the ground. That was a precedent we set. In the trial, we brought out the weapons they had. We are convinced that Brian was executed and that they knew what was happening. But you depend on the families, for if Alberta had said, 'No', I could have done nothing.

It was like blazing the trail, for people sit and watch you to see how you get on. That made it all right for Sally Hamilton to come to me and ask questions about her wee son who was shot dead by the RUC.

I had been building up a dossier on other people who didn't have a voice from years ago. So the Brian Robinson campaign sparked off other people. Ronnie Brennan was shot dead; Miller was shot dead; Hamilton—all shot dead in suspicious circumstances. At that time the inquests lasted five minutes and there was no-one there to say, 'Hold on a minute'. The police man in Hamilton's case said there was a gun in the car, when the car crashed; after they shot him, there was no gun found. That lad was out for the weekend on parole. He had been out drinking and he stole the car to get home. But it was a five minute inquest like all the others; there was nobody there to ask questions. But when we started investigating and raising the issue of a shoot to kill policy against loyalists, that's when these other people started to come forward.

Miller's case is even worse for there was a police informer; he was also the driver of the car. He informed the police about the operation and the police told him to go ahead. He told them the route they were going. In that area of the university where the shooting was there is a garden with hedges. The police waited behind the hedges and the driver was told to stop the car at that position and get out. He stalled the car at that position and got out of the car to look at the engine. The two other guys were still sitting in the car with the guns under the seats. The driver ran, the police came up from behind the hedges and emptied their guns into the car. That guy was removed from Northern Ireland, given anonymity and is away somewhere; he has never been seen since. While Bobby Morton was lying badly injured, he heard one of the peelers saying, 'There is one of the bastards still living. Will I finish him off?' But by that time a crowd had gathered and they couldn't do anything more. But there is another case where the police knew and actually designed it.

There were about twenty cases of shoot to kill in the loyalist community. But at that time nobody questioned the security forces because that wasn't the loyalist remit. So when nationalists talked about shoot to kill, loyalist politicians defended the security forces and when nationalists talked about internment, loyalists defended the security forces. When they talked about the supergrass trials, they defended the security forces and the state, even though we were subjected to all these things.

I was called a traitor for taking Brian's case up by some of my own people; it was unpopular. He had just shot dead a Catholic and he was shot dead himself and the state thought that it was wrapped up, finished. They didn't carry out an investigation after the shooting. I believe because of the attitude within the community, they probably thought they didn't have to bother. They thought, 'Sure, they will not say anything'. It was only because I had started an investigation. I was working in the community on a voluntary basis. From my release from prison, the police had not bothered me, but once I started to do this, the centre was raided with a search warrant for materials. They only got ordinary community things for I had removed all the material to do with the case from the office and my home. It's terrible that these things have to be done when you are only trying to seek the truth.

We have no political agenda. Nationalists have; they want to discredit the police, the courts and that fits into their agenda. It's very hard though to break through that cycle in the loyalist community. In the nationalist community that was par for the course.

But it gives other people confidence and it made our whole community aware of human rights issues. There is not this blind trust and faith in the RUC, the courts and the state. Protestants aren't the blind people they were. They aren't afraid to sue the police. It's far easier to do that now than what it was in 1989, ten years ago. Ten years ago you couldn't criticise the courts or the police.

17

PETER THOMPSON, JOHN MCNEILL AND EDWARD HALE
13 January 1990

Killed by undercover British soldiers

O
n 9 December 1989, joyriders from Twinbrook, West Belfast, stole a Vauxhall Nova car in the centre of Belfast and drove in it to the Homestead Inn at Drumbo, near Lisburn. Their intention was to steal another car from the pub car park in which to travel back the 10 miles or so to Belfast. They chose a Nissan, but inside it discovered two hold-alls containing guns and ammunition, as well as British army intelligence documents. It later emerged that the hold-alls were the property of the 14th Intelligence Company, an undercover unit of the British army. The joyriders took the hold-alls and left the scene in the Vauxhall. They immediately approached a gang of petty criminals based in the Dunmurry area nearby and sold the contents of the hold-alls to them for £200. The criminals quickly realised that the intelligence documents were too hot to handle and burnt them along with the car. The guns and ammunition, with the exception of one Browning pistol, were then transferred to a lock-up garage in Lurgan owned by a colleague of the Dunmurry gang.

The lock-up garage in Lurgan was raided by the RUC looking for stolen electrical goods on 15 December. They found the stolen weapons. The owner of the garage was arrested and held for questioning. Remarkably, he was released the following day. He immediately contacted the Dunmurry gang, stating that the RUC had told him that if the stolen Browning pistol and documentation were returned, no one would be charged. The gang apparently was suspicious, especially given the quick release of the Lurgan man, but did give him the Browning pistol. He passed it on to the RUC. Later he received a six-week jail sentence for handling stolen goods—but the stolen British army hardware was not mentioned in the charge.

There was no follow-up by the RUC in relation to the Dunmurry gang, which caused increased suspicion on their part. As a result, they decided to split up for a while and to get rid of any stolen goods they had. They believed they were under surveillance. After Christmas, however, they decided to return to business. A planned post office robbery was aborted, but on 13 January 1990, they set out to rob a bookmaker's shop at the junction of the Whiterock and Falls Roads in West Belfast.

There were five members in the gang, all of whom were well-known to the RUC as petty criminals. John McNeill (aged 42) had a string of convictions—28 in all, according the RUC—going back to the 1960s. Eddie Hale (aged 25) had two convictions and Peter Thompson (aged 21) six. In November 1987, Hale had been shot in the elbows, knees and ankles by the IRA for his 'anti-social activities'. These three agreed to take part in the bookie's robbery along with another member of the gang. The fifth member of the gang did not participate, unconvinced that there would be any money worth stealing in a bookie's that early in the day, despite Hale's assurances that a large sum of money was kept overnight. The fifth man was later jailed for eight years for possession of a shotgun which did not work and which was not in his possession.

The four members of the gang now committed to the robbery hid two replica guns, incapable of firing shots—a sub-machine gun and a starting pistol—and ski masks in the cemetery opposite the bookie's on the night of 12 January. The following morning, between 10.30 and 11.00, they retrieved the gear from the cemetery and drove to the bookie's in a stolen car. John McNeill, the driver, parked the car at the side of the bookie's and turned the engine off. If there was any sign of danger, he was to hit the side door of the shop loudly to warn the others. The three other gang members entered the shop through the front door with their ski masks rolled up on their heads like monkey hats. Hale carried the replica sub-machine gun and the fourth man the replica starting pistol. Thompson was unarmed, as was McNeill. Inside, Hale ordered the customers to lie on the floor while the fourth man began to fill a bag with money—as it turned out, there was only £428 on the premises at the time. Thompson stood by the front door. They heard loud bangs coming from the direction of the getaway car. Thinking it was a warning, they dropped the bag of money and ran out through the front door. In fact, the bangs were the sound of John McNeill being shot dead. He was shot six times from close range as he sat unsuspecting in the car. The fatal shot which hit him in the right side of the face was fired from a distance of less than two feet.

Peter Thompson, unarmed but still masked, came out of the bookie's first. He was shot ten times by the two undercover British soldiers who were waiting. Eddie Hale, carrying the replica sub-machine gun and also masked, came next and was shot 13 times. The autopsy report later suggested that both had been shot again as they lay on the ground. The fourth gang member merged with the customers in the shop and later escaped. He immediately went to a priest and from there to the RUC. He was arrested on 16 January and released two days later without charge.

The joyriders whose theft of a car had triggered off the chain of events were also arrested for questioning but released without charge. It was difficult to avoid the conclusion that the failure to prosecute was in order to avoid embarrassing court cases where members of the British army undercover unit would be called as witnesses and the contents of the stolen intelligence documents possibly revealed.

There were immediate accusations of a shoot-to-kill operation and parallels drawn between the killing of three IRA volunteers in Gibraltar in March 1988 and the shooting of Brian Robinson in Belfast in September 1989. Some commentators concluded that the same undercover squad—containing one woman operative and a number of men—was involved in both the operations. Brian Mawhinney, Northern Ireland Office Minister, stated: 'The only people who are conducting a shoot-to-kill policy in the province are the terrorists'. But at least 30 civilian eyewitnesses asserted, among other facts, that:

- there was a tremendous and unnecessary amount of firepower involved;
- there was no warning given to McNeill before he was shot, nor to the others as they emerged from the bookies;
- Hale and Thompson were 'finished off' on the ground;
- the shooting was carried out by two undercover soldiers from one car, but two others arrived in another car and gave their colleagues cover during the incident.

Ken Maginnis of the Ulster Unionist Party was quick to dismiss the eyewitness reports:

> My own experience is that when lead is flying about, you have a tendency to put your head down and keep it down, not to keep it up and do an objective appreciation of what is happening around you.

The initial British army statement was that two British soldiers were on surveillance duties monitoring the movements of known IRA members, when they saw two—note, not three—masked men, one of whom appeared to be carrying a sub-machine gun, get out of a car and run into the bookie's shop. One of the soldiers approached the driver of the waiting car who then 'made a movement as if he was reaching for something inside the car'. The soldier opened fire. The shots alerted the men inside the bookies who were shot as they emerged. There was a strong insinuation that the British undercover soldiers believed that they were dealing with an IRA group, not a criminal gang. This version of events was supported in a statement to the House of Commons by Secretary of State Peter Brooke on 15 January.

On 17 January the first connection was made publicly between the robbery of the guns and documents in December and the bookie's incident. The connection was made in a press conference held by Gerry Adams and Father Des Wilson, both of whom had interviewed the gang member who had escaped. This revelation added credence to an alternative interpretation of the bookie's killing. Members of the 14th Intelligence Company would undoubtedly have been reprimanded for losing guns and intelligence documents. Having got the guns back, they were clearly intent on recovering the documents. Thus, RUC raids on the homes of Eddie Hale and Peter Thompson were concerned solely with a search for documents, not arms. This would suggest that no one involved seriously believed that they were dealing with 'IRA terrorists'. But why kill the members of a criminal gang? It could be argued that the British unit was intent on saving face, or was seeking revenge; it could also have been intended as a warning to petty criminals to keep their hands off undercover cars and property.

The two soldiers involved directly in the shooting were questioned by the RUC for more than 12 hours, leading some commentators to speculate that charges might be brought. But this did not happen.

The inquest into the death of the three men opened in Belfast on 19 April 1993. It was revealed that the two killers—identified only as Soldiers A and B—would not appear and that only four of more than 30 civilian witnesses had been called to give evidence. At an early stage in proceedings the Coroner, James Leckey, refused to accept the Public Interest Immunity Certificate served by the MOD on the grounds that it was not specific enough, in effect allowing the MOD lawyers to use it at any point in order to impose a blanket ban on all oral evidence. Three days of legal arguments followed, with the Coroner still refusing to accept the PIIC. The Crown lawyers consequently applied for a judicial review of the Coroner's ruling, which resulted in the inquest being halted. The judicial review led to the Coroner's ruling being overturned. Lawyers for the families of the dead men appealed the finding of the judicial review, but were unsuccessful. As a result, the inquest could reconvene.

The reconvened inquest opened in Antrim court on 14 October 1994. According to Coroner James Leckey, Antrim was chosen because there was no suitable court room available in Belfast. As a result of the ruling in the judicial review, the Coroner now accepted the PIIC. It was announced that the two soldiers who carried out the killing would not appear and that other soldiers were to give evidence from behind a screen.

Much of what went on during the six days of the inquest centred around two points: the reason the soldiers were in the vicinity of the robbery, and their behaviour in relation to the killing of the three men. The statements of Soldiers A and B were read out. They repeated the official story put out initially by the British army and by Secretary of State Peter Brooke. On the second and third days of the inquest, the court was cleared of public and press while Soldiers C and G were installed behind a screen in the witness box. They stated that they were on routine duties at the time; as soldier C put it, there were three vehicles involved in a 'familiarisation operation' in West Belfast. They denied any foreknowledge of the robbery and also rejected suggestions that the killing was in revenge for the theft of documents and guns from a military car in Drumbo in December 1989. It was also denied that undue force had been used.

A number of civilian eyewitnesses stated that the soldiers shot the three men from very close range. One eyewitness said that one soldier had lifted up the bodies of Hale and Thompson before shooting them again at point blank range with a pistol. That McNeill was shot at close range—less than two feet distance—was confirmed by forensic evidence; he was hit six times. Hale was hit by 12 bullets, two of which went through his head. Thompson took 10 bullets; again two were in the head. One forensic scientist, Brian Thompson, stated on the fifth day that there was no evidence that Hale and Thompson had been shot from less than three feet distance. However, under cross-examination he agreed that a pistol shot from just over two feet away and a rifle shot from three feet away would not necessarily have left any powder traces on the bodies. One soldier had used two pistols, the other a rifle. The same scientist revealed that Soldier A—one of the killers—had given false details of the shooting. He claimed that he shot McNeill with one pistol and then returned to his car and got another pistol with which he shot Hale and Thompson. In fact, McNeill's body was found to have bullets from both pistols. Soldier A fired 24 shots in all. Soldier B fired 11 shots from a rifle which he claimed he had switched accidentally to automatic.

Another disturbing fact to emerge was that Soldiers A and B had spent considerable time with MOD lawyers before making their initial statements. Moreover, Soldier A had been advised by the RUC to alter his statement when it became apparent nine months later, as a result of available forensic evidence, that parts of his evidence did not correspond with the facts.

Overall, the evidence of civilian witnesses and forensic experts at the trial complemented each other on a number of crucial points, thus calling into question the soldiers' version of events. Errors in the soldiers' accounts included the following:

– three men entered the bookie's, not two;
– they did not wear masks as they entered, but only donned them once inside;
– only one of the men was 'armed' (with a replica gun); the others were clearly unarmed;
– no warnings were given;
– the overwhelming likelihood was that Hale and Thompson were shot at close range in the head while they lay on the ground;
– death was instantaneous, meaning the only movements of which they were capable were nervous death tremors.

The inquest was hampered by the absence of Soldiers A and B and by the production of the PIIC whenever any other military witnesses were questioned by lawyers for the families. Consequently, on the sixth day of the inquest, 20 October 1994, solicitors for the Hale and Thompson families withdrew. The Coroner took two hours to sum up and the jury of three men and five women withdrew for a long deliberation. Three times they returned to inform the Coroner that they could not reach a finding. Eventually, they were directed by the Coroner to reach a finding of lawful killing. Finally, over 12 hours after they had entered the court that day, they reached a finding. The three men had been shot by undercover soldiers who believed they were paramilitaries who posed a danger to the soldiers' lives. The men were encountered by chance by a routine patrol while they were engaged in a robbery. After being shot, they made movements which led the soldiers to fear that they were still a threat. There was, concluded the jury, no evidence of close-range shooting.

Lawyers for the one family who had remained (that of John McNeill) for the final day sought a judicial review at this point. The grounds were that, first, the marathon nine and a half hour session affected the jury's concentration and therefore their ability to reach a clear decision; and second, that the coroner had instructed the jury improperly, given that inquests in Northern Ireland can only deliver findings on the 'where', 'when' and 'how' of death, not its lawfulness or otherwise. In April 1995, Lord Justice Carswell quashed the inquest finding and ordered a new inquest. He concluded that four and a half hours was the maximum the jury could be expected to concentrate. He concluded that it was the responsibility of the coroner to run the court 'in such a way that the jury can consider their verdict in conditions which give them the opportunity to discuss the case and decide on their conclusions without undue time pressure and when they are fresh enough to give the case real consideration.' In addition, he agreed that the Coroner's instructions had overstepped the mark. Rule 16 of the Coroners' Rules prevent any finding other than relating to the facts of death. The Coroner's instruction that the jury reach a finding of lawful killing—in effect, justifiable homicide—was not permissible.

The new inquest took place over one and a half days in September 1995. No lawyers for any of the families were present. The inquest smoothly arrived at a finding about the facts of the deaths, once again agreeing with the British army version of events.

The families and relatives of the dead men have insisted from the beginning that excessive force was used by the undercover soldiers in apprehending the three men. The British army unit that day broke their own rules of engagement, as laid out in 'Army Code No. 70771—Instructions for Opening Fire in Northern Ireland', specifically:

- 'Firearms must only be used as a last resort.'
- 'A challenge must be given before opening fire ...'
- Weapons can only be used if someone is 'likely to endanger life and there is no other way to prevent the danger.'
- Specifically, the use of weapons is justified if 'there is no other way to make an arrest.'

On the basis of the activities of the British soldiers and the subsequent revelations during the inquests, campaigners conclude that there is enough evidence to bring charges of murder against Soldiers A and B. But no such charges have been recommended by the DPP. To the frustration of the relatives of the dead men, it is clear that this was a shoot-to-kill operation carried out with impunity. As John McNeill's sister put it shortly after the killings: 'He was no angel, but he was no terrorist either. They were not interested in taking prisoners'.

Mark Thompson, brother of one of the dead men, tells the story of the bookie's killing and the subsequent campaign, as well as of his own involvement in Relatives for Justice.

Mark Thompson

We are ordinary people who have come together in extreme circumstances and out of those experiences have identified a commonality which we feel we have to address. Against all the odds, against the state, against all the vilification, propaganda and all the disinformation, we have come up against it in a very resolute and dignified way.

It was a Saturday morning, the 13th of January 1990. Usually I would have been up and away to a football match, but at that particular time I hadn't been training and I had the morning off. My mum, dad and sister Joanne—who was seven at the time—had gone to Scotland. At around 11.00am, there was a rap at the door and on answering it, I found that it was two of Peter's friends. They asked to speak to my dad. I told them he wasn't in and could I help. They said, 'Pete's dead'. Just like that! I was suddenly bolt upright. I said, 'A car accident?' They said, 'No, the SAS killed him. It's revenge; we stole their gear'. They told me they were just involved in trying to rob a bookmaker's shop and got ambushed by the SAS and that it was all connected to them handling stolen undercover guns, maps and codes. 'We got their gear about a month ago. We returned it, but they have come back and done us; it's revenge because they didn't get their maps and papers.' I said, 'Was it just Peter?' They told me that Eddie Hale and John McNeill were dead too. Frank Turley, who subsequently became known as the third man, managed to stay inside the bookmaker's shop and he got away.

I was just kind of numb. With my dad being away, I phoned a couple of his friends. I wanted to be sure, for them to find it out for me. I had a sense within me, 'Let's not panic; it might not be him and if it is him, he may not be dead'. It was the afternoon when it was definitely confirmed. People started coming to our house and there was a realisation that this had happened. I didn't put on the TV or the news; I didn't want to deal with it. My sister Teresa was at work. We contacted her and told her to come home, there had been a bit of an incident. The ferry hadn't even docked in Scotland at this stage. Funny enough, friends of my dad's were working on the ferry at that time. They held the boat that was returning to Larne for a half an hour. They got word to my mum and dad; they got them on the phone. I went to the phone and said, 'Dad, something really awful has happened. Peter's been shot dead; the British army have killed him'. My dad's voice sank: 'Ah son, please don't tell me that'. I could hear my mum screaming in the background.

Some people set off to Larne to bring them back. It was dark by the time they came back. Earlier that afternoon around about two o'clock, our house was surrounded by the British army and the RUC. I looked out and the street was saturated with them. There was a plain clothes RUC man at the door and he told me he had a warrant to search the house. I said to him, 'My brother's dead. Can you confirm it? Can you confirm who you shot?' He told me he couldn't confirm anything, that I should go to the morgue to find that out. I said to him, 'I'll tell you what he looks like'—I was in desperation—'He had sandy coloured hair, a bit smaller than me, twenty three. You have to know who you have killed'. He said, 'We didn't kill anybody; it was the British army. We are just carrying out a search'. I looked out the back. We have a caravan and a shed out the back and they were tearing everything apart—the shed, the pot plants, the trees and bushes. They were in every room, the kitchen cupboards, opening the telephone book and going through it. They were taking the names of everyone in the house and by that time there were about fifteen people there. I'll always remember this RUC woman walking up; she had a big screwdriver. I'm trying to get information from this RUC man and she said, 'Have you any broken tiles in your kitchen or bathroom that would come off easy, that you would hide stuff behind?' I asked her what she was talking about. She told me they were looking for papers. Your man said, 'We are looking for papers, not weapons'. I told them I hadn't a clue what they were talking about. They must have been there for forty-five minutes.

Later my mum and dad arrived. As she came through the back door I looked at her, and for a few moments none of us were able to speak; there was this total silence and although the house was packed, those moments felt, and still feel like an eternity. It was as though everything else around us was suspended. She was being physically held upright by friends. There was an emptiness about her whole self and even recalling it, and the telephone conversation with my dad, still causes me great difficulty. Shortly after this my uncle Paul came back from the morgue. He had left long before my mum and dad had arrived. When he came into the room, there was this glimmer of hope—his verdict about identifying the body; it's all so clear even now. That glimmer, this last thread that everybody could be wrong and that somehow Peter was alive, maybe just hurt, and that the body was that of some other family, was still somewhere in the back of my mind and in the mix of thoughts kept the horribleness away. And I know that sounds awful but it's true. It was just like we could all sigh and everything we had gone through in the previous ten or twelve hours would be over. And yet this was just the final moment where no longer could I, my mum, dad, or anyone else push away the reality that Peter was dead. My uncle came into the room, and I'm picturing my mum; she looked at him and everybody looked at him, and as we all stared at him, waiting and not really wanting to hear, he walked to where my mum sat and took her hand. He didn't speak; he just nodded and the silence turned to sobs and cries. We all knew; that was it. I know how difficult that must have been for Paul and just over two years later he again made a similar trip to identify another nephew, also shot dead.

My dad kind of took control of the situation and he sent out for some of Peter's friends. He also sent for Gerry Adams MP and Father Des Wilson. They spoke to Peter's friends to try and establish exactly what had occurred, not only that day but over the previous weeks. It transpired that on December 9th 1989, joyriders had stolen two hold-alls from a parked car belonging to the 14th Intelligence Company just outside Lisburn. Contained in the hold-alls were a Heckler and Koch, a 9mm Browning pistol, stun grenades, ammunition, enlarged maps of west Belfast, notebooks with codes and references related to the maps, and various other items. The joyriders contacted Eddie Hale who purchased the hold-alls and their contents for two hundred pounds. Eddie had sent one gun to Lurgan to an associate, B.L., who had a rented lock-up garage, securing the remaining gun in Belfast. The maps, codes and notebooks were then destroyed. Stolen electrical goods, bought from a businessman who reported them stolen, were stored in the lock-up. B.L. had been casually selling some of these goods locally and it appeared that a local telephoned the RUC who in turn raided the garage looking for stolen goods and to their surprise found the weapon. They arrested B.L. and took him to Craigavon holding centre. He was later questioned by RUC Special Branch and members of British military intelligence. He was allegedly released into his own custody without assurances and told to recover the other gear, the weapon and particularly the papers. He phoned Eddie Hale telling him about the discovery, that he had been arrested, questioned, and released to recover the remaining items and if recovered, all would be fine. As soon as Eddie put the phone down and revealed the conversation to those involved who where also there, including Peter, suspicion arose. No way would he have been released; surely he had struck a deal or at the very least was being followed. As the discussion continued about B.L., the door knocked and he appeared. He arrived at their house in Belfast from Lurgan, allegedly, within the space of twenty minutes. A heated argument ensued and accusations were made. B.L. denied any deal that had disclosed their identities, or that he was driven to Belfast by those who questioned him. He claimed to have come alone. He was not driving. B.L., who was unaware of the maps and papers, kept saying that they wanted them back. According to those who subsequently provided this information there appeared to be more importance placed upon the recovery of these than the weapons.

B.L. was reluctantly driven to where the second weapon was hidden, given it and left on his own. According to B.L., he took a local taxi back to Lurgan, threw the gun in a field and telephoned the RUC who sealed off the area and recovered it. There was no record of anyone taking a taxi from either the depot he claimed or any of the three nearest taxi depots that day. Eddie, Peter and the others were aware of the significance of the loss and now in light of the discovery prepared for arrest.

A few days after the weapons were returned a small news item appeared on 5th January, linking the loss to an undercover unit of the British army and stating that no paramilitary connection was suspected. Chris Moore also ran the story on BBC Radio Ulster. There was no follow-up by the RUC, but despite this, Peter and his friends kept a low profile and suspected that the incident had not yet blown over.

It later transpired that those who had carried out the killings, the 14th Intelligence, had also been the same undercover unit that suffered the loss of weapons and surveillance material. Kevin McNamara revealed this information to our family and was himself in no doubt as to the connection. He stated that the surveillance material was of a 'highly sensitive nature'. Ironically two of the weapons used in the killings were a Heckler and Koch and a 9mm Browning pistol.

Gerry Adams held a press conference with Des Wilson in the Felons' Club. We put the radio on to listen to the response of the British government. We knew right away that they were lying, and that there was an immediate policy of disinformation at play—that they happened on a robbery, that there were just two soldiers in the area and that they were confronted by armed and masked 'terrorists', as they perceived them. That wasn't the case. There were three people who were in the bookmaker's and one outside in a car. My brother, who was unarmed, came out first. But there were difficulties getting these and other facts out, so in that sense we immediately began a campaign. I suppose it really started from Gerry Adams' press conference after leaving our house. It was us saying, 'Hold on, there is more to this than meets the eye. It wasn't just two British soldiers passing in a car on the Falls Road at 10.50 am on Saturday the 13th of January 1990 and seeing what they said were two armed men. There was a much more sinister background to the incident which posed serious questions.'

Peter Brooke on the 15th of January in the House of Commons, in response to a question from Kevin McNamara as to who was responsible for the killings, refused to reveal, but Kevin McNamara revealed that it was the 14th Intelligence Company. Brooke had stated that two soldiers happened to be passing and saw two armed and masked men going into the bookmaker's shop and that they took up positions. They said the driver of the car made a sudden movement; his hand moved as though to go for a gun. They were confronted by armed and masked men and as a result three of them were dead. Security forces had to operate in tight situations and had to respond to protect and save property and life. We knew that this was misleading and untrue. We called for a public independent inquiry. Cahal Daly and others echoed that call. Actually there was a range of political support for that, other than Ken Magennis and Sammy Wilson. Ken Magennis said that those who dress like terrorists can be expected to be treated like terrorists. Sammy Wilson said that the shooting was justified and that the soldiers were out to protect life. Surprisingly enough, John Alderdice of the Alliance Party asked a number of questions. We said that not only was there a shoot-to-kill policy, but this was a pre-planned, premeditated shoot-to-kill operation. They would shoot people, rather than arrest them. And the RUC were negligent in that they failed to arrest people for having a weapon, which carries a minimum sentence of ten years. Why weren't they arrested? Who took the decision for them not to be arrested and for an undercover operation to be put in place? We stated that we had no confidence in any RUC investigation. There were no grounds in the past to show that the RUC could carry out an independent investigation that would result in prosecutions.

The immediate days afterwards and dealing with bereavement and the media intrusion—that was hard to deal with. There wasn't a group as such we could go to for help. The first contact we had with anyone was Mike Ritchie from the CAJ. Mike came out to see the family and advised us what to do. The *Irish News* did a lot of work with us and we lobbied the BBC. Eventually a guy called Bruce Batten, a researcher and the editor of 'Spotlight', came to see the family and decided to do a programme about it. He visited every door in our street. For example, a week before Peter was killed we had a man call to our door with a pair of ladders asking to check the gutters and offering to clean them. He said he would leave his ladders as it was the weekend. On the Monday he never returned. On the day Peter was to be buried, this guy came to collect the ladders and I said I'd give him a hand to his van with his ladders. He said, 'No, I'm parked down round the corner' and there were two other people in the van. Someone said, 'That boy is a bit suspicious'. So as part of the research, 'Spotlight's' Shane Harrison from the BBC rapped every door in our street and asked if this person had called to any other house in the street. He hadn't.

The BBC actually did its programme. Senior members of the BBC, we were told, had serious problems with its content. They were told it was too suggestive and that it had to be edited, parts taken out. Actually 'Spotlight' had finished its scheduled run for that series and the programme still wasn't transmitted. They ran an extra week to broadcast this programme. Bruce Batten said that they'd invested too much for it to be pulled and was determined that it be screened.

Another strange thing was on the Thursday before the killing my mum went to drive out of the drive-way to pick up my sister from school at two o'clock. A red XR2 car, identical to one which my dad had previously sold, zoomed down our street and stopped, did a u-turn, let my mum drive out of the drive-way and the driver stared directly at her. He actually followed her to the school and sat while she went into shops and followed her back to our street. She thought, 'This is a car that Joe has sold and something is wrong with it and this man is up with a complaint'. My dad said that Agnew's Auto Exchange in Ladas Drive had bought the car and therefore it wouldn't be traced to us. Agnew's hadn't yet sold the car anyway. My mum gave a description of the guy; she got a very good look at him and in hindsight felt that there was a connection. We reported this and other incidents to the *Irish News*. We got a visit from the RUC two days after that article was published, Inspectors Meek and Molloy. They said they wanted to question my mum about her story in the *Irish News*, in particular the description of the man. My mum asked them why were they coming out to do that. 'I'm telling you why,' she said. 'It's because that person is one of the ones involved in killing my son, isn't it?' One of them put his head down and the other said, 'He could be'. My ma asked, 'Where are they now?' One of them said, 'They are out in the barracks in Lisburn and we are going out to interview them.' She had words with them and the two of them left the house.

A number of days later at seven o'clock in the morning our door was kicked continuously. It was a dark winter's morning. We got down and the RUC were all in the street. I'll never forget it; when we opened the door there was this big cop with a big grin on his face. He said, 'I have a warrant to arrest Peter Thompson'. We couldn't believe it. My da said to him, 'What are you talking about? I just buried my son. My son was murdered in one of the most public killings'. He just laughed and walked away. The other one was standing with his gun and my ma said to him, 'Just leave us alone'. The other cop said he had been on holiday and knew nothing about this. I never cried when my brother died—maybe once in my room. I thought I mustn't cry because my mum would then cry. It's just very hard.

It just never stopped. If it wasn't the RUC, it was the British army. My mum would have been stopped regularly going to her work at six in the morning. She was taken out of her car. The Brits would have come round and sat outside our house and threw pebbles at the window—all stupid things which didn't make sense because Peter wasn't in the IRA. He was an ordinary lad from a working class area. He came from a republican family but he wasn't a republican. When he was young, he would have been involved in the Bobby Sands Youth Movement but that was that. He had a separation with republicans in the local area and he didn't have any respect for some of them.

In July 1995 I went to the UN hearings in Geneva. The Sunday before I left I was in the Short Strand; it was the twenty-fifth anniversary of the Battle of Ballymacarret. There were two jeeps and as I walked past one jeep, the plain clothes RUC man in the back said to me, 'Alright, Mark, I hear you are off to Geneva'. I near died. He said, 'Long runs the fox', and he put his hand to his head as though he was putting a gun to his head and said, 'Remember, you can do all you like, but remember'.

We were contacted by Niall Farrell. Niall was hoping to put something together for the 6th of March 1991 for a protest at Government Buildings in Dublin on the ineffectiveness of the government in dealing with the issues of shoot-to-kill by the British army. There had been various incidents up until then—Armagh, Tyrone, Gibraltrar, us, Fergal Caraher. A full bus of relatives left Belfast and we all met up in Buswell's Hotel in Dublin. We went to Government Buildings and held a protest there for about an hour. People went by and we were chatting to them, telling them what we were about. I suppose Niall had a sense that there was a bigger issue here and we needed to organise ourselves.

That April, Niall, Father Murray and Peter Madden and others came together in Dungannon parish hall. There were 250 to 300 relatives there. We elected a committee and we became Relatives For Justice. We set a small programme of work—write letters lobby and so on, and perhaps provide a sense of support, not in the sense of counselling, but support to make publicity, get the issue up there, to protest, to rally round. You aren't on your own; there are people out there. There is an inquest in front of you; you need to be prepared for that. You need to call for independent inquiries, get the human rights groups to give you support. The key to it is to get information out. I suppose I had a sense of frustration on that, the lack of information put out. There was a form of self-censorship with the media particularly after 'Death on the Rock'. With the exception of a few, they were ignoring the clear patterns between all the killings—and also how they were subsequently managed through the system.

Before the DPP was to make his decision whether he would prosecute on the findings of an RUC investigation, the RUC leaked that they had recommended to the DPP that no prosecutions were to be taken in relation to the killings. Myself and a couple of friends then set about drafting a pre-inquest booklet. We printed a few hundred of those. We sent them to the States, to lawyers and human rights groups, anyone who was interested. It raised a number of questions: was it a pre-planned, premeditated operation? Was there a link between the weapons, maps and codes? Were the shootings justified, and was the force reasonable?

The first inquest was April 1993 and it was adjourned. James Leckey was the coroner. When we went into the court that morning, we sat there and it was rumoured that the soldiers may appear. In actual fact they weren't appearing. You had soldier A and soldier B who did the killings, soldiers C, D, E, F, G, etc. There were eight of them; there were three other soldiers and a commanding officer who were going to give evidence, evidence about I don't know what, for it was supposed to be one car with two soldiers who happened there by accident.

There was a Public Interest Immunity Certificate put on the inquest and we objected strenuously on the grounds that it would restrict our ability in an already restricted forum to find out what had happened. Leckey's objection wasn't towards the PIIC. It was that Malcolm Rifkind, the Minister of Defence who signed the application, hadn't clearly stipulated the guidelines in which it should be used. Those representing the British army and the RUC said that they could invoke the PIIC at any time of the proceedings and that it covered screening and oral evidence. But Leckey refused on the grounds that it was too vague. The RUC packed the courtroom and there was barely enough room for us, the families.

The inquest was adjourned and reopened in 1995. Surprisingly, it was moved to Antrim courthouse and the jury were picked from the garrison town of Ballymena. We felt a bit concerned; we thought, 'Why in Antrim?' This time the Public Interest Immunity Certificate was now accepted and Leckey voiced that he was glad to get the inquest under way. The Certificate had been cleared and it could be used by the Ministry of Defence to interject at any point. I had a tape recorder and I was going to start taping and I was called out of the court by the RUC and told to switch the recorder off or I would be held in contempt. I told him there was no stenographer in the court and we as a family needed some sense of what was happening. I took notes.

We never wanted an inquest, as most families don't. But you have to use the inquest for the media interest that is generated; you have to use whatever is at your disposal in terms of bringing a sense of awareness and raising issues. There were forty-seven witnesses and only three or four of them were civilian witnesses. In fact we actually brought a vital eyewitness whom the RUC claimed unable to find. The soldiers giving evidence totally contradicted initial claims that there were two soldiers on their own. There were four cars, a radio operator in the Henry Taggart Fort and various other pieces of information that contradicted Peter Brooke's statement in the House of Commons in 1990. It was a farce. Soldiers A and B, who never turned up, had their statements read out; they said that they left the barracks at nine thirty that morning. All the other soldiers said they left the barracks at ten o'clock. We wanted to know what they had done in the intervening half hour. A log provided proved that the two who carried out the killings had left earlier. One of the soldiers was driving around Twinbrook in a Volkswagen Golf at ten past ten that morning. The car used for the robbery left Twinbrook that morning. The second car containing two soldiers was in Andersonstown; they were all in radio contact. The third car did the shooting and was carrying the two soldiers, and the fourth car was at Beechmount Avenue. There was a DMSU [District Mobile Support Unit] mobile patrol that left the Whiterock British army base, there was a DMSU at the Donegall Road roundabout at the M1. There was a DMSU that left Andersonstown Barracks and there was a British army patrol at La Salle Drive and a VCP [vehicle checkpoint] at Beechmount Avenue-Falls Road junction. There was a helicopter out and a radio operator from the Signals who had control of all of this.

Most enlightening was the evidence from one of the first to provide medical attention, a British soldier, Private Mark Dickson of the Queen's First Regiment, from the nearby patrol in La Salle. His evidence was supposed to focus on the position of the bodies. However, we decided to question him about the nature of that morning's patrol and if any briefings were provided. He told the court that earlier that morning the patrol was introduced to a sergeant medic who was to direct the patrol and that they had found this both strange and highly irregular. He has never seen this person again.

After listening to the evidence, it only confirmed our belief that there was a pre-planned, pre-meditated operation to shoot them dead and that Peter, Eddie and John had been under surveillance. We walked out of the inquest. The inquest went on without us for another two days. It sat through a marathon session when it delivered its verdict; it sat from eleven in the morning to very late that evening, which is totally unprecedented. The reason was that John Major was flying in the next day.

Although Relatives for Justice was up and going, it hadn't really got a direction. We attended conferences and put out statements. We kept contact with people from Helsinki Watch and the American Lawyers' Guild. Father Murray's book about the SAS in Ireland carried a lot of weight. We also produced a collusion booklet; basically that highlighted the use of South African weaponry. Peter Madden, Father Murray and Martin Finucane went to South Africa to the Cameron Commission in 1995. Lawyers from there came over here and met relatives of those killed as a result of collusion.

We started to get a sense of the importance of the truth. The CAJ had Frank La Rue [a Guatemalan human rights lawyer] over and we talked about the issue of truth and what was emerging in South Africa with the Truth and Reconciliation Commission. We thought that this was something which was as important in Ireland; this is what we have been looking for. This was the vehicle which would address the whole issue. We formed the Campaign for the Right to Truth. The state has to acknowledge that they have acted outside the law, breached human rights and murdered people. A core part of conflict resolution is acknowledging our past and then beginning a process of addressing that. We were drawing, and continue to do, on the international experience of conflict resolution.

We were looking at other conflicts and becoming knowledgeable about what we wanted. We talked about reparation and restoration—not to be confused with retribution, for many relatives have no vengeance within them. They just need to find a sense of positive closure which allows for truth and justice. Tell us the truth. Don't keep adding insult to injury by telling us lies; don't perpetuate the suffering. We also want to positively contribute to a future society in which we are not left behind. If anything, we have a pivotal and central role to play in shaping our collective future. It is through our experiences that we will identify the failings of the past and set in place the safeguards which will protect and promote human rights. However, this can only come about with a careful examination of that past. Importantly reconciliation cannot be achieved in the absence of truth. Therefore we all have a vested interest in seeking the truth and no one should fear the truth. Such a process will also bring acknowledgement and recognition, ending the disparity of 'deserving' and 'undeserving' victims and survivors. A truth commission is the way to do this and we campaigned hard for this.

In 1995 the Forum for Peace and Reconciliation was up and running in Dublin. We had to struggle to get into the Peace and Reconciliation Forum; it wasn't an open door for us. We nearly had to come to the point of picketing. We chose a number of people to make submissions. Fianna Fail and surprisingly Fine Gael, we had very good responses from them. It came to Seamus Close [Alliance Party] and he sat; he didn't look. He talked a bit about drawing a line under the past. He said, 'A child cuts or burns her/his hand and a scab comes on that hand, then it heals. They have the sense to know not to pick that scab for they know if they do, it doesn't heal. And because they want it to heal, they leave it alone.' For me, he had missed the whole concept of conflict resolution. I was so angry and I was waiting to see what our people were going to say. Father Murray just looked up and said, 'I thank the learned gentleman for his comments. Now can we move on?' It was the perfect response. His analogy was so far off. Scars are never going to heal without truth and justice. I suppose that if we all listened to the likes of Seamus Close then the Bloody Sunday Inquiry and similar developments in the pipeline for relatives of the Dublin and Monaghan bombings would not have come about. We can't draw a line under the past when that past is the present and future because of the failure to present the facts and let unhindered due process takes its natural course— especially when it involves those supposedly there to protect, uphold the law and prevent such atrocities.

In July 1995 we were at the UN hearings in Geneva where they look at the issue of human rights within the jurisdiction of each signatory. Initially Father Murray, Martin and Michael Finucane and Peter Madden went out and presented the collusion pamphlet and other information concerning Pat's murder. They came back and then myself and Eilish McCabe went out to join Martin two weeks later. Ironically it was the same day that Mayhew released Clegg. We spent three days there and we lobbied extensively; if anything we harried and harassed. We presented evidence and views on patterns of shoot-to-kill, the failure of the judicial system to effectively handle cases concerning state killings, investigations and inquests and the need for the UN to act.

There was a Canadian guy who was an assistant to a Rapportuer. At one stage myself, Eilish and Martin were standing. He said, 'Take a seat'. He probably visualised a brief encounter with us. But if anyone knows Eilish McCabe or Martin Finucane or even myself, once we got our claws into him, there was no getting away. We told him about collusion, about Pat [Finucane] and the various things that were going on and he basically said that there was a chance of a Rapporteur being appointed on all this stuff after the hearings. We could not believe it. He mentioned a Malaysian judge called Cumaraswamy. We were very keen and extended an open invitation and exchanged contacts. On the basis of that first meeting in Geneva they appointed Param Data Cumaraswamy to come and carry out an investigation. Sometimes you try to assess yourself what impact you are making. It was totally out of the blue that we met that Canadian in Geneva, but out of that we now had a Special Rapportuer to come and investigate, and we all know what his findings were. The report talked about procedures of investigation, about inquests, about Castlereagh holding centre, shoot-to-kill and harassment. It made a number of recommendations. As you know, they were all side stepped.

The Brits are crafty. The UN committee were releasing their report on a Friday. John Major was coming to Ireland on the Tuesday to plan with Monika Wulfe-Mathies the Peace and Reconciliation Fund, which was special European money coming to Ireland, all tied up to the peace package. What John Major did was to put forward his visit to Ireland to the Friday to coincide with the release of the UN report. This meant that the report got lost in the media coverage of Major's visit. If they do things like that, it means what we are doing is right.

I am always mindful while I'm in Relatives for Justice, when I am meeting someone that it's not just me, that there are hundreds of other relatives; that I'm not just talking about my brother but that I am talking about every case and I think of those people when I am doing that. I think about the Forgotten Victims day. I was on the verge of breaking down, it was so moving. I think about the photographic project that Arthur [Fegan] and I started three years ago, which he has really carried on, particularly around the children. We went and visited a lot of them to get the photos and they open a wee tin box; in it there are photos, a piece of hair taken out of the coffin and they have it in a cellophane bag with a photo and a mass card. When they open that box, there is a ray of life that comes from them; that person comes alive for them for a while. The impact that photographs have made—people stand back and there is a different response when people see the faces.

I also saw a need for the relatives to be more proactive, particularly in the climate we are in now with developments within the peace process. We now have an office, a number of projects and volunteers which are not all campaign based and which provide for mutual support. I am now employed full-time by RFJ.

The Bloomfield Report was commissioned. Eventually he did agree to meet us. The first issue we raised was our objection to the way he had treated us; he had proactively engaged others, but he had to be nearly threatened to see us. We talked about truth. He mentioned twice the issue of compensation and quite obviously this was coming up from various other relatives' groups he had met before. Niall said to him, 'Listen, that is the second time you have mentioned money. We aren't interested in money; we want the truth'. He said to us, 'You know the IRA bombed my house and attacked my family'. I thought it was rather cheap of him and his mask slipped; he had a role as a professional person who would report on victims and in that he should have a sense of impartiality. He mentioned it again and I tackled him on it. I said, 'You had your house bombed by the IRA and frankly that is a matter for the IRA. Thankfully no-one was killed or injured. People round this table have lost relatives and that is the stark reality. We are here as a result of the security forces killing our loved ones. Your house was bombed and the forensic scientists came, the ballistics came, and the RUC scenes of crime officers came and went through your home with a fine tooth comb. They have opened files everywhere and, although I don't know if anyone was prosecuted for bombing your home, I can tell you every resource of every department is operating at maximum to apprehend those responsible, while those same resources are working in the opposite direction in relation to us. I find what you are saying offensive.'

Bloomfield published his report. He had a recommendation for everyone and rightly so—the disappeared, members of the security forces, RUC and prison officers. He talked about everyone and presented criteria to address their concerns. He didn't make any reference to our concerns and on the wider issue of truth, he sidelined it. He gave it back to the politicians; he didn't deal with it. We realised then that we were being squeezed out. We couldn't allow this to happen for it was in fact a basis for sowing the seeds for further excluding our experiences within a peace process which should have been redressing the issue and ending the inequality of that experience.

You can do one or two things about that: you can stand outside and shout, or you can go in and fight. We decided that, since we were calling for inclusivity, in no regard should we exclude ourselves. We got involved with the Victims' Liaison Unit. We raised the issue of membership of the Touchstone group. Adam Ingram, the MP and 'security minister', who was given responsibility for victims, himself had a problem with meeting the group; he wanted to meet Raymond [Murray] on his own. When we appointed Eilish to the Touchstone Group, it immediately caused problems for them. Given the broad section of people we represent, which included relatives of republican volunteers who were killed, they didn't want to see us as equals.

The one conscious move we have made, and we have been very vocal on this, is that we accept the suffering of everyone. We have carried that view into Touchstone. Last week myself and Eilish [McCabe] went to a Touchstone meeting. We raised a lot of issues, one being how the Loughgall families had been treated that Monday. We had a very interesting debate with Dave Clements from WAVE and also the Cost of the Troubles study. During the discussion on the Loughgall relatives, Dave Clements interjected and said, 'My father was in the RUC and he was gunned down and finished off while he was on the ground with his own gun. The Tyrone brigade of the IRA took that gun and had it at Loughgall.' When he had finished, I said, 'I recognise and accept the suffering you are going through. What happened to your father was wrong. The IRA needs to be accountable to you. It is not up to you to reconcile yourself with the IRA; they have to reconcile themselves with you.' I turned to Adam Ingram and said, 'In the same way, Mr Ingram, you have to reconcile yourself with me and with Eilish, with Brendan Bradley who is here and with three hundred other families'. He said, 'The truth is a two-edged sword'. I told him of course it was and that nobody should fear the truth. He said, 'It's who moves first in this process'. I replied that that was up to a sovereign power to move first. We are making a wee bit of progress about acknowledging and recognising all suffering and finding a common approach. But there is still a long way to go.

During the conflict many relatives and indeed communities suspended their grief, their emotions and I suppose in the cut and thrust of things every new day and week brought to others new tragedy. There was no space. People have now found that space as a result of the peace process and are now examining those hurts, beginning the necessary and difficult process of healing. There is a need for the truth as part of this process. As an organisation working with and for bereaved relatives and survivors we must design a strategic vehicle which delivers the truth, heals and provides the foundations for eventual reconciliation.

We are ordinary people who have come together in extreme circumstances and out of those experiences have identified a commonality which we feel we have to address. Against all the odds—against the state, against all the vilification, propaganda and all the disinformation—we have come up against it in a very resolute and dignified way. The truth will out and our struggle to tell that truth itself will be vindicated.

18

FERGAL CARAHER
30 December 1990

Shot by British army

On the afternoon of 30 December 1990, Fergal Caraher, aged 20, was shot dead by soldiers from the Royal Marines near an army checkpoint on the Tullynavall Road, Cullyhanna, South Armagh. His brother Miceál, aged 23, was seriously injured.

The brothers had gone in two separate cars, agreeing to meet up in a pub car park before driving on together to Dundalk. Fergal arrived at the car park first. It turned out that the British army had set up a vehicle checkpoint on the road near the car park. They were, however, stopping and searching cars going into the village; Fergal had driven out of the village.

As he sat waiting for Miceál he was approached by one of the soldiers, later known as Marine B. It has proven impossible to ascertain what went on between Fergal and the Marine. Army suggestions were that the Marine went to speak to Fergal about driving past the soldiers without stopping; on the other hand, eye witnesses claimed that Fergal's car was waved through by the Marines. Some altercation may have taken place, but it seemed to end amicably. As Miceál walked into the car park, having emerged from the other car a short distance away, he saw Marine B walk away from Fergal's car. Miceál got into the driver's seat and, as they drove out of the car park, two Marines, Richard Elkington and Andrew Callaghan, opened fire. Elkington fired nine shots and Callaghan 11. Nine bullets hit the car, three of which and a fragment of another lodged in Fergal's back. Miceál was also hit a number of times but managed to drive for about a mile before the car came to a halt. Miceál was brought to Belfast's Royal Victoria Hospital and Fergal was pronounced dead on arrival at Newry's Daisy Hill Hospital.

The army's initial statement was that the soldiers opened fire after the car failed to stop at a checkpoint. Two soldiers were said to have been injured by the speeding car, one of whom was hospitalized. Both soldiers, however, were back on duty the next day.

From the start, local eye witnesses challenged the army's version of events. All denied that the car broke through a checkpoint and that soldiers had been injured. All agreed that no warning had been given before the shooting began. One even stated that one soldier had taken up a firing position a minute before the car left the car park.

Despite an RUC investigation, no prosecutions seemed imminent. Relatives and local people in South Armagh formed the Cullyhanna Justice Group, and, with the assistance of the Irish National Congress, organised a public inquiry in June 1991. Six jurists from England, France and the USA—with Michael Mansfield QC as chair—considered evidence from medical and other experts. However, the RUC would not allow them access to the postmortem and forensic evidence. In their published report, the jurists concluded that there were sufficient grounds to charge the soldiers who fired their weapons with murder. One of the jurists, Veronika Arendt-Rojahn, stated:

> It is not at all comprehensible why the Director of Public Prosecutions has not been able up to now to make up his mind about whether to prefer charges.

Judge Andrew L. Somers Jnr of the USA went further:

> There are sufficient grounds to indict or charge with murder those soldiers who unreasonably fired their weapons with intent to kill Fergal and Miceál Caraher.

Shortly afterwards, the two Marines, Elkington and Callaghan, were charged with the murder of Fergal Caraher and the attempted murder of Miceál. Their defence was that Fergal had earlier ignored an army checkpoint and had subsequently driven away from the scene after an altercation with the soldiers. The car was said to have hit Marine B who was being carried off on the bonnet. To protect Marine B, the other two had opened fire. On 23 December 1994, Lord Justice Hutton announced his verdict. He concluded that the local witnesses from Cullyhanna had given untruthful answers on oath in the witness box when they said that they had not sought legal advice from a solicitor before giving statements to the RUC:

> [...]when assessing the truthfulness of the evidence of the civilian witnesses as to what they saw happen in the car park ... I have to bear in mind that they were prepared to lie in the witness box about the way in which they gave their statements to the police.

On the other hand, Hutton accepted 'that the two accused and Marine B had strong motives for supporting each other in the witness box and that Marine B had strong motives for giving evidence to help his two comrades, whether it was true or not'. In particular, he found it difficult to accept that Elkington and Callaghan had opened fire on a car ostensibly to protect their colleague whom, they claimed, was actually being carried on the bonnet of that same car. That said, Hutton stressed that 'an accused person can only be convicted if the court is satisfied of his guilt beyond a reasonable doubt, and, of course, this principle applies to the trial of a soldier just as much as it applies to the trial of any other person'. Consequently, he found the two British soldiers not guilty 'because I have reasonable doubt as to the guilt of each accused'.

The success of the Cullyhanna Justice Campaign was in applying pressure to ensure that the two soldiers were brought to trial, despite the fact that the outcome of that trial was not as the campaigners would have wished.

Margaret Caraher, the widow of Fergal, takes up the story.

Margaret Caraher

In many respects you can never let go; it's never a wound that gets to heal, because it's always unfinished business...Without an acknowledgement, I'll always think: "I did the very best I could, but it wasn't enough". There'll never be an ending to it; and things need an ending.

I was at home because Brendan and I had a cold. My sister and Fergal's doctor called into the house. This was maybe about half-five or six and I had been expecting Fergal back by then. When I heard the door, I thought, 'That's him now'. My sister came in and I did recognise that there was something wrong with her. She just said, 'There's no easy way to say this. Fergal's been shot'. I said, 'No, you've made a mistake'. And I thought, 'My God, how did they make a mix-up like this?' I really didn't take it in. And she said, 'No, there's not a mistake'. I didn't believe it, it was so ridiculous—for many reasons, not least that Fergal wasn't the aggressive type or he wasn't the sort you would imagine getting into any situations.

I went up then to Fergal's mummy and daddy's. That first night nobody seemed to know what happened or what way Miceál was going to be, whether or not he was going to survive. It was actually the day after that that some of the people came forward who had been in the cars at the checkpoint. And they said, 'We've been listening to the news and they're saying that Fergal and Miceál were at the checkpoint and they weren't. What do we do?' And Peter John's brothers said, 'Go to a solicitor and make a statement'.

They didn't come to notify us that Fergal had been killed. They wouldn't allow me access to the car; they wouldn't tell me where the car was. Brendan was just about a year old and I had a pram in the boot. Obviously they had forensic tests to carry out, but I only got the car back three and a half years later. As well as that, there were small things that make a difference—Fergal's tapes in the car, his jacket, things like that that I wanted.

At the funeral Peter John [Fergal's father] spoke for a few minutes and said there should be a public inquiry into what had happened. Some people from the Irish National Congress picked up on that and came forward after the funeral and said, 'We'd like to facilitate in whatever way we can'. And it was the first time we thought, 'What exactly do we mean by a public inquiry?' To say we hadn't a clue is really putting it mildly.

This area in its entirety is not an area that was policed by the RUC. The strongest feeling both myself and Fergal's family would have had was that there is no way we'll receive any justice. Very soon afterwards, as soon as we started moving about again, the police and the army would stop us and were making threats towards Fergal's younger brothers—'We'll do the same with you'—making sarcastic remarks; if you had any doubts that you were going to receive fair treatment from them, you weren't going to have them for too long. The idea that it would have been the RUC investigating the army wouldn't have made any sense to us either, because it's all the one. We needed to have something independently done, something that would have no influences from the RUC, although we recognised that it would have no power, except for the public power it would have. We went ahead and started to organise it. We called a public meeting, about March of '91; 80 to 100 people turned up and they all wanted to be on the committee. Nothing was too much for them to do. We decided we wanted to have it in Cullyhanna. There was an awful lot of organisation went into it. The first couple of months was trying to find out what our options were and from March on till the inquiry was held midway through June, it was organisation all of the time, with the last couple of weeks being full time. We targeted anybody—TDs, MPs, priests, nuns, anybody we thought would add any influence at all—all the human rights groups. We did obviously invite the RUC and the army to participate, but they declined.

A lot of work went into it, a lot of organisation—something that I don't think could be organised in a lot of areas. I think it's because it's a small area and the ripple of pure shock that went through people was very, very strong. Not to say that it's not the same in other areas, but because it's such a small close-knit community.

We held the inquiry over a weekend. We invited a panel of jurists using whatever network we could get from the INC who really did an awful lot of work for us, and Caitriona Ruane who worked for them at the time. Any contacts they had, anybody they knew—that was something we would have had no idea about. So we did get a panel of international jurists from France, Germany, America and England and set it up like a courtroom with terms of reference, solicitors, the witnesses giving their evidence and making their statements, and open to the public. It was a great success; it was very well attended. There were over 200 observers. We had a marquee set up on the outside of the hall. It lasted for two days, finishing up with a reconstruction of what actually happened on the day, which we tried to piece together. The jurists found that there were grounds to investigate and there were charges of murder answerable to, and there were serious questions to be raised around the issue of shoot-to-kill. We went on to publish a report with the jurists' findings and submissions from other organisations. That didn't come out until February of '92. About ten days after that, two soldiers were charged with murder and attempted murder.

In the beginning when we started out, I didn't think it carried too much weight. I was very surprised by the amount of power it turned out to have. I really wouldn't have banked on that. Just at the very beginning, when the soldiers were charged, people were saying, 'That's the report', and I was thinking, 'Aye, right!' But it's only really as years have gone on, I've seen the power it had. It was a way of channelling very negative emotions and a lot of anger into something positive. It was giving us something to do rather than sit there and wonder what was going to happen, with absolutely no input whatsoever.

A lot of politicians and media turned up thinking this is going to be a tiny, insignificant thing and were very taken aback that it was very well organised. I would have to say that wasn't the family's doing; that was the local people and the help from the INC and various groups. We as a family didn't have that kind of knowledge. Right down from having the road signposted, having a first aid caravan, accommodation, the local women in the school provided a three course meal on the two days for everyone who attended, and the actual professionalism of the inquiry itself and the way it was conducted. That made its impact.

Some of the locals discovered talents they never knew they had. As we came up to it, they were out putting up the marquee; they hooked up televisions to it; there was endless tea and biscuits; they set up an office with computers; all sorts of wee details—the name tags for people and press observers' badges. Everybody mucked in and helped out. Things just seemed to appear—like caravans and signs. And the amount of stuff people donated—'Here, take this. No, don't worry about paying. We'll cover that'. Like all the food; there were about 500 dinners made that weekend; all the food was donated; the school allowed the canteen to be used. Cullyhanna is a small village and it was just alive.

The power I got from it was in doing something. Very often then and since I felt, 'I'm up against a brick wall here. This is the British government who are very powerful, and they're not going to listen to wee me'. There's an awful sense of powerlessness there; this thing happens to you; you've got no choice about it, and then there's very little else you can do.

Myself and Peter John made submissions to the inquiry, and that was the first time I had ever spoken publicly; I was very much in two minds about whether I would or not. Through the inquiry we had met with other families and from that we started going to meetings or this protest or that protest. And then it became, 'Would you come along and talk at this meeting or conference?' At one point I would have been completely full-time going to one thing or another. And at the same time I was still working on Fergal's case.

We were invited by the American Senate—myself and Peter John—to go out and speak at a sub-committee hearing in September of '91. Myself and Peter John spoke along with John Stalker about the whole incident. That was in Washington. Then we went down to New York and did some talking. I never had done any sort of public speaking before.

We took every opportunity. We would have gone anywhere. We didn't know what the word 'no' meant. The initial statement went out from the RUC saying that this and this had happened. During the wake, we didn't really speak an awful lot to the press; we weren't really fit to do it. And during the funeral we had asked for no media presence; it's not something you'd want on national television. I certainly felt then that nobody had got to hear what really did happen. But it's very hard to keep the momentum going, because, unfortunately, it's a nine day wonder. Other things happen after that. Human nature being what it is, there are people who say, 'There's no smoke without fire. There must have been something to it. They don't go round shooting you for nothing'. The truth was that, yes, they do go round shooting you for nothing, but it's a very hard thing to win. So, I suppose in many respects, I felt I nearly had to convince the whole world that they do shoot you for nothing all too easily. I would have been as hard to convince as anybody else before that, if I'm honest.

It really did become my whole life. If I wasn't out talking, I was thinking about talking; if I wasn't out at a meeting, I was thinking about going to one. It was at the forefront of my mind all of the time. And while I might have been sitting somewhere, talking away to someone, smiling, acting as if everything was normal, that was all going through in my head over and over again. I felt that I had the whole world to convince and the whole world to tell. That was so very important to me. In this area you're surrounded with army bases and they stop you on the road all the time. And I found, very often I'd be thinking, 'Was it him?' It mightn't even have been the same regiment, but I would really think, 'Is that one of them?' It was really driving me crazy. One of the things that eased it was, after the soldiers were charged, they had to go up for a preliminary hearing and for the first time I actually got to see who it was. All along all I really wanted was to see who they were and I wanted to ask them, 'Why on earth did you do this?' They were taken into the Petty Courts to be charged with murder—by that stage it was over twelve months later. I had very mixed feelings about going up to the hearing. When I got there and saw them, I thought, 'So what, really? At the end of the day they're just a scapegoat really.' And for the first time I could see the bigger picture. For the first time I thought, 'Right, they're only one piece of this puzzle.' At the end of the day, it's the system that allows all this to go on. That took a bit of the heat out of it for me in my desire to see them and to see who they were. But it was very frustrating on the other hand, because obviously I couldn't talk to them; I wanted to be able to say to them, 'What on earth did you do this for?'

It was November 1993 when the trial started in Belfast. We had made requests for the car and all his things because we wanted to carry out forensic tests and we were still being refused. We actually had no input into the trial in that the Crown prosecuted the military. We were notified that it was on and where it was.

We all went down each day to observe the trial. That brought more work of asking people from different organisations and human rights groups to send an observer to monitor the trial. Then ourselves the family and the local people who had been very involved all along wanted to be there for the trial. So, it was a packed courtroom every day. They certainly didn't like it being a packed courtroom and they certainly didn't like having to let us in. It was this wee small courtroom with hardly any seats.

The first day of the trial, when we went into the canteen for a cup of tea, there were the soldiers sitting with no handcuffs, just sitting. The only table left was the one beside them. You could just feel people's blood pressure and tempers rising. There they were; they had tans.

The trial lasted three and a half weeks. If it wasn't such a very serious matter it would be absolutely comical. The amount of rubbish, lies, contradictions—it was really laughable. The soldiers gave evidence and contradicted one another. One of them, his story was that Fergal had knocked one of their soldiers down and carried him some distance on the bonnet and that they had fired to protect their comrade which, under the rules of the Yellow Card, they are able to do. So at one stage, one of these soldiers was stopping the car, he was jumping up onto the bonnet, he was running alongside, he was breaking the window with the butt of his rifle and he was breaking his fall at the same time; he was a real acrobat! Even the judge said once or twice, 'You're telling me you did this, this and this?' As he was demonstrating how he used the rifle, he used the wrong hand, and the judge pointed out, 'Actually, it's your right hand and you're using your left. Do you realise the mistake you're making?' It was ludicrous, to say the least.

They called the local witnesses, but not all of them. Miceál was in the car, but he was never called. They made a huge issue of the fact that most of the witnesses used the one solicitor; there is only one solicitor in Crossmaglen. A lot of these people hadn't been at a solicitor's before, so they just went to the nearest one. They tried to establish a pattern or plot—that we got together and plotted it all out—and really gave some of the witnesses an awful grilling. After three and a half weeks, they deferred the verdict and they gave the verdict on the 23rd of December, the day before Christmas Eve and it got lost in all the Christmas shopping. The judge found that, although he had serious doubts about the truth of the soldiers' statements, because the witnesses were from South Armagh, they couldn't be impartial. So, he had to find grounds for reasonable doubt and he acquitted them.

In many ways it was no surprise whatsoever; it was the verdict pretty much that we were expecting, but I suppose on the other hand, listening to the evidence, to see the flaws in it, you can't help but hope. I found the whole trial very difficult, emotionally draining—the implication at one stage that Fergal had been drunk—I found all that very upsetting. Whereas before I'd been feeling I had been doing something, working towards something, I really felt there and then I was banging my head off a brick wall. I really was very disheartened. It was difficult for quite a while after that.

The inquest couldn't be held because they were waiting on criminal proceedings. And then, because of the criminal proceedings, the coroner felt there weren't grounds for an inquest because the reason of death had been established in the criminal trial. So, we took a decision at that time; we could face ten years trying to get a decent inquest out of them. For some families, the inquest was the only type of trial they had; they didn't have a criminal trial, whereas we felt because of the criminal trial it wasn't going to have the same impact for us. So at that point we lodged the case in Europe. It's still there.

We still went on doing talks and that kind of thing, but eventually, because Brendan was getting bigger, I had to scale down. He thought my sister was his mammy for a while! I was just the person who arrived in the door after a while with a bag in her hand! I still tie in with other campaigns, but at nowhere near the same scale I used to. I don't do nearly as much now. Reality set in. I work now and so I have to miss out on a lot of stuff. But I still would take an interest and I would try as much as I can to make the Relatives for Justice meetings, and things locally that have come up through the peace process.

In many respects you never can let go; it's never a wound that gets to heal, because it's always unfinished business. I can say that the campaign moved us into areas that I know other families didn't have the opportunity of. I know in many respects we can consider it a success. But it never netted the results we wanted— for them to acknowledge that what they did was wrong, that all that rubbish about soldiers on bonnets was all wrong, that they had actually opened fire. The witnesses still maintain there were three soldiers. There were only two stood trial, so where did the other one go to? Who was it? We wanted justice; that's all we ever wanted. It makes no difference whatsoever to my life whether those soldiers serve time or don't serve time; it has no bearing on my day-to-day living. They took a life and there's nothing and no one can ever replace that, no amount of years served. But what would go an awful long way to helping this whole thing to heal would be a public acknowledgement of the wrongdoing. I may be wrong; maybe if I got that in the morning, it wouldn't be, but I certainly feel very strongly that it would be enough. I could really say to myself, 'Well, I've come to the end of the road now. I've got what I set out to do and I've come as far as I possibly can with this. Now I can leave it with a clear conscience.' Because otherwise I can't. It's always going to be there. I'm always going to feel that I didn't get to the end of it. For sanity's sake, I'm going to have to say at one point, 'Enough's enough'. I have a child here, I have bills to pay and I have to go on with my day-to-day life, but it will always be there for me. It just can't heal without that small acknowledgement. And it would be just as little as that, and as much as that.

In many ways it was the only road. I deeply resent having ever to go on that road. I deeply resent that as a family we could not have handed that over to proper authorities and been assured that every resource possible would have been used. And I deeply resent the really difficult things I had to do personally: how difficult I found it to speak publicly, how difficult I found it at certain times, especially very soon after Fergal's death, at a time when I couldn't even say his name, that I had to—I chose to because I felt I had no choice. It was difficult and it's totally not on for families to have to put themselves in that position. It was a positive way to channel anger, but I certainly never grieved properly, because I was out there being busy and I never stopped to actually grieve.

I think I'll always be glad because, although Brendan's a young fellow, if it ever comes to the point where he says, 'And what did you ever do about it?', I'd be able to look him straight in the eye and say, 'I did the very best I could. It maybe wasn't enough, but I did the best I could.' That's what a lot of it was all about at the end of the day. If I'm to be honest, I never could say I did it for everybody. At some point you do get involved in other people's campaigns and you do draw support from other families. But at the end of the day, I did it for Fergal and I did it for Brendan and at some point then I could see the benefits it had for me. But also its drawbacks. Without an acknowledgement, I'll always think: 'I did the very best I could, but it wasn't enough'. There'll never be an ending to it; and things need an ending.

19

KEVIN MCGOVERN
29 September 1991

Shot dead by RUC

Kevin McGovern was a 19 year old student at Loughry Agricultural College in Cookstown, County Tyrone. Although from Kinawley, County Fermanagh, he lived in Cookstown. On the evening of 29 September 1991, he left home with two friends, intending to go to a disco. They had been drinking beforehand and were carrying glasses of beer in their hands. Their route took them along Westland Road South on the edge of the town. It was about 11.30 p.m.

About forty minutes earlier the RUC had received a tip-off that an IRA attack was imminent in Westland Road South. The IRA later acknowledged that they had aborted a mortar attack after being spotted by a civilian. A large contingent of RUC personnel arrived in Westland Road South—locals said at least two dozen, many dressed in night-time camouflage and wearing balaclavas. They lay in wait. Kevin McGovern and his two friends walked into the ambush. Apparently they were ordered to stop and two did. Not unreasonably, given that there was no certainty that they were not being stopped on an unlit road by loyalist assassins, Kevin turned and ran. He was shot in the back and died on the spot. His two companions were arrested.

The RUC issued a statement that the shooting had occurred after the victim 'appeared to throw something at the police'. But the following day, this was retracted and the RUC acknowledged that Kevin McGovern was an innocent man shot by mistake. The RUC also released without charge Kevin's two companions who had been held in Gough Barracks, Armagh for twelve hours.

233

Local independent councillor Patrick McCaffrey issued a statement underlying Kevin McGovern's innocence:

> I can vouch for the fact that no member of the family would be involved in anything remotely regarded as illegal. I condemn the attempts by the RUC to cast a shadow of doubt by suggesting that Mr McGovern was possibly carrying an offensive weapon… Murder is murder and cannot be otherwise described, no matter who pulled the trigger.

Cardinal Cahal Daly called for an inquiry to be headed by a senior police officer from outside the RUC. Instead, the incident was investigated by the Independent Commission for Police Complaints; the inquiry was overseen by Fionnuala McGrady, a solicitor and niece of SDLP MP Eddie McGrady. Subsequently an RUC man, Constable Timothy Hanley, was charged with the murder of Kevin McGovern.

At his trial in February 1994, Timothy Hanley stated in his defence that he had opened fire because he honestly believed that his own life and the lives of his colleagues were in danger. He also argued that he was seeking to prevent the escape of a suspected terrorist. In assessing this defence, Mr Justice Nicholson focused on the first element of Hanley's assertion. He sought to ascertain whether Hanley's claim of an honest belief that he was in danger was sustainable. The judge pointed out that if the belief asserted was extremely fantastic or inconsistent, then it would be hard to conclude that the belief was reasonable. On the other hand, reasonableness alone was not the measure of the honesty of the belief. What appears reasonable in the clear light of day does not necessarily seem the same in a situation such as that experienced by Timothy Hanley as he waited to encounter armed IRA members.

The judge was in effect attempting the difficult—if not impossible—task of deciding whether Hanley's belief that lives were in danger, even if unreasonable, was not so implausible as to be dishonest. The problem was that there was in fact one major inconsistency in his evidence. In his notes written shortly after the shooting, Hanley stated that Kevin McGovern took up 'the standard aiming stance for a pistol/revolver'. The following day, in an interview with detectives, he elaborated further by stating that he could see Kevin McGovern's hands outstretched. Yet clearly Kevin McGovern did not have a revolver and would not have had any reason to take up a firing position. To believe that he did so would therefore appear to be unreasonable. So, was Hanley telling the truth about seeing outstretched hands? Judge Nicholson was sure he was.

> With hindsight, he may honestly have brought himself to believe that he saw Mr McGovern's hands though I am sure he was mistaken in any such belief. He assumed when he saw the face of Mr McGovern that the body was in a position in which he was in danger of being fired at and he reacted by firing. When he found that Kevin McGovern had no weapon he probably persuaded himself that he had seen him in a firing position and it was a short step to having a state of mind in which he believed that he had seen the man with a revolver or pistol in his hand.

Thus managing to infiltrate the mind of the accused and articulate his thoughts even better than the accused himself—Hanley did not appear in the witness box—the judge concluded that Hanley's account may have been inconsistent and even, with the benefit of hindsight, unreasonable, but it was not dishonest. He acquitted the accused.

Judge Nicholson pointed out that incidents such as the killing of Kevin McGovern would occur 'so long as the present campaign of terror goes on'. He surely did not intend to give a green light to the RUC to go out and murder; on the other hand, his remarks were a callous reminder that in this case, as in so many others, the RUC had killed with impunity. The blame for the death was, in effect, shifted from the RUC to the IRA. This conclusion was underlined by Hanley's subsequent career. He was immediately reinstated in the RUC and was not subject to any disciplinary investigation. In fact, five years later, in November 1999, he was interviewed on local BBC television as a spokesperson for a group of RUC officers heading off to be trained by the Gardai for peacekeeping duties in Kosovo. In February 2000 Hanley was also featured centrally in a Channel 4 documentary on the RUC, 'The Force'.

The McGovern family had been very active from the moment of Kevin's death. They arranged an independent post-mortem and lobbied the RUC to state unequivocally that Kevin was innocent. While unusually they were given the benefit of seeing a prosecution, the trial did not guarantee justice. As Sean McGovern, Kevin's brother, a hospital consultant, commented after the acquittal: 'While justice within the present system has been done, it is clearly corrupt'. And CAJ voiced the general concerns of many:

> What are they [the family] to think of a policeman whose reaction to a supposed threat to his life is to dash off in the direction of danger, discharging over twenty rounds from his weapon when none are fired at him? Moreover, what are they to think of a system that not only lets him away with such conduct, but warmly welcomes him back into a police uniform as soon as his acquittal is announced, despite the judge's comments that although he had acted honestly, he had not acted reasonably?

The story of the death of Kevin McGovern is told by his brother, Sean McGovern.

Sean McGovern

Our Kevin's dead. Truth and time help to heal but don't stop the hurt.

On Sunday night the 29th September 1991, Kevin had returned to Loughry College to start his third week. He had rented a room that was adjacent to a bar and there were two fellow students who asked him down to the bar for a drink. Kevin had a few drinks in the bar and then they decided to go on to a disco. They were walking through the Greenvale estate in jovial spirits. When the three of them started off walking, they had plastic glasses that they would have been given from the pub to finish their drink.

It appears that the police were that night on high alert; they had been warned of some IRA activity or other. The police drew up to where there were bollards. There was some shouting; there was a dispute as to whether there were shots or shouting or if it was shouting and then shots. The two students Kevin was with stopped. Kevin ran on. We have some description from a passer-by of Kevin running. He had heard the shots, stopped his car and was looking in his rear-view mirror at Kevin running down the road, very frightened. He saw Kevin run on as hard as he could. The next thing, he saw Kevin disappear out of sight. Subsequently we learned that the policeman who shot Kevin had fired in excess of thirty shots. Kevin was hit only once but that shot transected a major blood vessel in his chest. This would have resulted in immediate loss of consciousness and death within a few minutes. Kevin was essentially dead before he hit the ground.

There were people who said they heard Kevin shout, 'Help, help'. He could never have, because he was dead. But my mother and father found it distressing, thinking that he was lying there crying for help.

In terms of how we found out about it: my mother received a telephone call from Kevin's landlady saying that she should telephone the RUC in Cookstown. My mum telephoned the RUC in Cookstown. She was told by the police officer that they would return her call when they checked out who she was. An RUC officer telephoned her back and my mum said, 'What about Kevin?' 'You'll get his body in Magherafelt morgue', was the reply. 'What happened?' 'He was shot.' 'Whom by?' 'The police.' End of conversation.

It was the landlady again who telephoned me. I was in bed sleeping at six o'clock in the morning when the bleeper and the telephone went off. The landlady told me that Kevin had been involved in an accident. I asked, 'Was it serious?' She said it was. I asked, 'How serious?' She said, 'He's dead'. I asked her what had happened and she told me it was the police who had shot him. I drove down to Cookstown that morning, telephoned my mum obviously who was devastated—disbelieving and denying, as we all were.

The news reports at this stage were that the police were investigating a suspicious incident and came across three men, one of whom was shot and the other two were arrested. Quite clearly the inference was that they had got three 'baddies'.

When I heard the news I drove straight to Cookstown police station to enquire what had happened. I recall asking the senior officer if my brother was involved in any criminal or terrorist behaviour, to which I received the reply 'We have no evidence of that at the moment.' It seemed as if they were deciding how to play this event. It was suggested to me that Kevin had been an unfortunate by-stander to another incident and Kevin had been shot in the cross-fire. I challenged them to publicly state that Kevin was an innocent bystander.

The reaction of the security forces after such a death is to behave as if the family of the victim have done something wrong. I remember being asked about my family and what they all did. I felt more that I and my family were under investigation than being treated with the common decency that one would extend to a relative who had just heard his brother had been killed.

The police went into my brother Pat's flat in Cookstown. They searched his flat and never told him what had happened. He had a few drinks taken and was sleeping when they entered the flat, looked around, didn't get anything. They didn't tell him; he didn't know what was going on. Retrospectively we realised that they were desperately hunting for some evidence to connect Kevin or our family to a republican label. They weren't interested in what happened; they were more interested in a damage limitation exercise.

So the police propaganda machine went into full swing but it was more difficult than usual. We were a Catholic family with no republican connections—no cousins in Sinn Féin! The pressure was on them. I said that we were going to be asking for an inquiry. The family were in a strong position; this was going to be a major news story. To the British and English media, not the local media, this was a newsworthy story for prior to this, the propaganda machine had in the majority of cases been able to attempt to justify homicide by a policy of 'guilt by association'. 'Friend, cousin or neighbour of known/suspected republican.' Elements of the media saw this as a novel story. 'The police had shot a Catholic and no obvious escape route was available to them. It was actually somebody who was innocent and who was from a non-republican background, whose family were educated; one of them was even a doctor.'

Ironically some of my colleagues were saying, 'Well, we know that he was not doing anything at that time but...' It does come down to people who are fed on a diet of there are only two types of Catholics: those who are on active service for the IRA and those who are not—they are off-duty IRA members. It falls back into that mentality.

The police made a statement at our request later the day Kevin was shot, around twelve mid-day. The statement said that Kevin was not involved in terrorist or criminal activity 'at that time'. I had demanded that when I met with them earlier in Cookstown. Looking back it seemed that he had been off-duty that night; he was an off-duty terrorist. I was then interviewed by UTV news and I thanked the police for coming forward quickly with the statement in relation to Kevin but we needed to know publicly what had happened to Kevin that he could be shot on a night out.

Of course, this had the effect of turning the screw on the police even more then. This made our family appear in a very reasonable light. This was not a tirade of abuse against the RUC. It disarmed the police propaganda machine. People who were on the republican side asked, 'What are you thanking them for?' However, it was weeks, months later that the same people realised that this had put more pressure on the RUC.

They had used the media very effectively in the past to plant their version of events. In the past rarely if ever had the media been used effectively to apply pressure on the police to extract the truth. This was a whole different agenda now; it was being turned back on them and used against them in a way that they had not foreseen. We used the media. It was, 'Doctor, educated, Catholic, asking questions as to why his innocent brother was killed by the police on a night out.'

I think our family gained strength from being able to ascertain the truth. The independent post-mortem—we had a Dr Bolster, a forensic pathologist from Cork, perform the post-mortem. The independent post-mortem served three major purposes. Primarily it was great source of comfort to the family to know that Kevin would have died quickly. There were rumours about him crying for help but this could not have been the case. Secondly it allowed us to say that Kevin had received a single 'shot to the back'. Being shot in the back is always a news story. Thirdly by harnessing the media it also allowed us to send a message to the police that they were dealing with professionals now; Kevin's death was not going to go away. We were going to go out with the help of CAJ and get more information and they were going to have some explaining to do. The 'Counterpoint' programme we did was also sending them the message that Kevin's death was not going to go away. We were gaining more information about the circumstances of Kevin's death and they had no answers.

The ICPC [Independent Commission for Police Complaints] were really pathetic in their actions. The enquiry was headed by a Catholic solicitor. She was used by the ICPC; 'Here we go; it's a Catholic case—we'll get a Catholic'. She or the investigation never approached the family directly. Even their conclusions reached us via the media before the letter they sent to my mother arrived the following day. The whole exercise was about window dressing. Sir Hugh Annesley [RUC Chief Constable] actually refused to suspend the RUC officer who shot Kevin. He said he needed to be convinced of serious wrongdoing before he could suspend anyone. However, there could be no more serious wrongdoing than shooting somebody in the back. He was prepared to have the window dressing of an investigation. I know the phrase is overworked now but it's institutional; institutionally they can get off with this. 'We have got off with it before so there is no reason that we can't get off with it this time.'

After a period of time—I think it was around May or June of the following year, nine months after Kevin was killed—the police officer who killed Kevin, Timothy Hanley, was suspended from duty. The Crown Prosecution Service felt that there was enough evidence to charge Hanley with murder, a prima facie case to be answered. This was against the trend to charge their precious RUC men with murder while on duty; it is bad for morale. Eventually they caved into pressure, for, sooner or later they believed this McGovern boy will meet up with the right solicitor; some high profile solicitor who will take this case up. The RUC are only interested in protecting their reputation. Retrospectively their intentions in our case were not for the benefit of the family; it was the best strategic move that they had. If they allowed us to fester on, if we did not get some sort of resolution of it, then we would still be fighting and Mansfield or somebody would have taken the case on.

The RUC were beginning to realise that in time if we could bring this case up, this was the case that could bring them down. So they had to try to draw a line under it. They couldn't afford to keep this case open, for people were saying that they would use the McGovern case as a test case. They were going to find it very difficult to get out of this one.

This could not have happened in England where a policeman could shoot dead an innocent student in the back and not be suspended. It shows the depth of the institutionalised getting off with it, that they are outside the law, not the keepers of the law. Yes, the RUC have suffered a lot themselves and that has to be recognised, but they certainly did bring a hell of a lot of suffering on others. The history of the war will reveal that there are two sides and that a lot of people have suffered.

My parents are prayerful, straightforward folk, not engaged in any politics. They brought the family up and educated them. We as a family had 'stickability'. The family stuck together. We grieved in our own private and personal ways. We had the benefit of the court case, even though it never secured a conviction. The court case was not brought by us; it was brought by the DPP and we were left out of that process.

Do you know that the practice of the RUC is to get together immediately after a critical incident like this and start writing notes about what conceivably could have happened? All of them together! That was the first thing that they did and they admitted that in court. It is like that all the witnesses to a murder got together and got their story right before giving evidence. They went into a huddle and the general tone of it was, 'Now, what will we say happened?'. Then when it was proven that what they said they had seen they couldn't have seen, Hanley's notebook was suitably amended to make it fit. That came out at the trial. The judge in his summing up said that he [Hanley] was guilty of behaving unreasonably. I am a doctor and if I was found guilty of unreasonable behaviour resulting in death, I would be brought in front of the GMC [General Medical Council], disciplined and probably struck off and criminal charges brought against me. I certainly wouldn't be promoted. This is more evidence of the institutionalised way that these things are done. The trial result had the effect of killing Kevin again.

We are lucky that the trial got the truth out or as close a version as was possible. Kevin ran off; he was scared. The charge was murder, the level of proof being beyond reasonable doubt. Incredibly, a police officer who is on duty cannot be charged with manslaughter. This is something that has to change if the police officers are to be accountable.

The trial was a vehicle by which we could tease out the truth. It was there but it had to be teased out. He went berserk; he shot thirty times. I appreciate that the RUC have a difficult job to do but to fire thirty shots when there is nobody firing back! It would have been sensational if we had got a conviction; there would have been an appeal. He would have got out on appeal. They would never have let a policeman go down. The whole process demeans life, demeans the memory of individuals.

I don't think my mum and dad could have lived through another trial. It was like killing Kevin again when Hanley got off. There were propositions of remorse from his counsel but there was no tangible evidence of remorse. If he had been truly remorseful, he would have given up the RUC and left. He was a Queen's University graduate; surely he could have done something else.

Shortly after Hanley was charged Kevin was in the local paper, the *Fermanagh Herald*. Kevin's picture was on the front page with the headline, 'Policeman coming to trial soon'. In the middle pages there were photos of myself and my sister Deirdre. I had got my fellowship in surgery and Deirdre had graduated from Queen's in pharmacy. On the back page was an article about my sister Marie who had won an award for being the sports person of a local club. My dad said that if you had just read the front page you would spend the rest of your life depressed, so you had to 'read on'. It's funny that my impression is that not too many people ever get beyond the front page; they don't read on. They are in an endless spiral of wanting answers, an endless spiral of talking about 'Tommy', as if 'Tommy' is going to come through the door. They have never moved on; their lives stopped at that moment; they have just drifted into a wilderness. It's blinkered vision and abnormal grief reactions, fuelled by lack of evidence, fundamentally a lack of truth about what happened their loved one.

I think in terms of the need for reform of the RUC. I think there is an overwhelming case for it. It's going to take a number of generations before people can naturalise their trust; it's going to take a long time for it to set root.

Recently I was talking to my mother on the telephone. She told me that Timothy Hanley had been on the television speaking about the RUC training with the Gardai to go for peace-keeping duties in Kosovo. Later I received a phone call from the BBC warning the family that he was going to appear on television. Someone in the news room had recognised his name. The killer intruded into the home of my parents without warning, talking about peace in Kosovo. If there is a black humour in this world, it was brought to the fore by this man, none of whose actions in the court room ever suggested remorse. In fact many are convinced that because he was made to suffer the indignity of a trial, he would be later promoted. He is now a sergeant. More recently [March 2000] Timothy Hanley appeared on the Channel 4 programme 'The Force' talking about his great work as a police officer. Again Kevin's memory is soiled by his killer.

Our family have survived this experience through respect for Kevin and his spirit and having been able to have got close to the truth. We are grateful to the man who came forward as a witness at the trial, the CAJ, the media for their sensitivity in particular the team at 'Counterpoint'. Finally we are indebted to the members of other families in similar situations who were a source of support and comfort at the time of Kevin's death.

Our Kevin's dead. Truth and time help to heal but don't stop the hurt. Kevin's memory is with us and we are fresh from wounds of his death and the police handling of his death. We recognise that we all have to carry our crosses into a new future when deaths such as Kevin's will hopefully be a historical perspective and not a recurring theme and should such occur again those responsible are brought to proper account.

20

PETER MCBRIDE
4 September 1992

Shot by British army

Peter McBride, 18 years of age, was stopped by a British army patrol in Spamount Street, in the New Lodge area of North Belfast on the morning of 4 September 1992. He was walking back from a shop to his sister's house nearby and was carrying a bag containing crisps and a tee shirt. During the five minutes he was held, the British army patrol searched him and radio checked details of his age, address, etc. At some point, and for reasons that have never emerged, Peter started running away from the patrol and a number of soldiers pursued him. One of them was heard to shout 'Shoot the bastard'. As Peter McBride gained on them—running from Spamount Street to Hillman Street—two soldiers opened fire with SA80 assault rifles. These weapons have an effective range of 400 yards; Peter McBride was 70 yards away at the time. Five bullets were fired, two of which hit him in the back. Seriously injured, he managed to stagger through a house to the entry behind his sister's house in Hillman Street before collapsing dead.

Central to the soldiers' defence was the claim that they suspected Peter McBride of carrying a coffee jar bomb in his bag and that there was an altercation when they tried to search him. Despite that claim, they made no attempt to search the house through which Peter had run before dying, claiming that they were unable to do so because 'a lot of ladies threw ornaments' at them. A follow up search by the RUC revealed no coffee jar bomb, nor indeed any other weapon. It is not unreasonable to suspect that any aggression involved in the encounter

241

between Peter McBride and the British soldiers emanated from the latter rather than the former; one of their colleagues—24 year old Damian Shackelton—had been shot dead by an IRA sniper in the area a month previously, on 3 August.

An attempt was made by the RUC to question the soldiers on the spot, but they were removed to nearby Girdwood Barracks and were not available for questioning until ten hours after the incident. The following day, two soldiers, Scots Guardsmen Mark Wright and Jim Fisher, were charged with the murder of Peter McBride. At their trial, Fisher's defence was that he believed that Peter McBride was leading them into a trap where he would throw a coffee jar bomb at them. Wright went further and said that he believed that McBride had in fact opened fire on them. In short, their defence rested on a perceived threat from an unarmed man who was running away from them, a local man whose name and address were known to them and whom they had only just searched.

Passing judgement in February 1995, Lord Justice Kelly found the two soldiers' statements 'untruthful and evasive'. Fisher's evidence in particular 'strained credibility'. There was no threat. 'This was not a panic situation which required split second action or indeed any action at all', he said. Fisher and Wright were found guilty of murder and were sentenced to life imprisonment. Their appeal was dismissed in December 1995, and their move to appeal to the House of Lords was denied in March 1996.

Soon after their conviction, a sustained legal and political campaign to have them released swung into action. The campaigners argued that Peter McBride was a terrorist, or at least was suspected by the patrol of terrorist activity, that the soldiers were only doing their duty, and that there was no premeditation on their part to shoot the victim. It was also claimed, in the words of a barrister acting for the two Guardsmen in the Belfast High Court in 1998, that they had a 'legitimate expectation that in line with government policy they would be released after approximately three to three and a half years'. This argument was based on two previous precedents: that of Private Ian Thain, who served three years and eleven months for the murder of 22 year old Thomas 'Kidso' Reilly on 9 August 1983; and Paratrooper Lee Clegg, who spent three years and one month in jail for the murder of 18 year old Karen Reilly on 30 September 1990.

A number of high-ranking former and serving British army officers spearheaded the political campaign for the release of Fisher and Wright, including their former commanding officer Tim Spicer (later involved in the company Sandline which was implicated in the illegal supply of weapons and mercenaries to rebels in Sierra Leone). The military apologists were supported by a number of MPs—including former news reporter Martin Bell—and Lords, as well as by the *Daily Mail*. Ludovic Kennedy, well-known for previous campaigns against miscarriages of justice, was also prominent in the campaign. The British media in particular were eager to repeat the allegation that Peter McBride was at least suspected of 'terrorism'. The fact that the RUC had issued a statement shortly after the incident that he had no paramilitary connections was not stressed. And even the absence of the alleged coffee jar bomb did not dent the well-constructed story; for example, the *Daily Mail* on 19 October 1999 carried an extract from Tim Spicer's autobiography, *An Unorthodox Soldier*: 'Perhaps it was spirited away by the IRA, who often removed weapons or explosives to support claims that the Army had shot an innocent man.'

The campaign coincided with the lead-up to the early release of political prisoners resulting from the 1997 Good Friday Agreement. However, Fisher and Wright were not eligible for consideration under this early release scheme. Secretary of State Mo Mowlam assured the parents of Peter McBride as late as 1 September 1998 that the Guardsmen would not be among the first released from jail. But on the following day, 2 September 1998, she phoned Jean McBride to say that Fisher and Wright had just been released and had returned to their regiment. This was one week before the first political prisoners were released under the early release scheme. Mowlam cited the absence of premeditation as a key reason for the decision.

The McBride family had campaigned for the soldiers to serve a full sentence. On their release, the campaign shifted to demanding that they be dismissed from the British army. Jean McBride's first chance to make this demand was when she attempted to hand a letter to President Clinton during his visit to the Waterfront Hall in Belfast the day after the soldiers' release.

However, an Army Board, charged with considering the case of the two soldiers, ruled in November 1998 that they did not have to be dismissed. The Board stated that a soldier convicted of a custodial sentence must be dismissed unless there are 'exceptional circumstances' and concluded that such circumstances pertained in this case. The McBrides pushed consistently for a meeting about this matter with Armed Forces Minister Doug Henderson both to object and to ascertain the nature of the 'exceptional circumstances' involved. Finally Jean McBride, accompanied by Paul O'Connor from the Pat Finucane Centre in Derry, met Henderson in January 1999, and demanded the dismissal of the two soldiers. Henderson spelt out the 'exceptional circumstances', in particular the tense security situation in the area at the time, the fact that the soldiers had shown contrition and had paid the price for their error, that they had previously unblemished military records and that they were eager to continue serving in the army. Henderson was in fact doing no more than reiterating Ministry of Defence policy in the case from the beginning. Defence Minister George Robertson had over-ruled Mo Mowlam when she had urged that the Guardsmen should be dismissed from the army.

Furious at Henderson's response, in February 1999 the McBride family sought leave for a judicial review of the Army Board's decision to reinstate the soldiers. In a decision which made legal history, the Belfast High Court gave the McBrides leave to take a judicial review. The review was conducted by Mr Justice Kerr in

June 1999, and on 3 September 1999, almost seven years to the day after Peter McBride's murder, the court quashed the Army Board's decision. This was an unprecedented judgement but was, said Kerr, the only possible conclusion which could be reached on the basis of the outcome of the original criminal trial; the Board had 'failed to understand and give proper effect to the findings of the trial judge'. While Mr Kerr could not order the dismissal of the soldiers, it seemed that the only options open to the Ministry of Defence were to appeal Kerr's decision or to establish a new Army Board which would then dismiss the soldiers. In November 1999 the deadline passed without any appeal being lodged by the MOD.

While these events were happening, it was revealed in September 1999 that Mark Wright had been among the first NATO troops into Kosovo. In November 1999 he and Jim Fisher were reported to be serving with the British army in Germany.

Jean McBride, the mother of Peter, has been centrally involved in the campaign for justice for her son. She has been aided by the Pat Finucane Centre in Derry, and in particular by Paul O'Connor. Each of them now tells the story.

Jean McBride

The only mistake they made was that there were too many witnesses to my Peter's murder. Too many people saw it and the witness statements were all the same. The judge said that the witnesses were reliable and that the soldiers were liars. There were no loopholes. They couldn't get out of it. So when they got life sentences, I couldn't believe it, but I thought they would serve life sentences. I did expect them to do their time.

Peter was just getting over the chicken pox. He hadn't seen his two kids for I didn't allow her to bring the children over because they were so young and him with the chicken pox. So him and his girlfriend went out that day. When he came back, he had his dinner and he fell asleep on the settee. I kept coming back to check on him for he must have been so exhausted with being sick. I got up about seven o'clock that morning to go into the bathroom and I saw him sitting with a tin of coke and a Twix. I went in to talk to him. I would say I had a brilliant relationship with my son. I have a brilliant relationship with all my children. But he could have told me anything. If he was blamed on something and I asked, 'Peter did you do it?'—if he had said, 'No', then I knew he was telling the truth. Me and him were chatting and he told me he was going out that morning to buy himself a pair of gutties. He made me a cup of tea. He was going round to his sister's house to get a tee shirt he had left round there before he was sick. All he had on was a pair of jeans—no socks, no underwear—and a zip-up fleece, for he was ready to take a bath. So I threw him the keys and I said, 'Lock the door, son. I am going on back to bed again'.

I was in bed about half an hour and I could hear a girl shouting 'Jean, Jean McBride.' I live on the fifth floor and she was shouting, 'Jean, come on quick, come on down.' I asked her what was wrong and she said, 'Peter's been shot'. I thought, 'I never heard any shooting'. I grabbed my coat and me and her started to run down the stairs. As I was getting nearer the street, it was all cordoned off and I said to myself, 'What has happened here?' I said to somebody, 'Where is he? Where is he?' A fellow pointed down the entry. They wouldn't let me down the entry. When he was shot it must have been the adrenalin in him because, even though he was shot, he climbed over my daughter's wall into her yard and tried to get into her house. She was in bed and didn't hear him, so he came out and sat on her step. So I ran down the street and through my daughter's house for I knew he was at some part of the entry. When I went out, he was just lying there. I looked at him and thought, 'Jesus Christ! That couldn't be my Peter.'

On the way to the hospital I kept asking why the ambulance didn't have its sirens on. When we got to the hospital the priest came towards me. I didn't think he was coming to tell me he was dead; I thought he was just trying to comfort me. I kept saying, 'Don't tell me anything'. But the sister came into the room and knelt down beside me. She had all his jewelry in a bag. She handed it to me and I asked were they taking him to theatre for that was naturally enough what you would think. I kept on saying, 'Is he going to be alright?' She said to me, 'Mrs McBride, he has passed away'. I didn't know what she meant. I said, 'But sure, aren't you going to operate on him and he will be alright?' I kept saying for some reason, 'He is allergic to penicillin'. She said, 'No, he died'.

It turned out that my daughter and him walked to the shop together; the shop was on the corner of Trainfield Street. My daughter went up the way and he turned into Trainfield Street and was stopped by a patrol. Now he was searched, for every witness, their statements were the same; Peter was spreadeagled and searched. But Swift, who was the commanding officer at the time, conveniently didn't document in his book that he had searched Peter. For whatever reason Peter ran down the street. The two that shot him, the last two on the patrol, they took chase and ran after Peter. People in the street were shouting, 'Don't shoot'. Wright shouted, 'Shoot the bastard'. They said he had a bomb. My son's body was taken away to Forster Green [mortuary] and it was an army medical officer who did the tests on Peter. He said he was clean and could never have handled anything like that, but they insisted he was carrying this bomb, which was nonsense. All he had in his hand was a tee shirt. My daughter to this day still has the tee shirt in her house and it's funny, there wasn't a drop of blood on it. The judge said, 'You chased this man and you were in fear of your lives?' But when Fisher was asked what he did after he shot Peter, he told them he bent down to tie his lace. This was a man who was fearing for his life! My son was running further and further away from them. They could have got in touch with the foot patrol in the next street to pick him up. He had white jeans on him, red shoes and a bottle-green fleece; his hair was bleached white. My Peter would have been picked up anywhere.

Things come into your mind and you say to yourself, 'What did they say to my Peter to make him run? Did they threaten him?' For days later when they were searching young ones in the street, they were saying to them, 'Do you want to be another Peter McBride? Run!' When I had my Peter lying in the house, they tortured us, driving past, shouting, 'One down; one nil.' It ended up I had to phone the RUC and get them to take the army out of the area the day of Peter's funeral. Before the funeral, when I was told that they were getting charged with murder, I wasn't too worried about what was happening to the two soldiers for I had Peter here with me in the house in his coffin. Then I sat back after the funeral and I thought, 'Somebody is going to pay for what they have done. These two soldiers are going to go to jail for a long time for what they have done to my child and what they have done to me.'

I couldn't believe that they had got life sentences. The minute I walked out of the court I told any media there that this was not going to be another Karen Reilly/Clegg case. I knew what was happening, but I told them it wasn't going to work out like that. Do you see the campaign that they fought?—it was the dirtiest campaign. Do you see the people who came onboard with that?—Ludovic Kennedy, a man who was so well-respected, that man even put my address into an English paper and tried more or less to say that my son had guns in my home and I allowed it. I never had any reason to say that the British army ever raided my house until my Peter died. My house was searched after Peter died. Don't get me wrong, years ago your house was searched but then we all got searched. The peelers came here looking for Peter—I nearly knew every one of them by name; I was sick looking at them—but never the army. I would always say I'm as good a Republican as anybody but I'm a fireside one.

Do you see that Martin Bell?—I do not wish him well in anything he does for taking this case up. He said on GMTV that he was hesitant, that he wasn't sure to go ahead with it or not and that is the way they left it. He said that morning that Peter was 'shot dead'. I got the number of Martin Bell's office and I asked to speak to him. His secretary said he wasn't in but asked who was calling. I told her it was Jean McBride, the mother of the late Peter McBride. He got on the phone and told me he had written me a letter telling me he was on this campaign. I asked him if he wanted me to thank him. I told him that the next time he was speaking about my son, he was to get the wording right. 'My son was murdered, and they were convicted of murder.' He said, 'I'm not disputing that'. I asked him had he ever read the transcripts of the trial. He never answered me. I asked him again and he said, 'No'. I told him I would send them to him and he could tell me what he could see that made these two convicted murderers innocent of the murder of my son. He asked me to meet him in Belfast Airport for an hour to have breakfast and talk without reporters. I told him, 'No', when I would see him there would be plenty of reporters to hear what I had to say.

I'm not an educated woman by no means, but I'd love to get face to face with that man on an interview; I'd cut him to ribbons. When you are fighting for your own, you can't sway from it. Look at that man Ludovic Kennedy; look at the work he did for the Birmingham Six. Why did he take this case and discredit himself?

It was the dirtiest campaign I ever saw in my life. 'Newsnight' asked me to go on; they had one of the generals on and I said, 'No, I'd prefer Paul O'Connor to go on for us.' So they had Paul in a studio here and the general in the other studio. Paul went over the events of the day. He said, 'They had stopped that young man and searched him on the day'. The interviewer stopped him and said to the general, 'You didn't tell us he was searched'. That was it; the interview was stopped.

The only mistake they made was that there were too many witnesses to my Peter's murder. Too many people saw it and the witness statements were all the same. The judge said that the witnesses were reliable and that the soldiers were liars. There were no loopholes. They couldn't get out of it. So when they got life sentences, I couldn't believe it but I thought they would serve life sentences. I did expect them to do their time.

Mo Mowlam phoned me before they were released at a quarter to eleven at night. She said to me, 'Hello, it's Mo'. I said, 'Mo who?' She told me it was Doctor Mowlam and I asked what was wrong. I told her if she was going to release them, she was to tell me first. She said she would. She phoned me at a quarter past eight the following morning and told me they were going to be released. I was on my own; my son's anniversary was coming up the next day. I said, 'Do you know what you have done to me? I will not thank you for your call'. When she phoned me, they were on their way. They had been taken out of the jail at seven o'clock that morning. Paul O'Connor phoned me and I said to him, 'I have gone through all this—the trial, courts, all this. Everybody knocked them back, the House of Lords wouldn't give them leave to appeal and that bastard let them out!'

She promised me that they wouldn't be the first out of the gates. The media asked me about the early release of prisoners. I told them that they weren't released under the Good Friday Agreement. The Secretary of State let them out. I didn't care who got out but I didn't want them out.

The day we had had the meeting with her I came out buzzing. I thought her fair. Paul O'Connor said to me, 'Jean she is not to be trusted'. He was right. The day at the Waterfront [during Clinton's visit], she sat over in one of the boxes. We had eye contact. She couldn't have missed me and she had been told I would be there. I stared and stared but she looked everywhere but at me. I hoped that she would come over to me that day for I wanted to say to her, 'Do you know what you have done to me and my family? You have hit us a kick in the teeth'.

Paul O'Connor

That is the only way that miscarriages of justice are resolved—to make it abundantly clear that this is an issue that is not going to go away. If they think it will drift away, they will let it drift.

Our involvement was essentially a reaction to a growing campaign in the British media, especially the tabloid press, the *Daily Mail*, the *Telegraph* and others—this growing clamour for the two Scots Guards to be released. We felt that it was a terrible injustice that their campaign was getting so much publicity and the other side of the story wasn't being heard. So we contacted the McBride family and asked did they have an information pack on the case just to make it easier for it to be highlighted. As we suspected, they didn't. So at that stage we put together about a six or eight page information pack—what happened, the incident, the trial, the aftermath, the conviction and so on and the point of view of the family—and we put it up onto our web site. That began a process of more and more involvement with the family to a point, and it was a strange role for us, that we said to the media, 'Don't talk to the family; talk to us'.

We did that because it was requested of us and because we thought it was totally wrong that a mother of a victim was being asked to come on to radio and television programmes opposite high-level military people advocating that the two men who murdered her son should be released. Our view was that it would never be done if it were the other way round. If a political representative was arguing for the release of a particular group of IRA men who carried out whatever kind of an attack, that they would be put on television or radio constantly with the mother of a person who had died in that attack—it just wouldn't happen. We thought it was wrong, so we began to represent the family more and more.

We began bombarding the MOD with questions and queries. It's always been our style within the Centre, going back many years, to write to the RUC requesting statistics on recruitment, etc. When we asked how many plastic bullets were fired once, it caused a furore. Yet it seemed a very reasonable question to ask and no one had done it before.

We met with the Secretary of State, met with the Taoiseach and just kept drawing out different aspects of the campaign, such as the then Minister for the Armed Forces had agreed to meet their campaign but refused to meet the family. We asked the Taoiseach to put the pressure on, which he did. Very suddenly, with only forty eight hours warning, we were told we could meet the Minister for the Armed Forces, Doug Henderson, which we did in Belfast. Because the two soldiers had been released at this stage and because of our involvement, we kept on demanding reasons for their continued employment in the British army.

For the first time they provided their reasons, which were decided by an Army Board, which had included this Minister of State. They had never had to provide reasons before quite simply because no one had ever demanded it in the past. We got the reasons and they were so arrogant and so badly argued. I am not a solicitor but even I could see the weaknesses and massive contradictions in their arguments. It opened the door for us to go for a judicial review, which we then won last month. We are waiting for the MOD to appeal against it. I think ultimately we will win on a point of law, especially if it gets to Europe, and because it is so embarrassing. The decision has been criticised by the Independent Assessor on military complaints in his report a few months ago. The Alliance Party has criticised the decision. Privately unionists have told me that they are sickened by it for it diminishes their sense of being ordinary British citizens. It was such a blatantly racist decision because the victim was Irish and the perpetrators were British that I think it actually annoys quite a lot of people.

So that is quite threatening for the MOD and I think we will win. I also think it opens up the way for other cases. For example, we have now intervened with the MOD on the issue of Lee Clegg. When his case comes up in November [1999], the MOD have admitted to us that, if he loses his appeal, they have to begin dismissal proceedings against him.

This is Ireland; there is a different access to power. We get access to the Taoiseach, the US Congress and then it gets raised at the European Parliament and it's embarrassing for Britain. So it's not because of us but because of the levers that can be pulled. And because I think there is great support for this.

We went and met the Taoiseach. We didn't go to the European Parliament but it has been raised in the European Parliament by people like Patricia McKenna who is very good on human rights issues. We feel it's often better to go through her office for she is not constrained by all of the party politics down south. In the US it has been raised in Congress and the internet is certainly a massive campaigning tool.

Peter McBride spent time in Syracuse, New York on an exchange project. When he was killed, they actually named the St Patrick's Day parade in his honour. So there is already a base on which to build. A nephew of the family lives in the US; he is also called Peter McBride. So I think it's important to use all the levers we can to embarrass them. Also to use those in the Labour Party who are truly embarrassed by this decision. The problem is some people supported the Scots Guards because they believe the people really to blame are of higher ranks—particularly the commanding officer, Tim Spicer, who is involved in a controversial firm in London responsible for sending mercenaries to Sierra Leone. He was described to us as a 'gung ho' commanding officer, who created a gung ho culture within his regiment in North Belfast.

Some of the campaigners complained that the soldiers should have been charged with manslaughter, but it's a bit disingenuous for the people that changed the goal posts to complain that they had been changed. The reason no manslaughter charge was ever available for prosecuting members of the British army was to make it impossible to prosecute them. Then when they are not prosecuted under that manslaughter type charge, they complain it's not available. Well, it was them that changed the goal posts. However, at the trial the judge was of the opinion that they would not have qualified for the manslaughter charge anyway. They did not open fire in the belief that Peter McBride was a danger to them.

I think that the main lesson to be learnt in this case is not to worry about convincing all the people around you, gathering signatures and such—that's all valuable and important—but also to badger the people who were actually responsible. We sent a stream of faxes. We got the personal fax number of the Minister of State for the Armed Forces. We wrote to the Minister for the Armed forces and he made the mistake of replying to us once. We badgered him and badgered him and when we met them in Belfast we said to him, 'We are going to haunt your dreams'. He is now no longer the Minister of State. We told him that we were going to cling to his back until the decision was reversed. We told him we were not going away. That's why the Birmingham Six and the Guildford Four got out. That is the only way that miscarriages of justice are resolved—to make it abundantly clear that this is an issue that is not going to go away. If they think it will drift away, they will let it drift. But everything we did was guided the whole way along by the wishes of the McBride family. We have told the family that the moment they want us to stop we will drop everything. That has become our rule now; everything has to be guided by the families; they have to want this to happen. It has also to be made clear from the beginning that it's going to be a long, painful process.

This case is only where it is because Jean McBride hung in. The Lawrence case only got where it is because Doreen Lawrence hung in there. The Robert Hamill case is only there because of the activities of Diane and the rest of the family. I have sometimes seen people trying to hijack campaigns, jumping on families, trying to get them to do things when the family really didn't want to and that is totally wrong.

I think Jean has seen light at the end of the tunnel. I was away on holidays when she heard about the judgement. It must have been brilliant to sit there and hear a judge, especially of the Northern Ireland judiciary, vindicate the case put forward by the family.

21

PEARSE JORDAN
25 November 1992

Shot by RUC undercover squad

Pearse Jordan, a 21 year old from West Belfast and a member of the IRA, was shot dead on 25 November 1992. In what was clearly a carefully planned RUC undercover action, Jordan's car—a taxi which had been hijacked earlier in the day—was rammed by one of a number of police cars which were tailing him. As he emerged from the car and starting to cross the road, he was hit by three low-velocity bullets—once in the left arm and twice in the back—fired by a plain-clothes RUC men. He died shortly after admission to the Royal Victoria Hospital as a result of the severing of a main artery by a bullet which struck near his heart.

According to eye witnesses, Pearse Jordan was unarmed and no warning was issued by the RUC before shooting began.

Three hours after the incident, the RUC issued a short statement to the effect that a vehicle had been forced to halt, and that shots had been fired at the driver, fatally wounding him. However, a number of off-the-record statements to the media before that had served to muddy the waters. They all centred on the allegation that Jordan had been moving military equipment from one IRA 'bomb factory' to another when intercepted. One was to the effect that gloves, masks, guns and bombs had been found in the car. Another stated that Jordan had a previous prison sentence for possession of explosives. The incident was also linked to a raid at the same time on a house in nearby Arizona Street where a mercury tilt switch had supposedly been found. All these statements were untrue;

251

Pearse Jordan was unarmed and no military equipment or paraphernalia were found in his car. Speaking at the funeral four days later, Sinn Féin President Gerry Adams referred to this exercise in media manipulation by the RUC: 'None of this is true, yet this is the story that went out to the world'. The Committee on the Administration of Justice agreed: 'It now appears that as a matter of course immediately following such incidents misleading information is passed to the press in a systematic fashion'.

There were immediate calls from a number of human rights sources for an independent investigation of the killing, but this did not occur. Instead, the RUC announced that it would appoint a Detective Chief Superintendent from outside Belfast to investigate the incident. The investigation was to be overseen by the Independent Commission for Police Complaints.

There was a heavy police presence at the funeral on 29 November and some minor scuffles between the RUC and mourners. Giving the oration, Gerry Adams pointed out that the Jordan family had not yet been officially informed by the RUC of their son's death. Indeed, they only found out some time after the incident when some local young people came to their door to tell them.

Almost exactly a year after Pearse Jordan's death—on 18 November 1993—his parents, Hugh and Teresa, were informed that the DPP had concluded that there was to be no prosecution of any RUC personnel.

An inquest opened on 4 January 1995. The Coroner, James Leckey, stated that RUC Sergeant A of the Mobile Support Unit, who had fired the fatal shot, had refused to appear, but that notes from an interview with him would be read out. The jury, he said, would be within its rights not to attach much credence to his evidence. The ability of the inquest to arrive at the truth was further hampered by the decision of the Secretary of State for Northern Ireland Patrick Mayhew and Minister of Defence Malcolm Rifkind to issue Public Interest Immunity Certificates.

The effect of the PIICs was soon evident. One undercover soldier, giving evidence from behind a screen, admitted that they had been briefed before going out that day. He refused 'on grounds of national security' to say whether they had been told to expect 'terrorist activity' or if Pearse Jordan's name had been mentioned in the briefing. However, on the third day of the inquest, an RUC man answered the same questions, stating that 'terrorist activity' had been expected, but that Pearse Jordan's name had not been mentioned at the briefing. He stated that the purpose of the undercover operation was to identify 'the movement of munitions'.

On the second day of the inquest, lawyers for the RUC and MOD attempted to undermine the credibility of some civilian witnesses who reported seeing Pearse Jordan being kicked as he lay on the ground—by bringing up their previous convictions for IRA membership and assault on the RUC. This led lawyers for the

Jordan family on the fourth day of the inquest to seek equality of treatment. They contended that having the names of the RUC men involved would allow them to check if they had a criminal or disciplinary record and therefore assess their credibility as witnesses. Leckey rejected this move the following day, but added that no RUC witness had a criminal or disciplinary record, except for one conviction for careless driving!

Lawyers for the Jordans eventually sought a judicial review of a number of decisions of the Coroner, in particular, the granting of anonymity to RUC and British army witnesses, and the refusal to disclose witness statements to the Jordan's legal team in advance. As a result, the inquest was adjourned on 16 January 1995. On 8 November 1995, Lord Justice Carswell announced his decision that the Coroner had not erred in his ruling. In July 1996 the Court of Appeal in Belfast upheld Carswell's ruling. As is customary in Northern Ireland courts, the Court of Appeal did not grant leave for an appeal to the House of Lords. Instead, in October 1996, the Jordans' lawyers independently petitioned the House of Lords for leave to appeal. Such a route puts families at a disadvantage; the suspicion must be that the presumption of the Law Lords is that if the case was indeed worthy, it would have the backing of the local Court of Appeal. In late 1998 the House of Lords refused to grant leave to appeal. With all such avenues cut off, the way was now clear to reopen the inquest. A date was set for November 1999.

In the meantime, the Macpherson report into the racist killing of Stephen Lawrence in London led to a change in practice in British courts, requiring that in inquests lawyers for the families of the dead be given all the evidence available in advance. As this was one of the rights lawyers for the Jordan family had been seeking all along, they immediately asked for identical treatment. As of the time of writing, the RUC has still not reached a decision in relation to this request, and it may require litigation to encourage them to do so. As a result of the lawyers' move, the inquest was again postponed. Thus, more than eight years after Pearse Jordan's death, an inquest decision and a death certificate are still pending.

Meanwhile, Pearse Jordan's parents have taken every opportunity to campaign around the issue of his death. For example, in November 1998 they presented their case in both oral and written submissions to members of the Patten Commission, including Chris Patten himself, at a public meeting in West Belfast. Despite that, the Patten Report on the reform of the RUC stated on page 50: 'There has been no case of the RUC shooting anyone dead since 1991'. In October 1999, the parents met with the recently established Human Rights Commission and requested an investigation of the case. Their argument was that the original RUC investigation failed to meet international standards, such as those laid down in the European Convention on Human Rights, because it was not independent. The Commission agreed to provide senior counsel when the inquest was resumed; previously the Jordans had only had junior counsel representing them.

Six months after the original adjournment of the inquest in January 1995, the case was lodged with the European Court of Human Rights. In April 2000 the European Court heard evidence in relation to the death of Pearse Jordan. Three other cases were considered at the same time: that of the eight IRA members killed at Loughgall in 1987, the death of Gervaise McKerr in 1982, and the killing by loyalists, in collusion with the RUC, of Sinn Féin member Patrick Shanaghan in Castlederg, County Tyrone in August 1991. The argument of lawyers for the Jordan family is that the killing of Pearse by the RUC was a violation of Article 2 of the European Convention on Human Rights. The Court found that the British government had a case to answer in relation to all the deaths concerned, in itself a major victory for the campaigners. It was then open to the judges to move to a full hearing of evidence or to reach a judgement without such a hearing. As of the time of writing, this is where the case rests.

Hugh and Teresa Jordan, parents of the dead man, tell the story of their campaign for truth and justice.

Hugh and Teresa Jordan

Every time you see a cop in the street, you don't know if that's one of the ones involved in the killing of your son.

Hugh: The circumstances of Pearse's death are that on the actual night he was murdered, he was driving a car down the Falls Road. This was a busy time, about 5 o'clock at night. He drove past Andersonstown barracks, and there were two cars sitting outside the barracks. They followed the car he was driving down the road. When he got as far as St John's, one car cut in in front of him and rammed into the vehicle he was in. The other car rammed into the back of it. Pearse got out of the car into the middle of the road. I don't know if he was trying to make it to the other side of the road or if he was trying to get away or what. I don't know what sort of condition he was in. But before he reached the other side of the road, a guy stepped out of the back of the back car and put three bullets into his back. He was totally unarmed; there was nothing in the car. The RUC issued statements that there were bombs in the car, there were guns in the car, berets, gloves—but subsequently, it seems there was not a thing in the car. They also made statements that he had been coming from a bomb factory to another bomb factory and he was moving stuff from one place to the other place and he'd been doing this all day long and they'd been watching him all day. If they'd been watching him all day, they must have realised there was nothing in the car. It seems as if he was just set up for murder.

There were at least six cops between the two cars. At the inquest it came out that there was another car there as well, with some more Brits or cops in it.

It was such a well-planned operation. The only conclusion I can come to is that it was deliberate murder. They meant to kill him and they killed him. He could have been stopped rather than killed.

Teresa: They could have shot him in the leg. Two weeks before it happened, we were coming up the Falls Road in a small van. I had a baby shop in Smithfield and we were doing a clothes party. And Pearse came down with me to get the stuff to go up to the party. We were coming up the Falls Road; it was twenty five to six at night. We were coming up by Barrack Street, and there was one cop in plain clothes; he was standing along with the cops and there were two Saracens beside them; and he had a camera in his hand. He stopped the van and he took a photo of me and Pearse. He didn't search the van, just took a photo. And Pearse turned round and said to me, 'Mammy, you'd think they were setting me up'. And I said, 'Ach, Pearse, away and catch yourself on; what would they want to set you up for?'

Hugh: Round about the same time, he was along with two mates, walking down the Whiterock Road and they called his name. He turned around and they took another photograph of him. They stopped a car with him and two of his mates in it on the Hightown Road. They made them take their shoes off and stand in the rain, and they told them they were going to kill them. This came out afterwards from his friends.

There was a cop when I went up to identify Pearse's body. He asked me did I identify it as my son's body—his name, his age, that was about it. He looked more like a clerk than a cop. There was a very heavy presence at the funeral; there must have been close to 200 Land Rovers. The presence in the graveyard was overwhelming.

Teresa: A week later two Special Branch came to the door and one had a key in his hand. The key ring had a 'P' on it, which Pearse carried. He says to me, 'Do you know who owns this key?' I says , 'Sure, you know who owns the key'. He says, 'Try the key in the door; I don't believe you'. I said, 'I'm not trying the key in the door; that's my son's key'. And he says, 'Ah, fuck you and your son'. And they gave me the key and walked away; and they laughed going down the path. That was the way they approached me about Pearse's death.

Hugh: Nobody ever approached us until well over a year later. By this time we had started to try and find out the exact circumstances and if there were going to be any prosecutions over Pearse's death. Two cops came to the door—high-ranking cops—and they said they were just there to notify me that there were to be no prosecutions in connection with Pearse's death.

We had a reconstruction on the same day, same time a couple of weeks after the death; we leafleted people. It was more or less organised by friends. Pearse was a member of the republican movement. That's not in dispute. So, it was friends and people in Sinn Féin who got things organised. And it was because of that so many witnesses came forward. But the first time we actually met the witnesses was in the court.

Teresa: The night after the leaflets were given out at the bottom of the Whiterock Road, I was in the house here when a cop came to the door with a machine gun. He put the machine gun to my head and says to me, 'What kind of a mother are you?'

Hugh: There was a lot of harassment. Any time Teresa went out to the shops or down the road, the Land Rovers used to follow her very slowly. And when they were coming past the windows, at nights, they used to shine the lights through the windows. If I was walking down the road, they'd have shouted something at me. Or the young boy; he was threatened by the RUC and the Brits. They shouted at him, 'We'll fucking get you the same as we got your brother'. He was only 13 at the time. We've got a bit of harassment, but he has borne the brunt of it.

We found out practically nothing until the inquest. The witnesses were really harassed. They were verbally abused in the court. Their past records were brought up. Anything the cops had against them was aired in court. The witnesses who were giving their version of what happened that went against what the so-called security forces wanted, they were given a rough time. I felt sorry for them. Our solicitor and barrister made applications for statements from all of the witnesses so they could judge what questions they were going to ask them. They were told they wouldn't be supplied with any of the statements of any of the other witnesses because the witnesses might want to change their mind whenever they heard what our witnesses had said. The coroner seemed to think that that was quite acceptable. Our attitude was that, if this was the way things were going to go, there was no sense carrying on with the inquest. With the inquest system in Northern Ireland anyway, the only finding that they can come to is whether a person has been killed. They can't make any decision as to whether it was murder, manslaughter or anything else. That in itself has to be a farce; you don't need anybody to tell you that your son's dead.

Teresa: They put you through all that torture. They make you look at the photos; they put the photos on the table in a certain way so that you can see them. And they know that they're doing it to you.

Hugh: You're talking about full-scale photographs, full-colour. These are passed round the court. They were more flaunted than shown around. We were meant to see these things. The cops and the Brits, their personnel were behind a screen. You couldn't see them. They were giving evidence from behind these screens. And the microphones they were using were distorting their voices. They were classed as 'Soldier A', 'Soldier B', 'Soldier C'.

The witnesses said that, when they did shoot him, Pearse turned round. According to the pathologist, he couldn't have done that, because he died right away. He turned round, clutching his shoulder, and they ran towards him and booted him to the ground.

There were four fellows coming down the road from work in Milltown Cemetery. They said that the cop that did the shooting—he wasn't actually in uniform—got out of the back seat of the car that rammed into the back of the car Pearse was in, and he fired from the hip, a burst into Pearse's back. But according to the evidence of the pathologist, that couldn't have happened. The shooting was done from over the bonnet of the front car that had crashed into Pearse. The RUC said that Pearse had crashed into a road block. Anybody that passed down that road in front of Pearse would be able to verify that there was no road block there.

The coroner seemed to sit like Jack-the-Lad, swinging on his chair with his legs crossed, smirking and generally trying to make an idiot out of our barrister who happened to be a girl.

I made the decision: what's the good of being here if this is the way things are going to be treated? There's obviously no chance of getting a fair hearing. We pulled out of the inquest on the grounds that our people weren't being given the proper facilities in terms of the statements of the witnesses. We saw the way things were going, we saw the attitude of the coroner, the attitude of that wee monkey of a solicitor who was acting for the Ministry of Defence. The whole thing just seemed so loaded against anything that our legal team would try to put forward. There just was no sense in carrying on. We appealed the whole set-up of the inquest. It went to a judicial inquiry. At the judicial inquiry you had more or less the same shambles all over again. You had three judges sitting on the bench, and one of them just sat and picked his nose through the whole proceedings as if he was just disinterested. The inquest was never completed; the inquest still hasn't been resumed.

After that, an appeal was lodged with the House of Lords against the set-up of the inquest and the House of Lords rejected it. The inquest was supposed to resume then. That was four years ago. All the appeals were finished inside first three years, but in the past three years, except for the letters each Christmas to tell us the inquest was going to be resumed, there hasn't been anything. That's the way things stand at the present time.

Teresa: They sent us a letter last 10th of December, two days before Pearse's birthday—they did that three years in a row—to say that the inquest would be resumed in January. Then in January, they said it was postponed indefinitely.

Hugh: It's as if they're trying to put pressure on you over his birthday, over Christmas and the new year, to make sure it never leaves you.

Teresa: We've approached the European Court but there has to be an inquest first. You have to go through all channels before you can go to the European

Court. So, who's holding it up? I believe they are deliberately holding it up. That's why we wrote to Mo Mowlam, to ask her to speed up the process. We wanted to get it over with; we wanted to get it finished. We didn't want it to drag on another six years. You're just reliving it all the time; it never leaves you, but why should they keep on putting the hurt on to you? Stabbing us to death every day; they keep stabbing us. We've lost enough; we've lost our son; what do they want to do to us? We've no chance of justice in a British court. What justice have any of our people got in a British court over the years? They're talking now about peace. They don't want anything to rock the boat. It's too soon for them to bring Pearse's case up; it's still fresh in people's minds. They're trying to hold us back. They're not going to meet us half-way or even quarter-way.

Hugh: When you see you're not going to get justice, you start clutching at straws. You try to get whoever you can who is going to have influence to exert some sort of influence to get the thing sorted out. We lobbied for the disbandment of the RUC for starters. What sort of faith can we have in the RUC when there are at least nine of them involved in Pearse's killing? Every time you see a cop in the street, you don't know if that's one of the ones involved in the killing of your son.

For the first couple of years, you knew there wasn't any point trying to get in touch with any British politicians, because you had a Conservative government who were backing the unionist establishment to the hilt. Major's government was so weak, they wouldn't have gone against the unionists; they were relying on them to keep them in power. So it would have been futile to try to get them to give you some sort of justice. We were on the streets protesting about this, that and the other, particularly the disbandment of the RUC. It's only recently we've started again trying to see what this Labour government is made of. We sent a letter to Mo Mowlam, but the reply was that she had got the letter, she would be looking into it and we would hear from her eventually. This is about three months later, and up to now, we haven't heard anything. They've set up this Patten Commission, but I don't think that's going to do any good whatsoever. If you look at Patten's record; he was over here as a Conservative minister. He's going to keep his nose clean. He's not going to rock the boat too much.

We worked with Relatives for Justice. We sent a letter to Clinton; we never got any reply, so we don't know whether he ever received it or not. We've met Albert Reynolds, but nothing. Bertie Ahern—exactly the same. Bruton—he's a waste of space, so we didn't bother approaching him; he's just another Brit. Dick Spring is the same thing. If you haven't any faith in people, there's no sense in approaching them. You're only beating your head against a stone wall again.

Shortly after Pearse's death the Independent Commission for Police Complaints said they were looking into it. We had a press conference and I said there's no sense getting them to look into anything, because you know what they're going to come up with; which is exactly what transpired. The outcome was they decided that there wasn't going to be any prosecutions.

I don't want to see anybody spending any time inside—cops or Brits. To me that is just futile. What I would want is for the truth to come out. Just the truth.

Teresa: Just to say that they murdered him. It wouldn't make me feel any different about the RUC because I know what they are, but because he wore a uniform—our kids did time in jail for far, far less, just because they were maybe members of the IRA, or not. The cops have to be made accountable for their actions.

Hugh: When he was only about six months old, early 1970, there was a lot of trouble in the area. We lived in the Lower Falls at the time. The Brits pumped CS gas into the area. Pearse had to be rushed to the hospital, and it was IRA volunteers brought him to the hospital. The doctor in the hospital told him that they saved his life by bringing him to the hospital. His back was badly burned by the gas. He carried those scars all his life. Every now and again the scars used to break out. Even in the summer, as he was a kid, Pearse didn't ever take his tee shirt off.

It didn't surprise me to find out he was a member of the Irish Republican Army. All the things he saw when he was growing up. We lived in a mixed area; he was only about two, three years of age at the time, and we were put out of Roden Street. All those things imprint on a kid's mind. Seeing people being killed, and seeing people in the street, including myself, getting hidings from the Brits and RUC—he grew up with that all his life. He knew Kidso Reilly. Kidso's brother was a member of the group called Stiff Little Fingers. Kidso brought Pearse, Hugh and Colette down to meet Jim at the Ulster Hall, backstage. Stiff Little Fingers were their heroes. That was a big highlight in a kid's life. And then Kidso was murdered by Ian Thain. Passing the spot where Kidso was shot dead, he blessed himself. He wasn't religious, but he just blessed himself passing it; every time; should he pass that spot ten times a day, he'd bless himself. He knew Karen Reilly. Karen used to come in to the shop in Smithfield and speak to him. Karen was in a band and he used to go all the time with the band; he was never a member. When he saw people of his own age being killed by the Brits, and he saw the injustice, the way the killers were treated, it would have been surprising if he hadn't been a member of the Irish Republican Army.

Teresa: And even how many times they wrecked this house when they were babies. There was one night, to put them into bed we had to put two planks across the floorboards, they wrecked the room that much.

Hugh: One particular time, he was only about 8 or 9 years of age, the Brits stopped in the street and were talking to a group of kids. Next thing was, the Brits bounced into the house. They said to Pearse, 'Right, where are these guns you were talking about?' And he went over to the bed and lifted the pillow and says,

'There they are there'. It was Action Men guns. Out on the street, they must have asked him were there any guns in the house. That kind of thing—seeing what was happening in the areas, what was happening his friends and mates and relations, how could anybody be otherwise?

Teresa: They did it, the Brits did it. They made all our kids that way. It's their fault. They did it.

22

DIARMUID O'NEILL
23 September 1996

Shot by Metropolitan Police, Hammersmith, London

D iarmuid O'Neill, aged 27, was the son of Irish emigrant parents. Eoghan and Terry O'Neill had moved to Britain in the late 1950s and had lived and worked there until their retirement to a cottage in West Cork in 1995. Eoghan O'Neill told the *Irish Post* of their time in Britain: 'We loved it here. We had a very nice lifestyle. We are totally anti-violence. Violence never solved anything. We supported the police all our lives; they were there for our protection'.

Their son Diarmuid was a member of the IRA, the quartermaster for a unit in London. He was responsible for the procurement and storage of weapons and explosives for the unit. It is believed that the unit's plan was to carry out bombing missions in London.

Early in August 1996, the IRA unit was put under surveillance by the Metropolitan Police and MI5. In the next six weeks Operation Tinnitus, as it was code-named, became the largest and longest surveillance operation ever to occur in England and Wales. It involved numerous personnel, hidden video cameras, bugging of premises, etc. Using a master key, MI6 bugged the hotel room where two members of the unit—Brian McHugh and Patrick Kelly—lived. They also bugged Diarmuid O'Neill's car. The explosives and weapons of the group were traced to two lock-up garages. According to the police, six tons of explosives, two pounds of Semtex, three Kalashnikov rifles and ammunition, two handguns, 13 timer units and two under-car booby traps were found.

On 23 September 1996 officers of SO19, a specialist firearms unit within the Metropolitan Police, was sent to Room 303 of the hotel on Glenthorne Road, Hammersmith where Diarmuid O'Neill was staying the night with Brian McHugh and Patrick Kelly. At 4.30 in the morning they attempted unsuccessfully to enter the room using the master key. They then fired an 'enforcer'—a spring-loaded battering ram—at the door which succeeded only in blasting a hole in the door without breaking the lock. At this point CS gas was fired and quickly engulfed the whole area inside and outside the room. Few of the policemen wore gas masks and consequently had to vacate the building. One policeman, codenamed Officer Kilo, went back into the building. Despite being blinded and choked by the gas, he and a colleague ordered the men in the room to open the door. As Diarmuid O'Neill did so, Officer Kilo shot him twice; the bullets hit his spine. As Diarmuid fell, Officer Kilo shot him four more times. The police then entered the room and arrested Brian McHugh and Patrick Kelly. Forensic evidence later showed that they had also stood on Diarmuid O'Neill's face before dragging him out to the front of the hotel leaving a trail of blood on the front steps in the process. Twenty five minutes after the shooting, paramedics administered assistance, but Diarmuid O'Neill died later in Charing Cross Hospital.

Media misinformation began almost immediately. There were reports of 'armed terrorists' and a 'gun battle'. The *Daily Mirror* stated: 'Don't cry for him. He was going to blow up the Channel Tunnel tomorrow'. It soon became clear, however, that there were many problems with the official account of what happened. None of the three men in the room was armed and there were no explosives in the room. There was therefore no gun battle; only the police had fired shots.

At very least, this would seem to have been an arrest operation which had gone dreadfully wrong. Worse, it could be read as a shoot-to-kill operation from the outset. Either way there were serious questions to be asked. The Justice for Diarmuid O'Neill campaign proposed that an independent inquiry provided the best chance of answering those questions adequately. But such a proposal has been resisted by the Metropolitan Police and refused by the Home Office, leaving a number of potentially less satisfactory ways in which to arrive at the truth.

There were five others arrested at the time of the killing of Diarmuid O'Neill. Diarmuid's brother Shane was released after a few days. Michael Phillips was charged but acquitted. Brian McHugh, Patrick Kelly and James Murphy were sentenced to a total of 62 years imprisonment for conspiracy to cause explosions. At the trial the extent of the surveillance operation became obvious. In particular, an audio tape of the actual killing was revealed. It showed that the men in the hotel room had clearly stated that they were unarmed. They were also co-operating with the police when the fatal shots were fired.

Transcript of surveillance tape

Sound of breaking glass as CS gas canister fired through the window.

All: Jesus Christ!

Sound of police attempting to batter down the door and shouting.

All: All right, all right! We give up, we're unarmed, we give up. Whoa, whoa, whoa whoa. We're unarmed. Whoa, whoa, whoa.

Police: I'm a police officer. Get on the floor.

Diarmuid: Whoa, whoa, whoa.

Police: Open the fucking door now!

Diarmuid: Okay, we're down.

All: We're down, we're down.

Police: Open that door!

Diarmuid: Okay.

Police (shouting over Diarmuid's answer): Get to that fucking door now and...

Diarmuid: Okay.

Police: Show me your hands now!

Diarmuid: They're up, they're up.

Police: Get out here.

All: We're on the deck.

Police: Show me your hands through the door! Show me your hands through the door!

Diarmuid: Okay.

Police: Open it, open the door.

Diarmuid: I can't. It won't...

Police: Open it! Show us your hands!

Shouting by police, followed by short burst of automatic gunfire.

Police: Shoot the fuckers!

Diarmuid: Fucking hell!

Another burst of gunfire.

All: Whoa, whoa.

Sound of choking.

Police (entering room): Dead as a fucking rat! Just stay where the fuck you are. Just stay on the floor. Stay on the floor. One in the bathroom and one on the floor. Just keep your hands where we can see them, okay, and don't fucking move.

From the start the Metropolitan Police maintained that Officer Kilo only fired because he believed that Diarmuid O'Neill's actions were threatening. There was little evidence of that in this tape. Despite that, the Crown Prosecution Service, two and a half years after the shooting, determined on 26 April 1999 that there were no grounds to bring criminal charges against Officer Kilo:

> It is an established principle of law that when a man honestly believes that he is about to be attacked, even if that belief is mistaken, he is entitled to use such force as is reasonably necessary to defend himself. The officer who shot Diarmuid O'Neill has said that he did so in the belief that he was about to be shot by Mr O'Neill and that he was acting in self-defence. His belief was mistaken as Mr O'Neill was unarmed. However there is no evidence to show that the police officer's account is false or that his belief about the danger he thought he faced was not honestly held. The burden of proof lies with the prosecution and in the absence of any evidence— forensic, medical or eye witness accounts to contradict the officer's account—there is not a realistic prospect of conviction for any offence.

The inquest into the death of Diarmuid O'Neill opened in Kingston (not Hammersmith, for 'security reasons') on 31 January 2000 and ended on 18 February.

More evidence emerged which confirmed the campaigners' conviction that the operation was put together in such a way that it was virtually inevitable that someone was going to get killed. First, the members of SO19 where in a state of high expectation of a violent confrontation because of the briefing they had received immediately prior to the operation. For example, Detective Chief Superintendent Bunn, the commander of SO19 at the time and the man in overall charge of the operation, confirmed later that the firearms and detonators found in storage had been rendered harmless before the operation began and that the hotel room had been searched thoroughly, revealing no weapons or explosives. These facts were not conveyed to the armed policemen, who were instead warned that the IRA unit had guns and explosives and would not give up without a fight.

The decision to use CS RIP (Round Irritant Personnel) gas—a highly concentrated and penetrating version of CS gas—was taken at the last minute. That decision contradicted police regulations which maintained that CS gas should not be used when the suspects are thought to be armed. Those in charge of the operation claimed not to know this nor the regulations about how much gas to use. Because of the late decision, few of the policemen on the operation brought gas masks and fewer still wore them. Despite that, on the fifth day of the inquest, Michael Wood, QC for the Metropolitan Police, donned a gas mask and had the five men and five women of the jury do likewise, to demonstrate the difficulty of communication in such circumstances.

Officer Kilo continued to maintain that he had fired at Diarmuid O'Neill because he believed his own life was in danger. 'His body language suggested he was holding a weapon. He was bristling. This was a man who was going to kill me. He was standing in a classic boxer stance. His hands were down. My perception was he had a gun and I was going to die.' Despite the clear evidence of the tape which had been produced originally at the trial of the other IRA members, he said that Diarmuid O'Neill 'was not reacting to anything I said.' Along with nine other policemen who gave evidence, Officer Kilo claimed not to have heard Diarmuid and the others say they were unarmed and were giving themselves up.

The coroner, Dr. John Burton, in his summing up seemed to be very concerned with how the verdict could be seen and used politically. Despite the objections of Michael Mansfield, lawyer for the O'Neill family, he spelt out to the jury the implications of each of the decisions they might reach. 'He was killed unlawfully—which can be presented to say he was a martyr and it justified what the campaign set out to achieve. He was killed lawfully—which can be presented to show that it is lawful in England to kill people without a trial and that justifies and explains the conflict. Or you have an open verdict and that can be presented however the person can use it.' The coroner also argued with Michael Mansfield over the fact that the latter was one of the sponsors of the Justice for Diarmuid O'Neill Campaign. And he was at pains to understand the stress that the inquest had caused to the policemen involved. 'Society has required the police officers to take risks on our behalf. I have subjected them to three weeks' sustained attack without the protection afforded by the criminal court, with no pretence of natural justice, and there is nothing that I can do about it.' He made no such plea for understanding the plight of the O'Neill family.

The jury found that Diarmuid O'Neill had been lawfully killed. They recommended that there be a review of the way CS gas is used in such operations. For their part, the police did not think there were any lessons to be learned from the incident. DCS Bunn stated that he would not do things differently. And Detective Inspector Williams of the Firearms Branch told the inquest: 'I don't admit anything went wrong. Somebody's died, yes, but nothing went wrong'.

In their statement after the inquest the O'Neill family focused on the issue of lessons that might be learned. 'We are very conscious that nothing can bring our son back to life. But all of this could happen again. Our son is not the only unarmed person who has been shot by armed officers in recent years in London. Now that this inquest has finished and has uncovered decisions and actions that the police clearly are content to repeat, we suggest that a different form of public inquiry be held which can investigate all recent fatal shootings by armed police in order to ensure that lessons are learned, whether or not the police voluntarily agree.' In May 2000, the family lodged an appeal against the inquest verdict.

Before the inquest, Eoghan O'Neill told the *Irish Post*: 'We don't want Officer Kilo to go to jail for this. We don't even want him to be thrown out of the force. We want him to be reprimanded and we want an acknowledgement that the police made a mistake in the manner in which they tried to arrest my son'. The O'Neill family are still waiting for such an acknowledgement.

Paul Phillippou, a member of the Justice for Diarmuid O'Neill Campaign, tells the story of Diarmuid O'Neill's death and the subsequent campaign. This interview took place before the inquest.

Paul Phillippou

The Campaign's position has always been that Diarmuid's killing was totally unnecessary. If the police wanted to arrest Diarmuid and the others, they could have done so at any time. And they could have done so without violence.

It was the 23rd of September 1996. People awoke to reports on the radio and television that a gun battle had taken place on the streets of London, in Hammersmith, in a place just round the corner from where I used to live.

Later on, it appeared there wasn't a gun battle. What had happened was that a hotel on Glenthorne Road had been raided at 4.30 a.m. by the Metropolitan Police Firearms Squad and in that raid a young Irishman, Diarmuid O'Neill, 27 year old, was shot and killed by one of the police officers. Two other people were arrested in that house. Simultaneously that morning three other addresses were raided. Three other people—James Murphy, Diarmuid's brother Shane O'Neill, and Michael Phillips—were also arrested.

Over the next day or two, it became apparent that what the press had originally put out in terms of a gun battle, an arms find, explosives find, etc. was all misinformation. No guns or explosives were found at the hotel. The men inside did not resist in any way. We know now that the security forces had been watching Diarmuid and the other men for six or seven weeks. They had 50,000 hours of video and audio and surveillance evidence. It came out in the court case against Brian McHugh and the others. We were shown explosives and weapons held in a storage depot in Hornsey—weapons that had been made useless by the security services. These are the facts in the case.

The Campaign's position has always been that Diarmuid's killing was totally unnecessary. Diarmuid O'Neill lived and worked in Hammersmith. People knew him, knew what pubs and shops he went to. The police had been following him for weeks. To quote one police officer, 'Diarmuid O'Neill couldn't take a piss without us knowing'. The day before he was killed, he was up a ladder outside his parents' house in Fulham, painting the house. He popped into his local newsagent to buy a chocolate bar; the police knew what bar of chocolate he bought. If the police wanted to arrest Diarmuid and the others, they could have done so at any time. And they could have done so without violence. It would have been very easy. Instead, they chose a very different, more violent model of approach. In the early hours of the morning of the 23rd of September, police officers from SO19, Special Operations 19, the Metropolitan Police's firearms unit, were taken from the headquarters at Scotland Yard; they were briefed by senior members of the anti-terrorist branch, were then shown a video of the Canary Wharf bombing, a bombing totally unrelated to these men; they were shown footage of the lock-up where the explosives and arms were held and they were told that these men in this room were armed and dangerous. This was a complete lie. The security forces had been into the room in the hotel only two days beforehand and had searched it. They knew there were no arms there. They'd been following the men for six, seven weeks. They knew they had no weapons. They had bugged the room, they had bugged their cars. They knew all their pager messages, they knew all their phone messages. They knew they didn't have any weapons on them. They knew there were weapons in the lock-up, but they also knew that they had been disarmed by the security forces. Yet they whipped up these police into a frenzy. At the moment they needed to be at their most calm and professional, they were sent into a situation where they had good reason, so they thought, to fear for their lives.

In the Gibraltar killing, a case was taken to the European Court of Human Rights and the British government were found in breach of Article 2. You remember at the time they said, 'We shall ignore this judgement'. The significant thing is that Diarmuid was killed almost a year to the day after that judgement was made. It may be in a way, that's their way of ignoring that judgement. We've always believed that Diarmuid's case was a case of shoot-to-kill. Shoot-to-kill doesn't necessarily mean you plan an operation to target one man and go and do it. Shoot-to-kill can also be about your general approach and your general attitude. It was a consequence of the model the police used, the way they were trained and the way they were briefed, their approach, and it was a consequence of the political situation. When Brian and the others were questioned by police, they were told that Diarmuid was killed as a message to all second generation Irish in England not to get involved.

There was a bizarre issue over CS gas. The police officers were issued with RIP, which is the most powerful form of CS gas available to them and only available when the Home Secretary gives actual permission for it. It was meant to be used in case something went wrong. But the officers were then still given the option whether to take a gas mask or not. Some chose to take a gas mask and others chose not to.

4.30 a.m., they surround the house—officers at the back, officers at the front, officers with dogs, with all the support mechanisms around, including paramedics and ambulances. They had a key to the room in which the men were staying; it had been given to them by the hotel. I think it was actually the master key for the hotel. We know it worked a couple of days before because MI5 had been in the room with that key. But for some strange reason, it didn't work this time. The police officers then decided to use a device called an enforcer, which is a kind of pneumatic battering ram that you fire at a door that is locked and it breaks it down. Instead of knocking the door open, it merely made a hole through the door.

At this stage, the police officers made the decision to fire CS gas into the room through the back window and also through the front door. This gas soon spread out in the room and started pouring out through the hole in the door onto the landing where these police officers were, a number of whom didn't have gas masks on. They were overcome with the effects of the gas. Some of them were forced to retreat round the corner. Some of them were forced to go outside and be sick. The sergeant who was in charge of the operation was forced to leave the hotel; no one appeared to have operational command after him. Officer Kilo, who initially withdrew because of the effects of CS gas, then went back to the landing. The security forces had a bug in the room and what happened was on that tape; it was played in the court case. We know from that tape that Officer Kilo and one of the other officers were shouting instructions to the people in the room. We can hear on the tape the cries of the men in the room: 'We're down. We're on the deck. We're down. We're unarmed.' One of the officers insists that they open the door. Diarmuid O'Neill got up to comply with this request. The door of course has been damaged by the enforcer, so he's struggling to get the door open. The police officer is shouting, 'Show us your hands'—while other officers are shouting for him to get on the floor. The door is open, ajar, and Diarmuid is attempting to show his hands: 'They're up, they're up.' The police officer then says in court under testimony that he saw the figure of Diarmuid O'Neill crouching towards him or leaning towards him in some kind of aggressive stance. He said he felt his life to be in danger at that point and he fired. We know from the tape that either Kilo or one of the other officers at that moment shouted, 'Shoot the fuckers'. Initially there were two bullets discharged, then a further two bullets, and then a further two bullets. We can hear on the tape subsequently: 'Dead as a fucking rat'. One of the first few bullets pierced Diarmuid's spine, so he began to collapse backwards and the other bullets went into him at an angle as he was falling backwards. We know that from the pathologist's report. The police officers entered the room. At some point one of the police officers stood on Diarmuid's head—there's a boot mark on Diarmuid's head; we know that from the pathologist's report. They then took control of the two other men in the room, Brian McHugh and Patrick Kelly. They dragged Diarmuid out of the room, down the stairs and down the steps of the hotel into the street. We know he was dragged, not carried, not put on a stretcher, because we have seen on the media, in the newspapers, the blood streaming on the steps. We understand that he was not given immediate medical treatment. There were paramedics and ambulances on standby. Initially it was the police who administered first aid to him, not the paramedics. Eventually the paramedics were allowed in. He was then taken to Charing Cross Hospital where at 5.16, it was said that he was dead.

What I have said about the raid comes from the court case. But that trial wasn't about Diarmuid; it was about the other men. So the full facts of the raid have never really been gone into. Those police officers have never really been quizzed. It's our hope that the inquest would be the first time that the police officers involved could be questioned.

At the trial it was agreed that the police officers would all be anonymous. That's why, for example, I've described the policeman who shot Diarmuid as Officer Kilo, Officer K. They're known as Alpha, Beta, Hotel, etc. They had anonymity at the trial. It's almost certain that at the inquest the coroner will agree for them to have anonymity. The Metropolitan Police did lobby the Hammersmith coroner, John Burton, for anonymity for its officers. We of course argued against that. Senior officers from the anti-terrorist branch will not be anonymous; the men who gave the orders will appear in court and will be known.

One of the police officers involved was Steve Collins. He has since retired from the Firearms Squad and he's written a number of books, one of which is called *The Good Guys Wear Black*. It's about his exploits in the Firearms Squad. In the preface to the book he describes the raid on the house in which Diarmuid O'Neill was killed. He describes men in black in the early hours of the morning sneaking into this residence where highly dangerous terrorists are holed up. He uses a word which would imply that it was a gun battle. At the end of this, young Diarmuid O'Neill, terrorist, lies dead. And his last line is something like, 'You might think that this was in Lebanon or in Armagh, but you would be wrong. This was just another day for the boys of SO19 on the streets of London'. For him, the unnecessary killing of a young Irishman is 'just another day'. And he ends his book with the line something like, if it wasn't for him and others like him, we couldn't sleep soundly in our bed. Well, I certainly don't sleep soundly in my bed knowing that there are people like that on the loose.

In his book he publishes photographs of himself and other officers. The other officers, some of whom were almost certainly on the raid when Diarmuid was killed, have the customary black rectangle across the eyes. But he doesn't. He's full view in a number of photographs. He's been interviewed on the radio and the television. We know his name. And the book was produced with the acceptance of the Chief Commissioner of the Metropolitan Police. So we find that bizarre that he doesn't need anonymity. At the end of the day, these are public servants and they should stand accountable for their actions. If there had been threats, if there was a realistic threat of some kind of retaliation, then maybe the police would be justified in asking for anonymity. There's never been animosity expressed against him or any of the other police officers by the family. The family have always said, 'It's not Kilo we want to see banged up in prison. It is not revenge. We don't want to see this man punished. We want everyone involved to be accountable. We want the truth to come out'. So they cannot justify that there is a threat. I don't know of any other historical precedent in this country and certainly, given the present political climate, it's extremely strange. They've argued that perhaps Diarmuid's other comrades might want to kill this man. If Diarmuid's comrades were so dangerous, why is it that the British and Irish governments have let them out of prison? If these men pose a threat to Metropolitan Police officers, then why are they allowed out? They're allowed out because the British and Irish governments know that these men are not a threat to anyone.

Diarmuid was well known in the Irish community in Hammersmith. There are a number of people who knew him, knew the family, political people, progressive people who were either involved in the local trades council or community groups or in Irish political issues. Through them came the idea to set up a meeting at the town hall to launch some kind of campaign. A large room was booked at the town hall and 700 or 800 people turned up to that first meeting. People were asked to put their names down if they were interested in organising the group. After a number of weeks, those that were interested dwindled down to a smaller group, and correctly in a sense. The strength of the Campaign has always been that the members are quite diverse, quite broad. Some come from the Irish political spectrum, some come from the trade unions, and some are just friends of Diarmuid and the family. And because we have been small, I think it's made us very strong and efficient. I've seen many other campaigns over the years that are too big, too unwieldy, too many people with their own agendas. We made sure from the beginning that this campaign was about justice for Diarmuid O'Neill; it wasn't about other people's political policies. What often happens to these other big political campaigns in the past is that they get captured by people from different left wing parties and groups. They're pushing their own agenda and that's weakened the organisation and causes all sorts of problems. That's never happened in the group.

I came from a political background. I've been involved in politics since an early age. I've been involved in the local Labour Party in this area. I've stood for the council in this area. I'm a member of the local trades council. I'd also been involved with Irish political issues over the years—like the 'Time to go' initiative, Bloody Sunday, Guildford 4, Birmingham 6. I knew a number of the people who had called the first public meeting. A friend thought it might be a good idea for me to get involved in the Campaign and invited me to come along to the meeting—which I did, on the edge initially. Over the last four years I've taken more of a lead role in the campaign. It's not something I searched out to do. It's just emerged like that.

I have experienced individual intimidation—coming back from Dublin once, being stopped at Heathrow by the police, being told it's just a technical matter, they just want me to fill in a form. I filled in the form and they said, 'Could you just wait in this office while we just check your details?' I'm left in this room stewing for a while. And then a man and a woman come in. She introduced herself as PC Duffy from the Special Branch and he said he was from the security services. He looked like a train spotter. They started to talk about Diarmuid and my political involvement in Irish issues. They were trying to intimidate me. They were making threats, saying they could get information to prove I was a member of the IRA. I was a member of a lot of different groups, and they wanted me to tell them things about the groups. I was actually quite fearful. I didn't expect myself to be in the beginning. But eventually I got my composure and began to be more assertive and to question their right to hold me. I wasn't refusing to speak to them, but I had nothing to say to them because these are all legal political campaigns—and more importantly, it was none of their business. Eventually they let me go. I went to speak to Gareth Pierce and she told me this is very common. She said, 'I doubt if they'll ever contact you again', which they haven't done. It makes you think if they're doing that here, what have they got up to in the Six Counties in terms of intimidation, where they can get away with more?

What we realised at an early stage of campaigning is that we were up against it because we were dealing with a lot of prejudice. Diarmuid O'Neill was a member of the IRA. Those three letters cause a lot of people, wrongly, to step back. Rather than look at the questions we're asking, they would be frightened and wouldn't want to touch it. I'm not just talking about politicians. I'm talking about people in the community, Irish people as well. We thought, we have to be extremely professional. What we produce needs to be of the highest quality. We always try to maintain a high degree of professionalism in what we put out because we really want people to listen. We don't want any distractions from the point we're trying to make.

Probably our most successful campaign tool was the postcard that people could sign and send off to the Home Secretary to call for an inquiry. We knew that a useful image would be the image of the steps. Most of the newspapers had a picture in black and white. We needed a good quality image and we got it from *Hello* magazine's monthly news round-up! We wanted to get a picture of Diarmuid out. All of the newspapers had printed stolen photographs. When they raided that hotel where Diarmuid was staying, they also raided the family home and Diarmuid's flat. They took a lot of things, including photographs. These were given to newspapers and they picked photographs which you wouldn't pick yourself. They totally dismantled the family house. They knocked through all the plaster cornices. They took up all the floor boards downstairs—which have never been given back. They took up all the flagstones in the garden and took them away. They dismantled and did not put back washing machines and microwaves and cookers. They completely wrecked the house. They arrested Shane O'Neill, the brother. They questioned him for two or three days and told him that his brother was dead.

We produced something like 16,000 of the postcards. We know loads have been sent. We know they've been successful because we have a letter from the Home Office saying that they have received so many postcards and letters that it's impossible for them to write back to everyone and could we inform people of their standard line. As if we knew the names and addresses of all those people!

The kind of campaigning things we've done include writing to all the British MPs, MEPs, all the senators and congressmen in America, all the TDs, asking for affiliation or support for the Campaign. We've written to as many progressive, left or human rights groups all over the world that we can. Literally thousands of letters and faxes have gone out.

Diarmuid was an Irish citizen. Caoimhghín Ó Caoláin, the Sinn Féin TD, asked a question in the Dáil of David Andrews, the Foreign Minister, about Diarmuid. And David Andrews said, 'Yes, I think it would be a useful thing to have an independent inquiry'. That was a very powerful thing for the Foreign Minister of Ireland to do that.

One group that has been involved in the campaign separately from the beginning and has done sterling work is British Irish Rights Watch under Jane Winter's leadership. They operate very differently from us. We are much more of a grassroots campaign. Her work would be much more on the legal level. She's written a report to the Special Rapporteur for Extra-judicial Killings in the United Nations who is aware of Diarmuid's case and is investigating the issue. When she goes over to Europe to the Human Rights Committee, one of the cases she talks about is that of Diarmuid. If questions are asked in the United Nations of the British government about human rights abuses in their country, it makes them feel uncomfortable. It means they can't just brush the issue aside; they've got to address it. They do not want that; it's embarrassing. Similarly, we've lobbied quite strongly in America and we've got a lot of support.

We've made links with other groups. I remember a particular meeting where the four main issues were the Diarmuid O'Neill case, the Stephen Lawrence case—Suresh Grover from the Stephen Lawrence Campaign spoke—the Robert Hamill case—where Diane Hamill and Rosemary Nelson spoke—and the Ricky Reel case. You might have possibly thought those other people might have been uncomfortable being alongside the Diarmuid O'Neill Campaign. It was very significant that we could make those links with those other campaigns, who could see these things as human rights issues.

What we've really done over the last three and a half years is keep the issue going. What the police and the government have wanted is for the case to go away. We've never let it go and they know that. Despite their attempts to cover it up or put it to the side, we kept it going. Periodically we've been interviewed on the radio. We've been on television. We've had pickets outside the coroner's office, outside the headquarters of the Metropolitan Police's firearms squad and outside Hammersmith police station on a number of occasions, New Scotland Yard, Crown Prosecution Service, Downing Street. Every time we've done that, we've done our best to get as much media coverage as possible. This isn't very easy, because there is a problem in this country with Irish issues. Quite good journalists have been honest and said to me, 'I'm not going to write an Irish story. My paper doesn't want it'. But we've managed to keep the story in the local paper and the *Irish Post*. We've had good reports in the *Guardian* and the *Observer*, the *Sunday Mirror*, *Ireland on Sunday*, whose journalist Ann Cadwallader has written some brilliant pieces.

You're trying to keep this issue going. You're up against the resources of a state. You're trying to counter the lobbying of the Metropolitan Police, the government's refusal to act. When you think about what you've actually got available compared to a state, it's actually amazing. All praise to the group and everyone in it that we've actually managed to do what we've done. I know there were times when we could have been better, but we've always bounced back. We've always kept going.

Whenever someone is shot by a police officer, the Police Complaints Authority have to look at it. They have to write a report about it. They say that all reports should be complete in something like 120 days. Within hours of Diarmuid's killing, a member of the PCA visited the hotel and started the preparation for this report. But the thing about the PCA is, they don't actually do the investigation. They ask the police to do it. What would be normal in a case like this is to call in officers from a police force outside London separate to the force that took part in the raid. But in this case they invited officers from the Police Complaints Investigations Bureau, which is basically the Metropolitan Police's investigative section, to conduct the investigation. At the same time, the PCA dragged their heels. First of all, they said they couldn't really do anything because they had to wait for the trial of the other people arrested to take place. That didn't take place until over a year after the killing. I know that they can't complete their report until after the trial, but there's nothing to stop them starting.

About 18 months into this delay we started picketing the PCA. I thought we had a bit of a coup when we were allowed onto Greater London Radio to discuss the issue and to challenge the PCA who then responded. Peter Moorhouse, who was head of the PCA at the time, came on the radio about an hour later to say, 'There's not a delay. We're doing our best.' He invited the Campaign to come down to his office to discuss the matter—which we did. We discussed all our concerns about the delay. They explained the reasons for the delay and we pointed out things—had they looked at this? 'Oh no, we hadn't looked at this, but we will add that to the report.' We know from the trial that there was a video placed in the car park just opposite the hotel where they were staying. We could see people coming and going from the hotel. And we queried: was the video on the night of the raid? 'Oh, we didn't know about the video. We'll look into that.'

Eventually 23 months after Diarmuid was killed, the PCA finished their report. The final thing they did, right at the end, was to interview Officer Kilo. Their argument was that that's standard procedure, that you don't interview the police officer involved until you've talked to all the other witnesses and collected all the other data. I can understand that. I think that's fully justified if your investigation takes three weeks, four weeks—but not if it takes two years. That is absolutely appalling to do that. It's about getting the story right; it's about collecting all the evidence from the other police officers, making sure it's consistent and then feeding Kilo his lines.

Then the report gets to the Crown Prosecution Service who begin reading it. And they took something like seven months to read this report, to come to the conclusion that there is no evidence for any officer to be charged with anything. As far as they're concerned, that's the end of the matter.

So the next thing we wait for is the inquest. One would think that the inquest would start almost immediately. But now we have to wait for the coroner to read all the documentation. It's going to be three and a half years since Diarmuid died. It's an awful long time, given that the inquest was opened the day after he was killed. There's no excuse really.

Then the coroner writes a letter to the Home Office under new powers he's got post the Steven Lawrence case. He's basically saying, 'I feel this is a controversial issue. There should be a judicial review to look into it rather than an inquest'. This is a coroner at the end of his career, a very experienced coroner. For him to make that statement to the Home Office holds an awful lot of weight. The Home Office made the decision there was to be no judicial inquiry, I'm sure under pressure from the police. When we knew that the Home Office was considering it, we wrote to all our supporters telling them to write to the Home Office—ask them to consider it. The coroner said to Gareth Pierce that he was feeling pressure from the Campaign and asked her to sort of call us off! She's not involved in the Campaign.

At the inquest the jury could come up with a verdict of lawful killing, unlawful killing, or an open verdict. At the end of the day, in a way the verdict doesn't matter. What matters is the proceedings. It's the first opportunity for the family's lawyers—Gareth Pierce and Michael Mansfield—on behalf of the family to question those people involved, to try and find the truth, to expose to the British public and to the world what happened that day. That's what we want. We want the truth to come out. The police barristers will paint this picture of this very dangerous terrorist; the shooting was acceptable because of the danger. It's going to be very difficult for the jury to make an informed decision because there's going to be so much misinformation and so much prejudice and fear and bias. If the jury came out with unlawful killing, that's very important. There's the possibility of prosecution, there's the possibility of the investigation being reopened. But if there's an open verdict or lawful killing, obviously there's more to be done. It would be up to the family to decide what to do next. It's very difficult working with the family sometimes, because for me and for the other people in the Campaign, in a way we're dealing in an abstract way. When you talk to the family sometimes you catch yourself thinking, 'God, it's easy for me to discuss. But this is their son'. And every time something happens—like fighting for the PCA report to come out, fighting for the inquest, fighting for an inquiry—the family have got to relive the day of the murder of their son. They sat through every day of that trial. And now they're going to have to sit through this inquest for three weeks. They've never been allowed to move on from this. They've got to keep reliving it. I don't know if they're going to want to relive it again.

23

ROBERT HAMILL
8 May 1997

Kicked to death by loyalists while RUC were in vicinity

Robert Hamill was a 25 year old father of three - one child was born after his death - who lived in Portadown, County Armagh. At 1.30am on 27 April 1997, he left a Catholic social club in the centre of Portadown along with two cousins, Siobhan and Joanne, and Joanne's husband Gregory Girvan. They had only a short distance to walk to their home area—down Thomas Street, across Market Street and into Woodhouse Street—but would not normally have walked. Anyone heading towards Woodhouse Street would be immediately identifiable as a nationalist, and in staunchly loyalist Portadown, it was best for a nationalist not to be so public about their destination. However, Robert Hamill and his friends had been unable to get a taxi for the journey home.

There was a crowd of loyalists gathered in the centre of the town. Their presence had already been noticed by a man who had left the social club shortly before Robert. This man had approached four RUC officers sitting in a parked Land Rover at the entrance to Woodhouse Street and advised them to keep a lookout as there would soon be other nationalists leaving the club and heading home. The RUC did nothing to disperse the crowd or make the area safe for nationalists. Despite the presence of the loyalist crowd, Robert Hamill and his friends walked towards Woodhouse Street, reassured by the RUC presence. As it turned out, their confidence was misplaced.

Robert and Gregory were attacked by 30 or so loyalists, knocked to the ground and kicked repeatedly. Many in the crowd focused their attention on Robert, jumping on him and kicking him about the head. The four police officers in the armoured Land Rover parked fifteen yards away—Constables Neill and Atkinson, and Reserve Constables Connett and Sharpe, the last of whom was female—did not intervene, not even when Siobhan went over to the Land Rover and sought their assistance. They only emerged from the Land Rover when the crowd gave up and an ambulance and RUC reinforcements had arrived. By that time, both Robert and Gregory were unconscious. Gregory regained consciousness the following day, but Robert did not. He died 12 days later, on 8 May 1997, of skull fracture and brain injury resulting from repeated blows to the head.

There were 19 armed RUC officers on duty in Portadown that night and four British army units available within ten minutes. During the incident one mobile British army unit radioed Portadown RUC station and offered assistance, but was told their help was not needed. When the RUC eventually intervened they took no statements, questioned no suspects—even though they temporarily held one of those later charged, Wayne Lunt, to check his identity—and did nothing to make it clear that this was the scene of a crime.

Initial RUC press reports were of a fight in Portadown between two rival factions, rather than of an unprovoked attack on four innocent people going home. Police were said to have moved in to separate 'rival factions' at which point they supposedly came under attack themselves. The Hamill family succeeded in getting the true story out. But it was May 7, the day before Robert Hamill's death, before the 'rival factions' explanation was dropped and the RUC acknowledged that a sectarian attack had taken place.

Two days after Robert's death, five men—Stacey Bridgett, Wayne Lunt, Dean Forbes, Allistair Hanvey and Mark Hobson—were charged with his murder. On the following day, a sixth man, Rory Robinson, was also charged. They were remanded in custody. Hobson, Lunt and Bridgett were housed in the LVF wing at the Maze Prison. In leaflets distributed in Portadown the LVF, notorious for a campaign of sectarian assassination and intimidation in the area, referred to the accused as 'the Portadown Six': 'We would like to take this opportunity to wish you all success in your trial. Everyone of us know that the charges against you are outrageous... You have been criminalized for defending yourselves against an unprovoked attack.'

At the end of October 1997, three of the accused—Forbes, Hanvey and Robinson—were released for lack of evidence. The magistrate said: 'It has been a terrible ideal for all three of you'. He did not address any such remarks to the Hamill family. Shortly afterwards charges against Lunt and Bridgett were also dropped. The last remaining accused, Mark Hobson, went on trial in February 1999. The main prosecution witness was Constable Alan Neill, one of the RUC personnel in the nearby Land Rover. He stated that he saw a man similar to Hobson shouting at Robert as he lay on the ground; he also saw him swinging his foot towards Robert's head, but could not swear that he had made contact. Neill re-introduced the 'rival factions' explanation for the events of 27 April.

In his judgement, Judge McCollum criticised the RUC for not acting on the early warning provided by the man who had left the social club shortly before Robert Hamill and his friends. As regards allegations of police inaction, McCollum said that he was 'unable to resolve the question whether the police officers remained in the Land Rover during the attack'. However, he did not have to resolve this question as it was in his view immaterial to the issue of whether or not Hobson was guilty. 'Even if alerted at the earliest moment by the occurrence of the attack itself, it is unlikely they would have been able to dismount and intervene in time to save Mr Hamill'. The Judge found it impossible to be satisfied of Hobson's guilt, although he did conclude that 'it is probable that he intended and did strike' Robert Hamill. He found Hobson guilty of causing an affray and sentenced him to four years in prison. As Hobson had already served almost two years on remand, under the 50% remission rule, he had only 46 days to serve. He was released on 10 May 1999. He later appealed the sentence but on 26 October 1999, the Appeal Court judges upheld the conviction, concluding that the sentence was not excessive.

It has been the contention of the Hamill family from the beginning that RUC negligence contributed to Robert's death. A timely intervention could have saved his life. Specifically, they point out that the RUC,

- ignored warnings of a potential incident;
- ignored pleas for them to intervene during the attack;
- did not fire into the air or attempt to disperse the crowd;
- did not administer first-aid;
- did not declare a crime scene, collect forensic evidence or take statements from witnesses;
- detained one suspect but released him after a few minutes;
- did not make any arrests until two weeks after the event.

The family's insistence on RUC culpability has led to them being the focus of sustained RUC harassment and intimidation.

Speaking to the US Congress House International Relations Committee on 22 April 1999, Diane Hamill, sister of Robert, began her testimony thus: 'I am black, I live in Alabama and the year is 1962'. At the end of her submission, she returned to the point:

> I want a police force I can call upon when I need to but more especially I want a police force that will protect me and not leave me to be murdered because I am a Catholic. I am not black, I do not live in Alabama and the year is not 1962, but you tell me the difference.

On 30 September 1999, the DPP announced that there would be no prosecutions brought against the RUC personnel in the Land Rover that night.

However, the possibility was left open that an internal RUC inquiry could lead to some disciplinary action. For the Hamill family, the only options in the pursuit of truth and justice were to continue to demand a rigorous and independent inquiry or to pursue a private prosecution of the police officers concerned. Both avenues were being pursued by the Hamill family's solicitor Rosemary Nelson before she too was murdered by loyalists on 15 March 1999. On 24 April 2000, two weeks before the third anniversary of Robert's death, the campaign was given a significant boost by the announcement of the Irish government that it was urging British Prime Minister Tony Blair to set up an independent public inquiry into the murder.

Diane Hamill, Robert's sister, has been at the forefront of the campaign since the beginning. She now tells her story.

Diane Hamill

I want them to face criminal charges and I want them put out of the RUC. I'm a nurse and if someone had died because of something I didn't do, I would have been suspended. They are the best equipped police force in Europe and they couldn't do a thing to save our Robert's life.

It was the 27th of April 1997. I was working up in a nursing home in Carnlough and I had my mummy and my brother John up staying with me. It was lovely up there in the countryside. I was working nights and about six o'clock in the morning, mummy came to the nursing home and said Robert had been hurt. I thought it couldn't be our Robert, for our Robert was over six foot and well-built. She said, 'Diane, there were thirty of them and the police just stood there and let it happen'.

What had happened was, about half-one that morning, he was making his way back from St Patrick's Hall in the centre of the town with my cousins Joanne and Siobhan and Siobhan's husband Gregory; they had to go through the centre of Portadown. They had phoned for a taxi but there were no taxis. As they came down to a junction, they could see there were a couple of lads hanging about, but they could see there was an RUC Land Rover parked at the top of the street so they felt safe to go on ahead. As they got to the junction, the boys were attacked. The police have told us the figures range from forty to fifty of them, male and female. So they pulled the boys and beat the boys; they concentrated on Robert for some reason. We were hoping that he was knocked out with the first blow for they beat him around the head. The police didn't get out of the vehicle. People coming out of Catholic pubs some two hundred yards away tried to get the boys away from them and still the cops stayed in the vehicle. One of the fellows actually came out of the pub and opened the door of the Land Rover and pulled one of the cops out and said, 'You sat and watched this happening'. The cop got back into the jeep again. I don't know how long the attack actually lasted for, but

I know that the crowd got fed up. They stood in a circle around Robert as he lay on the ground. I think he lay with his chin to this chest, not getting any oxygen. The ambulance came, I don't honestly know how long after, but that was the first first-aid he got. At that point the cops got out because they saw the ambulances coming, I think one of them approached Siobhan and said, 'Turn him on his side'. Siobhan hadn't a clue what to do.

The cops never even fired a bullet in the air; they never did anything. We found out later, about ten minutes before Robert went down the road, a fellow had come out of the same club and seen the crowd. He approached the RUC vehicle and said, 'They are coming out of St Patrick's Hall and there is a crowd here. You had better watch out'. They never came up the road to stop people coming down. What scares me most is that those people, thirty or forty of them, knew they would get away with doing something within fifteen yards of the police.

Robert was taken to Craigavon Hospital and the CT scan wasn't working, so they had to rush him down to the Royal. He went to the Royal on the Sunday morning and they did a brain scan on him and told us it was clear. We thought he was going to be okay. They were reducing all his drugs. They were expecting him to come round anytime. We were going to get a camera and take a photo of him just to show him what he had put us through. As the hours went on, you could see him starting to come round a bit. You could see his fingers and feet starting to move a bit. But by three o'clock that afternoon he hadn't woken up and he should have woken up. On the Monday I was talking to one of the nurses. Robert would get really agitated and he would thrash around. He wasn't opening his eyes but he was semi-conscious. I kept saying to that nurse, 'Why isn't he waking up?' She said to me, 'Did you ever consider how long he was lying on the ground without oxygen?' Then it clicked with me; they thought he was brain damaged. On the Tuesday morning they moved him out of intensive care. They thought that because Robert could breathe, he didn't need intensive care. They moved him up to the neurological ward and basically there he suffered immensely for ten days in extreme pain. It was like he knew he was caught in this body and couldn't get out of it. Our Robert was such a big, lively fellow. He took no orders; he was quite assertive. To see him lying there knowing he couldn't get out of it! Each day we thought he was getting better and the doctors told us he was off the critical list; he wasn't going to die. But they didn't know whether he would regain full ability or whether he would stay the way he was. We were prepared for all that.

Twelve days after he was hurt, I decided I would go back to work and that was the Thursday. There were some of us with him all of the time. Daddy had stayed with him on the Wednesday night and I couldn't get away until four and I was going to take mummy over on the way home from work. As we were walking into the ward about four o'clock, I could see there was an emergency trolley beside his bed and I tried to speed up, but I didn't want to scare the heart out of mummy. I thought it couldn't be him. There was an old man across from him who had been sick and I thought he had died. People had been in that ward a long time and the relatives get to know each other. A woman came out and said, 'Don't go down there, love'. I went round and there was a doctor standing there. Robert had literally just died. I think the nurses came in to change the sheets because he perspired so much from thrashing around and he had arrested. They tried to resuscitate him but he died. That was the Thursday the eighth of May. He was buried on the Sunday.

Our priest had got up on the altar the day after our Robert was hurt and preached to people about going into the town and fighting. The police had spoken to him.

In their first coverage the newspapers picked up the police statements. Then gradually over the days their statements changed because we were talking to the newspapers and giving our side of what had happened. The girls actually gave a statement to the *Irish News* before Robert died and told how the police had stayed there. So the RUC had to change their story. The very last statement they released said it was an unprovoked sectarian attack. After Robert died, the media were down in our house the next morning. They wanted daddy to talk and he wasn't going to do it, but we wanted to get the story across. Other people might have told them to clear off, but I knew from the day Robert was hurt that if you wanted to get anything done, you had to use these people like they use us. Daddy sat down and I just jumped in beside him in case he broke down. I remember him telling them they jumped on his head. He told them about the cops. I noticed everything was very sympathetic initially. There was a hearing then to see if there was evidence for a trial and one of the police officers gave a statement and talked about 'scraps'; he had gone back to the initial RUC statement that Robert was fighting. The next day a reporter came and asked about the fights and the two groups taunting one another. I was disgusted but I was ready for them doing something like that.

I just thought about the police not helping him and I thought, 'You pigs, you aren't getting away with this'. I went to a solicitor in Portadown, and I said, 'Will I phone the police station?' He said, 'No, that's what I'm here for'. He phoned over and he spoke to some sergeant or whatever and it was all sort of jollity. A day or two later I went back to see the solicitor and nothing really had changed. I went with my boyfriend and as we were coming out, he said to me, 'Diane, he couldn't look you in the eye'. I was saying, 'What can we do?' and he just said, 'We could sue them for defamation of character'. I didn't want that. I wanted some sort of action. They let him be attacked and then tried to say he was in a fight. So I went to Rosemary Nelson and she was for us straight away. She just knew straight away what to do. I knew this was a cut and dry case; there was no way they could get out of it. They can't deny the fact that they were there and that he was attacked fifteen yards away from where they were and that they didn't do anything at all. All they had to do was stick one arm out of the jeep and fire a bullet in the air. They had no excuse whatsoever.

We started to gather petitions to get the officers suspended, for they weren't even suspended. Over a few weeks we collected twenty thousand signatures; we could have got a lot more if we had gone berserk on it, but I thought twenty thousand was enough. We met Mo Mowlam a couple of times; she never did anything; she pretends to care but she doesn't. The officers were never suspended. I think they were out on the sick for some time. We got this anonymous call—we believe it was a police officer. He gave us the names of the cops who were in the jeep that night. He told us the officers had gone off on sick leave and that they had claims in for trauma.

I had never had any dealings with the cops. I didn't know how malicious they could be, how they could trick and twist. But within days of Robert's attack, I knew they couldn't be trusted at all. We had asked about video evidence for there are four banks and building societies around the junction where he was attacked. They told us there was nothing, only the vehicle on one of them. I don't actually know where the video evidence is; I reckon they destroyed it. They waited so long before they arrested anyone there was no forensic evidence left.

A couple of days after Robert had died, there were six fellows lifted and charged with murder. That was May. In October three of them were released on the grounds that people were reluctant to give evidence against them. Then in November they let two more go; they said it was mistaken identity, even though they didn't give anyone a chance to pick them out of an identity line. They let Stacy Bridgett go; his blood was on our Robert. That was enough to keep him in for six months but it wasn't enough to take the charge any further. So now, when we walk round Portadown, we bump into Stacy Bridgett regularly. There is one fellow still in jail, Mark Hobson; he has had five different hearings. Allistair Hanvey stood in a room outside the courtroom in front of my mummy and kicked a banister; they knew what they were doing—they were imitating the attack on Robert. They have sat in the court and very subtly stamped their feet on the carpet, not enough for the people around them to realise but enough for us to know what they are doing.

I wrote loads of letters to politicians looking for support for an inquiry. Ken Magennis wrote back to me; he sympathised, but he said he couldn't do anything. But my MP, David Trimble—I wrote to him and got no response. I wrote again a few months later and I got a response. He said that he had written a letter to the RUC after the first letter and it was still in the hands of the RUC. It was four lines; he didn't sympathise. I met David Andrews, the Irish foreign minister; he was quite good.

We had a vigil on Robert's first anniversary and they sent a representative, a senator in the Irish government. Brid Rogers [SDLP] was there; Gerry Kelly

[Sinn Féin] was there. I attempted to get the mayor of Portadown and various unionist MPs; they ignored me. One Alliance politician told me that I was on very dodgy ground and I needed to be careful. A few hundred people turned up and we just moved off to the spot where Robert was attacked, just a few of us for we knew the whole crowd couldn't go in case of an attack. We stopped half way up Woodhouse Street, and just the family carried a wreath to the spot at the top of Woodhouse Street where Robert had been attacked. We had put flowers on the lamppost where he had died every day for a month after he died and everything was totally destroyed. Mummy wanted us to do it but she was getting upset. We wanted to defy them but it was just tearing her apart. We stopped that June, but it was his birthday on the twelfth of September and we did it then, but they pulled them down again. The sad thing about that was it was just after Diana's death and there were flowers everywhere, but they wrecked Robert's. On the thirteenth of July 1997, I had to go up the town, myself and my boyfriend. He had told me not to go, but me being me went ahead. He pointed out some flowers on the pole. We thought, 'Imagine someone thinking of him now a couple of months down the line!' We went over. There was a card stuck beside the flowers and it read, 'For the Portadown Six Heroes'. That's how evil they were; someone had actually sat down and thought of that. There was a white hankie there and I had no idea what it was for until the following Sunday. We live near a loyalist area and there was a fellow shouting over to us, pretending to pull someone to the ground and kick their face. He was shouting, 'Did you get the white hankie to wipe your tears away? Did you'se get it?'

We have tried publicity, the petition and the Irish government. It's been over a year and a half and we don't seem to be getting anywhere so we have decided on a private prosecution. We think there is bound to be enough evidence there to prosecute everyone, those involved, the RUC officers. I feel they were just as guilty as the ones who attacked Robert. They were duty bound to act but they didn't do it. They could have at least protected him or helped him and I believe they decided not to do it. They knew rightly Robert was a Catholic because of where he was walking. I believe they wanted a bit of fun and to see a fenian being beaten.

We have discussed a private prosecution with Mike Mansfield. He is going to do it for us but he is really busy. It's just a matter of waiting for Hobson's trial to finish and for the DPP to decide whether there is going to be any disciplinary action against the RUC officers. I had been watching the television and the Stephen Lawrence case was on and I knew how his family were feeling. We held a press conference and read out statements about a private prosecution. We advertised for donations in the *Irish News*. We opened an account and called it The Robert Hamill Justice Fund and took out a half page advert in the paper. Someone sent us a five thousand pounds anonymous donation. I was really unsure at the start of whether to do it, for a lot of people who had started campaigns got nowhere and were really devastated.

I went to the Aidan McAnespie annual dinner in the GAA club [in Boston]. I did an article for the *Boston Herald* as well while I was there. The *Guardian* did a really good article for us. Jeremy Hardy writes for the *Guardian* as well and he has got us good publicity. The 'Insight' programme did a documentary for the TV. I was really afraid that they would go out of their way to make the RUC look good. I don't know how they would have done that—they would have had to tell lies—but they were really truthful and I think that helped the campaign.

We get a lot of harassment. Daddy would have been walking down the street and the RUC would drive by and slow down. My brother was standing at the end of the street talking to a couple of girls and the RUC in one of their cars stopped and stared right at him. It is real provocation. One time he was standing with two of his mates and two Land Rovers came along, just when the campaign started. Eight RUC men got out of the Land Rovers, all dressed in their riot gear; at least two of them had plastic bullet guns. They lined up across the street and just stared at the boys. They were looking to aggravate them into doing something. Another time he was just walking along a little foot bridge and they came driving through in a Land Rover and hit him on the ankle with one of the wheels. One time I was stopped at traffic lights and there were three lanes. I was in the middle lane and the RUC were in the next lane. As the lights turned green, they pulled off and swerved out in front of me. All the media coverage has made our faces known in Portadown. My two young cousins were in the shopping centre a few months back with their children. They were recognised and chased out of the centre. One of the children wet herself with fear. We got a wee pup in January and we went up the town centre to get some squeaky toys for him. As we left the shopping centre, there was a loyalist protest and there were about twenty of them. One of them recognised me and started shouting, 'You fenian bastard? Where's Robbie now?' I phoned the police and they did nothing. It's hard when someone did you wrong and then the people who are supposed to do something don't do anything.

I have been to Scotland and London to a Socialist Workers' Union rally. When we had a vigil for Robert, Monica McWilliams from the Women's Coalition turned up there. I met a fellow who works with Kevin McNamara and he is helping us word the parliamentary questions to be asked, but there is nothing really much happening at the minute. With these cases, it's so political it depends on the atmosphere at the time whether people actually take an interest in you. There were things that happened in Robert's case and the media just didn't cover them because they didn't think it was right at the time. The media say to me, if anything happens let me know and I would let them know and they didn't report it. This Patten Commission which has been set up; my brother wrote to them, but we got a letter back from an official in October [1998] and they refused to look at it because it was sub-judice. But it's not sub-judice for the cops haven't been charged with anything. At a public meeting with the Patten Commission later, I again asked for a private meeting. This time we got one.

Ideally I would like the RUC to face criminal charges. I'd like them to be charged with murder. They could be charged with common purpose, but I'm not sure how that works. I want them to face criminal charges and I want them put out of the RUC. I'm a nurse and if someone had died because of something I didn't do, I would have been suspended straight away and an investigation would have taken place. There is not another police force in the world who would get away with this. They are the best equipped police force in Europe and they couldn't do a thing to save our Robert's life.

If we had not stood up and said this was wrong, they would probably not have given us as much hassle. They hate us for some reason. I do feel hated by the RUC. I would never regret doing what I do. I'm glad they hate me; I want them to hate me for then I know that I'm having an effect on them, you know, actually getting somewhere. Robert was worth too much to let it go. Sometimes you get really exhausted and down and you think, oh my God, how are you going to go on with this. But you just go on; you have to. I think they are hoping we will just give up on this and go away but we can't. All this talk of peace is good, but it makes people want to forget what the RUC have done. That Patten Commission are supposed to investigate the RUC but they don't want to hear. How can you learn from the past if you're not told what they have done?

24

Raymond Murray

We didn't have to do the job all the time of condemning paramilitaries for everyone was doing that—the media, the church. But who was to do the other narrow focus where people in charge of the law were breaking the law?

L ike everybody else, I was interested in the northern situation as part of the northern community. I was ordained in 1962. I was on loan in Belfast in St Teresa's on the Glen Road. I talked one day at Mass about injustices— lack of promotion in the civil service, about the unemployed and things like that, and I remember very clearly afterwards a number of people approaching me and saying how true this was. I suppose it was a kind of instinct in me. Next I was appointed in 1967 to Armagh Prison as prison chaplain; I was a curate in Armagh and the prison work was a part-time job. We also had the beginnings of the Campaign for Social Justice, Doctor Conn McCluskey and his wife Patricia. I knew of them and was interested in what they were doing. I invited them over to a little debating club which met once a month in Armagh, to talk about the work they were doing. From time to time we would listen to the anti-partition nationalist politicians. The McCluskeys were pointing out how useless it was to feed people the jargon of grievances without being able to produce the proof. It wasn't enough to say the thing but you had to produce the proof. They had been working at that and they invited me to their house and showed me how they would make books of newspaper cuttings on Irish problems and have them copied. At that stage there was a little group of Labour MPs who were interested in the North. They kept supplying them with this information from the newspapers. They went on to publish a number of pamphlets, including *The Plain Truth*, where they produced the statistics. That was their message: social justice was important and if you talked about that, you needed to publish, canvass, lobby and gather a crusade.

Everything would have to be a crusade. When you get the one-lined reply from officialdom, you must never leave it at that. You must be like a terrier to keep on and on pursuing the issues. You find, generally speaking, officialdom and the state, especially in crisis, rarely judge from a moral point of fair play and justice; they go on expedience; if the pot is not stirred, they will leave things as they are. That was a situation that you had in the North of Ireland since 1922, where there was a monolithic party and the grievances were very great. Everything was sewn up; Westminster wasn't interested and people were too weak.

I remember very well after the Falls Road Curfew—3-5 July 1970—going down the Falls Road into the little side streets. The barricades were still up and I said to myself, 'Where were we all for so many years that there wasn't a concerted campaign? Where were the social ethics people, where were the theologians, where were the unions and the churches? Where were they all?' Those who had, never thought it should be shared and those who hadn't got it, more or less thought it was their lot. That's the way the world was, a hangover from the last century where inequality was almost accepted.

I suppose when the civil rights movement started there was a tremendous excitement amongst everybody. I was in the march in Armagh on 30 November 1968. There were a lot of rumours going around about what was happening. After I did my half seven Mass, I drove round the town, round Ogle Street, English Street and Market Street. There were great groups of Paisleyites with sticks and nails in the sticks, obviously there from early morning and no one was going to disperse them; they were there to do a job, to stop the parade. The parade went on with huge crowds; everybody was there. That was the thing about the Civil Rights movement at that stage—rich and poor were there and everybody mixed with a great air of excitement. The march went off but it was stopped in Thomas Street. Again it was an indication of how these things were going to be handled; the nationalists had never walked through Armagh City and they weren't going to be allowed. Orange men and unionists were going to run Armagh as a capital plantation city, which was a blind notion for by this time Armagh, population-wise, had altered; it had a majority of Catholics. But the old mentality was still there.

The police notion was not to disperse the Paisleyites; it was always the same in all these early marches. If you look at the film footage of the time in Dungannon, Armagh or wherever, the police have always got their backs to the loyalists who are behind them with their flags waving and they are facing the civil rights people.

The marches coincided with the new media, with television. This could have happened in 1926 and nobody would have seen it. The pictures flashed around the world. One had to be prepared that the media would be censored and controlled. But for all the faults the media has, it is one of the main outlets for those interested in civil rights. You have to break the paper wall barrier and get in there for, as I say, government is not that concerned whether it is right or wrong. When you go on a crusade, you have to harness enough counter-power so that you make it counter-productive for whatever violation there is. If you do that, they will change it, not from its merit but because of their good name. The British government was always sensitive about its good name abroad and didn't like any kind of bad publicity abroad. As long as the lid could be kept on the trouble here, they would continue to violate human rights. That is a major feature now, when other countries show an interest, for instance, the United States. The State Department there is no longer sewn up by the British Embassy. You have sympathetic people now in the international community and the whole situation has opened up. But in the early stages it was always difficult to break through.

On the night of the 14th of August 1969, there was a civil rights meeting in the town hall in Lower English Street in Armagh. I was at my house in Abbey Street. My room was three storeys up and I could see a little portion of the area of Lower English Street where the meeting was taking place. I could see this loyalist mob who had gathered outside the town hall and it became very menacing. The people in the hall called the meeting to an end and advised people to go home. When they came out, they were driven down the street by the police. Some of them were pushed on further down Cathedral Road and by this time the B-Specials had driven down in two cars into Edward Street nearby. Just outside the parochial hall, they fired on the people who were coming down Cathedral Road. Some of them were running for the police were running after them and one who had been running to the Cathedral was shot dead—John Gallagher (29), a young married man with three children. There was a fellow Moore injured. We heard the shots, the two priests and myself. Within minutes the phone rang and Father Clarke went down to where the man was shot. Very shortly afterwards, the ambulance came to the General Hospital which was there at that time, opposite our house. I went over into the ambulance and looked down on John Gallagher who was lying dead with a bullet hole to his chest, one mark. I prayed there with him. All the details came out later in the Scarman Tribunal.

I remember going down to the court house to the Tribunal and the day I was there, B-Specials were being cross-examined. I noted Scarman's style; he was in no way belligerent and he would entice them to talk with a sympathetic nod or the expression on his face so that he would almost invite people to tell their story. But there is where the rot set in. Here was one of the first men to be killed; Samuel Devenney was beaten but John Gallagher was the first to be shot. Everybody knew who shot John Gallagher and they were completely unjustified in shooting him. They had gone back to the barracks to clean their weapons and there were policemen in charge there who knew what they were doing. All this came out in the Scarman Tribunal but there was immunity there. That was the pattern set.

I was in Spain when internment broke out. There were 22 interned from our own parish, two of them among 'the Hooded Men'—Brian Turley and Patrick McNally. Of course it was so ridiculous when you consider the people they lifted—Irish-language people, GAA, incredible! People were lifted and interned; it didn't matter who they were, they were all expendable. It was just to teach a lesson to the public: no matter what happens, we can do this and you could be the next. It was always a stronger lesson if it was people only slightly involved in nationalism; there was that menace behind it.

I think the thing that really changed me utterly was in December 1971, when the overflow from Crumlin Road Jail—for Long Kesh wasn't opened until August 1972—was brought down to Armagh. Father Faul had got wind that they had been transferred and he told me to go in there. The Association for Legal Justice had been formed; Father Brian Brady was the main instigator of that. There were a few solicitors with Frances Murray, Ann Murray, Paddy Kelly, Clara Reilly, Father Faul and myself and a few others. I went in for about a week and took statements from these men, about forty of them. A pattern emerged. They had been arrested under emergency laws, brought to Holywood and Girdwood Barracks, badly beaten, unashamedly brutalised—beaten by batons and made to sit in these little pens with white walls and when they moved they were beaten. Numerous other stories emerged of use of electric shocks and simulated executions. The sight of these people shocked me. I made them show me their wounds, so I saw for myself. Cardinal Conway wanted me to record these things and I made a dossier. Doctor Oliver Woods went into the prison to examine these men so we had an independent witness. Later on, of course, the prison authorities wouldn't allow any independent doctor in. It is an indication of how arrogant they were that they didn't even care, for at that stage the Special Branch and British army had beaten around four hundred prisoners. They only learned later, as the media became aware and we put it on record, that they had to be more careful.

It was a very good dossier, for we had around half a dozen of the worst cases and coloured photographs of some of those injured that had been taken to the Mater Hospital, Belfast. We put together a booklet called *British Army and Special Branch RUC Brutalities*. That was about March 1972. The prison authorities in Stormont attacked me in correspondence for I had gone to Dublin to see editors of newspapers to try to interest them and I had these statements with me. Some of the papers carried the statements and the authorities came at me that I had broken prison rules for carrying this stuff out. When I wrote back, I asked them why didn't they stop the brutality now that they knew it was going on.

We followed this up with all kinds of books about the problems in Long Kesh and different jails which led right up to the Hunger Strike. We documented problems with the families and because we were priests, a number of people tried to help us. In the early '70s even the people in RTE helped us and sent a little money to assist us. But they were different people then, not like now; the older people in RTE were part of that noble, concerned people who were interested in Ireland and justice. All that changed later on, so that it was almost impossible to get any kind of single programme on RTE about the SAS or plastic bullets. They would never do a single programme about these; they would throw them in with other issues. The more the IRA went on the offensive, the more doors were shut because people then didn't want to get involved in issues of human rights and state violence. There were very many years when the whole unionist campaign was to smear people who were searching for legal justice as IRA fellow travellers.

People weren't all that educated about their rights, what was law, what wasn't law. The thing again was to break the paper wall of silence on the violation of human rights. At the early stage the main problem was internment so we went over to England, Father Faul, myself and Father Brady. We went to Birmingham University, to Preston and Portsmouth. We also went down South to Leitrim, Cavan and different places. That was the early years. Then I went to the United States in 1977 and 1978. I did two major tours each time and of course Rita Mullan was there. We lobbied a lot of Congressmen, met Sean Donlan who had been in the Foreign Office and who used to come North looking for information as to what was going on. Things in the United States had been changing because you had Father Seán McManus and the National Caucus who were working on human rights and they were in close association with the Ad Hoc Committee on Ireland who were in Congress—Mario Biaggio, Lester Wolff, Benjamin Gilman, Hamilton Fish and people like that. Then you had Northern Aid who were associated with the republicans. The Irish government's attitude in the beginning had been not to awaken the United States to the Northern Ireland problem. We on the other hand, because we welcomed any interest and publicity, were trying to cultivate it. So there was a clash there and that resulted in Sean Donlan sending a letter to Hamilton Fish, whom I had interested in the Birmingham Six case, saying I was not a suitable person.

I went around Philadelphia, Washington, Detroit, Chicago, New York, Phoenix, Arizona—sometimes two places in one day. You went to the television stations, the radio. They were very hectic trips. I also went to New Zealand; my brother was active in the Irish Civil Rights movement there. I went to Germany; there were good relationships there. I spoke in France and in later years in northern Italy. I was in Norway also in later years. As the war went on and the more savage the whole thing became, the more difficult and dangerous it became. Because of the paramilitary atrocities, our work of human rights became more difficult; people were turned off by violence. So if you were pleading the cause of some little girl killed by a plastic bullet, you weren't always getting people to listen to you.

So it was the whole thing of internment and ill-treatment that led us on to all the other problems that came after them. All the time part of our ideal was to get it down on paper, get the facts. Because I was a trained historian, I always believed in putting things on record, for things can be easily forgotten or lost. I found that with that went a consolation for people who had suffered injustice, that at least they knew that the truth was told, documented in some way.

That led to a lot of work and when you are young, you are more able to do that. Our facilities were almost nil. If you wanted eight copies of something you had to write the whole thing eight times. When you took statements, you wrote them out, typed them out, got them signed again and took them to solicitors—or tried to. It wasn't always easy interesting doctors or solicitors in people's problems. Then they didn't always want anything to do with this type of stuff. I remember ringing a doctor about a serious situation of a fellow from Belfast who was in Castlereagh and he said to me, 'It's all right for you. I have no time to write books'.

We were never in any trouble from the church authorities, were never in any way political. People might see us as that, but we weren't. It was very strict with myself, Father Brady and Father Faul that we were concentrated on human rights only. Also you were a priest in a parish where it would be wrong to show any kind of party feelings, where you had SDLP, unionists, Catholics who were prison officers and policemen. These were often hurt by what we were doing, but in time they learned the truth themselves. I would say it would be wrong if a priest showed any favouritism to any particular party.

One got a lot of nasty remarks and hundreds of anonymous letters; that was a kind of suffering in itself, but that was part of the whole thing. Our superiors never stopped us, but neither did they give us much encouragement. I suppose there was an advantage in that for, if you had a committee, you would have to be answerable to them. We had no time to discuss things, no time. We just worked on, on our own and we got together from time to time and put out joint statements and opposed particular things. This left us with a tremendous independence and in the end that was a great advantage. As time went on the church authorities were glad that there was the likes of us who had been there to do that work for there was a lot of criticism of the church from people who were suffering and this wasn't always justified. Bishops from time to time made strong statements, but they also made strong criticisms of violence and because of that, people from the republican side didn't always give them credit. We didn't have to do the job all the time of condemning paramilitaries for everyone was doing that—the media, the church. But who was to do the other narrow focus where people in charge of the law were breaking the law?

We noticed that all down the line the state authorities always had a short-term serious problem that absorbed your energies. There were so many other things we would have liked to do; there was the whole issue of the long-term political settlement, the main issue, but they never allowed that to the surface in those years. All the time they kept sapping people's energies by short-term issues. Look how long the rubber/plastic bullets thing has gone on. If they had any decency, if Sir Ronnie Flanagan had any decency in this present climate, he would stop the use of plastic bullets.

All down the line, from John Gallagher on, when it was the question of an unjust killing by a policeman or a soldier, whether it was because he was a bad policeman or a bad soldier, or because it was deliberately carried out in a planned ambush or whatever, they were not going to in any way injure their morale by sending them to jail. It showed you that the people in charge had no honour and honour is supposed to be a high-ranking thing with the army or police!

Even so the question is, 'How strong is the case for the prosecution?' It is as strong as they make it but it is also as weak as they want to make it. I found that out to my utter disappointment in the case of the Roddy Carroll and Seamus Grew killings. After taking seventeen statements and, as I thought, filled in a whole picture from the early morning until they were shot and fitted in an important witness whom Stalker mentions in his book, I thought they all would have been called to the trial. When they weren't, I wrote to Barry Shaw in the DPP and asked why they weren't. He said they didn't have to be called. I had thought there were some very strong witnesses there, so the prosecution case is only as strong as they want to make it.

In later years, the Association for Legal Justice sort of faded out. We have another group, Relatives for Justice, which concentrates on those killed directly or indirectly by security forces through collusion, murder and unjust killing. A number of people are very closely involved on the committee. We have Clara Reilly, whose brother was killed just a few days after surveillance by the security forces; that was James Burns. Then we have Pat Finucane's brother Martin and Niall Farrell, brother of Mairéad. We have Arthur Fegan who does research. We produced booklets on plastic bullets, collusion and shoot-to-kill. We made a submission to Mitchell on decommissioning and met the Patten Commission. I went to Washington twice and I was back this year to make an oral submission to Congressional hearings. There are great changes there. We have good friends there; Ben Gilman, our old friend, is now the chairperson of the Committee on International Relations in the House of Representatives. We have changes in the State Department too; when Reagan and Thatcher were there, it was different. We aren't a big group but we try to do things throughout the year to keep the issues alive and now we have an office. Hopefully we will be able to organise things better.

So much of what I have told you I have put down in my book, *The SAS in Ireland*, the *Hard Time* book and *State Violence in Northern Ireland*; that last book brought together issues I have written about in the past thirty years.

I was disillusioned and often frustrated because of the deafness of government authorities. You knew the state knew and the police knew that the evidence was there. You were trying in your own way to gather information. Your energy was spent in trying to reveal and find the truth and their energy—which it shouldn't have been—was directed in trying to keep the truth covered up, destroying it, investigating it in a half-hearted manner. That was frustrating. This was on a massive scale, not a few wee things down the years. I can think, for example, of soldiers taking a fellow away in a Land Rover and him jumping out a mile or two up the road into a river, and then coming to me exhausted. I got in touch with the police and the army; I wanted a criminal process for this was a kidnapping. The policeman who came in when I was up at the barracks covered it up. I had statements and took them to a solicitor and the man was compensated in a civil action, but there should have been a criminal prosecution.

One could talk of hundreds of examples—one's own experience of going round people's houses taking statements, talking to the little people in their own little homes. One couldn't do much but one did one's own little bit to console them. I had my parish and my own duties so it was very hard to do much. Before I knew it, thirty years of my life had passed! I wrote an essay last year on a United Irishman and I looked at the date on top of the documents that I'd gathered from the Public Records Office in Dublin and 1974 was the date. Twenty-five years had passed since I was going to write this!

You see, one does a thing not for profits or praise, but like the Good Samaritan. The Good Samaritan never heard of Christ; he just saw another human being. Human rights mean that you have to pursue things; but there is a tremendous fulfilment in it. You meet people and they are the most wonderful people in the world. You see other worlds that people don't know about. I was chaplain in the prison for twenty years so I know what prison is like, but I find it hard to talk to people about prison; people outside don't know what prison is like. People who are outside in different worlds never think of prisoners. I have met the most wonderful people and made great friends. You might not see them for a long time but when you do, it's like yesterday! You see, people who suffer and who have suffered have something added to them, there is something really extraordinary about them—people like Emma Groves, who was blinded by a rubber bullet. With all these people you have a great brotherhood and sisterhood. The girls out of the jail, for example—it's like family when we meet.

The truth has its own extraordinary way of coming out. The old phrase I always used was that of George Bernard Shaw, 'Truth like blood comes out from under the door'. And you never know how it is going to come out but the truth will out. As regards justice, it is very hard to get it; you are depending on the institutions of state to give justice. I suppose being a historian I concentrate on the truth. This is a sort of an in-built thing, which is independent of state justice and legal justice. If the truth is told, people will read it and judge and that is an important justice, the justice which flows out of truth itself, independent of the courts and all these mandates. That is why I wouldn't be keen to say, 'Oh, it's all over now. I'll get back to poetry and history and I'll throw out *Hard Time: Armagh Jail 1971-1986* and I'll throw away *State Violence: Northern Ireland 1969-1997*'. I'll let them stay in order to let some of the justice flow from the truth. That is why I still stay with these issues; it's justice, you see.

25

Clara Reilly

I believe that evil can only flourish when all good people remain silent, so we can't remain silent. We have to speak up. We are beginning to feel the rewards of that, slowly but surely. There is still a good bit to go but there is no going back. We are up off our knees and we are staying there. There is no way that we will allow any of our children or our grandchildren to be treated as second class citizens in their own country, no way. That is what has motivated me.

In 1971 when internment happened, my father, who was in his sixties, was arrested. I felt anger like I never had before. I thought, 'Why the hell would they come and arrest my daddy? My daddy wouldn't hurt anybody.' He was an ex-internee of the forties. Subsequently four of my brothers were interned. We were one of the few families who had so many interned at the one time. They released my father; they said that his name was the same as his son's. When my four brothers were interned, I started campaigning against internment. I remember the army coming to the house looking for a brother called Kevin. I had six brothers. Kevin wasn't there but my young brother Pat was there. They turned around to us and said, ' If we can't get Kevin, then Pat will do'. Pat was arrested and got a very, very bad beating which resulted in kidney injuries from which he still suffers to this day. Another young brother of mine who was thirteen got arrested. So I was involved on a personal level because of the injustice of what happened to my family. I felt someone had to do something for this was all happening to our people and no-one wanted to know—not the church, not people in high places, nobody. I felt we had to do something ourselves. The Association for Legal Justice came into being around that time, so I joined the Association and it was a nightmare.

The Association of Legal Justice was made up of a few doctors and lawyers but it was mainly housewives like myself who had absolutely no experience whatsoever. I had six kids and I was working part-time. In those days, my kids recall laughingly now, they never got a meal in peace. We had only a living room and a kitchen and if the kids were at their dinner, you could bet that the door was knocked. We were knocked up at four, five, six in the morning by mothers crying, saying, 'Sorry for coming to you at this time of the morning Clara, but my son has been arrested'. I brought them in, made them a cup of tea and you knew there wasn't much you could do at that time but at least you could document their details. If someone came and said, 'My son has been brought to Fort Monagh', I would ring Fort Monagh over the next two or three days or whatever it took. I kept on at them until that person was either released or charged. If they were released, I would ask if they had been ill treated or threatened and if they had any allegations to make, I documented them.

I covered a good lot of West Belfast with Ann Murray. Each of us had our own books of all the arrests. I have arrest books which go back all those years. There are dozens and dozens of people in the books who are now dead. There was hardly a day when we got peace. I think maybe the only day we didn't get any complaints was Christmas Day.

My husband threatened to divorce me hundreds and hundreds of times! As I said, you would sit down to a meal and someone would come to the door. But compassion took over. Here were people in need that none of the powers that be wanted to help and even as a Christian you felt you had to help these people in need. When people came and told me that their life had been threatened in the police stations, I would say, 'Okay, now let's make a complaint to the police'. Then these people would have to go and make the complaint. I went with them. People knew at the end of the day that they weren't going to get anywhere with the complaint; you could have papered the walls with the pieces of paper that came back saying, 'No prosecutions'. But people continued to do it because they hoped one day that there would be a breakthrough and that someday someone would listen to their stories. All these thousands of statements are history and the next generation coming up will have to say, 'We have to put something good back into our country for a lot of people suffered very greatly for it, suffered with their lives, suffered great brutality that they will never get over.'

We had gone to the Irish government over the cases of the 'hooded men'. We asked them to take an inter-governmental case against Britain for torture. The Irish government was not convinced so we had to convince them. We supplied them with the statements taken from the men and they were finally convinced. They agreed to take the inter-governmental case. In 1976, Britain was found guilty of torture. They gave an undertaking that these methods would never be used again. But as the years progressed the Association for Legal Justice found that there were people coming out of Castlereagh detailing very, very bad stories of brutality. We invited Amnesty International over to investigate. We took them to the Lake Glen Hotel and for three days we brought people to them who had been held in the interrogation centres. They listened, took documentation and medical evidence and found that ill treatment had taken place.

We found then that we were dealing with everything that happened—like when they started to use the supergrass system; we had the situation in jails, the dirty protest, the blanket protest. You were getting letters out from the prisons; you were trying to highlight the inhumane conditions that the prisoners were held in by contacting every human rights group, the United Nations, anyone who was prepared to listen. In the beginning, we were all very naïve; we thought that all we had to do was expose it and it would stop. We asked the *Irish Times* to carry each of the hooded men's stories, one a week. We really thought when people knew what was happening, it would have to stop.

We set up an international tribunal on plastic bullets for this was of great concern to us. Plastic bullets were being fired like confetti and people were dying, especially during the hunger strike when seven people died over that period, including several children—Carol Ann Kelly, Julie Livingstone. We set up the tribunal in the Balmoral Hotel. We had a panel of lawyers and doctors who physically examined people coming in off the street who had actually been hit with plastic bullets. At the tribunal we were handed a video by a girl who said it had been shot by a Canadian film crew and that it was actually of the incident involving Nora McCabe. We knew the solicitor in the case was Pat Finucane and I rang Pat to tell him that we had the video and that he was welcome to have a look at it. So he looked at it and asked who knew about it. We told him very few people, for we didn't use it at the tribunal. He asked us to keep it quiet for he may have been able to use it, and we did. When Nora McCabe's inquest came up, the most senior RUC officer in West Belfast, James Crutchley, said that any plastic baton rounds fired that morning were fired under his orders and that none were fired in Linden Street where Nora McCabe was killed. He said that they had come under petrol bomb attack, stone throwing, the road was littered with beer barrels, etc. All the police officers were allowed to give evidence. Then Pat Finucane introduced the video and the policemen were absolutely shocked; some of them stormed out. The inquest was halted and a senior policeman was appointed to go and speak to the Canadian crew who made it. When the inquest resumed, he said it was a true and authentic account of what actually had happened. What was shown on the video was a panoramic view of the Falls Road, the two police Land Rovers coming up. It showed the first one turning into Linden Street and the plastic bullet being fired out of the side slit of the Land Rover. It showed an ambulance arriving on the scene and Nora McCabe being taken to hospital.

So Jim McCabe thought that these people would have to be charged with involvement in his wife's death and also with perjury. Absolutely nothing happened and when the DPP was contacted by Jim's solicitor, he said he couldn't bring charges because he couldn't identify which police officer in the Land Rover actually fired the plastic bullet that killed Nora. How is that for justice? That was the nub of the whole thing; people never got justice. Jim McCabe never got justice. The senior policeman involved was promoted to Assistant Chief Constable and mentioned in the Queen's honours list the following January. Jim McCabe, who was never involved in any campaigning group, is one of our most active members now.

That sense of injustice is like a festering sore that eats away at you. People just want the truth and justice. No compensation can bring his wife back. He had three children; the youngest, Áine, was three months. Áine, who is now sixteen, wrote a poem about peace. She lives in West Belfast; she has never known peace. She listens to the government telling the IRA to put away its guns, but it wasn't the IRA who killed her mother. It was the RUC who shot her down in cold blood; they destroyed her life; they destroyed the family's life. That has been eating at that child since she was a baby, growing up without a mother.

In 1984 when the plastic bullet group was set up, I was nominated onto it for I had done some work on the plastic bullet issue and I was interested in it. Why I was interested in it was that I had been a witness to Brian Stewart's death. Brian Stewart was only thirteen. I was actually out calling my kids on the streets of Turf Lodge; it was about six o'clock, supper time. I saw two of them down the street bunking marlies. You know what boys are, they were so engrossed in what they were doing they didn't hear me. So I started to walk down the street to get them and I heard the bang. I was unsure what it was. Then I saw a soldier coming round the corner and I knew it was a plastic bullet. The boy fell, the wee girls were screaming and I thought 'Jesus, that child has been hit with a plastic bullet'. I ran and the guy in the second house came out and ran down; the two of us got to Brian Stewart at the same time. The side of Brian Stewart's head had caved in and there was blood coming down his nose. I knew he was bad. We lifted him into the house and did all we could for him. The ambulance came and took him away and he was placed on a life support machine; he died two days later. I went to court and testified as did eight other independent witnesses. We told that the situation in that street was quite normal at that time; my kids were out playing in the street. It seems there had been rioting earlier on in the day and the soldiers were in an aggressive mood. But at that time there was absolutely nothing happening.

Eight of us went to give evidence and not one of us was believed, not at the coroner's inquest, nor at the civil case that Mrs Stewart took subsequently against the Ministry of Defence. The soldiers' versions were believed and we were not. It leaves an awful sense of anger and injustice. But I'll never forget that child and what actually happened afterwards. People all came out when they heard that a child was injured; there were crowds waiting outside the house as the child was brought out. It was only then that the riot developed. There were bottles and stones thrown but it was as a result of the child being injured; it wasn't beforehand. An army major came on the news that night and said that his soldiers had been attacked by a crowd of five hundred and they had to fire plastic bullets to get themselves out of a situation. Curious enough, at the inquest they changed their story and at the next court case they had changed it again. None of the media were picking up on this. The soldiers always got their story out first and that version of events is the one that always stuck in people's mind. Then the families came in later to get their version out, but by then it was too late.

That is one of the reasons we did the wee booklets; there are dozens of these booklets on a lot of the killings. I always remember Danny Barrett from Ardoyne; he died during the hunger strike. This fifteen year old kid was outside his own door when he was shot by a British army sniper from Flax Street. He was sitting on his own wall with his father. Weeks later this child was on my mind and I said to Father Faul we would have to get up to Ardoyne to see this family for this child's death has been lost in all the publicity about the hunger strike. So we went up to Ardoyne to talk to the mother and father and they were so grief stricken but so, so grateful that somebody had come to listen to their story. We documented the evidence and brought the witnesses together and put the booklet out, *Danny Barrett: A British Army Murder*. I'll never forget the inquest—no reporters there, nobody gave a damn. The soldiers got up to give evidence and Danny Barrett's father vaulted out of the chair, over a table and dived on top of a soldier. There was pandemonium. That night the papers were full of it. When the inquest resumed the next morning, you couldn't get into the court house for reporters. So I keep saying to people: if you want publicity, vault over a table in the court, punch a police man or a soldier and you will get all the publicity you want! Not that he was thinking that way at the time; it was a reaction. Danny Barrett was a totally, totally innocent child and they got away with it. No soldier was ever charged. You could repeat that over all the deaths.

Young Carol Ann Kelly was killed while her mummy watched from her window. The first jeep stopped and her mummy saw it. She saw the gun coming out and the child falling. She was screaming from the top window. A soldier ran up out of the second jeep; he was heard to say, 'Oh my God, it's only a little girl'. He threw his gun down to try to attend to her. Everyone was screaming at him to leave her alone and the mummy was saying, 'Please, please let him help her'. He took the packs out and tried to stem the flow of blood from the child's head. His commanding officer ordered him away from the child and reprimanded him for throwing down his rifle. The fact that he threw down his rifle meant he felt under no threat; there was no riot situation. He was nearly in tears. He was ordered back to the jeep. So there was one soldier who had a bit of humanity and compassion in him. Carol Ann was put on a life support machine and died five days later. The heartache of all the families, it never goes away.

The plastic bullet group has travelled the world. We even picketed one of the factories that made plastic bullets. We found out which factories manufactured plastic bullets; one was a fireworks factory in Dumfries in Scotland. We hired a minibus and went over. We handed out leaflets to the workers saying, 'Your fireworks give great delight to children in Great Britain but some of your other products are killing and maiming children on the streets of Northern Ireland.' That was a success story, for Eileen Kelly, who was the sister of Carol Ann Kelly, had a meeting with the directors of the company and they assured her that they would not be renewing their contract with the Ministry of Defence. We had travelled over there for four years and we thought, 'Great! Victory!' Emma Groves also travelled over to America for there were plastic bullets being made in Ohio and there was a shareholders' meeting taking place in New York. Emma went over along with a lad called Alec McLaughlin from Derry who had lost one eye. Emma addressed the shareholders. She told her story and told them exactly what rubber and plastic bullets were doing. They immediately stopped the production of plastic bullets. They were two small victories in a way for what actually happened with the fireworks company, another company took over the production of them.

We also got involved with shoot-to-kill, the Armagh killings. Then we took up the Sam Marshall killing, where there was obviously RUC collusion, and we had a big tribunal on that. We brought American lawyers over for that. Kadar Asmal, who is now very much involved with the South African government, chaired it. Their findings were very, very strong that there was a shoot-to-kill policy going on in Northern Ireland at the time.

We were constantly round at people's houses taking statements. We worked very closely with Father Faul and Father Murray at the time. Father Murray is still very much involved. Father Faul sort of does his own thing now. We were very much involved during the hunger strike, visiting the families—very, very committed years.

I don't know where we drew our strength from, but my motto always has been that the truth comes out no matter what. No matter how long, it always comes out in the end. I also felt very angry over the years that I was denied my Irishness. I come from a very nationalist, republican family. My father was interned with Tom Williams; he was still in Crumlin Road Jail the morning that Tom Williams was hanged. My mother was outside the jail saying the rosary. My mother taught us to be very proud of our country, very proud of our culture and heritage. We grew up with that pride and I was angry that I was not allowed to express it. I instilled it in my kids: 'You are no better than anyone else but I'm bloody sure you are no worse. Don't expect more but take no less.' So what my mother instilled in us I have instilled in my kids, that they should be proud of their country. I love Ireland, its people, its culture and everything about it and I would defy anything that would stop me from expressing my love of that. I think that is what drove me over the years. It was anger too that motivated me. But I also believe that evil can only flourish when all good people remain silent, so we can't remain silent. We have to speak up. We are beginning to feel the rewards of that, slowly but surely. There is still a good bit to go but there is no going back. We are up off our knees and we are staying there. There is no way that we will allow any of our children or our grandchildren to be treated as second class citizens in their own country, no way. That is what has motivated me.

A lot of people suffered. My own brother was shot dead. I blame the RUC, for two days before he was killed the British army were caught taking a video tape at the back of his house. He lived down in St James's and the houses down there all look the same. My sister who lives a couple of doors away saw them. It seemed irrelevant at the time, but two days later loyalists from the Village area came over at half four in the morning, broke in through the back of his house and shot him while he was in bed. Then the whole thing clicked and I remember going to the complaints department of the police and asking just how far on with the murder investigation were they. 'Who have you interviewed? Is there any evidence? What about the gun?' They rang me and asked me to go to Springfield Road police station to meet a senior police officer. I went and told him that I believed there had been RUC collusion in my brother's death. He went away and investigated and said he couldn't even find who the ones were that day with the video camera. Then the supergrasses came and two men were jailed for life for my brother's murder, but then Bennett retracted his evidence and they got out. There was no serious investigation into my brother's murder.

I had a cousin, Brendan O'Callaghan, who was only 21 who was shot dead by the British army just down here by the Hunting Lodge. He was an only son. To this day my Aunt Teasie has to get out of Belfast when his anniversary comes. Like my mother, she lived in the same street as my brother. She had to pass his door every day and we saw her over the years, her health going down because of it.

I was arrested by the British army in 1981. They came to my home in Turf Lodge, got all of my six kids up, my husband up, guns drawn and so on. But because of my experience with the ALJ, I knew my rights. I knew what they could and couldn't question me about. I drew on that and I challenged them from the time they entered my home. I told my kids not to give them their names. I went to the phone to ring my solicitor; they told me I couldn't do that. They put the gun to my back. I remember lifting the phone and saying, 'Shoot away'. Poor Pat Finucane was my solicitor and I told him the army was in my home and that they were arresting me. They took me down to Springfield Road army barracks and put me into a cubicle with a curtain. There was a military police woman there and she told me to go in and sit facing the wall. I walked in, turned the chair round and pulled the curtain back. I told her there was no way I was sitting like that, so I argued with her for about fifteen minutes. A soldier came in and sat on a chair like he was judge on a pedestal. He was bombarding me with questions, not questions about a crime but about me, my family, what motivated me to do the work. I was known to the British army and the RUC, for when I rang up to make inquiries about fellows, they would say, 'We were waiting on your call, Mrs Reilly'. They would also say to the fellows when they had them in, 'I suppose you are going to go to that Clara Reilly and she is going to write a statement and make a complaint'. As a matter of fact, when a new regiment came in, the other ones would tell them, 'That's Clara Reilly and if you step out of line, she will be complaining about you'.

The time they lifted me I told them to mind their own business. I told the medical orderly to get the hell out. They kept me for four hours and when I walked out, the major said to me, 'Goodbye, Mrs Reilly. I will see you in two weeks'. I turned to him and replied, 'Goodbye, major. I will see you in court'. I went immediately to the RUC station and wrote out a long statement of complaint. What they had done was illegal. They didn't once question me about a crime; they questioned me about what motivated me. A year later the case came to court and I said to Charlie Hill, the barrister, 'I'm not interested in compensation. I want this clarified that the army is acting illegally when they lift people for screening.' It was clarified in the courts and it's in the records that due to my case it was made clear that lifting people for screening was illegal. After that, we told everybody: if you're lifted by the British army or even the RUC and they're not asking you about a crime, sue them; take an action against them.' A lot of people did that.

I found that then my family started to suffer. They came to the house to arrest my 13 year old daughter. She was standing in her uniform, going out to school. My husband stood in front of them with a hurley and said 'The first one who tries to put a hand on her will have to come through me'. The neighbours had gathered outside and I was shouting out to people, 'They're arresting my Colleen; she's only 13; she's in her school uniform.' The people came out with their bin lids, rattling them. The British army officer in charge knew he was in for a fight that day; we stood our ground. He said, 'We'll go away; there might have been a mistake made.' He went away and I immediately rang the RUC in Andersonstown, lodged a complaint and asked them to find out what exactly was going on. They came back and said, 'We don't know what they're on about. There was no order issued for the arrest of your daughter'. That was harassment of me.

My son Terry, who was only 16 at the time, attended Gort na Mona School and he was always very interested in electrical work. The careers teacher had put up a notice that appeared in the *Belfast Telegraph* for apprentice electricians and I said,'Terry, put in for an application for that'. There were 15 boys out of his class went for an interview and he was the only one recalled for further interviews, aptitude tests and medical exams over a three to four month period. The final thing was a climbing test at the Northern Ireland Electricity Service up in Aldergrove because the job entailed erecting overhead cables. There were a couple of lads from Derry there too. The supervisor told them that they had more or less got the job because they didn't get to that stage unless they had been chosen, but that it was official policy to wait on a letter. So we all sat back to wait on the letter for we were delighted for Terry. All his mates had left school and were unemployed and he had said, 'There is no way I'm going on the dole'. I will always remember, it was a Saturday morning that the letter came and I brought it up to him in bed. I stood waiting for him to open the letter. I sat down on the bed and watched his reaction as he read the letter. I saw his eyes fill up. He said to me, 'Mummy, I didn't get it'. I took the letter from him, a run of the mill letter: 'Thank you for your interest but we regret to tell you this time you were unsuccessful, blah blah.' I tell you I never felt so angry. If I had been in the IRA I would have blown up all the power stations, that's how angry I felt! I said to my son, 'Terry, I am sorry that at 16 years of age you have to find out what discrimination is about for that's discrimination'. I went to the Fair Employment Agency to take a case against them. Over a three month period they were corresponding with the Northern Ireland Electricity Service. Then I got a letter from the Fair Employment Agency saying that they couldn't proceed with the case because the Secretary of State James Prior had signed an order stating that my son, who was sixteen years of age, was a risk to national security. A wee boy who had never been in trouble in his life, who was an example to other boys of his age, who had no interest in politics and they were saying he was a threat to national security! 'Spotlight' did a programme about it and what they found out was that two of the Derry boys who had been up at the training day with Terry were also turned down. One of their fathers was on the H-block Committee and the other was always on the marches. It was obviously information given by the RUC on the families, and our children were made to suffer because of our activities. I said that I was sorry that our Terry had to suffer because of my activities but if they thought that they could silence me, they would have to think again. Terry later went into a firm on a YTP scheme. The employer was so impressed with his ability that he gave him a permanent job. He worked himself up to management and he now owns his own company.

I have never regretted it once. Down through the years I have met some great people. What always impressed me is the dignity of the families who have borne all this great suffering. No one has a monopoly on suffering; suffering is suffering right across the board. The families of soldiers, their suffering is not less, but it's also no greater than ours. But there are some marvellous people I have met through the years and we still keep in touch. I think slowly but surely things are changing but we still have a long way to go. What I am really concerned about is the RUC because if we don't get a proper police force that people have respect for, that people from the nationalist community can join, who will be impartial and who we know won't be sectarian, then we are going nowhere. If it doesn't happen, we can just go and close our doors for nothing will change. We have a long way to go but I have every confidence we will get there in the end.

Those policemen who have been guilty of torture should never have a place in any police force. The ministers who were involved, right up to the highest level, when torture was going on should never ever have a say in the creation of a just society over here. I feel that our people are so strong now, politically, for we have matured so much. When I think back to my mother's time, nobody spoke out. You accepted it as a way of life. But no longer. I think our people have come a long way now and that we are challenging what we see that is not right. We will challenge it and keep on and on until there is change.

26

Denis Faul

That's the lesson of state terrorism; if you drag people too far, they will explode... They said the Catholic people were mad Provos but they were driven mad by all the torture and shooting.

John Gallagher was killed on the fifteenth of August 1969 outside the Cathedral in Armagh by the B Specials. On the same night there were nine people killed in Belfast during the invasions. In the autumn of 1969 I condemned the Northern Ireland judiciary, because no one was charged with the invasion of the Falls Road. The two IRA men who tried to defend the Falls Road with the only two guns they had, Frank McArt and Billy McKee, were arrested and put in jail. In Dungannon, John Arthurs was arrested and put in jail. In Omagh there was a big case, seventeen witnesses against one policeman and his word was taken. So I wrote that the judicial system was not fair and this caused an uproar. At that time they were all ex-ministers for Home Affairs and ex-Unionist MPs who failed to administer justice in parliament. How could you trust them to administer legal justice when they couldn't administer social justice properly? I also said the jury system was rotten. You had to have property to be a jury member. In a county like Tyrone, which was nearly all Catholic, the juries were all Protestant. In the Arthurs case the jury was eleven to one and they were all B-Specials, sitting on a case which was all about the B-Specials. The judge took the word of one uniformed policeman over that of 17 civilian witnesses. The Cardinal silenced me but I knew I was right and he later apologised to me. Indeed ten years later the Bishops made a statement against the judiciary and in particular against Judge Gibson for the remarks he made.

It really was when internment came along in August 1971 that we got involved because of the torture; that was state terrorism. The people were terrified. You

303

were arrested, tortured and put in jail without trial and left to lie there. A week after internment began, the Association for Legal Justice was formed at a meeting in St Mary's Hall in Belfast by Father Brady, myself and several others. We met in St Mary's Hall in Belfast a week after internment and formed this little group. Then we started to get statements out from the camps. On the 25th of August, myself and Father Brady went to the Grand Central Hotel in Belfast with an account of the sensory deprivation and we gave it to a man from the *Sunday Times*; it wasn't published. We gave it again that September to a man called Campbell, also associated with the *Sunday Times*, and again it wasn't published. Finally at the end of October, Austin Currie, who was an MP and a past pupil of mine, arrived at the house with a man called John Whale of the *Sunday Times*. I gave him this again and it was published; he got a prize for the big scoop!

What I think happened during the summer is that the British said to the Northern Ireland government, 'Give us two months and we will destroy the IRA. We will take them in, get the information, torture and intern them'. We are convinced that the British put a 'D' notice on this torture, the worst in Europe since the Gestapo, and the papers were not allowed to publish it. We gave the information to the most prestigious English newspaper, the *Sunday Times*, three times before they published.

There is a book called *The Mailed Fist*; that was the first book Dr McCluskey and I put out. The prisoners were put on the Maidstone and in Armagh because there was no room for them. Long Kesh wasn't opened at that time. I went to Father Murray about December and asked Father Murray to get statements from the prisoners for he was the chaplain of the prison.

I visited family after family here all over the north of Ireland, clocked up a lot of miles. And when you went into their homes they literally were in a state of shock; they were terrified out of their wits. The army came at six o'clock in the morning, wrecked the house, took the young boy or young girl and they didn't know where they were. They didn't know what was happening. The only lifeline they had was myself and Father Murray and Jim Canning from Coalisland. We were the only sort of link with sanity. Dublin didn't give us much of a hearing. We got no hearing from the Brits; they thought we were Provos. Not one of the Provos was ever grateful; their families were, but the Provos are unforgiving, ungrateful; you make one mistake with the Provos and you're out. When I settled the hunger strike, they never talked to me since; but their families do. I left Long Kesh in 1997 after twenty-five years. But after the hunger strike the Provos wouldn't allow me to say Mass. Oh, full of themselves! They wanted to stop the hunger strike themselves but they couldn't do it. Never mind, that's history; it doesn't worry me.

Internment was nearly as bad as death. Fellows just disappeared. 'What are they doing to him? Are they torturing him? When is he getting out?' You don't know - he could be there for twenty years. We produced a book called *Whitelaw's Tribunals*, and about twenty leaflets about what to do when you were arrested. People had no one to help them. Lawyers never moved an inch. There were a few like Pascal O'Hare and Paddy McGrory, but they were only two. There was another solicitor called Donal Murphy who was very good; he resigned from the Police Authority over some torture cases. And Jack Hassard in Dungannon is a very interesting man; he is a Protestant. He was in the British Legion and he fought in the Burma War. He resigned from the Police Authority over the torture of a man called Rafferty who lives out here.

Internment lasted on and on and then, with the Workers' Council Strike, the Executive was abolished. We were very annoyed, myself and Father Murray, so when it came to the [Constitutional] Convention, we said there should be a boycott until everybody was released from internment. The SDLP didn't like that. They complained to the Cardinal about us. The Cardinal spoke to Father Murray, and the Dean in Dungannon spoke to me; he laughed. I'm not saying Cardinal Conway was wrong. I was right and he was right. He was doing his job and I was doing my job. The SDLP are great fellows for liberty and free speech. They said, 'We are not a sectarian party. We welcome Protestants as well'. But they wanted the sectarian vote, so they got mad when a priest spoke out on a different line.

We went to America and gave evidence to the Rosenthall hearings. That was February 1972. I carried on a non-stop campaign in the *Irish News*. Sometimes they were reluctant to publish, so we published our own books and leaflets. Amnesty International came over in December and January 1971-72. They had hearings in the Midlands Hotel in Belfast. They went back and issued a devastating report. Then we persuaded the Dublin government to collect evidence and they took the English to Strasbourg. In 1976, Britain was found guilty of torture, of cruel and inhuman treatment. But the torture continued. The Brits simply shifted themselves from Palace Barracks to Castlereagh. So we brought Amnesty over again in 1978 and they issued a very critical report. The British of course pretended not to take heed of the Amnesty Report and they appointed their own commission, called the Bennett Commission. Then Bennett came out with his findings which were the same as Amnesty's. The British say, 'Aren't we the lovers of fair play and justice that we would come out and acknowledge the reports against ourselves? Aren't the Irish so lucky to be ruled by us?' Hypocrites to the teeth! Oh yes, it was their Commission that 'discovered' it after we had Amnesty over twice.

It took eight years and Amnesty's two visits plus the European Court and Commission on Human Rights, plus endless publicity and distribution of our book all over America to end the torture - myself, Father Murray, Father Brady, the Murrays and Clara Reilly.

In the mid-seventies you had assassination squads involving Sergeant Weir and a fellow called McCaughey. Both were members of the RUC. They were caught eventually by a Catholic detective called Mooney from Dungannon for a murder in Ahoghill and a catalogue of sins in Cushendall. Whether this fits into state terrorism it's hard to say for they were caught and sentenced. Even if they worked independently, they certainly had the benefit of access to police records and information. They killed a grocer called Strathearn in Ahoghill. The loyalist hit man called the Jackal, who died about six months ago, killed Strathearn but they were there. They also kidnapped Father Murphy the time that Turbitt the RUC man was shot and his body hidden near Sturgan's Brae. They were actually coming to my house to kidnap me but they met the British army. They told Father Murphy: 'If you'd been Faul, he wouldn't have survived'. Those were bad boys, whether you'd class them as state killers or not - they were probably operating on their own, but Weir's statement suggests they were recruited from within the RUC as likely men, they were so bitter and so loyalist.

In 1986 or 1987, I went over to see Albert Baker in Albany Prison on the Isle of Wight. He was an ex-British soldier and he talked to me about 1972. It was about the worst year of all, with a large number of assassinations on both sides. The assassination of Catholics in Belfast was so bad that Whitelaw, who had taken over in March of that year, put a ring of steel around Belfast to prevent the weapons getting into the Falls Road or up to Ardoyne or any of these places. According to Baker the assassins' guns were brought in by the RUC men, detectives, who simply showed their police card and went through the road blocks. The guns were used to shoot Catholics. Now he had written statements about all this which I took home and sent them to Chief Constable, Sir John Hermon, and to the Taoiseach. I sent them to the *Irish Press* as well, but I never heard another word.

There was another document which came into my possession about the early eighties. It gave a list of 45 people who were alleged to have been assassinated by the British themselves during the 1970s, by British agents under the cover name of the loyalist groups. These stories were probably true but it was difficult to prove that the British were working under cover of the UDA, murdering people. At the same time there was a thing called the Four Square Laundry, who were British soldiers working undercover, and the IRA caught on and assassinated them.

We also have the publications of Michael Holroyd and Colin Wallace. Holroyd worked with Captain Nairac and he gives a whole lot of information. For example there was a case here in Donaghmore of Columba McVeigh; it's a very sad case. He was a boy of seventeen. The British army brought him in. They wanted him to spy. They decided they would get him arrested on a false charge and get him into jail. They went to his house and left a few bullets, came back a day or two later, found the bullets and arrested him and sent him to Crumlin Road Prison. Of course the IRA tortured the poor fellow in jail. His mother went down to visit him and he was black and blue; he said he ran into the door. Then he got bail, which was unheard of for a man caught with bullets. As Holroyd said in his book, 'Father Faul said it was a death sentence'. He was in Dublin. But the IRA took him away and killed him. He is one of the bodies we are looking for. In a sense he is a victim of British state terrorism, for when they take fellows, terrorise them and then they are killed by the IRA, they really are as much victims of British terrorism as they are of IRA murder. In the late seventies there was an awful lot of that going on, a murky underworld.

The crucial decade was 1971 to 1981; that's when all the dreadful things took place, right up to the hunger strike. Our people thought they had no protection; the IRA recruited as many as they liked. That's the lesson of state terrorism; if you drag people too far, they will explode. We said to Douglas Hurd, 'Treat the Catholic people with generosity and they will respond'. The British got the message. Now they are all for the Catholic people and they have learned what they could have learned in 1969. The Catholic people voted 100%, north and south, for the new Agreement, the Protestant people voted 50/50 for and against; they can see quite clearly now who the trouble makers are in Northern Ireland. They said the Catholic people were mad Provos but they were driven mad by all the torture and shooting. But the state has recognised that the Catholic people are innocent and hard working people; by their baptism into the church, they are non-violent people. They drove them crazy, torturing their brothers, shooting their brothers, putting them in prison without trial. They did that from the very start; they ruled with an iron fist. I'll tell you something about torture; the man who is tortured might not be so resentful, but his brother will be. His brother will grab a gun and go out to kill. The tortured man might not be so vexed but his brother will be and his family will be; they will go after you.

If you are nice to the Catholics, they respond immediately. Catholics are not mad over partition; all they want is fair play. All they ever wanted was fair play. The reason they joined the IRA was not about the border; it was because they were ill-treated. I used to visit a lot of IRA men down in the South and they would say, 'We would like to go back to the North'. When I said, 'Why do you want to go back for you could be shot?', they'd say, 'We think our families are better off for education and health.'

During the seventies we also took on the Birmingham Six case, the Guildford Four case, Annie Maguire's case and Judith Ward. After the bombing of Birmingham in 1974, the British passed the Prevention of Terrorism Act and it was a case of 'any Irish will do'. They grabbed these six men in Birmingham and they knew well they didn't do it. I remember Mrs Hunter sent for me. She lived somewhere on the Oldpark in Belfast; it was a slum, the poorest place and this wee woman, her legs were like two sticks, a little old woman, said, 'My son Gerard is innocent. Will you do something about it?' I got Father Murray, Father Brady and Sister Sarah Clarke in England and we went to Birmingham. Then we produced a book called *The Birmingham Frame-Up* in 1977.

If there had been capital punishment, the Birmingham Six, the Guildford Four and Judith Ward would have been hanged. Annie Maguire was the most innocent person you ever met in your life. And poor old Guiseppe Conlon - I visited him in Wormwood Scrubs six months before he died. When it came to his funeral in 1980, the hypocritical British workers at Heathrow Airport refused to handle the coffin. It had to be sent to the RAF base at Norfolk and they wouldn't handle it.

Charlie Haughey said that the coffin was to be brought to Dublin by Aer Lingus and the hearse brought it to Belfast. Mrs Conlon had a bill of over £1000, which myself and Father Murray paid from the money that we made on the books.

Then we come on to the hunger strike. One must remember, there were sixty people killed outside during the period of the hunger strike. We were all warned by the police at that time. Then there was the shooting of Bernadette Devlin and the killing of John Turley, an SDLP Protestant man, and Miriam Daly. Very suspicious - they were able to walk into her house and kill her. So we were in danger; we had to be fairly careful of all your movements. What was the point of stopping? You had to go on. The people needed you. Basically for about ten years the people had nobody else.

They say in Maynooth, 'Keep your mouth shut'. Well, you have to make up your mind what you are going to do, what you are going to say. You know it can get you into trouble, you know it will block all this promotion business, but as a priest you are not interested in those things. You are interested in fair play and justice for the people, Catholic and Protestant. You just do it; it has to be done. You are not looking for reward in this life. You can stand back and be cagey and say, 'I'm going to do nothing' and go far in the church; but that's not the object of life - to do nothing and say nothing and lick up to everybody.

I have great freedom because I am celibate. There are a lot of people, even solicitors, who would like to speak out but they have wives and children so they have to be careful. A priest has great freedom if the bishop doesn't shut him up. Cardinal Conway may have been a bit cautious. I think he let myself and Father Murray ramble away. We were rebuked twice and another time he came after us; we didn't care. Then we had Cardinal Ó Fiaich and he was as bad as we were! Cardinal Daly, a cautious man, made us both Monsignors; he was very angry about Drumcree.

Since 1968 no RUC man has served a day in jail for killing innocent or unarmed people, or for ill-treating prisoners, and the British army have only put six people in prison and most of them got out within two to three years. We can give a list of one hundred and fifty unarmed people killed by lead or plastic bullets in a thirty year period. They paid several million pounds worth of damages to people tortured in the seventies and people falsely interned, but they would not convict a single person. And they talk about justice! Sure, we just laugh at them!

The terror was that England was going to back her soldiers and police no matter what they did. For fifteen years they did every thing they could, then they caught on. That was 1986 and the Anglo/Irish Agreement; up until that it was state terrorism all the way. They got frightened when the Provos started to hit home. I'd say the Brighton bomb scared the Brits; when they saw that the Provos could bomb England, they soon shut up and started looking for peace. They thought they could crush the Irish with terrorism; it was a very wrong, illegal and immoral procedure. Now is the time for peace and reconciliation, respect for everybody's rights and the healing of the hurts of the past.

CONCLUSION:

STATE KILLINGS, TRUTH AND DENIAL

How do you reach the truth if lying has become a habit?
(Ariel Dorfmann, 'Death and the Maiden')

As this book was being written, there were numerous calls from British Prime Minister Tony Blair for the IRA to reassure unionists by stating unequivocally that 'the war is over'. Yet for most of the 30 years that that war persisted, the British state emphatically denied that the conflict in the North of Ireland could be termed a war, even a low-intensity war. Instead, what was happening was represented as 'terrorism'. The state could thus engage in the most belligerent language without resorting to a declaration of war. For example, after the IRA killed three people in Coagh (one of whom they alleged was a leading loyalist), British Home Secretary Douglas Hurd stated:

> I believe that, with the Provisional IRA and some of the Middle-Eastern groups, it is nothing really to do with a political cause any more. They are professional killers. That is their occupation and their pleasure and they will go on doing that. No political solution will cope with that. They just have to be extirpated. (*Belfast Telegraph* 9 March 1989)

In relation to the Irish conflict, the British state's self- representation was as a democracy under siege from a 'terrorist conspiracy', often international in character, to destroy the democratic state itself. The state's actions were therefore merely a reaction to the threat, not a derogation from democracy. Moreover, in this view the state cannot itself be accused of 'terrorism', no matter how harsh its actions, because it is merely acting to protect democracy. This representation was invaluable in terms of international reputation, especially in other states which accepted or even used the discourse of 'terrorism' themselves.

In the Irish case the discourse of 'terrorism' became a totalising one in at least two important ways. The first was in relation to the definition of 'the terrorist'. Obviously the label can be said to fit when state forces are confronted by armed insurgents. But in a war of insurgency, such set-piece encounters are not the norm. The applicability of the label therefore quickly extends to take in the family and friends of 'the terrorist', the geographical areas in which they live, and any commentators who refuse to preface their political remarks with a robust condemnation of 'terrorism'. The second way in which the discourse is total is in relation to its inability to allow space for criticism, and certainly self-criticism. Even 'war' is not so rigid a concept. In war, the state can accept that there are mistakes or that what is referred to euphemistically as 'collateral damage' (that is, unintended civilian casualties) can occur. The armour of 'anti-terrorism' allows for no such chinks. The state must close ranks to justify the killing of innocent victims as ritualistically as it does the killing of armed insurgents.

The culture of denial, ingrained in the very heart of the state's management of mass and later armed opposition in the North of Ireland quickly percolated through all of the institutions of the state. Resorting to 'terrorism' as an explanation for political conflict thus led to the erection of a complex system based on denial and obfuscation. An essential part of that system is the vilification of the good name of the victim.

Representing the Death: Misinformation

By far the clearest pattern to emerge from the stories recounted in this book is the way in which the state has been quick off the mark to disseminate a version of the incident which depicts the activities of its forces in the best possible light. The surest way to achieve that goal is to broadcast as negative a picture as possible of the victim. In a number of cases, where the victim was a republican (and in one case a loyalist) activist, that task was made somewhat easier because of the pre-existing and all-pervasive discourse of 'terrorism'. But even if the victim was not connected in any way with a paramilitary group, the same picture emerged. Misrepresentation, misinformation and vilification were evident in every single story. For example, Kay Duddy, whose brother was shot dead on Bloody Sunday, has a unique story to tell; at the same time, her conclusion fits for all the victims considered here: '… my brother was murdered and as well as murdering him, they then besmudged his name'.

In each case of state killing there have been two diametrically opposed versions of the event in circulation, the first being that of the state, the second that of relatives and human rights campaigners. Given the state's ideological and institutional advantages, its version was often the first and most widely disseminated. In the face of a popular consensus that the state version was right, relatives and human rights campaigners were relegated to the position of being judged to be either too traumatised or too sympathetic to 'terrorism' to be taken seriously. They were either mad or bad. In a situation where it was their word against that of the state, they faced overwhelming odds. The contest was unequal. Even when alternative evidence—eye-witness, forensic, video—emerged to support their version over that of the state, they had to work to establish the credibility of that version without the same institutional and ideological currency available to the state.

It might be argued that in the case of two diametrically opposed versions of the same event, it is impossible for the uninformed observer to ascertain the truth. For example, were Charles Breslin, Michael Devine and David Devine in Strabane the victims of a planned undercover operation by British troops? Or were they shot dead after chance encounters with routine British army patrols, at which point they made sudden threatening moves which required the use of lethal force? Was Kevin McGovern a young man out for a drink with friends when he walked into an RUC ambush? Or was he shot after he appeared to throw something at the police?

There is one potential way out of these dilemmas. The state has the resources to be much more than an uninformed observer. It has the means to investigate these killings as systematically as those of every other person killed in the conflict. Did it do so in relation to state killings?

Investigation

Eleven people who tell their stories in this book make specific reference to the failure of the police to adequately investigate the killing. It is likely that others who did not refer to this point could also have pointed to inadequacies. There is thus no doubt that all could have agreed with Ní Aoláin's (2000: 117) conclusion: 'From the outset there is the presumption that no crime has been committed by the state agent when a person is killed by lethal force'.

William Smith, in the case of the shooting of Brian Robinson, noted that: 'There were a lot of things that weren't done which are normally done at the scene of a shooting. If you go to any scene of a shooting in Northern Ireland, you will see rings round bullet holes. You can look at the photos in the newspapers and you'll see nothing like that. The car was moved before forensics got near it. The police never asked for any witnesses.' Similarly, campaigners in the case of the death of Louis Leonard, pointed out that the RUC made no 'attempt to seal off the scene of the crime... There was no investigation... Louis' case was a murder in a small village and it was never treated like you would imagine a murder to be treated.' The experience was similar for the family of Carol Ann Kelly: 'There was never a proper investigation into Carol Ann's death. They didn't do any measurements or take statements from witnesses. A lot of the local people went to Woodburn Barracks to give statements and they were told it wasn't necessary.'

Even the most obvious of police routines—the interviewing of those involved in killing—was often ignored. The SAS men who killed the three IRA members in Gibraltar were whisked back to England immediately afterwards and were only interviewed two weeks later. Likewise, following the killing of eight IRA members at Loughgall, the soldiers involved were flown away from the scene in helicopters and were not interviewed until they had a chance to consult with army lawyers. These lawyers were also present when each soldier later dictated a statement to the police. The two RUC men involved in the death of Seamus Duffy only made official statements after they had viewed the video which was used later in the inquest to attempt to prove that Seamus had been rioting. And in the case of Peter Thompson, the two soldiers who fired the fatal shots spent considerable time with MOD lawyers before making their initial statements. One of these soldiers was advised by the RUC to alter his statement when it became apparent nine months later, as a result of available forensic evidence, that parts of his evidence did not correspond with the facts.

In some cases, even the professionals who had a right and duty to investigate were thwarted in their attempts to do their job. During the Gibraltar inquest, the crown pathologist stated that he was not allowed to see ballistic reports, nor even the results of the blood and urine tests he himself had sent for analysis. The crown forensic expert charged to gather evidence following the shooting of three IRA members in Strabane reported at the inquest that he was prevented by the RUC from examining part of the field in which the shooting had occurred.

Loretta Lynch, a campaigner in the case of Louis Leonard, summed up the conclusion of many relatives: 'Not only was there no investigation, but there was a concerted effort not to investigate'. And yet, the abnormality of it all only became apparent in retrospect, as Corina Breslin pointed out.

> ...nobody came to get a statement from us. I mean, it was a fatal shooting and there was no investigation. Not that we expected it, for we knew the score. But sitting now and looking at the Stephen Lawrence case, why the hell wouldn't we expect it? Why wouldn't we be expected to be interviewed and to be asked was there anything suspicious about all this? We just took it as par for the course.

Police officers who were more attuned to normal police procedures were less prone to accept that the practices in relation to the investigation of state killings were acceptable, none more so than John Stalker when he examined the RUC's investigation of the killing of six men in North Armagh. 'The files were little more than a collection of statements, apparently prepared for a coroner's inquiry. They bore no resemblance to my idea of a murder prosecution file.'

Why should such a systematic refusal to conduct or to hinder investigations have existed in relation to state killings? In part it surely derived from the sympathy of police investigators for colleagues under investigation. But it was undoubtedly much more fundamental than that. As Stalker himself came close to concluding, the decision to ignore professional police investigation procedures derived from political decisions enacted by top personnel in the RUC itself. There was no intention to puncture the discourse of 'terrorism' by conceding that these deaths were comparable to those of other citizens. Or, as Tommy Carroll, whose brother Roddy was one of the victims investigated by Stalker put it:

> No policeman goes out to shoot anybody hoping that in retrospect it will all be ratified; you can't do that. In this system, you know that when you pull the trigger, it's okayed before you do that.

Harassment

In most cases, those interviewed stated that they have never been officially informed by the RUC or anyone else that the incident occurred. Others were informed by the RUC or British army in the most callous of ways. After the killing of eight IRA men at Loughgall, the UDR drove through the local nationalist estate with a banner reading 'Eight nil'. As Peter McBride's body lay in his house awaiting burial, the British army drove past shouting 'One down; one nil'. Even a personal approach did not guarantee more sympathetic treatment; when Kevin McGovern's mother phoned the RUC to inquire about her son, she was told, 'You'll get his body in Magherafelt morgue'.

For relatives in six of the cases considered here, the first intimation of the death was a raid on their home by the RUC. In most cases, no reason was given for the raid. Even when, as in the cases of Michael and David Devine, and of Gervaise McKerr, the raiders were asked why they were there, they refused to answer or said they did not know. In only one of these cases did the RUC state that the raid was linked to the death of a relative; Peter Thompson's brother Mark already knew of the death when the raid started. 'We didn't kill anybody; it was the British army', they told him. In retrospect it became clear to the Thompson family that the purpose of the raid was to search for missing British army intelligence documents. In other cases, it would appear that the police were on what might be termed a 'fishing exercise', searching for some information which might allow them to tarnish the name of the victim and thereby excuse their own involvement in the killing. For instance, take the raid on the flat of the brother of Kevin McGovern:

> Retrospectively we realised that they were desperately hunting for some evidence to connect Kevin or our family to a republican label. They weren't interested in what happened; they were more interested in a damage limitation exercise.

Eleanor McKerr had a similar experience.

> They just kept on searching my home, going through my cupboards, all my personal belongings... All the time during the search I was hoping Gervaise would come home. There was not one place on my house that the police did not search. I kept asking them what they were looking for; it seemed so pointless, as I knew there was nothing in my home that could possibly be illegal. At 2.45 they left my home with not a word. I still didn't know what

was going on. But looking back now, the policemen who came to my home deliberately concealed the death from me and were apparently looking for evidence to support the theory that they had shot a terrorist in action.

Such raids were only one manifestation of a campaign of harassment which many of the families experienced. Interviewees spoke explicitly of harassment in fourteen of the stories told here. The harassment was usually verbal and highly offensive. Seamus Ludlow's sister was visited by the British army two days after her brother's death; the soldiers made insulting remarks about Seamus. British soldiers frequently drove at night to the monument erected to teenage plastic bullet victim Carol Ann Kelly. 'Wee Irish bitch' was one of the comments they made. Gervaise McKerr's wife Eleanor experienced frequent raids and was advised on one occasion by the RUC that she ought to emigrate to America. The family of Charles Breslin was subjected to numerous taunts such as 'Charlie's a Tetley tea bag', a reference to the fact that he was shot at least 13 times. Some time after the killing, his young sister Linda was stopped one day and subjected to a cruel hoax when she was told, erroneously, by the RUC that they had just shot another brother. Mairéad Farrell's boyfriend, Seamus Finucane, was stopped by the RUC and taunted: 'Well, you won't be fucking Mairéad anymore'. Seamus Duffy's brother was frequently abused by the RUC: 'Do you want to be next?' Pearse Jordan's teenage brother experienced similar harassment.

It is important to stress that this harassment was not confined to relatives of republican activists. The taunts and harassment were par for the course whether your brother was an IRA man attacking a supposedly empty RUC barracks or a bachelor killed near the border as he returned from a night's drinking. Nor were the families of those who might in other circumstances be represented as prototypical innocent victims spared—teenage girls like Carol Ann Kelly and mothers like Nora McCabe or middle class students like Kevin McGovern. The harassment started from the moment of the death, as Kevin McGovern's brother Sean was acutely aware.

> The reaction of the security forces after such a death is to behave as if the family of the victim have done something wrong. I remember being asked about my family and what they all did. I felt more that I and my family were under investigation than being treated with the common decency that one would extend to a relative who had just heard his brother had been killed.

Moreover, the harassment continued the more the relatives became involved in political action to achieve justice. Peter Thompson's brother Mark was accosted by an RUC man the day before he went to present evidence to the United Nations in Geneva. '... he put his hand to his head as though he was putting a gun to his head, and said, "Remember, you can do all you like, but remember".' William Smith, who campaigned over the death of Brian Robinson, was clear that as an ex-prisoner turned community activist, 'the police had not bothered me, but once I started to do this, the centre was raided with a search warrant for materials'. Robert Hamill's sister Diane put it even more emphatically: 'If we had not stood up and said this was wrong, they would probably not have given us so much hassle.'

Consequently, many of those interviewed were clear that their dead relatives were not the only victims in the various stories. As a result of the attention of the same armed forces of the state which had killed their loved ones, they too were victimised. Gary English's father Mickey, was direct on this: 'We have become victims through the deaths of our loved ones and those of us who expected truth and justice after the death became further victimised by the state'. Nora McCabe's husband Jim is equally articulate:

> We as the victims of state violence were ignored by the state from the day and hour it happened. We became victims of the state and, as I said all along, 'When you become a victim of the state, you become an enemy of the state and you are treated in that way whether or not you wanted to be'.

Once the discourse of 'terrorism' is employed, it cannot admit of any error, no matter how innocent the victim.

Experiencing powerlessness

At every stage relatives experienced an overwhelming sense of powerlessness in the face of the odds against them. It began with frustration over the misinformation disseminated about the incident but continued as each level of the process emerged.

For example, a number of those interviewed referred to the way in which the state moved to claim ownership of the incident, the body and the belongings, thereby refusing access to the relatives. The body of Mickey English's son Gary was lifted into a British army Land Rover and driven to an army barracks where it was examined by an army medic. Only later was it delivered to the local hospital where relatives could be close to it. Anna Magliocco was slapped on the face by a policeman as she tried to get close to her husband Antonio's restaurant; it was the following day before she finally traced his body in the morgue. Eilish McCabe was told by the RUC not to touch the body of her brother Aidan McAnespie as he lay on the border road, presumably on the grounds of not disturbing forensic evidence. She ignored the instruction. Jean McBride found her way to her son Peter's body blocked by the British army unit which had killed him, but managed to get through a neighbour's house and out into the alley where Peter lay.

The issue of ownership was also central in relation to a number of funerals. In the case of Charles Breslin, Michael Devine and David Devine, the RUC dictated the route when the bodies were brought from the morgue to the family homes; they also appeared at Charles Breslin's funeral in huge numbers to enforce the decision that the funeral could not be a paramilitary one. The RUC also dictated the route and pace as the bodies of Mairéad Farrell, Dan McCann and Seán Savage were returned from Gibraltar; they held the cortege on the motorway and abused mourners, as well as forcing the cortege to slow down as they passed loyalist areas.

The clothes of the victims were never returned to the Breslin and Devine families; they were destroyed 'for health reasons'. The same reason was given for the destruction of the clothing of Patrick Kelly, shot dead by the SAS at Loughgall. Eleanor McKerr fought for 12 years for the return of her husband Gervaise's belongings and the car in which he was shot dead, but only received back a wallet and a wedding ring. Margaret Caraher got the car back in which her husband was shot dead three and a half years after the incident, but not his jacket and audio tapes that were of personal value. In the case of Aidan McAnespie, the RUC later took the keys from the clothes he had been wearing when shot dead, returned to where Aidan had parked his car before the incident and, without telling the family, took the car. Most disturbing of all, Aidan's sister Eilish later discovered that part of the ribcage of her brother was kept by the pathologist after the post-mortem; although it was allegedly shown to a pathologist from the South at a later point, it was never returned to the family for burial with the rest of the body.

One reaction to this sense of powerlessness noted by some of those interviewed was a feeling of guilt. From the state's point of view, such a reaction was politically useful, for it meant that the relatives of victims pointed the finger of blame at themselves rather than at the perpetrators. For some, the guilt related to some aspect of the process which they wished in retrospect they had handled better. For example, Jim McCabe, Nora's husband, said: 'In a way I still feel guilty because I did not do enough. Maybe I should have tried the private prosecution; maybe I should not have accepted compensation and would have been able to go to the European Court.' Eilish McCabe, sister of Aidan McAnespie, referred to an equally specific issue: 'I suppose one of the things I regret in the campaign is going ahead and allowing the state pathologist in the South to carry out the second autopsy... I'm sorry we didn't go for someone international'. For others, the guilt was potentially much wider than solely in relation to their own relative. Take Kay Duddy, sister of Jackie:

> I find the saddest part of all was that they were prepared to sacrifice all
> those lives over the years for this cover-up... there were people went out
> and did things in the name of Bloody Sunday. That's not what we wanted.
> I felt so responsible for so many deaths. Then I thought, 'How dare they
> do that to me? That's their burden, not my burden'. It took me a long time
> to convince myself of that.

Another consequence of the powerlessness they experienced was that many of those interviewed stated that they had not been able to grieve properly. As Ciaran Leonard put it: 'I would say we never grieved. I remember we just stopped having Christmases'. Kay Duddy recognised that she had not yet come to terms properly with her brother's death, even though she had done so in relation to the death of her parents. 'I would love to be able to go and see the priest, get his mass said, go up to the cemetery, say a wee private prayer—to have peace to grieve, deal with it, the same as we did with our parents and then hopefully, get on with the rest of my life.' The experience of Eileen Kelly, sister of Carol Ann, was similar: 'We are coming towards Carol Ann's eighteenth anniversary and it's like there is no end and that grieving process has never ever stopped.' 'It's a wound that never gets to heal', concluded Margaret Caraher.

A day in court?

There is a powerful myth in democratic societies that victims will achieve some satisfaction and redress in having their day in court. But another casualty of war in the North of Ireland has been the rule of law. Early in the war, the state's knee-jerk reaction was to respond to conflict as it had normally done in Ireland through at least the previous century. The rule of law was in effect suspended in crucial ways, most notably through the introduction of internment. But in the face of increased conflict and international criticism, a more sophisticated strategy was introduced. The façade of normal law was retained, but the details were altered to harness the law as a weapon in the war. Jury trials were abolished, and the burden of proof in 'terrorist' offences was reversed; a person caught in possession of explosives or guns was taken to be guilty until they could prove innocence. The period suspects could be held for interrogation was increased to seven days, and evidence acquired by methods of 'interrogation' short of torture was deemed acceptable. Eventually the right of silence in 'terrorist' cases was altered in such a way that refusal to answer questions under interrogation could be taken as evidence of possible guilt.

This was the distorted legal system which faced relatives of state killings when they sought their day in court. Such was the distortion that the chances of them achieving satisfaction or redress were practically nullified.

For a start, there were very few prosecutions in relation to state killings. And where there were, it was clear that there was a presumption that the defendant was innocent. This presumption was often evident not only in the behaviour of the DPP and prosecution, but also of the expert witnesses and the judges themselves. In the case of the judges, it was not merely a matter of case hardening, exaggerated by the absence of the possible tempering effect of a jury. More, the distortion of the law to enable it to act as a weapon against 'terrorism' clearly led to a dilution of ideals on the part of judges. Ní Aoláin (2000: 113) cites some outrageous examples of this. Lord Diplock expanded the notion of self-defence to cover the situation in which the victim was shot by British soldiers who believed that if he was allowed to get away he could 'join armed fellow-members of the Provisional IRA who might be lurking in the neighbourhood...' In another case, Justice Jones accepted that the British soldier had shot the victim in self-defence on the basis of the following specious logic:

> ... if the deceased ... had been permitted to run away when legally called
> upon to halt ... there might ... have been a resultant discomfiture of the

forces of the law, and encouragement of the Provisional IRA to further resistance to the Army, and it could be seen by those in the area hitherto uncommitted to the IRA as a demonstration that the Army was ineffective to enforce its authority.

Of the cases considered in this book, there were only prosecutions on six occasions: the shoot-to-kill deaths in North Armagh, and the deaths of Gary English, John Downes, Aidan McAnespie, Fergal Caraher and Peter McBride. In only one case—that of Peter McBride—did the prosecution lead to a custodial sentence. Even then, the soldiers concerned were released within a few years despite the imposition of a life sentence.

Within those trials, as those interviewed sometimes recount, the attitude and behaviour of the judges added insult to injury. The judge in the case against the two British soldiers accused of killing Fergal Caraher rejected the evidence of civilian witnesses as unreliable because of the widespread support for republicanism in South Armagh. And, most notoriously of all, Judge Gibson commended three RUC men for bringing three IRA men—Gervaise McKerr, Sean Burns and Eugene Toman—'to the final court of justice' by shooting them dead.

For others whose stories are recounted here, the only venue where there was even a remote chance of disclosure of the facts of the killing was the inquest. But the collective experience of the inquest was a frustrating one. As a result of changes in the coroners' rules for Northern Ireland introduced in 1981, inquests are unable to reach conclusions as elsewhere in the United Kingdom; for example, they cannot reach a finding of 'unlawful killing'. Instead, they can only record their findings regarding the identity of the dead person and about how, when and where he or she died. Even further restrictions were imposed in practice. Relatives were not entitled to legal aid, while the MOD and RUC could afford the most expensive of legal representation. Lawyers for the relatives worked at a disadvantage to lawyers for the state forces; the latter had documents and statements in advance, while the relatives' lawyers did not, thus making the task of questioning witnesses extremely difficult. In addition, Public Interest Immunity Certificates were issued in relation to three of the inquests considered in this book—the Loughgall killings, the Gibraltar killings, and the killing of three men at a bookmaker's shop in Belfast. These prevented the disclosure of information on the grounds of national security, thus further curtailing the chances of lawyers for the families uncovering the truth. Countless RUC and British army witnesses were called at these inquests, but often fewer civilian witnesses. RUC and British army witnesses, especially if implicated in the death, did not have to appear, but could send unsworn statements which were read to the court. The evidence of civilian witnesses was sometimes treated as suspect by the Coroner, as also happened in a number of trials. For example, in the inquest on Pearse Jordan, lawyers for the RUC and MOD attempted to undermine the credibility of a number of civilian witnesses by interrogating them about their previous convictions.

As with the judges mentioned earlier, the attitude and behaviour of coroners sometimes left much to be desired as far as a number of relatives were concerned. Hugh Jordan recalled:

> The coroner seemed to sit like Jack-the-Lad, swinging on his chair with his legs crossed, smiling and generally trying to make an idiot out of our barrister who happened to be a girl.

The coroner in the case of Diarmuid O'Neill apologised to the Metropolitan police officers present for subjecting them to 'three weeks' sustained attack without the protection afforded by the criminal court, with no pretence of natural justice...'; they had been cross-examined, as was permitted, indeed expected in an inquest, about killing Diarmuid.

Finally, those state personnel accused—by name in a trial, or by implication in an inquest—were frequently rewarded by promotion, honours, or, as in the case of the killers of Peter McBride, reinstatement in the British army. If relatives did not know it before, they certainly realised as a result of their experience of the attempt to acquire legal redress through the criminal or coroner's courts, that the system was stacked against them.

Resistance

Despite—but also because of—the odds against them, many relatives fought back. Their first act of resistance was the rejection of the state's account of the killing. But for many, an important turning point in terms of resistance was involvement with groups campaigning for justice and truth. The experience was often cathartic, for they found that they were not alone, that others acknowledged their loss, that they were neither mad nor bad. After joining the United Campaign Against Plastic Bullets, Jim McCabe was exuberant:

> For the first time I could sit down and talk of my fears and concerns and put forward suggestions to make it better for all of us... You weren't different. For once you were a piece of a jigsaw that filled in; you weren't a square peg in a round hole anymore.

Brenda Downes discovered a similar release when joining the same group: 'For the first time I realised that I wasn't the only one who had suffered'.

Through campaigning, their private ills were transformed into public issues. Their individual experience became a spur to political action. Most of the people we spoke to were not just involved in their own case, but in wider political issues through groups such as Silent Too Long, the United Campaign against Plastic Bullets, Relatives for Justice, Justice for All, the Campaign for the Right to Truth, VOICE, the Bloody Sunday campaign. From that political involvement they drew the strength to continue struggling for truth and justice in their own individual cases.

As a result, they could point to a number of victories. William Smith was pleased that the jury in the inquest into the death of Brian Robinson went beyond their brief to agree that Robinson could have been arrested rather than killed. The Caraher family and the community in Cullyhanna managed, through a well-organised public inquiry, to ensure the prosecution of two British soldiers for the killing of Fergal Caraher—even if the soldiers were subsequently acquitted. The McBride family got court backing for their argument that the two soldiers who killed their son Peter should be dismissed from the British army. After a long struggle, relatives of the IRA members shot dead in Gibraltar achieved a unique and impressive victory when the European Court of Human Rights found the British state guilty of contravening Article 2 of the European Convention which upholds the right to life. And after an even longer struggle, the relatives of those killed on Bloody Sunday prevailed on the British government to institute the Saville inquiry; no matter the outcome of this inquiry, its very existence is a repudiation of the findings of the original inquiry into the events, the Widgery inquiry.

The rate of success in these campaigns should not be exaggerated. Often the victories were relatively minor, and often their significance was symbolic rather than a harbinger of substantial change in the system. At the same time, the victories should not be dismissed as irrelevant. At very least they convinced those in all the campaigns, not just the successful ones, that it was politically realistic to make demands and to continue struggling for them, despite the odds.

What do they want?

Some of those interviewed were adamant that they did not want to see anyone imprisoned for killing their relative. Tony Doherty was one such person: 'I wouldn't like to see the soldier who killed my father go to prison...' Hugh Jordan spoke likewise: 'I don't want to see anybody spending any time inside—cops or Brits. To me that is just futile'. For Margaret Caraher, there was nothing which could compensate for the death of her husband: ' It makes no difference whatsoever to my life whether those soldiers serve time or don't serve time; it has no bearing on my day-to-day living. They took a life and there's nothing and no one can ever replace that, no amount of years served.' Others insisted that they were not seeking revenge. For example, Jim McCabe stated: 'It has gone beyond the point of revenge... There is no sense of satisfaction to maybe sit in a court one day and see some guy be sentenced to life imprisonment for Nora's murder'. Ciaran Leonard was equally emphatic:

> We are not out for revenge... At times I really hate the British army, the RUC and the UDR for what they have done to our people and the years of suffering they have inflicted on us in the name of the law. But in human terms, I wouldn't want to see any of their relatives suffer what we've suffered.

Although it was clear that most relatives realised that the chance of prosecution was at best slim, those who ruled out prosecutions and revenge were not merely making the best of a bad situation. For people who had suffered so much, they showed remarkable tolerance and magnanimity.

There was another group of people interviewed who specifically insisted that they wanted to see prosecutions. Eileen Kelly pointed to the stark difference between how the killing of her sister Carol Ann was treated and the approach to other killings: '... murder is murder is murder and it didn't apply in our case nor in any of the other plastic bullet cases. I would like someone to have to stand trial'. Mairead Kelly was similarly determined in relation to the killing of her brother Patrick and others at Loughgall by the SAS: 'I would like to see them indicted for murder, whether they would ever serve a sentence for it'. Although Diane Hamill had witnessed the prosecution of some loyalists for the death of her brother Robert, she wanted more: 'Ideally I would like the RUC to face criminal charges. I'd like to see them charged with murder'. For Niall Farrell, charging those who actually pulled the trigger to kill his sister Mairéad was not enough: 'People think I'm daft when I say Thatcher should be prosecuted for killing my sister, but why not? The Spanish Minister of the Interior found himself in jail for a similar crime and as we talk, Pinochet is in the dock. So why not Thatcher?' And Kay Duddy stated that she would like to see Ted Heath, Prime Minister at the time of Bloody Sunday, prosecuted.

At a superficial level, there is a seemingly stark division here: prosecution versus non-prosecution, a criminal justice model versus a more humanitarian model, hawks versus doves, revenge versus forgiveness. But in fact, beneath the apparent dichotomy is a remarkable unanimity on the part of the relatives. Although there are disagreements about ideas of justice and how it can be achieved, all those interviewed clearly want the same thing in the first instance; they want the truth. There is no coincidence in the timing of this demand now that the war is over. Mark Thompson states this succinctly:

> During the conflict many relatives and indeed communities suspended their grief, their emotions and I suppose in the cut and thrust of things every new day and week brought to others new tragedy. There was no space. People have now found that space as a result of the peace process and are now examining those hurts, beginning the necessary and difficult process of healing. There is need of the truth as part of this process.

At one level 'truth' refers specifically to the facts; there is no closure without disclosure. But fundamentally, whether the facts of the case are already well-known or not—and in many cases they are—relatives demand an official acknowledgement of wrongdoing. Kathleen Duffy, mother of plastic bullet victim Seamus, puts it as follows: 'I just cannot understand how we don't get recognition. It's the same hurt, the same as any other murder... I want the same recognition as everyone else. I don't want to be any different. I want to be on the same footing as any other mother whose son has been murdered. I think I have the right to that.'

Margaret Caraher sums it up:

... what would go an awful long way to helping this whole thing to heal would be a public acknowledgement of the wrongdoing... I could really say to myself, 'Well, I've come to the end of the road now. I've got what I set out to do and I've come as far as I possibly can with this. Now I can leave it with a clear conscience.'... It just can't heal without that small acknowledgement. And it would be just as little as that, and as much as that.

Truth and justice

How can the relatives achieve the official acknowledgement they seek? One obvious mechanism would be an apology from the British state. But, although some of those interviewed specifically referred to the possibility of an apology, it was clear that much more than an apology was demanded. In fact, for some, the possibility of an apology was rejected as an affront. Tony Doherty, for example, recounts that the Bloody Sunday campaigners worked hard to prevent the Labour Party persuading Tony Blair that he should issue an apology: 'The idea of an apology had a certain amount of currency; it was quite an effort for us to keep the emphasis on the truth.'

No matter if delivered with solemnity and fanfare, an apology would be too easy. An apology is not only a statement about past wrong, but also must convince the offended party that the wrong will not be repeated in future. The surest way that that can be guaranteed is not merely through a verbal promise but through the establishment of mechanisms to ensure that it cannot happen again. An apology for past abuses is useless in a situation where the system which spawned the abuses remains intact—or, to paraphrase Brecht's reference to fascism, while the bitch that bore them remains in heat. As Jim McCabe concluded, 'an apology from the RUC or the British government would be an insult at this stage'.

One mechanism which has been tried in at least 19 societies in the past two decades—including most recently South Africa and Guatemala—has been the establishment of a truth commission. A number of those interviewed for this book suggested that a truth commission for Ireland would be appropriate. It is not difficult to see why they should have done so. A truth commission marks a significant symbolic break with the horror of the previous regime. It states unequivocally that what the state did—torture, disappearances, killings—was wrong and should never happen again. In fact, 'nunca mas'—'never again'—has been the title of the publications of at least two of those commissions. In conjunction with other legal and political changes, it is hoped that the truth commission marks a turning point. Although it may appear simply a symbolic device, it is intended to underwrite a new consensus about human rights. Without such a consensus, there is no assurance that the future will be any different from the past.

There are some who have argued that we are already at that point in Ireland and that the elements of a definitive break with the past are present in a number of the mechanisms established as a result of the Good Friday Agreement of 1998. The Patten Commission on the reform of the RUC was said by a number of its members to be our equivalent of a truth commission. Some commentators have suggested that the Saville inquiry into events of Bloody Sunday has the potential of developing into a mini-truth commission. Kenneth Bloomfield reported on the situation of victims and recommended a number of policies to allow relatives access to education and business start-up; similar policies emerged, for example, from the truth commission in Chile after Pinochet handed over power to a civilian government. The Good Friday Agreement led to the criminal law review which recommended a broad range of reforms. And finally, out of the same Agreement came a Human Rights Commission and the decision to incorporate European human rights instruments into domestic law.

But what distinguishes the current situation in the North of Ireland from that in most societies which had a truth commission is that there is no widespread consensus on the legitimacy and purpose of these innovations. There are three distinct ways in which these events are being represented. First, the changes are at best unnecessary, and worse, an attack on respectable institutions which have proven their worth in the defence of democracy against 'terrorism'; in effect, they represent the victory of 'terrorism'. This is the position of a major proportion of unionism. Second, the reforms are a welcome and appropriate recognition of the political changes which have occurred. The 'terrorist menace' shows the potential of being gone forever, so there is now the opportunity to professionalise and modernise institutions. Such changes do not constitute any criticism of the past actions of those institutions. This position is held by the British government. Third, the changes are cosmetic and likely to be merely superficial. They do not yet represent the root and branch change that is necessary if a significant break from the past is to be accomplished. This is the position of republicans and a proportion of nationalists.

So, we are not even at the stage where other countries have been at when they established their truth commissions. Nor does it follow that if and when we arrive at that point, a truth commission will magically solve all our political problems. The case of the South African Truth and Reconciliation Commission (TRC) proves that.

Although it gained wider support in the society than might have been imagined and led to remarkable instances of both disclosure and reconciliation, the TRC was criticised by some of those whom it might have been expected to help most. Thus, the family of murdered activist Stephen Biko objected to the trade-off inherent in the TRC—amnesty in return for disclosure. But even those who reluctantly accepted the necessity of such an historic compromise ended up feeling a sense of anti-climax. There were at least two elements to this deflation. The first was an over-emphasis on the goal of reconciliation. Some perpetrators went along with the event not out of genuine remorse for past wrongs but because of what was on offer, amnesty. In such a situation, it was not easy for victims to believe that there was any hope of reconciliation with perpetrators. Second, all the eggs, as it were, were placed in one basket. No one event, no matter how wide-ranging, could hope to give everyone a sense of accomplishment. Especially for those who had suffered at the hands of the apartheid state there was the realisation that some of those responsible were never going to own up, that the truth would not be total, and that there would be often little more than a begrudging acknowledgement of the injustices perpetrated on them, their families and communities. And because the TRC was a one-off event, there was no second chance for them to experience an event which could bring about closure.

All of which might appear to spell out a pessimistic message—there will be no truth commission for Ireland, and even if there is, it is likely to fall short of the ideal for many relatives of people killed by the state. On the contrary, the conclusion is one of realism, not pessimism: whether or not there is a truth commission for Ireland, the relatives must continue to struggle for truth and justice. They will tell their stories in many venues, including those organised by themselves. They will continue to demand acknowledgement for past wrongs through current state institutions, including any new institutions which emerge as a result of the peace process.

Some—such as the relatives of victims of the Dublin and Monaghan bombs, of Pat Finucane and of Seamus Ludlow—will continue to demand independent public inquiries, a demand which in one case, that of the relatives of those killed on Bloody Sunday, has been realised. The belief is that such an independent forum has the potential to guarantee truth and acknowledgement which is not otherwise available in the current political and legal system.

For others the mechanism of disclosure identified is that of prosecution, whether of those who pulled the trigger or those in political positions who gave them the authority to do so. It is misleading to label such relatives as vengeful in supposed comparison to the others who are deemed to be more forgiving. Attractive as it may be to dismiss aspirations to prosecution, especially in a time of peace when the goal seems to be to empty the prisons and move on to a new era, relatives should not be denied this aspiration. Prosecution remains the strongest symbol in a democratic state of societal disapproval. It unreservedly conveys the message that there is no impunity, even for the forces of the state; no one is above the law. Moreover, in a situation where prosecution has been used relentlessly for three decades (and more) as a mechanism against their community, why should relatives be required now to expect less? Ultimately, the struggle is not about prosecutions per se. There is no fetishisation of the criminal justice system on the part of these relatives. Like an inquiry, a court case is seen as a means to an end, namely truth.

It may even satisfy the desire for justice. That said, truth and justice are not coterminous. As developments in those countries which have had truth commissions reveal, truth may require less than full justice, especially in terms of prosecutions. In those societies, victims of state killings and torture have been prepared to accept less than justice for past offences in return for building a future society where the protection of human rights is central.

The relatives interviewed in this book are not passive victims, but active human rights campaigners. Although they never volunteered, once the state killed one of their family, they had no choice but to speak out. Silence was not an option. As one of them, Margaret Caraher, puts it:

> In many ways it was the only road. I deeply resent having ever to go on that road. I deeply resent that as a family we could not have handed that over to proper authorities and been assured that every resource possible would have been used. And I deeply resent the really difficult things I had to do personally—how difficult I found it to speak publicly, how difficult I found it at certain times, especially very soon after Fergal's death, at a time when I couldn't even say his name, that I had to—I chose to because I felt I had no choice—it was difficult and it's totally not on for families to have to put themselves in that position. It was a positive way to channel anger, but I certainly never grieved properly, because I was out there being busy and I never stopped to actually grieve.

In Chile they learned to their cost the consequences of silence. They had a truth commission which managed to solve some issues about the acknowledgement of past state human rights abuses and of compensation for victims. But while military power remained intact, there was no consensus about the past and the future; above all, the truth commission did not lead to reconciliation. In the absence of reconciliation, there was a widespread conspiracy of silence about the past. Chilean writer Isabel Allende recounted the debilitating legacy of that silence two decades after the truth commission (*Observer*, 24 January 1999).

> For years Chileans have lived in a fragile peace based on silence and prudence; few desire confrontation. Because of fear we have swept memory under the rug. We feared words, we feared calling things by their names, we walked on eggshells, we spoke in euphemisms, we treated each other with caution and suspicion.

If in Ireland we manage to come to the point where no one can write that of us twenty years into a peace process, it will be due in no small part to the fearlessness of the relatives of state killings. They have been vilified and marginalised, when in fact they should be commended for helping to bring about a better society—one rooted firmly in a culture of human rights.

BIBLIOGRAPHY

Introduction

Fay, Marie-Therese, Morrissey, Mike and Smyth, Marie. *Northern Ireland's Troubles: the Human Costs*, London, Pluto Press 1999

Fegan, Arthur and Murray, Raymond. *Collusion 1990-1994: Loyalist Paramilitary Murders in the North of Ireland*, Belfast, Relatives for Justice, 1995

Krog, Antje. *Country of My Skull*, London, Jonathan Cape 1998

McKittrick, David et al. *Lost Lives: the stories of the men, women and children who died as a result of the Northern Ireland troubles*, Edinburgh, Mainstream Publishing 1999

Ní Aoláin, Fionnuala. *The Politics of Force*, Belfast, Blackstaff Press, 2000

Sutton, Malcolm. *Bear in Mind These Dead: an Index of Deaths from the Conflict in Ireland 1969-1993*, Belfast, Beyond the Pale Publications 1994

Chapter 1: Bloody Sunday

Bloody Sunday and the Report of the Widgery Tribunal: the Irish Government's Assessment of the New Material, presented to the British government, June 1997

Bloody Sunday Justice Campaign website, http://freespace.virgin.net/nash.family/

Bloody Sunday Justice Campaign, *Bloody Sunday: A Miscarriage of Justice*, Derry, nd.

Bloody Sunday Justice Campaign. *The Breglio Report*, Derry, 1997

British Irish Rights Watch. *Submission to the Special Rapporteur on Summary and Arbitrary Executions: the Murder of 13 Civilians by Soldiers of the British Army on 'Bloody Sunday'*, 30th January 1972, London, 1994; available on http://cain.ulster.ac.uk/events/bsunday/birw.htm

Broken Covenants: Violations of International Law in Northern Ireland, Report of the Northern Ireland Human Rights Assembly, 6-8 April 1992, London, NCCL/Liberty 1993, p. 19

Doherty, Tony. 'Bloody Sunday Campaign Continues', *Just News* 7(10), November 1992, p. 2

Gartner, Joelle. 'Anger at the Heel: the Legacy of Bloody Sunday', in Trisha Ziff (ed), *Hidden Truths: Bloody Sunday 1972*, Santa Monica, Smart Art Press, 1999, pp. 117-131

McCann, Eamonn. *Bloody Sunday in Derry: What Really Happened*, Dingle, Co. Kerry, Brandon, 1992

McCann, Eamonn. 'Bloody Sunday truth "was known 25 years ago"', *The Observer*, 19 September 1999

McKittrick, David et al., op. cit., pp. 143-149

Mullan, Don. *Eyewitness Bloody Sunday*, Dublin, Wolfhound Press, 1997

Mullan, Don. 'The Eyewitness', in Trisha Ziff (ed), op. cit., pp. 33-48

Saville inquiry website, http://www.bloody-Sunday-inquiry.org.uk

Walsh, Dermot. *Bloody Sunday and the Rule of Law in Northern Ireland*, Dublin, Gill and Macmillan, 2000

Chapter 2: Louis Leonard

MacDonald, Darach. 'VOICE speaks for truth, not revenge', *Ireland on Sunday*, 7 March 1999

MacDonald, Darach. 'A butcher's death', *Ireland on Sunday*, 7 March 1999

McKittrick, David et al., op cit., pp. 286-287

'Unanswered questions over the death of Louis Leonard', *An Phoblacht/Republican News*, 18 December 1997

Chapter 3: Dublin and Monaghan Bombs

A Place and a Name: Report of the Victims Commission, Dublin, Stationery Office, July 1999

Holroyd, Fred. *War Without Honour*, Hull, Medium Publishing Co., 1989

McKittrick, David et al., op. cit., pp. 447-453

Mullan, Don. 'The experience of the bereaved and maimed of the Dublin and Monaghan bombings', http://www.serve.com/pfc/dubmon/1974.html

Mullan, Don. 'End Game', *Magill*, April 1999

Murray, Raymond. *State Violence: Northern Ireland 1969- 1997*, Cork, Mercier Press 1998, pp. 107-110

Chapter 4: Seamus Ludlow

A Place and a Name: Report of the Victims' Commission, Dublin, Stationery Office, July 1999, pp. 16-17, 43

Bonner, Aeneas. 'Collusion inquiry "to shake Republic"', *Irish News*, 24 May 1999

Cadwallader, Anne. 'What's the truth?', *Sunday Business Post*, 14 February 1999

McKittrick, David et al., op cit., pp. 642-644

Moloney, Ed. 'The murder of Seamus Ludlow', *Sunday Tribune*, 8 March 1998, 15 March 1998, 30 August 1998

Murray, Raymond. *The SAS in Ireland*, Cork, Mercier Press 1990, pp 175-176

Seamus Ludlow campaign web page: http://www.adon89.care4free.net/chronology.htm

'The abduction and murder of Mr. Seamus Ludlow 2nd May 1976', Pat Finucane Centre, January 1999; http://www.serve.com/pfc/ludlow99.htm

Walsh, Liz. 'Murder, Collusion, Lies', *Magill*, April 1999, pp. 38-42

Chapter 5: Gary English

Gifford. Tony. *Deaths on the Streets of Derry*, London, National Council for Civil Liberties, 1982, pp. 11-21
McKittrick, David et al., op. cit., p. 855

Chapter 6: Carol Ann Kelly

Curtis, Liz. *They Shoot Children: the Use of Rubber and Plastic Bullets in the North of Ireland*, London, Information on Ireland, 1987
Harker, Bob. *The Killing of Carol Ann Kelly*, Unpublished, July 1994
Holte, Joe. 'The Killing of Carol Ann Kelly', *Just News* 9(7/8), July August 1994, p. 6
Livingstone, Robin. Lecture at West Belfast Festival, August 1999; see http://www.serve.com/pfc/Robin.html
McKittrick, David et al., op. cit., pp. 864-865
United Campaign against Plastic Bullets, *A Report on the Misuse of the Baton Round in the North of Ireland: Submission to the Mitchell Commission on Arms Decommissioning*, Belfast, January 1997, pp. 30-31

Chapter 7: Nora McCabe

Broken Covenants, op. cit., p. 20
Committee on the Administration of Justice, *Plastic Bullets: a Briefing Paper*, Belfast, June 1998, p. 4
Faul, Denis and Murray, Raymond. *Rubber and Plastic Bullets Kill and Maim*, August 1981, pp. 33-34
Irish Information Partnership, *Agenda*, London, case A9108110
McKittrick, David et al., op. cit., pp. 870-871
United Campaign against Plastic Bullets, op. cit., pp. 29-30

Chapter 8: Shoot-to-kill, North Armagh

Asmal, Kadar, chair. *Shoot to Kill?*, Cork, Mercier Press, 1985, pp. 31-43, 90-93
Beirne, Maggie. 'Coroner Continues to Battle for Truth', *Just News*, 9(5), May 1994, p. 2
Campbell, Kate. 'The McKerr Inquest: Judicial Review', *Just News*, 7(7), July/August 1992, p. 7
Gallagher, Philomena (ed). *Troubles and Joys: an Anthology of Craigavon Women Writers*, 1992
Irish Information Partnership, Update 1987-1989, London, 1990, pp. 76-90
McKittrick, David et al., op. cit., pp. 920-921, 926, 929-930
Ní Aoláin, Fionnuala. 'Update', *Just News*, 7(6), June 1992, p. 3
O'Brien, Martin. 'Stalker Inquest and Appeal', *Just News*, 3(11), December 1988, p. 4
Stalker, John. *The Stalker Affair*, London, Penguin Books, 1989
Urban, Mark. *Big Boys' Rules: The SAS and the Secret Struggle against the IRA*, London, Faber and Faber, 1992, pp. 151-160

Chapter 9: John Downes

Irish Information Partnership, *Update 1987-1989*, London 1990, pp. 120- 122
McKittrick, David et al., op. cit., pp. 993-994
Sinn Féin Publicity Department, *The Slaying of John Downes*, Dublin, Republican Publications 1984
Springhill Community House, *The Best Documented Killing*, Belfast 1988
United Campaign Against Plastic Bullets, *A Report on the Misuse of the Baton Round in the North of Ireland, submission to the Mitchell Commission on Arms Decommissioning*, 1998

Chapter 10: Strabane shootings

Irish Information Partnership, *Update 1987-1989*, London 1990, pp. 143-156
McKittrick, David et al., op. cit., pp. 1010-1011
Murray, Raymond. *The SAS in Ireland*, Cork, Mercier Press 1990, pp. 333-348
O'Brien, Martin. 'Full Inquest Sought', *Just News* 3(5), May 1988, p. 3
Urban, Mark. *Big Boys' Rules: The SAS and the Secret Struggle against the IRA*, London, Faber and Faber 1992, pp. 196-205

Chapter 11: Patrick Kelly

Irish Information Partnership, *Update 1985-1989*, London 1990, pp. 175-191
Loughgall – A Case to be Answered, Dublin, Loughgall Truth and Justice Campaign, n.d.
Mageean, Paul. 'The Alphabet Killers', *Just News* 10(6), June 1995, p. 1
Murder on their Minds: British Government found Guilty of Premeditated Murder, Dublin, Loughgall Truth and Justice Campaign, n.d.
Murray, Raymond. *The SAS in Ireland*, Cork, Mercier Press 1990, pp. 376-396
Taylor, Peter. *Provos: the IRA and Sinn Féin*, London, Bloomsbury 1997, pp. 268-273
The Events of May 8th 1987, Dublin, Loughgall Truth and Justice Campaign, n.d.
Urban, Mark. *Big Boys' Rules: The SAS and the Secret Struggle against the IRA*, London, Faber and Faber, 1992, pp. 227-237

Chapter 12: Aidan McAnespie

A Place and a Name: Report of the Victims Commission, Dublin, Stationery Office, July 1999
Broken Covenants, op. cit., p. 19
Irish Information Partnership, *Update 1985-89*, London, 1990, pp. 192-209
McCabe, Eilish. 'The Shooting of Aidan McAnespie', in Raymond Murray, *State Violence in Northern Ireland 1969- 1997*, Cork, Mercier Press, 1998, pp.187-191
McKittrick, David et al., op. cit., pp. 1110-1111

Chapter 13: Gibraltar

Broken Covenants, op. cit., pp. 19-20
Farrell, Niall. 'The Gibraltar Murders', in Raymond Murray, *State Violence: Northern Ireland 1969- 1997*, Cork, Mercier Press 1998, pp. 191-204
Jack, Ian. 'Gibraltar', *Granta* 25, Autumn 1988, pp. 13-86
Mageean, Paul. 'Gibraltar Families Clear First European Hurdle', *Just News* 8(9), October 1993, p. 1
Mageean, Paul. 'The Final Court of Justice', *Just News* 10(10), October 1995, pp. 1-2
McKittrick, David et al., op. cit., pp. 1112-1116
Mitchell, Jack. *Gib: A Modest Exposure*, Dublin, Fulcrum Press 1990
Murray, Raymond. *The SAS in Ireland*, Dublin, Mercier Press 1990, pp. 396-437
Tomlinson, Mike. 'Gibraltar and beyond', *Statewatch*, September- October 1995, pp. 18-20
Third Party Intervention by British Irish Rights Watch, CAJ, Inquest and Liberty (NCCL), November 1994

Chapter 14: Pat Finucane

Amnesty International, *Political Killings in Northern Ireland*, London, 1994, pp. 23-34
Fegan, Arthur and Murray, Raymond. *Collusion 1990-1994: Loyalist Paramilitary Murders in the North of Ireland*, Belfast, Relatives for Justice, 1995
British Irish Rights Watch, *Justice Delayed: Alleged State Collusion in the Murder of Patrick Finucane and Others*, London, February 2000
Broken Covenants, op. cit., pp. 20-21
Lawyers' Committee for Human Rights, *Human Rights and Legal Defence in Northern Ireland: the Intimidation of Defence Lawyers, the Murder of Patrick Finucane*, New York, February 1993
McKittrick, David et al., op. cit., pp. 1159-1162
Moloney, Ed. 'The murder of Pat Finucane and how the RUC could have stopped i', *Sunday Tribune*, 27 June 1999
Murray, Raymond. *State Violence, Northern Ireland 1969- 1997*, Cork, Mercier Press, 1998, pp. 219-244

Chapter 15: Seamus Duffy

Barron, Sandy. 'No Prosecutions in Duffy Case', *Just News* 5(4), April 1990, p. 4
Barron, Sandy. 'Seamus Duffy Inquest', *Just News* 5(7), July/August 1990, p. 1
Irish Information Partnership, *Update 1985-1989*, London 1990, pp. 225- 230
McKittrick, David et al., op. cit., pp. 1175-1176

Chapter 16: Brian Robinson

Davies, Nicholas. *Ten-Thirty-Three: the inside story of Britain's killing machine in Northern Ireland*, Edinburgh, Mainstream Publishing, 1999
Irish Information Partnership, *Update 1985-1989*, London 1990, pp. 231-233
O'Connor, Maggs. 'Brian Robinson Inquest', *Just News* 7(6), June 1992, p. 1
McKittrick, David et al.. op. cit., pp. 1177-1178

Chapter 17: Peter Thompson

Dickson, Brice. 'The Whiterock Killings', *Just News* 5(2), February 1990, pp. 1-2
Broken Covenants, op. cit., p. 16
Gilmore, Anthony. 'Death Knell of the Inquest?', *Just News* 10(5), May 1995, p. 1
Irish Information Partnership, *Update 1985-1989*, London 1990, pp. 235-247
McKittrick, David et al., op. cit., p. 1191
Ní Aoláin, Fionnuala. 'Update', *Just News* 8(5), May 1993, p. 3
Pre-Inquest Statement on the Killings at Sean Graham's Bookmakers on the Falls Road in January 1990
Thompson, Joe. *Submission to the Independent Commission on Policing*, October 1998

Chapter 18: Fergal Caraher

Broken Covenants, op. cit., p. 17
Cullyhanna Justice Group and Irish National Congress, *Report of the Public Inquiry into the Killing of Fergal Caraher and the Wounding of Miceál Caraher, 30th December 1990*, 1991
Hutton, Lord Chief Justice. The Queen v. Richard Elkington and Andrew Michael Callaghan, December 1993

McEvoy, Kieran and Ritchie, Michael. 'Law of Legerdemain: Caraher family's fight for justice goes on', *Just News*, 9(1), January 1994, p. 1
McKittrick, David et al., op. cit., pp. 1221-1222
'Minimum Use of Force?', *Just News*, 5(11)/6(1), December 1990/January 1991, p. 1
Morrissey, Joe. 'Public Inquiry into Caraher Death at Cullyhanna', *Just News*, 6(7), July/August 1991, pp. 1-2

Chapter 19: Kevin McGovern

Broken Covenants, op. cit., pp. 18-19
McKittrick, David et al., op. cit, pp. 1250-1251
Wolfe, Martin. 'McGovern judgement disappointing', *Just News*, 9(2), February 1994, pp. 4-5

Chapter 20: Peter McBride

Greenslade, Roy. 'Give this family justice', *The Guardian*, 22 November 1999
Ní Aoláin, Fionnuala. 'Lethal Force and Accountability', *Just News* 7(9), October 1992, p. 5
Pat Finucane Centre, Derry, 'The murder of Peter McBride', http://www.serve.com.pfc
Ritchie, Michael. 'Peter McBride killed by British soldiers', *Just News* 7(8), September 1992, p. 6

Chapter 21: Pearse Jordan

Committee on the Administration of Justice, *Submission to the United Nations Special Rapporteur on Summary or Arbitrary Executions*, October 1993, pp. 1-7
McKittrick, David et al., op. cit., p. 1303
Ní Aoláin, Fionnuala. 'The Final Court of Justice (Again)', *Just News* 7(1), December 1992, p. 1
Ritchie, Michael. 'No Prosecution in Jordan Case', *Just News* 8(11), December 1993, p. 1
The Independent Commission on Policing for Northern Ireland, *A New Beginning: Policing in Northern Ireland* (Patten Report), HMSO, September 1999
The Patten Commission: A Submission by the People of West Belfast at Whiterock, November 1998, Upper Springfield Development Trust, 1999, pp. 17-20
Winter, Jane. 'An Overview of the Inquest System', *Just News* 11(7/8), July/August 1996, p. 2

Chapter 22: Diarmuid O'Neill

Diarmuid O'Neill Campaign website, http://go.to/justicedoneill
McKittrick, David et al., op. cit., p. 1399

Chapter 23: Robert Hamill

Hardy, Jeremy and O'Docherty, Malachi. 'Did this man have to die?' *Observer*, 21 February 1999
McKittrick, David et al., op. cit., pp. 1406-1407
Pat Finucane Centre, *First Report to the United Nations Special Rapporteur on Extra-judicial, Summary or Arbitrary Executions concerning the Death of Robert Hamill*, August 1997; see http://www.serve.com/pfc/hamill1.html
Pat Finucane Centre, *Second Report to the United Nations Special Rapporteur on Extra-judicial, Summary or Arbitrary Executions concerning the Death of Robert Hamill, May 1998*; see http://www.serve.com/pfc/hamill2.html
Robert Hamill Justice Campaign, *Justice for Robert Hamill*, Portadown, n.d.
Robert Hamill Justice Campaign website; http://www.bigwig.net/hamill
Testimony of Diane Hamill to the US Congress House International Relations Committee, 22 April 1999; http://www.serve.com/pfc/hamillusa.html

Chapter 24: Interview with Raymond Murray

Murray, Raymond. *The SAS in Ireland*, Cork, Mercier Press, 1990
Murray, Raymond. *Hard Time: Armagh Jail 1971-1986*, Cork, Mercier Press, 1998
Murray, Raymond. *State Violence: Northern Ireland 1969- 1997*, Cork, Mercier Press, 1998
Murray, Raymond and Faul, Denis. *British Army and Special Branch RUC Brutalities*, December 1971-February 1972, 1972

Chapter 26: Interview with Denis Faul

Campaign for Social Justice, *Northern Ireland: The Mailed Fist – A Record of Army and Policy Brutality from August 9 to November 9, 1971*, Dungannon, 1972
Faul, Denis and Murray, Raymond. *Whitelaw's Tribunals: Long Kesh Internment Camp, November 1972-February 1973*, 1973
Faul, Denis and Murray, Raymond. *The Birmingham Frame- up: Six Innocent Men Framed for the Birmingham Bombings*, 1977

INDEX

14th Intelligence Company x, 207, 215, 216, 220

Ad Hoc Committee on Ireland 289
Adams, Gerry 106, 171, 209, 215, 216, 252
Aer Lingus 165, 308
AfrI (Action for Ireland) 42
Ahern, Bertie 11, 21, 47, 138, 258
Alderdice, John 216
Allende, Isabel 325
Alliance Party 216, 221, 249, 282
Amnesty International 29, 83, 139, 159, 169, 187, 203, 293- 4, 305
An Crann/The Tree xv
Andrews, David 272, 281
Anglo-Irish, Agreement 122, 308; Secretariat 20
Annesley, Hugh (Chief Constable) 177, 178, 238
Arendt-Rojahn, Veronika 226
Argyll and Sutherland Highlanders 24
Armstrong, Robert 7
Army Board 243, 244, 249
Arthurs, Declan 130, 140
Arthurs, John 303
Askin, Patrick 32
Asmal, Kadar 296
Asquez, Kenneth 159, 163-5
Association for Legal Justice (ALJ) 98, 288, 291, 293-4, 299, 304
Atkinson, Constable 276
Austin, Joe 165

B-Specials ix, 188, 287, 303
Badger, The; see McCoy, John
Baker, Albert 306
Barrett, Danny 297
Barrett, Mr 297
Barrett, Seán 165
Basque separatists 167
Batten, Bruce 217
Battle of the Bogside 1
BBC 168, 217, 235, 240
Belfast Telegraph 66-7, 204, 300, 309
Bell, Martin 242, 246-7
Bennett Commission 305
Biaggio, Maria 289
Biko, Stephen vii, 323
Birmingham Six 15, 203, 247, 250, 270, 289, 307
Birmingham Frame-Up, The 307
Blair, Tony 6, 9, 14, 21, 188, 278, 309, 322
Blanket protest 22, 157, 295
Bloody Friday bombings xv
Bloody Sunday ix, xi, 1-22, 39-40, 41, 43, 171, 186, 195, 270, 310, 316, 320, 321, 322, 323, 324; commemoration 10, 15-6; Initiative 186; Justice Campaign 5, 9, 40, 41, 186, 319
Bloomfield, Kenneth xii, xiii, 196, 223, 323
Bobby Sands Youth Movement 218
Boer, Keith 151
Bolster, Doctor 238
Bookmaker's shop killings 207-24, 312, 313, 318
Border Roads Campaign 153-4
Borza family: Claudio 36; Savina 36, 38-9; Vittorio 36

Boston Herald 283
Boyle, Harris 34
Bradley, Brendan 224
Bradley, Josephine 31
Bradshaw, George 32
Brady, Father (Brian) 289, 290, 304, 305, 307
Brady, Kevin (Caoimhin Mac Bradaigh) 156, 166, 167
Brannigan, David (Constable) 89, 101
Brecht, Berthold 322
Breglio, Robert 6, 43
Brehon Law Society 187
Brennan, Ronnie 201, 205
Breslin, Charles 115, 116, 117, 119-27, 312, 313, 314, 315
Breslin family: Corina 119-127, 312; Joseph (junior) 119, 120, 122; Linda 120, 123, 314; Marie 123; Mr (Joseph senior) 119, 120, 121, 122, 124, 125, 127, 128; Mrs 119, 121, 122, 123
Bridgett, Stacey 26, 281
Brighton bombing 308
British Airways 165
British army: collusion with loyalists 24-5, 26, 34-5, 41-2, 53- 4, 176-8, 188; harassment of victims/campaigners 72-3, 227, 246, 256; killings ix, x-xi, xvi, 2-4, 8-9, 19, 24, 55-6, 58-9, 65, 66, 67, 68, 115-7, 119, 130, 135, 137-8, 143, 151, 152- 3, 155, 162-4, 199, 200, 202, 204, 208-9, 210-1, 212, 216, 220, 225, 231, 241, 242, 245-6, 259, 294, 295, 311, 313, 315, 320; members charged with murder 24, 144, 145, 148, 226, 242-4, 250, 318; members charged with other offences 56-8, 59-60
British Army and Special Branch RUC Brutalities 288
British army bases, Forkhill 49; Fort Monagh 292; Girdwood 242, 288; Holywood/Palace Barracks 288, 303
British Information Services 3, 4
British Irish Rights Watch 6, 18, 29, 52, 139, 178, 187, 272
British Military Intelligence x, 27, 34, 35, 41, 53, 155, 157, 168, 176, 186, 188, 199, 207, 209, 215, 216, 220, 230-1, 232
Brooke, Peter 189, 209, 210, 216, 220
Brown, James 55, 57, 58, 59, 60, 61, 62, 63
Brown, Mark 190, 194
Bruton, John 20, 258
Buchanan, Sergeant 120
Bullock, Stephen 162, 163
Bunn, Detective Chief Superintendent 264
Burke, Tracey 68
Burns, James 291, 299
Burns, Sean 87, 91, 92, 93, 95, 97, 98, 101, 318
Burton, John (Doctor) 265, 269
Buswell's Hotel, Dublin 46, 52, 170, 218
Butler, Marie 31
Buzzard, Stephen (Lance Corporal) 56, 57, 59, 60
Byrne, Ann 31

Byrne, Gay 4, 173
Byrne, John (Sergeant) 24
Byrne, Pat (Garda Commissioner) 42
Byrne, Seamus 52

Cadwallader, Ann 272
Cahill, Thomas 57, 62
Calamati, Silvia 36
Callaghan, Andrew 25, 226
Cameron Commission (South Africa) 221
Campaign for Social Justice 285
Campaign for the Right to Truth 221, 319
Campbell, Justice 201
Campbell, Thomas 32
Canary Wharf bombing 267
Canning, Jim 304
Caraher family: Brendan 227, 231, 232; Margaret 227-32, 316, 320, 321-2, 325; Micheál 225, 226, 227; Peter John 148, 229
Caraher, Fergal 148, 218, 225-32, 318, 320, 325
Carroll family: Mrs 102-5; Tommy 102-5, 313
Carroll, Roddy 87, 88, 91, 92, 102-5, 291, 313
Carson, Derek 200
Carson, Doctor 152
Carswell, Justice 93, 108, 118, 212, 253
Carver, Michael (General) 8
Casalattico 36, 38, 42-3
Casey, Eamonn (Bishop) 173
Cassidy, Seamus 191
Castlereagh Holding Centre 176, 184, 222, 290, 294
Channel 4 19, 20, 235, 240
Chestnut, Iain (Lieutenant Corporal) 24
Chetrit, Simone 31, 42
Chile, Truth Commission 323, 325
Civil rights movement 1, 96, 286
Clarke, Christopher 8, 9
Clarke, Sarah (Sister) 307
Clegg, Lee xvi, 222, 242, 246, 249
Clements, Dave 224
Clements, William (Reserve Constable) 129
Clinton, Bill 243, 247, 258
Close, Seamus 221, 222
Claudy bombing xv
Collins, Frank 124, 125, 128
Collins, Gerry 145
Collins, Steve 269
Comiskey, Nora 40
Committee on International Relations (US) 291
Committee on the Administration of Justice (CAJ) 18, 131, 137, 139, 171, 187, 203, 217, 221, 235, 238, 240, 252
Communist Party of Ireland 169
Congress (US) 11, 111, 249, 277, 289, 291
Conlon, Guiseppe 307-8; Mrs (Sarah) 308
Connett, Reserve Constable 276
Connolly House 106, 108
Constitutional Convention 305
Convery, Mrs 68

Conway, Cardinal (William) 288, 305
Cooney, John 32
Corrigan, Owen (Detective Sergeant) 46
Courtey, John (Chief Superintendent) 47, 53
Cosgrave, Liam 33
Cost of the Troubles Study x, xv, 224
Council of Europe 173
'Counterpoint' 238, 240
Covert Methods of Entry Team (CME) 177
Craig, Bill 32
Craig, Colin 200
Crane, Jack (Professor) 132
Croarkin, Thomas 32
Crossan, Declan 115-6
Crowley, Eugene (Garda Deputy Commissioner) 145
Crowley, Joe (Congressman) 43
Crown Prosecution Service 263-4, 274
Crutchley, James (Chief Superintendent) 76, 77, 79-80, 83, 295, 296
CS gas 2, 77, 259, 262, 264, 267, 268
Cullyhanna Justice Campaign 226, 227, 228-9
Cumaraswamy, Param Data 181, 222
Cummings, Kenneth 140
Cuomo, Kerry Kennedy 11
Curran, Brendan 101
Curran, Gerry 87
Currie, Austin 144, 145, 304
Curry, Inspector 27

D Notice 304
Dáil 32
Daily Express 161
Daily Mail 6-7, 242, 243, 248
Daily Mirror 126, 262
Daily Telegraph 248
Dalgaard, Jorgen (Professor) 57-8, 61, 63
Daly, Cahal (Bishop, later Cardinal) 173, 200, 216, 234, 308
Daly, Edward (Father, later Bishop) 4, 56
Daly, Miriam 308
Dargle, John 31
Davies, Nicholas 199
'Deadly Intelligence' 187-8
'Death on the Rock' 158, 159, 162, 219
Death on the Streets 60
Democratic Unionist Party (DUP) 130, 133, 203
Dempsey, Concepta 31
Department of Foreign Affairs 140, 170
Department of Justice 50
Derry City Council 17, 18, 20
Devenney, Samuel 287
Devine, David 115, 116, 120, 127-8, 311, 313, 315
Devine family: Antoinette 127, 128; Billy 122, 127-8; Cathy 127, 128; Sheila 127; Mrs 27, 128
Devine, Michael 115, 116, 119, 120, 127-8, 311, 313, 315
Devlin, Bernadette 2, 13, 308
Dickson, Mark (Private) 220
Diplock, Lord 317
Director of Public Prosecutions 46, 47, 58, 76, 77, 81, 90, 91, 99, 116,

130, 140, 144, 148, 179, 180, 181, 190, 213, 219, 239, 277, 282, 291, 295, 317
'Dirty War, The' 178
Disabled Police Officers Association xv
DMSU (District Mobile Support Unit) 220, 252
Doherty, Kieran 156
Doherty, Patrick 2, 4, 5, 7, 9
Doherty, Tony 9, 15-22, 320, 322
Donaghey, Gerard 2, 5, 7
Donaldson, Andrew (Justice) 116
Donegan, Michael 46, 47-54
Donlon, Sean 289
Donnelly, Seamus 130, 132, 136-7
Dorfmann, Ariel 309
Douglas, Thomas 32
Downes family: Brenda 83, 84, 108-14, 319; Claire 113; Gerard 111
Downes, John xi, 82, 106-14, 191, 197, 318
Downtown Radio 149
Drumcree 84, 111, 308
Dublin-Monaghan bombings xv, 31-44, 171, 222, 324
Duddy, Jackie 2, 4, 5, 7, 9, 10-1, 12, 14, 316
Duddy, Kay 9, 10-4, 310, 316-7, 321
Dudonis, Ken 43
Duffy, Henry 67, 75
Duffy family: Brendan (junior) 192, 193-4; Brendan (senior) 189, 190, 194; Bronagh 193; Kathleen 84, 191-8, 321
Duffy, Seamus 189-98, 312, 314, 321
Duffy, Thomas 32
Dundalk Democrat 48
Dunseith, Derek 13

Elkington, Richard 225, 226
Elliott, James 67, 68, 70, 76, 93, 99, 190
Elliott, Robert 115
Ellis, John 45, 50
Emergency Provisions Act (EPA) 123
English family: Charles 64; Michael 57, 58-64, 315
English, Gary 55-64, 315, 318
Enniskillen bombing xv, xvi, 168, 171, 179
Entwhistle, Superintendent 76, 80, 81
ETA 165
Ethnic cleansing xiii
European Commission on Human Rights 161, 172, 305
European Convention on Human Rights 95, 133, 161, 172, 173, 254, 320
European Court of Human Rights 73, 83, 85, 95, 118, 132, 133, 137, 161, 169, 172, 231, 254, 257-8, 267, 305, 316, 320
European Parliament 83, 249
Eversheds (solicitors) 12, 13

Fahey, John 124, 125-6, 128, 184
Fair Employment Agency 301
Falls Road curfew 286
Families Acting for Innocent Relatives (FAIR) xv, 133
Families Against Intimidation and Terror xv
Farrell, Mairead xi, xiii, 155-74, 176, 291, 314, 315-6, 321

Farrell, Niall 158, 162-74, 218, 291, 321
Faul, Denis (Father) xvii, 69, 65, 131, 288, 189, 297, 298, 303-8
Faulkner, Brian 8, 32, 183
Fay, Marie-Therese x
Fay, Patrick 31
Feeney, Brian 195
Fegan, Arthur x, 223, 291
Fermanagh Herald 240
Fermanagh Partnership 29
Fianna Fáil 33, 138, 221
Fine Gael 20, 32, 47-8, 49, 165, 221
Finucane family: Dermot 175, 182, 185-6; Geraldine 175, 185; John 177, 183; Martin 153, 171, 181-8, 221, 222, 291; Michael 222; Mrs 185; Seamus 166, 175-6, 183, 185, 314
Finucane, Pat xi, xvii, 79, 81, 93, 94, 95, 99-100, 101, 110, 111, 175-88, 222, 291, 295, 299, 324
'First Tuesday' 77, 81
Fish, Hamilton 289
Fisher, Jim 242, 243, 244, 245
Fitzgerald, Elizabeth 31
Flanagan, Ronnie (Chief Constable) 290
Forbes, Dean 276
'Force, The' 235, 240
Ford, Robert (General) 8
Foreign Office 156
Forster Green mortuary 193, 245
Forum for Peace and Reconciliation 221
Four Square laundry 306
Fox, Tommy 47, 48
Fraser, William 133
Free Derry Corner 1, 2, 13
'Friendly Forces' 34
FRU (Force Research Unit) 176-7, 178, 181
Funerals 11, 26, 36, 38, 45, 49, 56, 78, 97, 98, 102, 115, 121-2, 145, 156, 166, 200, 227, 246, 252, 315-6

GAA (Gaelic Athletic Association) 23, 27, 143, 152, 283
Gabriel, Peter vii
Gallagher, John 287, 290, 303
Galvin, Martin 106, 107, 110, 114
Gannon, Sergeant 49
Garda Siochana (Gardai) 33, 34, 35, 37, 41-2, 45-6, 47, 48, 49, 50, 51, 52, 53, 145, 146-7, 150, 156, 165; Special Branch 33, 54, 146, 165
Garrett, Brian 189
Gartner, Joelle 5
Garvey, Ned (Garda Commissioner) 34
Gib: A Modest Proposal 158
Gibraltar killings xi, 155-74, 176, 205, 209, 218, 267, 311, 312, 318, 320
Gibson, Cecily 90, 130: Maurice (Lord Chief Justice) 90, 101, 105, 130, 303, 318
Gibson, Terry 27
Gifford, Tony 56, 60
Gillen, Mrs 185
Gilliland, George (Constable) 129
Gilman, Ben 44, 289, 291
Gilmore, Hugh 2, 7

Girvan, Gregory 275, 276; Joanne 275
GMTV 246
Golden, Father 193
Good Friday Agreement xii, xv, 22, 132, 141, 243, 247, 323
Good Guys Wear Black, The 269
Gonzales (Spanish Prime Minister) 167
Gormley, Michael 130
Gough Barracks 18, 103, 184, 233
GPA (airline) 165
Grace, Bernadette 31
Greater London Council (GLC) 82
Greater London Radio 273
Greater Manchester Police 91, 94; Committee 92
Gregory, Tony 170
Green, John 34, 96
Green, Mary 95, 96-7, 98, 99, 100-2
Grenadier Guards 144
Grew, Seamus 87, 88, 91, 92, 102-3, 291
Grover, Suresh 272
Groves, Emma 85, 111, 112, 195, 294, 298
Guatemala 221, 322
Guardian 272, 283
Guildford Four 15, 250, 270, 307
Gunn, Helena 42

H-Block Committee 301
Hailsham, Lord 7, 19
Hale, Edward 207, 208, 209, 210, 211, 213, 215, 220
Hamill family: Diane 250, 272, 277, 278-84, 315, 321; John 278; Mr 279, 280, 283; Mrs 278
Hamill, Robert xi, 250, 272, 275-84 315, 321
Hamilton, Justice 35
Hamilton, Paul 89
Hamilton, Sally 205; Stephen 201, 205
Hanley, Timothy (Constable) 234, 235, 238, 240
Hanna, William 34
Hanvey, Allistair 276, 281
Harbinson, John 45, 48, 125, 145, 150, 151, 152
Hard Time: Armagh Jail 1971-1986 291, 292
Hardy, Jeremy 283
Harker, Bob 73
Harney, Mary 11
Harper, Archibald 32
Harrison, Shane 217
Hart, Justice 180
Hartley, Tom 86
Hassard, Jack 305
Homes United by Ruthless Terror (HURT) xv
Hooded men 287, 292
Hathaway, Stanley (Staff Sergeant) 24
Haughey, Charles 71, 152, 165, 170, 171, 308
Heath, Edward 7, 8, 14, 19, 321
Hegarty, Nigel 107, 110, 112, 114
Hello magazine 271
Helsinki Watch 29, 83, 220
Henderson, Doug 178, 243, 248
Hermon, John (Chief Constable) 66, 80, 91, 92, 94, 104, 137, 180-1, 306
Heseltine, Michael 114, 161, 173
Hibernian Civil Rights Coalition 132

'Hidden Hand: the Forgotten Massacre' 33
Hierarchy of victims xiii-xiv
Higgins, Michael D. 170
Hill, Charlie 80, 81, 300
HMSU (Headquarters Mobile Support Unit) 87, 88, 89, 90, 91, 117
Hobson, Mark 276-7, 281, 282
Hogg, Douglas 176, 180, 181, 184
Holden, David (Private) 144, 145, 152
Holland, Mary 131
Holroyd, Fred 34, 41, 306
Home Office 176, 262, 274
Hoskings, Paul 46, 50
Hospitals, Altnagelvin 10, 55-6; Charing Cross 262, 268; Craigavon 279; Daisy Hill 225; Mater 192, 288; Royal Victoria 65, 75, 77-8, 80, 107, 109, 225, 251
House of Lords 93-4, 100, 101, 118, 126, 128, 242, 247, 253, 257
Howe, Geoffrey 157
Howes, David (Corporal) 156
Hoyt, William 6
HQ 39 Infantry Brigade 131, 135
Hughes family: Anthony 130, 131, 133, 135, 138, 139, 140; Brigid 131, 139; Oliver 130, 131, 135-6, 138, 139
Human Rights Watch 187
Hume, John 17, 18, 20, 77
Hunger strike 55, 63, 65, 67, 75, 96, 156, 175, 288, 295, 298, 304, 308
Hunter, Gerard 307; Mrs 307
Hurd, Douglas 77, 307, 309
Hutton, Brian (Justice) 56, 108, 118, 226

Independent 173, 181
Independent Commission for Police Complaints (ICPC) 189-90, 234, 238, 252, 258-9
Ingram, Adam xii, 133, 140, 141, 142, 224
INLA 87, 88, 89, 200
Inquests 4, 25, 27, 48-9, 61-3, 67, 70, 75-6, 79-80, 81, 87, 93, 99-100, 101, 102, 103, 111, 116-8, 122, 124-6, 128, 131- 2, 134-5, 136, 137, 145, 152, 155-6, 159-61, 163-4, 167-9, 172, 190, 194, 200, 204, 210-212, 219-220, 231, 252-3, 255, 256-7, 264, 274, 295, 297, 312, 318-20
INQUEST 159
'Insight' 283
International Association of Democratic Lawyers 159
Internment 1, 183, 189, 206, 287-8, 293, 303-5, 317; commemoration 106, 108-9, 190
IRA, members killed ix, 23, 24, 29, 87, 89, 95, 115, 116, 118, 129-31, 133, 134-5, 137-8, 139, 155-60, 165, 174, 191, 201, 202, 224, 251-9, 261-5, 266-8; operations xv, xvi, 67, 91, 115, 116, 129-31, 155-60, 223, 224, 233, 236, 306309
Ireland on Sunday 272
Irish Council for Civil Liberties (ICCL) 52, 139
Irish Echo 43
Irish Independence Party 56
Irish National Caucus 289

Irish National Congress 226, 227, 228-9
Irish News 217, 280, 282, 305
Irish Post 261, 265
Irish Press 116, 123, 306
Irish Times 131, 170, 295
Irish Voice 43
ITV 52

Jack, Ian 160
Jackal, The; see Jackson, Robin
Jackson, Robin (The Jackal) 34, 54, 308
Jewish Weekly 43
Johnston, John 2
Joint Intelligence Committee 157, 181
Jones, Justice 317-8
Jordan family: Hugh 252, 254-60, 319, 320; Teresa 252, 254- 60
Jordan, Pearse xii, 95, 133, 251-60, 314, 318
Joyriders xvi, 207, 209, 215
Justice for All 201, 203, 319
Justice for Diarmuid O'Neill Campaign 262, 264, 266, 270, 271-2, 274
Justice for the Forgotten 34-5, 36

Kairos xv
Kearney, Brendan 62
Kee, Robert 173
Kelly, Carol Ann xii, 65-74, 295, 297, 298, 311, 314, 321
Kelly, Charles (Chief Constable) 93
Kelly, Eugene 130
Kelly family: Eileen (junior) 68-74, 298, 321; Mrs (Eileen senior) 67, 68, 297
Kelly, Gerry 281-2
Kelly, Justice 242
Kelly, Mairead 132, 133-42, 321
Kelly, Michael 2
Kelly, Mr 121
Kelly, Oliver 67
Kelly, Paddy 288
Kelly, Patrick 95, 129-42, 316, 321
Kelly, Patrick 261, 262, 268, 269
Kelly, Roisin 139
Kennedy, Helena 61, 62
Kennedy, Hugh 62
Kennedy, Ludovic 242, 246, 247
Kennedy, Teddy 11
Kenny, Pat 173
Kerr, Justice 132, 243, 244
King, Tom 93, 130, 143, 178
Komac, Ed 43
Korff, Douwe 171, 172
Kosovo 235, 240, 244

La Mon bombing xvi
La Rue, Frank 221
Labour Committee on Ireland 82
Lambert, Aidan 179, 180
Law Society, of Northern Ireland 181; of Republic of Ireland 181; of England and Wales 178, 181
Lawrence, Doreen 250
Lawrence, Stephen 123, 253, 274, 282, 312
Lawyers' Alliance 187
Lawyers' Committee for Human Rights 181, 187
Leckey, James 94-5, 104, 200, 210, 219, 252, 253

Lenihan, Brian 152
Leonard family: Betty 23, 25, 26; Barry 23; Ciaran 23, 25- 30, 316, 320; Desmond 24; Hugh 23, 26;
Leonard, Louis 23-30, 311, 312
Liberty/NCCL 5, 19, 159
Little, Tommy 176
Livingstone family: Archie 72, 195; Robin 66
Livingstone, Julie 65,66, 72, 75, 293
Livingstone, Ken 82
Londonderry Victim Support xv
Loughgall killings 95, 129-31, 133, 140, 203, 224, 254, 313, 316, 318, 321
Loughgall Truth and Justice Campaign 132-3, 137-8
Loughry Agricultural College 233, 235
Loyalist Volunteer Force (LVF) 276
Ludlow family: Kevin 48, 49, 51, 54; Paddy 48
Ludlow, Seamus xi, 45-54, 314, 324
Lunt, Wayne 276
Lynagh, James 130, 134
Lynch, Denis 139
Lynch, Jack 33
Lynch, Loretta 23-30

Mac Aonghusa, Prionsais 170
Macpherson Report 253
Madden and Finucane (solicitors) 12, 183-4
Madden, Peter 183, 184, 218, 221, 222
Mageean, Paul 131-2
Maginn, Loughlin 177, 201, 202
Maginnis, Ken 180, 209, 216, 281
Magliocco family: Anna 36-8, 42-3, 315; Corrado 37, 38; Marinella 38; Mario 36, 37, 38; Tommassino 36, 38, 39
Magliocco, Antonio 31, 36-9, 42-3, 315
Maguire, Annie 307
Maguire, Frank 28
Mailed Fist, The 304
Major, John 12, 17, 18, 220, 222, 258
Mallie, Eamon 149
Mallon, Seamus 130-1, 184
Mambo 46, 47, 51
Mansfield, Michael 61, 62, 226, 264, 274, 282
Marchant, William 34
Marley, Larry 166
Marren, Ann 31
Marshall, Sam xvi, 298
Marshall, Tom (Professor) 57, 60, 61, 62, 63, 89, 116, 125
Massey, Anna 32
Maudling, Reginald 2
Mawhinney, Brian 209
Mayhew, Patrick 92, 104, 222, 252
Maynard, Joan 77
McAleese, Mary 36
McAnespie, Aidan 143-54, 283 , 315, 316, 318
McAnespie family: Mr 148; Mrs 148
McArt, Frank 303
McAtamney, Michael (Deputy Chief Constable) 89, 103
McAteer, Fergus 56
McBride, Henry 103-4
McBride, Jean 243, 244-8, 250, 315

McBride, Peter xi, xii, 241-50, 315, 318, 319, 320
McCabe, Eilish 146-54, 222, 224, 315, 316; Paul 146, 147
McCabe family: Áine 79, 296; Jim (senior) 77-84, 110, 111, 195, 295, 315, 316, 319, 320, 322; Jim (junior) 78, 79
McCabe, Nora 75-86, 110, 295, 314, 315, 316, 320
McCaffrey, Patrick 234
McCann, Daniel 155, 157, 159, 160, 162, 163, 164, 166, 169, 172, 315-6
McCann, Eamonn 5, 7, 16
McCarthy, James 201
McCartney, Robert 195
McCaughey, Sergeant (William) 305-6
McCauley, Martin 87, 90-1
McClean, Raymond (Doctor) 6
McCloskey, Father 120, 127, 128
McCloy, Alan 89
McCluskey, Conn (Doctor) 285, 304; Patricia 285
McCollum, Mr (later Justice) 57, 132, 136, 277
McConnell, Brian 133
McCorrigale, Rosie 121
McCoy, John 34, 41
McCracken, Kevin 156, 165
McCreesh, Raymond 65
McCrory, Damien 115, 116
McCullough, David 199, 201, 202, 204, 205
McDaid, Michael 2, 5
McDermott, Sean 156
McDonald, Henry xv
McDonnell, Joe 75, 76
McErlean, Thomas 156, 166
McElhinney, Kevin 2, 5, 7
McElwaine, Seamus 125
McGeever, Jenny 166
McGlinchey, Dominic 88
McGonnell, Anthony 147
McGovern family: Deirdre 240; Mr 240; Mrs 236; Pat 237; Sean 235-40, 313, 314
McGovern, Kevin xii, 233-40, 311, 313, 314
McGrady, Eddie 234
McGrady, Fionnuala 234
McGrory, Barra 172
McGrory, Paddy 156, 158, 159, 160, 168, 169, 171, 172, 205, 305
McGuigan, Bernard 2, 4, 5, 7
McGuinness, Martin 20, 166
McHugh, Brian 261, 262, 266, 267, 268
McKearney, Patrick 130; Mrs 148
McKee, Billy 303
McKenna, Mary 32
McKenna, Patricia 249
McKenna, Patrick 199, 200, 201, 203
McKerr family: Damian 96; David 95, 96, 97, 100; Eleanor 93, 94, 95-100, 104, 105, 171, 313, 314, 316; Jonathan 95, 96, 97, 100
McKerr, Gervaise xii, 87, 91, 92, 93, 95-102, 133, 134, 145, 175, 254, 313, 314, 316, 318
McKinney, Ciaran 192
McKinney, Gerald 2, 7
McKinney, Michael 7, 12
McKinney, William 2, 5, 7

McKittrick, David ix, 200, 201
McLaughlin, Alec 298
McLaughlin, Detective Inspector 131, 135
McLernon, Roger 145
McLoftus, Doctor 152
McManus, Seán (Father) 289
McNally, Patrick 287
McNamara, Kevin 216, 283
McNeill, John 207, 208, 209, 211, 212, 213, 220
McShane, Dermot ix
McVeigh, Columba 306
McWilliams, Monica 283
Media coverage of state killings and campaigns xii, xiii-xiv, 6-7, 33-4, 46, 48, 51, 52, 66-7, 73, 76, 77, 107, 10, 126, 140, 141, 142, 148, 150, 151, 152, 157, 158, 159, 161, 162, 163, 166, 217, 219, 228, 229, 237-8, 240, 242-3, 247, 250, 252, 262, 272, 280
Meek, Inspector 217-8
Mehaffey, Bishop 60
Metropolitan Police, London ix, 165, 262, 262, 263, 264, 266- 7, 269, 270, 272, 273, 319
MI5 91, 92, 157, 181, 261, 267
MI6 33, 41, 157, 261
Miami Showband 34
Miller, Billy 201, 205, 206
Ministry of Defence (MOD) 6, 9, 62, 116, 117, 118, 135, 158, 169, 210, 211, 219, 243, 244, 248, 249, 252, 257, 296, 300, 312, 318
Mitchell, Senator (George) 291
Mitchell, Jack 158
Molloy, Inspector 217-8
Molloy, Jim (Chief Superintendent) 46
Moloney, Ed 46, 51, 179, 180
Molyneaux, James 130
Montgomery, Mr 125
Montgomery, William (Sergeant) 89, 101
Mooney, Detective 305
Mooney, Jean 76, 80
Moore, Chris 216
Moorhouse, Peter 273
Mordue, Robyn 163
Moriarty, Gerry 123-4, 126
'Morning Ireland' 166, 173
Morris, Dorothy 32
Morton, Bobby 206
Mowlam, Mo 12, 21, 105, 243, 247-8, 258, 281
Mulholland, Neil 179, 180
Mullan, Don 4-5, 6, 11, 12, 19, 20, 39-44
Mullan, Rita 289
Mulligan, Patrick (Garda Commissioner) 51
Murphy, Donal 305
Murphy, Father (Hugh) 306
Murphy, James 26
Murphy, Jim 25, 28
Murphy, Ted (Chief Superintendent) 46, 51
Murray, Andrew 24, 27, 28
Murray, Ann 288, 294, 305
Murray, Frances 288, 305
Murray, John 156, 166
Murray, Raymond (Father) x, xvii, 52, 59, 66, 105, 170, 171, 218, 220,

221, 222, 224, 285-92, 298, 304, 305, 307

Naan, Michael 24, 27, 28
Nairac, Robert (Captain) 24, 25, 34, 54, 306
NCCL; see Liberty
Nash, William 2, 5
Neill, Alan (Constable) 276-7
Nelson, Brian 176-7, 178, 186
Nelson, Rosemary 186, 272, 278, 280
New Statesman 107
News Letter 66
'Newsnight' 247
Ní Aoláin, Fionnuala x-xi, 311
Nicholson, Justice 94, 234, 235
Noraid (Irish Northern Aid) 106, 289
Norris, David 139
Northern Ireland Bar Association 62
Northern Ireland Civil Rights Association (NICRA) 1, 5, 169
Northern Ireland Electricity Service 301
Northern Ireland Human Rights Commission 253-4, 323
Northern Ireland Office 147, 157, 180, 209
Northern Ireland Policy Authority 93, 305
Northern Ireland Terrorist Victims Support xv

Ó Caoláin, Caoimhghín 138, 272
Ó Cuaig, Seosamh 170
Ó Cuiv, Eamon 138, 170
Ó Fiaich, Cardinal (Tomas) 144, 145, 152, 186, 308
O'Brien family: Anna 31; Anne Marie 31; Jacqueline 31; John 31
Observer xv, 160, 272, 325
O'Callaghan, Brendan 299
O'Callaghan, C.G. (Superintendent) 27
O'Callaghan, Gerard 130, 140
O'Connor, Paul 52, 244, 247, 248-50
O'Doherty, Colette 32
O'Doherty, Ronnie 57, 62, 116
O'Donnell, Michael 52
Offences Against the State (Amendment) Act (1972) 32
Official Secrets Act 89, 990
Officer Kilo 262, 263, 264-5, 268, 268, 273
O'Hara, Patsy 65
O'Hare, Billy 77
O'Hare, Paschal 305
O'Loughlin, Christina 32
Omagh bombing 41, 85
O'Neill, Brenda 170
O'Neill, Diarmuid ix, 173, 261-74, 319
O'Neill, Edward 32
O'Neill family: Eoghan 261, 265; Shane 262, 266, 267
O'Neill, Greg 35
O'Neill, Hubert (Major) 4
Operation Tinnitus 261
O'Reilly, Mr 57
Owen, Nora 35
Oxford Island bombing 89, 91

Pace University Law School 132
Paisley, Ian 195
'Panorama' 126, 178

Parachute Regiment/paratroopers xvi, 1, 7, 8, 13, 242
Pat Finucane Centre 10, 19, 52, 186, 187, 244
Patten Commission 84, 114, 196, 253, 255, 258, 283-4, 291, 323
Payne, Donald 111
Peace and Reconciliation Fund 222
Peake, Martin xvi
Percival, Robin 16
Pervost, Jean Guy 76
Phelan, Marie 32
Phillippou, Paul 266-74
Phillips, Danny 47
Phillips, Michael 262, 266
Pierce, Gareth 203, 271, 274
Pinochet, General 173, 321, 323
Pizzarello, Felix 159, 161
Plain Truth, The 285
Plastic and rubber bullets x, xi, xiv, xvi, 2, 65, 66, 67, 69, 70, 71, 72, 73, 74, 75, 76, 77, 78, 79, 80, 81, 84, 85, 86, 106-14, 189, 190, 191, 192, 194, 195, 196, 197, 248, 288, 289, 291, 295, 296-8
'Plastic Bullets: the Deadly Truth' 86
Plouffe, Jean Pierre 76
Police and Criminal Evidence Act 190
Police Complaints Authority 273
Police Federation 90
Porter, James 8
Press, John (Doctor) 190
Prevention of Terrorism Act 72, 180, 184, 307
'Primetime' 34
Prior, James 301
Prisoner releases 141, 243, 247
Prisons, Armagh 156, 285, 292, 304; Albany 306; Crumlin Road 288, 298, 306; Long Kesh 103, 156, 175, 183, 288, 304; Maidstone 304; Maze 279; Portlaoise 185-6
Proetta, Carmen 158, 159, 162, 163
Progressive Unionist Party 201
Pryor, David 165
Public Interest Immunity Certificates 94, 104, 136, 159, 168, 169, 210, 211, 219, 252
Public Record Office, London 6, 7, 18

Queen's First Regiment 220
Queen's University, Belfast 113, 156, 240
Quick Reaction Force 117, 120
Quinn, Sean 89

Radio Four 7
Radio Ulster 216
RAF ix
Reagan, Ronald 291
Red Hand Commando 46, 51
Reel, Ricky 272
Reese, Captain 24, 25, 26
Reilly, Clara xvii, 82, 84, 110, 195, 288, 293-302, 305
Reilly, Karen xvi, 242, 246, 259
Reilly, Terry 300-1
Reilly, Thomas 'Kidso' 144, 242, 259
Relatives for Justice vii, viii, 86, 153, 171, 187, 195, 213, 218- 9, 220, 222-3, 231, 258, 291, 319
Restorick, Rita 14
Reynolds, Albert 258
Rice, Siobhan 32
Rice, Tom 26

Rifkind, Malcolm 219, 252
Ritchie, Mike 18, 20, 217
RM Distribution 6
Robert Hamill Justice Fund 282
Robertson, George 6, 243
Robinson family: Alberta 203, 205; Margaret 200
Robinson, Brian xvi, 199-206, 209, 311, 314, 319
Robinson, Frederick (Constable) 89, 101
Robinson, John (Constable) 88, 89, 91, 103
Robinson, Mary 11, 85, 171
Robinson, Mrs 69
Roche, Dick 138
Rogers, Brid 281
Rogers, Henry 131, 134
Rooney, Cornelius vii
Rooney, Patrick vii, viii
Rosenthall hearings 305
Royal Anglian Regiment 6, 8
Royal Marines 225, 226
RTE (Radio Telefís Éireann) 34, 52, 166, 173, 288-9
Ruane, Caitriona 228
RUC (Royal Ulster Constabulary) collusion with loyalists 27, 29, 33, 41, 44, 47, 52, 133, 167, 176, 177, 178-9, 181, 184, 188, 200, 254, 291, 296; harassment of victims/campaigners 18, 102, 112-3, 117, 121-3, 128, 131, 149-50, 156, 166, 192, 193-4, 206, 218, 227, 236-7, 255, 256, 283, 313-5; investigation of state killings 23, 26, 28, 46, 50, 53, 77, 92, 104, 125, 140, 149, 189-90, 195, 196, 217, 220, 226, 227-8, 234, 238, 241, 242, 252, 311-3; killings vii, ix, x, 75-6, 77, 78, 79-80, 81, 83, 87, 88-91, 102-3, 105, 107, 109, 126, 129-30, 135, 137, 189, 190, 194, 198, 201, 205-6, 233-5, 236, 238, 251, 254-5, 257, 293-4, 303-4, 306, 311-2, 313; members charged with murder/manslaughter 89-90, 101, 103, 107-8, 109, 110, 114, 234-5, 238, 318; raids on relatives 97, 100, 119, 120, 127, 214, 313; reform/disbandment of 196, 240, 258, 290-300; Special Branch 18, 46-7, 50, 53, 88-9, 90, 91, 92, 176, 177-8, 179, 180, 215, 255, 288
RUC stations, Andersonstown 110, 166, 220, 254; Ballygawley 129; Birches 129; Carrickfergus 177, 181; Cookstown 236; Loughgall 134, 135, 137-8; Oldpark 193; Rosemount 55; Springfield Road 86, 297-8; Tennent Street 204; Woodburn 70, 311
Ryan Air 165
Ryan, Brendan 170
Ryder, Chris 67
Rytka, Helen 24

Sampson, Colin (Chief Constable) 92, 94, 99
Sandline 242
Sands, Bobby 22, 55, 63, 65, 67, 75, 96, 122, 126, 175
SAS x, 51, 54, ;105, 115, 117, 126, 129-30, 131, 132, 133, 135, 137-8, 139, 140, 155, 156, 157, 158, 159,

160, 161, 162, 167, 169, 176, 213, 288, 311, 316, 321
SAS in Ireland, The 52, 220, 291
Savage family: Mr 166; Mrs 170
Savage, Seán 155, 156, 157, 159, 160, 161, 162, 163, 164, 166, 167, 169, 172, 315-6
Saville Inquiry 6, 7, 8, 9, 12, 21-2, 222, 320, 323
Scarman Tribunal 287
Scots Guards 242, 243, 248, 249
SDLP 17, 144, 147, 195, 234, 290, 305, 308
Shanaghan, Patrick 95, 133, 254
Section 31 166
Senate (US) 83, 229
Shackleton, Damian 242
Shannon, Rosaleen 84
Sharkey family: Jimmy 46, 47-54; Nan 48
Sharpe, Reserve Constable 276
Shaw, Barry 291
Shaw, George Bernard 292
Shields, Maureen 32
Shiels, Maureen 9
Shoot-to-kill, against loyalists 201-6; at bookmaker's shop 207-24; in Gibraltar xi, 155-74; in North Armagh x, xi, 87- 105, 123, 130, 144, 145, 175, 291, 296, 312-3, 316; in South Armagh 227-32; in Strabane 115-28, 311, 312, 313; of Diarmuid O'Neill 267
Silent Too Long 59, 60, 319
Sinn Féin (Official) 15
Sinn Féin (Provisional) 15, 17, 18, 25, 77, 106, 144, 165, 166, 195, 254, 256, 281
Smith, Hugh (Colour Sergeant) 56, 57, 59, 60
Smith, Jean Kennedy 11
Smith, William 201-6, 311, 314-5, 319
Smyth, Sammy 32
Snowball, Andrew (Captain) 24
SO19 262, 264, 266-7, 269
Somers, Andrew (Judge) 226
Somers, Edward 6
Socialist Workers' Union 283
Somerville, Wesley 34
South African weapons 177, 221
South Down Action for Healing Wounds xv
Spanish police 157, 158, 159, 162, 167
Special Rapporteur; see United Nations
Spicer, Tim 242, 243, 249
'Spotlight' 217, 301
Spring, Dick 20, 173, 258
Springhill Community House 108
Stalker, John (Deputy Chief Constable) 91-2, 93, 94, 99, 101- 2, 103, 104, 105, 291, 312-3
Stephen Lawrence Campaign 271
State Violence in Northern Ireland 291, 292
Stephenson, Billy 141
Stevens, John (Chief Constable) 177-9, 180, 181, 201, 202
Stewart, Brian xvi, 196
Stewart, Ian 166
Stewart, Kathleen xvi, 84, 296
Stiff Little Fingers 259

Stobie, William 179-80
Stone, Michael 156, 166
Strasbourg 73, 170, 171-2, 305
Strathearn, William 306
Sun 159, 161
Sunday Business Post 8
Sunday Life 179, 204
Sunday Mirror 272
Sunday Times 9, 177, 181, 304
Sunday Tribune 46, 52, 179, 180
Sunday World 143-4, 146
Sunningdale Agreement 32, 41
Supergrasses 157, 206, 295, 299
Survivors of Trauma xv
Sutton, Malcolm ix, 201

Taggart, John 57, 60, 61, 62
'Talkback' 13
Taylor, John 180
Taylor, Kevin 92, 105
Tennyson, Francis 131, 138
Thain, Ian (Private) 144, 242, 259
Thames Television 157, 158, 162, 163
Thatcher, Margaret 71, 83, 142, 157, 162, 167, 170, 173, 174, 181, 291, 321
'This Week' 157
Thompson, Brian 211
Thompson family: Joanne 213; Mark 153, 213-24, 313, 314, 321; Mr 213, 214, 215, 218; Mrs 213, 214, 217-8
Thompson, Peter 207-11, 213-5, 217, 218, 220, 312, 313, 314
Thorpe, Jeremy 3
Tighe, Michael 87, 90, 91, 92
Time to Go initiative 270
Times 159
Tinney, Mark 118, 121
'Today' 7, 168
Toman, Eugene 87, 89, 90, 91, 92, 93, 95, 97, 98, 101, 104, 130, 318
Toman, Malachy 90
Touchstone Group xv, 224
Toxteth 77
Travers, Jack 32
Treacy, Diana 163
Trimble, David 281
Troops Out Movement 59, 61, 104, 195
Truth and Reconciliation Commission (South Africa) vii-viii, 221, 322, 323-4
Turbitt, Constable (William) 306
Turley, Brian 287
Turley, Frank 213
Turley, John 308
Turner, Breda 32
Turner, Detective Inspector 180
TV3 52

UDA (Ulster Defence Association) 32, 46, 176-7, 179, 181, 202, 306
UDR (Ulster Defence Regiment) ix, 28, 30, 34, 41, 46, 51, 53, 54, 96, 115, 133, 175, 177, 170, 313, 320
UFF (Ulster Freedom Fighters) 176, 177, 181, 185, 201
Ullger, Joseph (Deputy Chief Inspector) 162
Ulster Democratic Party 181
Ulster Unionist Party 130, 203, 209
Ulster Vanguard 32
Ulster Workers' Council 32, 305

United Campaign against Plastic Bullets 82, 83-4, 111-2, 170, 195, 319
United Nations 153, 218, 222, 314; Special Rapporteur 153, 181, 222, 272, 295
Unorthodox Soldier, An 243
Urban, Mark 129
Urwin, Margaret 40
UVF (Ulster Volunteer Force) 32, 34, 46, 199, 200, 201, 203
UTV (Ulster Television) 237
Valenzuela, Rayo 167
Victim Support Northern Ireland xv
Victims' Commission, Northern Ireland 84; Republic of Ireland 35, 40, 47, 145
Victims' Liaison Unit 141, 224
Victims of Trauma 196
VOICE 24-5, 28, 29, 319

Wallace, Colin 34, 306
Walker, Johnny 16
Walsh, Dermot (Professor) 6
Walsh, John 32
Ward, Judith 307
Ware, John 178
Watson, Alan (Professor) 155, 158-9, 163, 164
WAVE xv, 224
Weir, Sergeant 305-6
Welsh Guards 24
West Belfast Festival vii, 113
Whale, John 304
White, John 181
White, Keith 195
White, Margaret 32
Whitelaw, William 77, 304
Whitelaw's Tribunals 302
Widgery Tribunal and Report 3-4, 5, 6, 7, 8, 9, 11, 13, 14, 16, 17, 18, 19, 22, 320
Wilford, Derek (Lieutenant Colonel) 7
Williams, Detective Inspector 265
Williams, Tom 298
Williamson, George 32
Wilson, Des (Father) 108, 209, 215, 216
Wilson, Harold 3
Wilson, John 35, 40, 43, 47, 145
Wilson, Sammy 130, 216
Winter, Jane 6, 7, 18-9, 52, 187, 272
Withers, Paul 60
Wolff, Lester 289
Women's Coalition 283
Wood, Derek (Corporal) 156
Wood, Michael 264
Woods, Oliver (Doctor) 288
Wray, James 2, 5, 7
Wright, Alan 90
Wright, Mark 242, 243, 244, 245
Wulf-Mathies, Monika 222

Yellow Card, rules of engagement 116, 212, 231
Yorkshire Ripper 24
Yorkshire Television 33, 77, 81
Young, John 2, 5
Younger, George 157
YTP (Youth Training Programme) 301